Italian Studies
in Shakespeare
and His Contemporaries

International Studies in Shakespeare and His Contemporaries

Jay L. Halio, General Editor

French Essays on Shakespeare and His Contemporaries, ed. J. M. Maguin and Michèle Willems

Russian Essays on Shakespeare and His Contemporaries, ed. A. Parfenov and Joseph G. Price

Shakespeare and His Contemporaries and Central European Studies, ed. J. Limon and Jay L. Halio

Strands Afar Romote: Israeli Perspectives on Shakespeare, ed. Avraham Oz

Italian Studies in Shakespeare and His Contemporaries, ed. M. Marrapodi and G. Melchiori

Japanese Studies in Shakespeare and His Contemporaries, ed. Yoshiko Kawachi

Editorial Advisory Committee

Jay L. Halio, Chair
University of Delaware

Professor J. Leeds Barroll III
University of Maryland

Professor Werner Habicht
Institüt für Englische
　Philologie
University of Würzburg

Professor Yoshiko Kawachi
Kyorin University

Professor Arthur F. Kinney
University of Massachusetts

Professor Jerzy Limon
University of Gdansk

Dr. Barbara Mowat
Folger Shakespeare Library

Professor Stanley Wells
The Shakespeare Institute
University of Birmingham

Professor George Watson
　Williams
Duke University

Italian Studies in Shakespeare and His Contemporaries

Edited by
Michele Marrapodi
and Giorgio Melchiori

Newark: University of Delaware Press
London: Associated University Presses

© 1999 by Associated University Presses, Inc.

All rights reserved. Authorization to photocopy items for internal or personal use, or the internal or personal use of specific clients, is granted by the copyright owner, provided that a base fee of $10.00, plus eight cents per page, per copy is paid directly to the Copyright Clearance Center, 222 Rosewood Drive, Danvers, Massachusetts 01923. [0-87413-666-0/99 $10.00+8¢ pp, pc.] Other than as indicated in the foregoing, this book may not be reproduced, in whole or in part, in any form (except as permitted by Sections 107 and 108 of the U.S. Copyright Law, and except for brief quotes appearing in reviews in the public press).

Associated University Presses
440 Forsgate Drive
Cranbury, NJ 08512

Associated University Presses
16 Barter Street
London WC1A 2AH, England

Associated University Presses
P.O. Box 338, Port Credit
Mississauga, Ontario
Canada L5G 4L8

The paper used in this publication meets the requirements
of the American National Standard for Permanence of Paper
for Printed Library Materials Z39.48-1984.

Library of Congress-in-Publication Data

Italian studies in Shakespeare and his contemporaries / edited by
  Michele Marrapodi and Giorgio Melchiori.
    p. cm.
  Includes bibliographical references (p.   ) and index.
  ISBN 0-87413-666-0 (alk. paper)
  1. Shakespeare, William, 1564–1616—Criticism and interpretation.
2. English drama—Early modern and Elizabethan, 1500–1600—History
and criticism.   3. Shakespeare, William, 1564–1616—Contemporaries.
I. Marrapodi, Michele. II. Melchiori, Giorgio
PR2979.I7I83 1999
822.3'3—dc21   98-36115
                                                                                CIP

PRINTED IN THE UNITED STATES OF AMERICA

Contents

Introduction: Shakespeare Studies in Italy Since 1964 MICHELE MARRAPODI	7
With a Postscript by Giorgio Melchiori	18

Part One: Theory and Practice

A Midsummer Night's Dream: An Example of Shakespeare's Specularity MARCELLO PAGNINI	27
Bonds of Love and Death in *The Merchant of Venice* ALESSANDRO SERPIERI	44
The Interdiction of Eroticism in Shakespeare's Histories FERNANDO FERRARA	57
Shakespeare's Discursive Strategies and Their Definitions of Subjectivity ANGELA LOCATELLI	76

Part Two: Theme and Culture

In a Time of Unrest: A Role for the Theater in *Measure for Measure* VITO AMORUSO	97
Shakespeare's Uncultured Caesar on the Elizabethan Stage CLAUDIA CORTI	109
Shakespeare's History Plays as a "Scene" of the Disappearance of Popular Discourse LAURA DI MICHELE	128
"Now I play a merchant's part": The Space of the Merchant in Shakespeare's Early Comedies MARIANGELA TEMPERA	152
Three Kings, Herod of Jewry, and a Child: Apocalypse and Infinity of the World in *Antony and Cleopatra* GILBERTO SACERDOTI	165

Part Three: Language and Ideology

A National Idiom and Other Languages: Notes on Elizabethan Ambivalence with Examples from Shakespeare — 187
VANNA GENTILI

"But thou didst understand me by my signs": The Instability of Signs in *King John* — 206
ROBERTA MULLINI

"Let her witness it": The Rhetoric of Desdemona — 220
MICHELE MARRAPODI

"Great mischiefs mask in expected pleasures": The Rhetoric of Expectation and the Rhetoric of Surprise in English Baroque Theater — 245
FRANCO MARENCO

From Shakespeare to Dryden: Three Dramatic *Incipits* — 258
VIOLA PAPETTI

Bibliography — 279
Contributors — 288
Index — 291

Introduction: Shakespeare Studies in Italy Since 1964

MICHELE MARRAPODI

Any introduction to such a wide and peopled area as "Italian Studies in Shakespeare and His Contemporaries" must, of course, originate from some definitions, limitations, and acknowledgments. I will consider these in turn.

This collection of essays offers, with a variety of perspectives and methodologies, a wide-ranging picture of the present state and prospects of Elizabethan critical work in Italy. It should be emphasized from the outset, however, that the papers collected here only in part represent the nature and extent of the Italian contribution, since, for editorial reasons, this selection does not include articles already published in English or which have appeared in internationally known publications.

The aim of both the editors and the series as a whole is to gather a multifaceted group of significant essays which otherwise might not reach a worldwide readership. The editors have selected the critical production of several relatively young scholars, together with writings by some well-established critics that have been specially translated on this occasion. After a brief survey of the course of Shakespeare studies in Italy, the present inquiry mainly considers the particular trends and body of work produced by and associated with the critics represented, within the larger movement of Shakespeare scholarship in Italy. The achievements and richness of the Italian scene may make such a limitation a flaw, but a systematic investigation of all the methodologies and accomplishments cannot be encompassed within the space of an introduction.

With the exception of the chapters by Angela Locatelli, Vito Amoruso, and Franco Marenco, who have provided their own English versions, the difficult task of translation has been perceptively undertaken by Peter Dawson, in close collaboration with the editors and the authors themselves, while the updated bibliographical section appended to the volume has greatly profited from the generous assistance of James L. Harner. To both, the editors express their profound gratitude. Thanks are also due to the editors of the relevant journals and collections for permission to reprint in translation expanded or revised versions of published, though not copyrighted, material.

I have to record a sad loss which occurred during the final editing of the volume: the death of Fernando Ferrara, the inspirer and founder of a most original and active school of cultural studies at the Istituto Universitario Orientale of Naples. From the very beginning, he had approved with enthusiasm the idea of producing this book. Inclusion of his contribution is the best way of keeping his memory alive.

"Shakespeare e la critica italiana" is the title of a cogent article by Agostino Lombardo on Shakespeare criticism in Italy, which, significantly, appeared in the year of the quatercentenary celebrations.[1] As no other thorough contribution to the field has been published since then, I begin with his documented account, taking it as a temporal line of demarcation for a reassessment of the subject matter. Lombardo's essay provides a historical survey of Italian appreciation of Shakespeare—from the first adaptations and translations in the eighteenth century to the critical views and defenses of the early and late Romantics, estimators, and interpreters (V. Alfieri, I. Pindemonte, V. Monti, U. Foscolo, N. Tommaseo, A. Manzoni, G. Mazzini, A. Boito, F. De Sanctis, etc.), leading up to the aesthetics of Benedetto Croce and the fine scholarship of Mario Praz, the first modern critic of authentically international rank that Italy has produced in English studies. Praz has long been the reference point for all Italian *anglistica*, and most subsequent scholars came from the orbit of his influence. To limit this considerable offspring to the most distinguished names, I just mention Gabriele Baldini, Benvenuto Cellini, Carlo Izzo, Salvatore Rosati, Alfredo Orbetello, Augusto Guidi, Aurelio Zanco, Vittorio Gabrieli, Elio Chinol, and Nemi D'Agostino. Even now, two of Praz's former students—Agostino Lombardo and Giorgio Melchiori—are the leading Shakespearean critics and the most representative exponents of Italian scholarship abroad.

As I have written elsewhere, Agostino Lombardo, who holds the only chair of Shakespeare criticism in Italy, is highly influential throughout this country as an inspiring critic and scholar; he is particularly acclaimed as a fine translator of Shakespeare and other dramatists for stage productions.[2] His kind of historicism comes close to certain instances of existentialism and cultural materialism because of a marked tendency to emphasize the ideological links with our century, establishing an implied parallel between Shakespeare's contemporary political situation and the moral and political crisis of modern man. Lombardo's method helps define an "ideology of crisis" that reverberates throughout the canon. Among his analytic studies on almost every aspect of Shakespeare's production, his book on *Macbeth* best exemplifies his thematic-historical approach, rigorously based on the text, from which he derives an impressive amount of evidence for a coherent political interpretation, blending the dramatist's universal issues with the uncertainties and concerns of our age.[3]

Giorgio Melchiori, the most eclectic Shakespearean, has produced seminal contributions to the field of textual studies and interpretative commentary on Shakespeare and his contemporaries. He has written on a wide range of Renaissance authors, employing diverse methodologies and critical viewpoints in relation to the aims and targets of his research. Among the critical perspectives adopted, Melchiori deals with structuralism and semiotics, historical and neo-Marxist approaches, and formalist and textual analyses. He has also undertaken a successful, experimental harmonizing of a variety of critical methods to reach a pluralist interpretation.[4] He is internationally known as a textual scholar and editor of Renaissance plays as well as of a bilingual, nine-volume edition with translations by various hands, of Shakespeare's complete plays.

Besides Lombardo's and Melchiori's distinguished presence in the current critical debate, three major schools of criticism characterize the Italian scene, although it is not always possible to discern a clear-cut separation or to isolate them from other theoretical trends. This is because literary criticism in Italy has emerged from largely idealistic and post-Crocean roots, transformed and updated by the influence of European cultural materialism and neo-Marxism, on the one hand, and the Prague structuralist school and American formalism, on the other. Thus, the structuralist-semiotic school is surely one of the most influential. This is characterized by a marked tendency toward theoretical discourse, most notably on methodology and critical practice, and has as its founders Marcello Pagnini and Alessandro Serpieri, and among its leading members Paola Pugliatti and Keir Elam, as well as other dedicated scholars of different cultural formation, such as Angela Locatelli, Claudia Corti, Romana Rutelli, and Roberta Mullini. Pagnini may rightly be considered the introducer of post-structuralism in Italy, as his famous essay on the interpretation of Sonnet 20 demonstrates; his chapter on *A Midsummer Night's Dream* in this collection provides a sound example of his critical ability to delve into the comedy's dramatic construction.[5] Serpieri's semiotic approach has gathered a group of scholars, mainly from the universities of Florence, Pisa, and Bologna, who have published collective works on Shakespeare's dramaturgy and its sources. These scholars have successfully wedded semiotics to theatrical practice, conducting pioneering research on the segmentation of the theatrical text and producing a massive four-volume study on Shakespeare's transcodification of his narrative sources.[6] Among other semioticians, Paola Pugliatti is widely known for the application of her theoretical premises to the rhetorical-ideological structures of *King Lear* and the history plays, while Keir Elam's various books and essays on the semiotics and intertextuality of the dramatic text have been echoed throughout Italy and abroad.[7]

Historical Marxism has produced in Italy a second important trend of Shakespeare studies which in varying degrees initially revolved around the works of Franco Moretti, Paola Colaiacomo, and Marcello Cappuzzo, the last of whom has put into practice the Marxist aesthetics of the internationally known critic Galvano della Volpe in a stimulating book on *Macbeth*.[8] More closely bound to neo-Marxist ideology, Moretti's numerous essays of Shakespearean interest have been extensively translated into English, whereas Colaiacomo's largely thematic approach has mainly focused on a variety of dramatic and literary texts ranging from Shakespeare's *Hamlet* to the theater of Samuel Beckett.[9] Other scholars have produced outstanding contributions to Elizabethan studies consonant with the cultural-sociological field: Rosa Maria Colombo's *Le utopie e la storia* draws attention to wider ideological implications that can be read in the symbolical opposition between Iago's and Othello's utopian worlds.[10] Laura Di Michele's articulated work on Shakespeare's histories successfully combines politics and ideology with theatricality, while Rossella Ciocca's volume on the same group of plays deals with more ritualistic-anthropological features.[11] Other productive investigations are the thematic-psychoanalytic analyses of Silvano Sabbadini and Vito Amoruso. As already pointed out, however, the critic's adherence to one school or another is not easily determined; nor does it appear clearly monistic and one-sided. Although the primary critical influence may sound immediately familiar, individual application has often shifted from its origins, developing into myriad perspectives.

Many have passed from a largely historical–sociological approach to closer attention to formal structures. This third group of scholars has variously focused on the rhetorical and ideological uses of language. Grouping the most prestigious names in relation to common areas of interest, I cite Vanna Gentili's valuable investigation into the role of madness in Elizabethan and Jacobean drama, to which we may add Roberta Mullini's own considerations of the (meta-)linguistic function of Shakespeare's fools. Other stimulating critical inquiries emerge from the ideological political concerns of Giulio Marra, Paola Bottalla, and Loretta Innocenti; from the largely historiographical practice and cultural analyses of Franco Marenco and his collaborators; from the deeply intercultural and linguistic methodology of Mario Domenichelli and Viola Papetti and the wider interdisciplinary proposals of Masolino D'Amico and Gilberto Sacerdoti. As I have already hinted, a particularly important contribution to Italian critical theory and practice has been (and still is) provided by the school of wide-ranging cultural studies founded in Naples some thirty years ago by Fernando Ferrara. In the specific Shakespearean field outstanding results have been achieved by Ferrara himself, by the already mentioned Laura Di Michele and Rossella Ciocca, and by the relatively younger scholars who have contributed to the journal *Anglistica,* edited by Ferrara with Lidia Curti and Laura Di Michele, a journal to which the present writer's interests in the general construction of the dramatic text, its rhetoric, and intertextual legacies are certainly indebted.[12] Performance theory and dramatic criticism are represented in the numerous collections of essays on Shakespeare's individual plays, edited by Mariangela Tempera, and in the new series "The Renaissance Revisited," edited by Tempera and Patricia Kennan.

Though condensed, this survey of certain Italian critiques of Shakespeare and some of his contemporaries reflects a wide range of approaches, demonstrating the main features of the Italian contribution to Shakespeare studies. I turn again to the results of this kind of achievement in the context of the international scene. Here, I must emphasize that I can speak only of general tendencies, since, in most of the chapters, we may find more than a single focus contributing to a clearer overall interpretation or to the posing and solving of a particular issue or query. Bearing this peculiarity in mind, I would say that most Italian scholarship is creatively theoretical and propositional, on the one hand, and largely thematic and ideological, on the other, moving generally from the enunciation of a proposed methodology to the critical confrontation with the chosen text. Some exponents of the semiotic-structuralist field have profited from the teaching of Umberto Eco in the application of their theoretical premises, and have produced rewarding structural investigations into the world of Shakespearean drama. Other scholars have proved especially effective in the treatment of specific issues or aspects or themes, and have given detailed accounts of the linguistic and rhetorical strategies, suggesting an ideological design in Shakespeare's dramatic construction either in line with or in dissent from past and recent positions expressed in the international debate.

In recent years, Italian textual criticism has produced several new detailed editions of Shakespeare's plays and those of his fellow dramatists. Giorgio Melchiori's editorial activity on the works of Shakespeare and Renaissance drama in general is well established in the international forum. Accurate editions of selected Elizabethan and Jacobean plays have been published by Mario Praz, Grazia Caliumi, Anna Busi, Mary Corsani, and many others. Giorgio Melchiori, Alessandro Serpieri, and Elio Chinol have provided editions of Shakespeare's sonnets, while a number of scholarly editions of individual plays have been done by Elio Chinol, Nemi D'Agostino, Agostino Lombardo, Sergio Perosa, and Alessandro Serpieri, among others. In his *Teatro Completo,* Melchiori provides new critical editions of *Edward III* and *Sir Thomas More.*

The division of the present volume into three sections—the first focusing on theoretical and methodological issues, the other two centering on the thematic, linguistic, rhetorical, and ideological levels—may broadly indicate the variety and nature of the major trends of contemporary Italian scholarship.

The opening chapter by Marcello Pagnini is a subtle investigation into the multiple plot structure of *A Midsummer Night's Dream*. Pagnini reveals in the comedy a structural design which serves as a dramatic unity and contributes to the richness of meaning. Carefully related, all the plots follow four comedic subgenres: an opening "classical" action, which provides the setting; a "romantic" love-story of two pairs of lovers; a "popular" entertainment based on the artisans' show-within; and a "magical" narrative line concerning the fairies of the wood. The characters' names reflect this distribution; their stage worlds are consonant with topical comedic experimentation, ranging from Lyly's euphuistic affectations and Greene's or Sidney's romance plots to Plautine farce and medieval fairy tale or Tudor masques. All this obeys a general structural design that gives the play dramatic coherence by means of a perfect game of symmetry, specularity, and correspondences which throws new light on the comedy's deep structures and diverse ideologies. The semiotic construction of Shakespeare's comedy is also examined in Alessandro Serpieri's discussion of *The Merchant of Venice*. At the core of the play's linguistic and thematic universe is the idea of a personal and public contract, the "bond," which dominates the characters' concerns and interactions, investing the represented social order at all levels. Despite the ideological opposition between Venice and Belmont, and their dual symbolical significance, these two stage worlds are ruled by the same prescriptions and limitations, founded on the power of gold and the strict rigor of social contracts. The dramatic function of the bond thus gives circularity to a play characterized beginning to end by a "strange" ambiguity and sense of loss. Private and public obligations abound; they dominate the action and involve all characters and dramatic situations, disclosing unsettled social tensions and ideological conflicts that are a metaphor for the structural transformation of Elizabethan England. Fernando Ferrara's chapter deals with the dramatic function of the abolition of eroticism from sacred regality, operating in a number of Elizabethan history plays—to be precise in those he calls the "archaic" histories (the three parts of *Henry VI, Richard III, Edward III,* and *King John*), the "modern" histories (*Richard II, 1* and *2 Henry IV,* and *Henry V*), and the "mythical" histories (*Henry VIII*). In this repression of sexuality, Ferrara sees a wider epistemological crisis, involving a self-confident and demanding superego, and the interdiction imposed on eros by politics and power, signaling the social conflict about eros in terms of a transition from one epoch to another. Henry's repudiation of Falstaff obeys the strict rigor of this law, and Shakespeare's entire dramaturgy, to a great extent, follows this same pattern indicated in the histories. In the archaic histories of the English kings, the interdiction of eroticism contributes to the formation of a cultural taboo, concerning the incompatibility between eros and power. Thus, the opening dispute between Lady Faulconbridge's legitimate and natural sons in *King John* provides a wider conflict between sexuality and the ethics of power that reverberates throughout the history plays. From Ferrara's analysis of the socio-cultural implications of the Tudor myth, we move, with Angela Locatelli, to a critical definition of subjectivity in both social and textual terms investigating the dramatic idea of subject in Shakespeare through a number of critical categories, arising from rhetorical and largely new historicist and cultural materialist discourse. Shakespeare's ethics of subjectivity denies any partial interpretation of history and provides, in Locatelli's words, a "double enunciation" that opens up to a verdict of interpretative indeterminacy, eschewing "black and white" statements. Individual utterances and general enunciations are thus aligned in light of the play's entire textuality. Katharina's final speech in *The Taming of the Shrew* offers a formidable example of Shakespearean "double enunciation," as is the case of *Julius Caesar,* in which the historical "truth" is refashioned into Tudor-Stuart terms, and the ideological rivalry of both parties is accurately balanced through a series of dramatic devices. Individual utterances in *The Merchant of Venice*—and, more important, the "framing" level of dramatic enunciation—give the play its notorious ambiguity. Once we move beyond the characters' utterances and consider the entire enunciation, we find a dual perspective in the comedy that equates Shylock's murderous vengeance to Antonio's moral contradictions and mocks the play's patriarchal universe by means of Portia's "masculine" role, which she eloquently accomplishes in a man's attire and frame of mind.

The opening chapter of Part Two, by Vito Amoruso, explores the multifarious levels of ambiguity that the social and political world of *Measure for Measure* unfolds. Starting from the Duke's concealment and the choice of his deputy, Amoruso sees this act as a deliberate disruption of the social structure whose precariousness attracted Shakespeare because of its topical political connotations. The critical analysis of this stage world is seen from the viewpoint of the courtier's ideology, pointing to an institutional crisis and to the loss of identity of the ruling class. The play's climate mirrors the social and religious tensions of the age: Puritan hostility toward the theater and growing social discontent. The new genre itself, tragicomedy, theorized by Guarini, helps express all the ambivalences. The very words with which the Duke explains to Angelo why he is the chosen deputy reveal a profound ambiguity, in the same way as Isabella's playacting, suggested and prompted by Lucio, unfolds something which is at the same time real and feigned. Ironically, Bernardino's unreadiness to die mocks the disquieting reality of the play's social world. Wider cultural implications are at the center of Claudia Corti's chapter on the characterization of Caesar on the Elizabethan stage. Shakespeare's *Julius Caesar* depicts the eponymous hero as a weak, superstitious, timorous leader, many of whose human frailties are stressed by evidence of physical infirmities in direct or reported speeches. The devaluation of the figure of Caesar obeys both ideological responses intrinsic in the dramatic voices of the drama and a well-established theatrical tradition. By following this tradition and interpreting the textual data, we give full meaning to Shakespeare's constructive strategy and his methods of individual characterization, whereas Shakespeare's major deviations from it testify to his political views in line with the ideological and epistemic attitude of anti-Catholic and anti-papist Anglican intellectuals. Laura Di Michele focuses on the history plays, particularly the figure of Falstaff, to analyze the dramatic function of the disappearance of popular discourse from the social environment represented. When the popular class does appear, its presence is parodistically vilified by a clownlike role, as is the case of the Jack Cade episode or the more telling and longer presence of Sir John Falstaff in the Henry IV plays. Shakespeare places the popular discourse in the foreground, intermingled with other social and political discourses, to guide and extol the affirmation of regality. Thus the "heavy, fearful materiality" of Falstaff and the popular world he represents must be known, dominated, and, in the end, rejected by Hal once he acquires his kingly role. This growing maturity in the new prince is dramaturgically explicit in the episode of the "play extempore," when Falstaff inverts roles and situations and mocks royal authority; but his attempt to conclude the harangue in his own favor is prevented by Hal, thus anticipating the subsequent rejection and the moral and political significance implied in the definitive separation from Falstaff's disordered universe. In a similar field of inquiry, Mariangela Tempera explores the roles of the merchant class and the gentry in a group of Shakespearean comedies in which higher authority, represented by a duke, appears to be absent or ineffectual as regards the social structure. *The Comedy of Errors, The Taming of the Shrew,* and *The Merchant of Venice,* all characterized by a mercantile society dominated by the laws of the market, offer an interesting case in point. They may help define the space of the merchant and that of the gentleman, and the shifting of identities between the two social classes. The process toward the rise of the mercantile gentry that these plays represent does not lead to a real integration, and the frequent acceptance of the merchant's part in the characters' interactions only reveals an attempt at social cohesion which, in the comedies' final harmonization, is still far from complete. The ensuing chapter by Gilberto Sacerdoti provides another stimulating interdisciplinary analysis of Elizabethan episteme by delving in detail into the puzzling exchange between Antony and Cleopatra on the precise "bourn" of Antony's love (I.1). Sacerdoti follows a learned cultural trajectory which, from the Scriptures, moves to the Renaissance religious controversy over the finiteness or infiniteness of the world, leading to the philosophy of Thomas Digges, John Dee, Giordano Bruno, and the Hermetic tradition. Together with other textual traces emerging from Charmian's oracular fantasies in the ensuing scene, Sacerdoti finds a common syllogistic method in the kind of linguistic strategy adopted by Shakespeare and Bruno, demonstrating an affinity of thought between the two authors that is not yet fully recognized.

The relationship between national idiom and other languages and the use of translation are investigated in Vanna Gentili's chapter, which opens Part Three, "Language and Ideology." Referring to some items from the Elizabethan cultural context and commenting on various Shakespearean examples, most notably as regards the linguistic ability of certain characters in *Richard II*, *Henry V*, and *The Tempest*, Gentili questions the specific nature of Elizabethan translation and the dramatic function of Shakespeare's interplay with other languages. In their working with words, Shakespeare's fools provide the most eloquent case of translation as appropriation and indeed as a thorough change, a definitive passage from one condition to another. This distortion, as either an attenuating or an amplifying process, marks the idea of Elizabethan translation as an imaginative practice comparable to Shakespeare's dramaturgical metamorphosis of his source material into an overall creative construction. In Roberta Mullini's chapter on *King John*, the theme of illegitimate kingship is seen through the epochal historical milieu and the textual traces suggesting the indeterminacy, confusion, and uncertainty that characterize John's doubtful royalty. In the clash between expression and content that the King's word ironically manifests, Mullini sees evidence of the instability of signs indicating the kingly symbols of authority. John's loss of the necessary "biunivocal correlation" between the plane of expression and that of content represents the fragility and precariousness of his body politic. Michele Marrapodi studies the strategies of character construction in *Othello* to challenge some traditional readings of Desdemona as a passive, childlike figure in past and recent interpretations. The rhetoric of character construction demonstrates Desdemona's fundamental role if it is seen in opposition to that of Iago and for the salvation of the Moor. A comparison between the two antagonistic characterizations of Iago and Desdemona and their rhetorical strategies may throw fresh light on the tragedy's overall symbolic dimension and allow Desdemona to be freed from the artificial displacement of the other characters' opinions, speaking with her own "voice" to the audience. From this perspective, Desdemona becomes Iago's most natural and direct antagonist, her more active role being necessary for the dynamics of the action and decisively influential for the final recovery of Othello's spiritual knowledge. Franco Marenco's essay questions the contrasting nature of English baroque theater in the rhetorical game of expectations and surprise of much Jacobean drama and finds its nearest archetypal models in the first version of Sidney's *Arcadia.* The two antithetical denouements, characterized by miraculous recognitions and surprises, produce in this work a solution that leaves the real offenses of the princes' story unpunished and the inherent ethical questions unsolved. The bafflement of the reader's expectations and Sidney's ironic devices become a mockery of faith and virtue in most Jacobean tragedies. The very nature of baroque theater, its poetics of "mischiefs and expected pleasures," originates from Sidney's moral allegory in the clash between predictability and surprise, between grotesque prophesy and peripeteia. Shakespeare's *Richard II* and *Macbeth* represent the most notable antecedents of this inversion of perspectives that we find more structurally conceived as a disruption of social values in Webster's and Middleton's Italianate tragedies. The final chapter by Viola Papetti discusses the openings of three Shakespearean plays—*The Tempest, Antony and Cleopatra,* and *Troilus and Cressida*—in an analytical comparison of the parallel sequences of their late seventeenth-century remakes by Dryden. Papetti proposes a contiguous reading of texts which, set side by side, generate a metatext that involves all the variants of stage practice, theatrical tradition, and diverse ideology. The protatic comparative analysis thus conceived sheds fresh light on Shakespeare's opening strategy, providing at the same time new, critical perspectives on the study of Dryden's dramatic *incipits* and his creative modifications of Shakespeare.

Notes

1. Lombardo, "Shakespeare e la critica italiana," *Sipario* 218 (Giugno, 1964): 2–13, 65.

2. See Marrapodi, "Elizabethan Studies in Italy in 1993 and 1994," *Cahiers Elisabéthains* 48 (October 1995): 53–74, and "Galvano della Volpe's Marxist Aesthetics and the Interpretation of *Macbeth,*" *Nuovi Annali della Facoltà di Magistero dell'Università di Messina* 8–10 (1990–92): 451–70.

3. Lombardo, *Lettura del "Macbeth"* (Vicenza: Neri Pozza, 1969).

4. Melchiori, *L'uomo e il potere* (Turin: Einaudi, 1973); translated as *Shakespeare's Dramatic Meditations: An Experiment in Criticism* (Oxford: Oxford University Press, 1975). See also, in this regard, M. Marrapodi, "A New Approach to Shakespeare's Sonnets: A Note on Pluralist Criticism," *The Blue Guitar* 3–4 (1977–78): 195–202.

5. See Pagnini, "Lettura critica (e metacritica) del sonetto 20 di Shakespeare," *Strumenti critici* 3 (February 1969): 1–18, reprinted in *Critica della funzionalità* (Turin: Einaudi, 1970). See also his *Shakespeare e il paradigma della specularità* (Pisa: Pacini Editore, 1976).

6. Serpieri et al., eds. *Come comunica il teatro: dal testo alla scena* (Milan: Il Formichiere, 1978); and *Nel laboratorio di Shakespeare: dalle fonti ai drammi.* 4 vols. (Parma: Pratiche Editrice, 1988).

7. See, respectively, Paola Pugliatti, *I segni latenti: Scrittura come virtualità scenica in "King Lear"* (Messina-Florence: D'Anna, 1976), *Shakespeare storico* (Rome: Bulzoni, 1993), *Shakespeare the Historian* (London: Macmillan, 1996); Keir Elam, *The Semiotics of Theatre and Drama* (London: Methuen, 1980), *Shakespeare's Universe of Discourse: Language-Games in the Comedies* (Cambridge: Cambridge University Press, 1984), and his numerous collections of essays edited with Alessandro Serpieri (see Bibliography).

8. Cappuzzo, *Da Duncan a Malcolm: la tragedia di Macbeth* (Messina: Peloritana Editrice, 1972).

9. Moretti, *Signs Taken for Wonders: Essays in the Sociology of Literary Forms* (London: Verso, eds., 1983); P. Colaiacomo, *La prova: saggi da Shakespeare a Beckett* (Rome: Editori Riuniti, 1993).

10. Colombo, *Le utopie e la storia: saggio sull'"Othello" di Shakespeare* (Bari: Adriatica, 1976).

11. Di Michele, *La scena dei potenti. Teatro, Politica, Spettacolo nell'età di W. Shakespeare* (Naples: Istituto Universitario Orientale, 1988); R. Ciocca, *Il cerchio d'oro: i Re sacri nel teatro shakespeariano* (Roma: Officina Edizioni, 1987).

12. See the various entries in the Bibliography for these and other critics mentioned.

Postscript: Present and Future
by Giorgio Melchiori

The papers collected in this volume by Michele Marrapodi, to whom I acted as adviser, set out to present some contributions to Shakespeare studies in Italian that, scattered through a number of publications not available outside Italy, might have escaped the attention we feel they deserve. Regrettably, for a number of reasons, we were unable to secure some particularly significant studies, but the samples—representative but by no means exhaustive—we managed to collect may convey a sense of the vitality and of the extreme variety of critical and scholarly attitudes in this field.

Practically all contributors to the present volume are university teachers, and this is somewhat misleading, inasmuch as it does not give the measure of the deep-seated and wide-ranging interest in Shakespeare present in the Italian public at large, even more outside than inside the academic world—and of the progressive narrowing of the gap between the scholars' or textbook Shakespeare, on the one hand, and the people's and the stage Shakespeare, on the other. Until about thirty years ago in Italian universities, Shakespeare was simply the dominating figure of English literature. His plays were approached with considerable—at times, indeed, brilliant critical and philological—skill as literary works which happened to be written in dramatic form. The translations available in print were at times philologically impeccable, literal renderings, intended for the reader in the study, not for the actor on the stage. Acting versions were a separate genre, adaptations the scholar regarded with suspicion, as being unfaithful to the received canonical text. There were exceptions. The achievements of a militant Italian playwright, Cesare Vico Lodovici, who translated the complete plays with a view to the stage, and of Gabriele Baldini, a brilliant scholar and the master of an original style, who translated all Shakespeare's works, cannot be ignored. Besides, poets like Eugenio Montale, Salvatore Quasimodo, Mario Luzi, were commissioned by men of the theater or by academics, like Mario Praz, who were also major literary figures in their own right, to translate Shakespeare, on the ground that a great poet could be rendered into Italian only by other masters in the same profession—and the results were indeed gratifying. But the scholars looked at them with some misgivings. For a while, the reciprocal mistrust between scholars and men of the theater remained: the latter preferred to do their own translations and adaptations or to entrust them to other theater people, the former were wary of letting show-business people manipulate the translations they had prepared for the reader in the privacy of the library or the study.

The breakthrough came in the late sixties, when academics keenly interested in the theater, like Masolino D'Amico and Elio Chinol, began producing stage-oriented translations of theatrical texts. The result of such experiences was the emergence in Italy of a global view of Shakespeare studies in which textual studies, literary criticism, literary theory, translation studies, theater and social history and the performing arts are seen as indispensable parts of a unified scholarly endeavor. This awareness, which opens a new avenue toward the future of Italian Shakespeare scholarship, is felt in all the academic institutions throughout the country; here, I can provide only a few instances.

Credit for the new approach and for the tremendous impulse Shakespeare studies have received in Italy must go, first, to Agostino Lombardo, a major, well-established Shakespeare critic, whose activities extend over the years to a number of ever new initiatives. His admirable translations of several plays for great theater directors (his memorable *Tempest* for Giorgio Strehler was only a beginning—I must mention at least his *Timon* for Luigi Squarzina and his *Titus* for Peter Stein), the numerous conferences and seminars on the Elizabethan and Jacobean theater he promoted in Rome, Milan, Verona, Vicenza, and elsewhere in connection with major Italian theatrical institutions, as well as the inclusion in the *Biblioteca di Studi Inglesi,* in the periodical *Studi Inglesi,* and in other series of scholarly publications that he edited, of his own works and of those of his colleagues and pupils, make him the leading figure in Shakespeare studies and an inspiration to the younger generations of Italian Shakespeare scholars. As holder of the first chair of Shakespeare criticism in Italy, his work and influence is projected into the future: on the one hand, he has undertaken to complete the translation of all Shakespeare's plays in individual volumes; on the other, he founded (in 1991) and edits the series *Piccola Biblioteca Shakespeariana,* which issues twice or three times a year short monographic studies by scholars belonging to all critical schools.

No less of a promise for the future are the activities centering on the University of Florence, but extending to those of Pisa, Bologna, and other seats of learning, promoted in the first place by Alessandro Serpieri. Serpieri, whose original approach to semiotic studies was already apparent in his analyses of Shakespeare's nondramatic works, culminating in his monumental annotated edition of the *Sonnets,* has created a school of semiotics of the theater centering on the study of the ways in which the theater communicates. He not only collaborated with several directors (beginning with a full-length *Hamlet* directed by Gabriele Lavia) but, at times in connection with Keir Elam and Paola Pugliatti, promoted several international meetings, seminars, and conferences, in Florence, Taormina, and elsewhere in Italy, on intertextual and editorial theory and practice, always seen in the light of stage performance. His critical alertness to all the most recent developments of the theory of literature in respect of the theater is a constant stimulus for the growing number of young Shakespeareans in Italy.

Shakespeare studies are flourishing throughout Italy; but special mention is more than deserved by the Center for the Study and Teaching of the Shakespearean Theater established in 1991 at the University of Ferrara. The creation of the Center, a unique blend of experimental teaching methods and scholarship of the highest order (as shown by the "International Shakespeare" conferences and lecture courses held in Ferrara since that date) was the culmination of ten years' work by Mariangela Tempera, who launched the project in 1982. She conceived it as a total involvement, not only of her students, and of teachers and boys and girls at all school levels, but of the town of Ferrara itself each year in the reconsideration of a different play of Shakespeare, inasmuch as, alongside lectures, films, and exhibitions illustrating the play, she set up a theater laboratory in which at first visiting English University Drama Groups, and later the Ferrara students themselves, were invited to present their own original reelaborations of the texts.

Shakespeare studies in Italy have reached remarkable standards of scholarship, even sophistication; their greatest strength, however, lies in the close alliance they have established with the men of the theater, internationally known directors such as the late Giorgio Strehler, Luca Ronconi, Luigi Squarzina, Gabriele Lavia, Franco Zeffirelli, and many others, and the more adventurous Carmelo Bene, Giancarlo Nanni, Leo De Berardinis, Gigi dall'Aglio— the constant exchange between the world of academe and that of the stage is the best augury for the future.

Italian Studies
in Shakespeare
and His Contemporaries

Part One
Theory and Practice

A Midsummer Night's Dream:
An Example of Shakespeare's Specularity
MARCELLO PAGNINI

A Midsummer Night's Dream is complex in structure. On careful examination, the play offers two related lines of inquiry: verification of its unity and its amazing richness of meaning. There are four plots in the play, all perfectly blended together—for the first time in the evolution of Shakespearean comedy—suggesting that the playwright had reached his full maturity. The first plot consists of the slender theme of Theseus and Hippolyta's imminent wedding, the second of what we might call (later on, we shall return to this point) "the love quartet." The third is provided by the rehearsals of the artisans' play, the fourth by the love of Oberon and Titania. These plots possess generic qualitative features. Respectively, we have "classical action," which also provides the setting of the main play; a "romantic" play, if such we may call it, based on the impassioned yet fickle feelings of the four lovers; a "popular" play; and a "magical" play. The names of the characters naturally reflect this distribution: ancient Greek names for the first two plots (Theseus, Hippolyta, Egeus, Lysander, Demetrius, Hermia, Helena); Elizabethan popular names and nicknames (the artisans); and names from medieval folklore tradition for the fourth (Oberon, Robin Goodfellow or Puck). The context of the plots also involves interesting typological-historical considerations: the first constructed on the cultural premises of recent local comediographic experimentation, in the manner of John Lyly, with overwhelming euphuistic affectations of lofty elegant language (overwhelming as regards the plot, which itself is extremely slim). The second reveals an underlayer of a romance à la Robert Greene or Sir Philip Sidney, with gallant language and complicated intrigues, exchanges of person, disguises, symmetries and mechanical denouements. The third harks back to Plautine farce, with its recurrent use of coarse language—dialect forms, solecisms, grammatical improprieties; and the fourth and last reveals the clear recourse to Celtic myths and medieval fairy tale as well as to forms of the English masques which themselves were derived from performances in Italian Renaissance courts, abounded in encomiastic apostrophes to the audience or to some illustrious person present, presented exotic characters, and had plenty of music and dancing.

The diagram below sums up this structure. It may help the reader to appreciate the elaborate framework of the comedy while offering an opportunity to pause on the theme of the relationship between heterogeneity and cohesiveness. In my view, this is basic to understanding Shakespeare's challenging artistic undertaking, which is directed at the integration of discordant, contradictory elements.

Plots	Description	Type	Derivation
A	Wedding of Theseus and Hippolyta	Classical	English Elizabethan comedy
B	Quartet of love	Romantic	Romance à la Greene or Sidney
C	Artisans' performance	Realistic	Plautine farce
D	Quarrel and magic of Oberon and Titania	Magic	Medieval popular traditions; masque

The technical audacity of this integrative plan is clear. The question is whether we have merely an indiscriminate, superficial hodgepodge of elements, or whether we can speak of deep structuring—that is, of interfunctionality. The desire to integrate such heterogeneous traditional data is due, I would say, not only to the attempt to create a multifaceted, brilliant spectacle—with all the concomitant multiple social appeal, inasmuch as this theater was meant for all levels of Elizabethan society, from the court to the groundlings—but also to the culturally more profound and typically baroque desire to produce a work of art manifesting the macroscopic paradox of *variety* in *unity*.

We might say that plot A creates the occasion and the space for the other plots, in addition to being—in all probability—a witty metaphor of the motivation of the entire play with regard to an external event: another noble wedding about to be celebrated. Plot A is, however, related to plot B because, as a result of Hermia's refusal to vow obedience, Theseus becomes personally involved as the supreme authority in Athens with regard both to the initial punishment and to the final pardon. Plot C is clearly inseparable from plot A, as the artisans' performance is intended for the wedding of plot A. Plot D is related to plot A, inasmuch as the intervention of the fairies is occasioned by the wedding of Theseus and Hippolyta. Elizabethan popular tradition recognized a link between the world of fairies and household spirits and the good or bad fortune of marriages. It was a good omen for a young couple—as, for example, can be seen in Spenser's *Epithalamion*—if elves and witches, not to speak of owls and crows, did not spoil the festivities with their evil doings. Plots C and D thus bear practically the same relationship to A. From the point of view of *topos,* space B—that is, the forest (chosen by the lovers for their elopement or their mutual pursuit, and by the artisans for their rehearsals)—is also the natural setting of all the action of plot D.

From a formal point of view, it is not difficult to see that plot A is typologically opposed to plot D, as one is regulated by the laws of men and the other by the laws of the fairies: on the one hand, an ordinary, objective world, and, on the other, an extraordinary fantastic world. Plots B and C are also antithetical, one being a "romantic" plot and the other "prosaic." The same antithesis is produced by plot C as regards B and D, since the prosaic and material quality of the groundlings is opposed to the refined and ideal quality of the nobility, just as it is opposed to the ethereal and supernatural quality of the fairy tale. All four plots have one thing in common, the theme of love or, rather, the love relationship that encompasses them. A = Theseus-Hippolyta; B = Hermia-Demetrius-Helena-Lysander; C = Pyramus-Thisbe (a demystification of the "romantic" theme); D = Oberon-Titania. It is a heavily overemphasized love, reiterated and varied, which oversteps the bounds between the single plots to become a dominating cohesive element—plot A and plot D come into close and indissoluble contact with plot C by virtue of the fact that the magic spell causes Titania to fall in love with Bottom. Another point to be noticed (and I shall return to this) is that plot A is antithetically opposed to plot B as regards their erotic symbology: A concerns controlled and dominated love, posed for its constitutional legalization, while B constitutes what might be considered a prior phase of love A, the phase of uncontrollable, ingenuous sensuality, of whim and instinct.

From the distributional point of view, the montage is clearly of the usual alternating type; but the succession of the segments of the plot is ingeniously skillful in stabilizing the reciprocal relationships and in tying and untying all the knots of each plot in a single overall solution. The succession of the segments of the play is strictly geometric:

A   BCD   BCD   BCD   A

Here we see the formal, framework function of the Theseus-Hippolyta plot, which encompasses the whole play, and the succession of three regular triads, in each of which the other plots regularly alternate. This also means that we have the same impartial number of presences of the single plots: three times for B, three for C, and three for D.

Another important element in the structure of the play is the use—quite common at the time—of the play-within-the-play, with its powerful mirror-image effects, as in *Hamlet*. We must also consider homologies with real-life situations. Performances would often be given which portrayed contemporary historical events—as George Chapman did with French history. It could also happen, as in *A Midsummer Night's Dream,* that the play not only contained a play-within-the-play (the *Pyramus and Thisbe* episode), which was homologous to the plot of the four lovers, but was also a play-within-the-play of life—in this particular case, feigned and fanciful nuptials homologous to a royal wedding.

Let us move directly to the structural interpretation. It is not difficult to detect a basic opposition between the space of ATHENS and the space of the FOREST: topological but also, and more importantly, semantic ambits. The entire action of the play takes place within them, with the following sequence:

A (Athens)   B (Forest)   A (Athens)

Note that Athens is opposed to the forest through a series of symbolic attributes: it is a city, therefore rationally ordered, both architecturally and as regards its laws and institutions. The forest is not rational: it is chaotic and mysterious. It is the place of a sort of *madness* that is counterposed to the *rationality* of the *polis*. The symbolic role of Athens is strengthened by its being the city of Athene, the goddess of wisdom and reason. It is no coincidence that Athens is illuminated by the *sun* while the forest, the place of magic spells and errors, is lit by the *moon*. This can be shown in another diagram:

ATHENS	versus	FOREST
Rationality		Irrationality
Sun		Moon
Laws, customs *(culture)*		Waywardness, impulse, instinct *(nature)*

The uncultivated forest is traditionally a symbol of bewilderment and error. In *A Midsummer Night's Dream,* we have a "wild forest." The *topos* occurs frequently in Shakespeare. In *Two Gentlemen of Verona,* Valentino, leader of the outlaws, prefers to live in the forest; in *As You Like It,* the banished duke has retired to the forest of Arden. In *The Merry Wives of Windsor,* all the magic spells and jests take place in Windsor Forest. In medieval and Elizabethan English the word *wood* also meant, as an adjective, "mad" or "lunatic." The expression "to be in a wood" meant "to have lost one's way," "to be in a predicament," "to be at a loss." In the city—in Athens—we are immediately presented with three institutional relationships: that of *husband and wife,* which is about to be realized in the marriage of Theseus and Hippolyta; that of *parent and daughter,* which provides the first basic conflict (the transgression of the law of filial obedience); and that of *political authority and subjection,* as represented by Theseus and the Athenians. Theseus denoted, in the allegorical medieval interpretation (and in the emblematic Renaissance interpretation), the hero who subjugated unruly nature: the Minotaur, the Centaurs, the Amazons (Hippolyta is an Amazon constrained by Theseus to abide by the laws of the *polis*); the Duke's pack of hounds (4.1) bays harmoniously, which is another metaphor for the reduction of natural chaos to rational order. Theseus, it should be noted, does not believe in the existence of fairies—indeed, he plainly declares his disbelief in "these fairy toys" (5.1.3). Not unpredictably, Theseus' preferred space is the *polis,* Athens.

The standards which Hermia's transgression offends are thus the laws of Athens, as a symbolic complex. A number of antitheses are immediately evident in the charges made by the *senex*. Egeus accuses Lysander of bewitching the bosom of his daughter by rhymes and music. In other words, the expedients of poetry, the enchantments of the imagination, have subverted Hermia's rationality. The antithesis is clearly presented at the level of manifestation: it is Hermia who speaks, bewailing her father's lack of understanding; it is also Theseus who recalls her to the order of reason:

> *Hermia*
> I would my father look'd but with my eyes.
> *Theseus*
> Rather your eyes must with his judgement look.
> (1.1.56–57)

Here we may note the antinomy EYES (symbols of deceit, appearance, hallucination) versus WISDOM (reason, order, law, hierarchy).

The play thus opens with a *rebellion against the law,* such a passionate and stubborn rebellion that not even the threat of the cloister or death can stem it. Indeed, the threat provokes escape, *flight* to a more congenial environment. The entire play rests on the struggle between these two principles, which constitute the customary archisemic dichotomy so dear to Shakespeare:

REASON versus MADNESS

with its various sememes:

ATHENS	versus	FOREST
Law, custom	versus	Illegality, transgression, freedom
Theseus	versus	Young lovers
Obedience	versus	Rebellion
Sun	versus	Moon
Conscious	versus	Unconscious
Objectivity	versus	Fantasy (poetry, music, fairies)

On the level of manifestation, the antithesis is:

"cool reason"   versus   "shaping fantasies"
(5.1.5–6)

Reason and *Love,* as Bottom observes, seldom go hand in hand: "And yet, to say the truth, reason and love keep little company together nowadays" (3.1.138–39).

With regard to this antithesis, I think it may be useful to open a brief parenthesis to consider the significance of *Midsummer,* which, in my view, has a much richer meaning than is commonly accredited. Midsummer Day falls on June 24th, the day of the summer solstice (which occurs more precisely on June 21st). Various festivities used to be observed in England on this date to mark the passage from spring to summer. In Act 4 (1.132), Theseus speaks of the "rite of May," which did not necessarily take place on the first of May nor was observed on a single day. The rite of May had remote origins in magical practices. It was believed possible, for example, to discover by means of dreams or divination which young persons were destined to be joined in marriage. The May games included walks in the woods, where often the night would be spent amid various fun and games, undoubtedly erotic in nature, in a traditional carnivalesque abandonment to sensuality and fantasy. Midsummer was also a period of the moon favorable to metamorphoses and misunderstandings. Old records refer to the midsummer moon as frequently a time of madness. There used to be an expression "to have a mile to midsummer," meaning "to be nearly off one's head," while the expression "midsummer madness," actually used by Shakespeare in *Twelfth Night* (3.4.55), referred to a kind of madness that was furious and incurable. Therefore, if my interpretation is correct, Midsummer day symbolically represents the passage from innocence and pubescence, which are the metaphoric and mythical characteristics of springtime, to the physiological potency and maturity—and fertility—of summertime. This is, indeed, the central theme of the play, in which this metamorphosis affects the young people of the "love quartet" who, in the end, find their passionate instincts placated in the civilized and legally recognized bonds of matrimony—just like Theseus and Hippolyta. The title of the play itself refers not to Midsummer day but to Midsummer night, with an entire series of connotative implications. Night is an evident symbol of irrationality, blindness, error, and dream. It should also be noted—and here I conclude this parenthesis—that the dream is the space where the two worlds of reality and irreality meet and blend together.

Let us now consider what I have called the "love quartet." This definition seems to me apt, for if we consider the relationships between the four young lovers they indubitably present the characteristic features of a composite piece of music, in which four instruments play together, with alternating fortune. The lovers have little psychological depth. Generally speaking, characters are not strongly drawn in comedies, in which more attention is paid to the dynamic of action and dialogue. In *A Midsummer Night's Dream*—unlike, for example, *As You Like It*—the characters are little more than pieces on a chessboard (the only exception is Bottom, who is psychologically deeper). This is probably due to the fact that the play—dedicated, as is widely accepted, to the celebration of a noble wedding—displays a strong tendency to adopt the traditional features of the masque. The most drastic simplification of character is precisely in the four young lovers—that is, the four characters around whom the action mainly revolves. They are types or figures in a game governed by the dynamic rule of *equivocation,* a game that progresses by a process of *subverted order*—a series of equivocations—which is then reestablished. The passages are as follows:

ORDER→DISORDER→ORDER

Again by analogy with music, one may recall the sequence: consonance→dissonance→resolution.

As the play represents *love* in all its aspects, this youthful quartet represents the antithesis of *rational love*—i.e., *blind love*—impulsive, fickle, mad. It often displays the features of *fanciful love,* which, like poetry (it may even resemble poetic fury, *divinus furor),* has the power to transfigure the things of this world and invent nonexistent forms. Because this is the emotion of passion and deceit, Shakespeare places it in relation to the eye, through which, according to medieval tradition, the passion of love reaches the heart. Titania, in love with the Ass, declares:

> Mine ear is much enamour'd of thy note;
> So is mine eye enthralled to thy shape.
>
> (3.1.133–34)

And the juice of love-in-idleness is laid on the *eyelids* of the young lovers asleep in the forest, a philter that works blind and absurd enamourments.

The characterization of the four actors in the love quartet is extremely simple. They are distributed in antithetic couples that are not distinguished merely by sex. The two girls are contrasted on the basis of antinomies related to (a) temperament, (b) height, and (c) hair color and complexion:

Hermia (a)	versus	Helena (b)
harsh		gentle
short		tall
dark		fair

The two young men are contrasted only on the grounds of temperament:

Demetrius (α)	versus	Lysander (β)
harsh, aggressive		calm, poetic

This basic situation, which, as it were, marks the four pieces in the game, gives rise to four possibilities governed by the rule of heterosexual couplings:

A MIDSUMMER NIGHT'S DREAM

1) a/α
2) b/α
3) a/β
4) b/β

All these combinations are, in fact, used in the various phases of the transformation of the quartet. To the rule of coupling can be added another that concerns reciprocal feelings, which can be either *returned* (+) or *unreturned* (−). On this basis, we could in theory have sixteen possibilities:

(1) a+/α+   (9) a+/β+
(2) a−/α−   (10) a−/β−
(3) a+/α−   (11) a+/β−
(4) a−/α+   (12) a−/β+
(5) b+/α+   (13) b+/β+
(6) b−/α−   (14) b−/β−
(7) b+/α−   (15) b+/β−
(8) b−/α+   (16) b−/β+

In actual fact, however, Shakespeare's game is played out only as follows:

PHASE ONE: The situation at the beginning of the play (the arrow indicates the direction of love; nonreturn of love is not indicated):

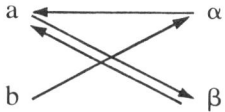

Notes: Hermia loves Lysander, and her love is returned. However, their love encounters the obstacle of the *senex*. Demetrius and Lysander love the same woman and are therefore enemies. The coupling a/β signifies the union of opposite characters. Helena is unloved.

At this point, they all take to the forest: Hermia and Lysander in order to be together, despite Egeus' opposition; Demetrius to follow Hermia and kill his rival, Lysander; and Helena to follow Demetrius.

PHASE TWO: the situation created by the first magic spell:

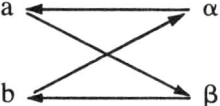

Notes: Lysander, now bewitched, no longer loves Hermia: he loves Helena. No one is unloved, but no love is returned. Demetrius and Lysander remain enemies, and Hermia and Helena become enemies.

PHASE THREE: the situation created by the second spell:

Notes: Demetrius, now bewitched, no longer loves Hermia: he loves Helena. Hermia is unloved. The coupling b/α signifies the union of opposite characters. The two women and the two men remain enemies.

PHASE FOUR: situation created by the third spell:

Notes: Lysander is bewitched again, by a counterspell. Demetrius remains bewitched. A perfectly harmonious resolution of the quartet combination. All loves are returned. The two couplings signify the union of opposite characters. Hermia makes peace with Helena. Demetrius is reconciled with Lysander.

This last situation, phase four, terminates the vicissitudes of the four lovers. The obstacle of the *senex* is overcome; love has triumphed.

The symmetrical game of combinations has an evident connotation in the playful nature of this carefree juvenile affection, in its impulsive, madcap season. On closer examination, however, it also contains a measure of good-natured irony toward the upheavals perpetrated by the solstice. If we recall the situation prior to the action of the play, we realize that the final phase of transformations has merely re-created the original situation, inasmuch as Demetrius loved Helena before he transferred his attentions to her. Thus, in reality, *nothing has happened.* The young people have simply undergone the influences of this seasonal madness, which acts through the movements of the stars and in dangerous collaboration with the world of the spirits, of the secret forces of Nature.

We may therefore conclude that the overall transformational model is still:

$$A \to B \to A$$

in which B represents the transitory moment of "confusion" as compared to "order" (A).

The geometric precision of the combinatory mechanism of this sentimental quartet is paralleled by a strongly formalized language; in a certain sense, it too is *geometric*. The social class to which the four lovers belong is that of the nobility; thus, the language that characterizes them is a genteel, affected, precious speech rich in antitheses and parallelisms.

A typical example of this type of language can be found in Hermia and Lysander's dialogue after the drastic verdict pronounced by Theseus (1.1.128–40). Another example is the oath taken by Hermia, in which the moral solemnity required by the circumstances is nullified—deliberately, of course—by the cloying artificiality of the speech (1.1.168–78). Or we might cite the antiphonal structure of the dialogue in which Helena asks Hermia what arts she has used to captivate Demetrius (1.1.194–201). It is also useful to consider that this manner of speech is parodied in the lines of the artisans, who, in the tragicomedy, speak a language filled with euphuistic devices (5.1.146–48, 168–79). With reference to the theme of the maximum exploitation of every expressive possibility offered by language, it should also be noted how the dimension of the forest—so unsuited to the normal behavior of courtly persons—alters the euphuistic preciousness of the young lovers, stripping them, as it were, of their rhetorical distinctive feature just as it has stripped them of the other attributes of their specific social level. The language, when in contact with the more naturistic order, becomes more paratactic, more direct and lexically less complex. An example is to be seen in the way Lysander tries to get rid of Hermia, who has become an object of hatred for him (3.2.260–64).

As we have already seen, the artisans' plot (C) should be seen as a parody of the plot of the four lovers (B). At the beginning the two dynamic spheres appear unconnected; yet, little by little, one comes to reflect the other, to be its antinomic homologue. We will not here consider the skillful and complex diegetic mechanism which elegantly develops the two plots, weaving them progressively closer and closer; we will consider, instead, the ambiguity constituted by the contemporary presence of synonymy and antinomy.

The two plots are synonymic in the sense that they overlap and present the same thematic and dynamic elements. I am not referring to the interrelation with the clowns but rather to the fact that the story of Pyramus and Thisbe is in some ways the same as that of the quartet of noble lovers. In both cases we find that: (1) two lovers are thwarted; (2) they decide to flee the city for the forest; (3) they carry out their plan in the moonlight; and (4) in the forest they fall victim to an illusion. While Thisbe is waiting for her lover, a lion follows her and tears her mantle. Pyramus sees the garment, is convinced that the beast has devoured his beloved, and in a paroxysm of passion takes his own life. Thisbe stabs herself over the body of her young lover. What substantially distinguishes the two plots is the conclusion: a happy ending in the one case, a tragic outcome in the other, almost as if Shakespeare wished to suggest that the chosen comic mask might also conceal the mask of tragedy. But, in any case, the possible tragedy is made innocuous by the manner of its performance, which is comic in every sense. The artisans are totally incapable of playing any role requiring culture or refinement of feeling. For this reason, the antinomy—internal in this case—can be presented as follows:

| TRAGIC | versus | COMIC |

and as:

| Necessity of cultural experience | versus | Absence of cultural experience |
| Necessity of romantic sensitivity | versus | Absence of romantic sensitivity |

The grotesque preparation of the play, and the actual performance of such a prestigious work (of Ovidian or Chaucerian derivation) in the hands of rough plebeians, offered Shakespeare the opportunity for a glancing irony on the way theater could be presented in his day. But it contains other implications as well. The rehearsal of a refined classical tragedy of amorous disaster takes place in a space which, representing Nature, is the antithesis of Culture. It is also the place where all that is form, propriety, and civility gives way to impulse and vulgar desire. Nature runs blindly to satisfy its whims; it affords no space to courtesy, gentleness, and sentimentalism. Not only can the young courtiers chase each other with indiscriminate passion, but even she who is presented as the most ethereal of the fairy creatures, Titania, can fall head over heels in love with Bottom, the lowest of all creatures—an ass. For this reason, in this space represented by Nature, sentiment and gallantry clearly count for nothing. The episode of Titania's love for Bottom is coarsely erotic and suggestive, and the crafty eye of Priapus gleams in the weaver's ass-head. Thus, we have malapropisms and poor grammar, misuse of words, bad rhyme, halting metre, a total inability to act anything involving pathos, and every sort of vulgarity imaginable.

The world of Nature is represented by the fairies, in a hierarchy which, from its princely, aristocratic peak, passes down through the common people and reaches an underworld that swarms with obscure passions, provokes illusions and fantasies, and triggers impulses. In the cosmology underlying the play—as is frequently the case in Shakespeare—the characters are subject to two distinct impulses that subvert their powers of reason and induce them to behave as they normally never would. On the one hand, there is the influence of the stars—in this case, the solstice and the moon; and, on the other, the action of hidden forces, animistically and mythopoietically represented by the world of the spirits. This too is a full-scale kingdom, constructed precisely like that which is at the peak of the hierarchic scale. It has its king (Oberon) and queen (Titania), who have their fool (Puck) and their subjects. The kingdom of Theseus administers rationality and is "classical," while the kingdom of Oberon administers impulsiveness, caprice, passionality, and eroticism and is "Celtic," "medieval," "romantic." The reason for the intervention of the world of the little people on the occasion of Theseus and Hippolyta's wedding is clearly revealed in Titania's words to Oberon:

> Why art thou here,
> Come from the farthest step of India,

> But that, forsooth, the bouncing Amazon,
> Your buskin'd mistress and your warrior love,
> To Theseus must be wedded, and you come
> To give their bed joy and prosperity?
>
> (2.1.68–73)

Bearing in mind the mirror-image antinomy, we can see how poetry naturally belongs to Oberon's kingdom and not to that of spent passions governed and administered by the law. The workings of the subcultural animist world certainly have no moral purpose. The juice of love-in-idleness simply has the power to make men and women dote on the first person of the opposite sex they set their eyes on. It is, therefore, amoral and insensate. But this world is rich in poetry and fascinating, like the power of the magic philter, thanks to the fantastic spectacle that unfolds before the spectator's eye, with its floral mythopoetic Nature, artfully enriched with music, songs, and dances. This is poetry par excellence, albeit of Renaissance decorative style. We might call it a sort of *poésie pure*. In the symbological rigor of the play it represents the fascination of fantasy *tout court*—what we might today call the subconscious, or the oneiric, as we find not only preternatural happenings but also the fulfillment of what are clearly repressed desires. We thus see that, hierarchically speaking, the young lovers waver between the world of reason, morality, and the law and that of instinct, impulse, and fantasy.

Shakespeare handles the two levels of reality and dream with great mastery. A question arises: did the events in the forest really occur, or were they all part of a dream? The four noble Athenians, once their problems have been resolved, are convinced they have dreamt it all. Hermia says:

> Methinks I see these things with parted eye,
> When everything seems double . . .
>
> (4.1.188–89)

And Demetrius wonders:

> Are you sure
> That we are awake? It seems to me
> That yet we sleep, we dream . . .
>
> (4.1.191–93)

then adds, after calling on the others to follow Theseus into the city (Theseus significantly reappears in the forest at *dawn,* intent on the hunt):

> And by the way let us recount our dreams.
>
> (4.1.198)

They must have been amazed when they found that their dreams coincided perfectly!

It is interesting to note that none of the *human* characters actually sees the fairies. The only exception is Bottom, who, however, thinks he has been dreaming. The game of illusions is specular; this is also evident on other levels, in what is like a series of perspectives. Both the story of Pyramus and Thisbe and the fantastic adventure of the four lovers appear to the spectator as two *irrealities,* within the fiction of the comedy, as fiction it is. But the first of the two, in its blatant fiction, succeeds in bestowing—in a play of perspectives—a degree of concrete reality on the second, which, in fact, is pure dream. Both in the end appear fiction and irreality to the eyes of Theseus, who is however not a real person but a mythological figure and therefore another fiction himself. The epilogue compounds everything in illusion. Puck addresses the audience in the following terms:

> If we shadows have offended,
> Think but this, and all is mended,
> That you have but slumber'd here
> While these visions did appear.
>
> (5.1.409–12)

The play of mirrors also produces refractions. An example of this is to be found in the last act of the play, when the spectators of the *Pyramus and Thisbe* interlude are not just Theseus and Hippolyta and the four young nobles but also ourselves, spectators throughout the ages. It is easy to conclude: *shadows* with *shadows,* when we know that the stage is frequently compared by Shakespeare—following an ancient *topos*—to the world. That is, it is seen as a *mirror of the world;* men are all considered "such stuff as dreams are made on." In *As You Like It,* we read:

> All the world's a stage,
> And all the men and women merely players.
>
> (2.7.139–40)

In *Macbeth* man is compared to:

> a poor player
> That struts and frets his hour upon the stage,
> And then is heard no more.
>
> (5.5.24–26)

And in *King Lear* the world is called "this great stage of fools" (4.6.181).

But let us return to the basic antinomy:

REASON versus MADNESS

In the final act (1.2–17), Theseus makes an oft-quoted declaration. As the play approaches its conclusion, Shakespeare presents the various *points of view* of the major characters as regards what happened in the forest or what is said to have happened. Theseus is skeptical, Bottom believes what he hears, the young lovers believe and disbelieve. Hippolyta remarks that the story is improbable but yet must contain something true (5.1.27). For Theseus, "lovers," "poets," and "lunatics" are "all compact." There are, however, in the follies of art and love certain truths far more profound than those that rationality apprehends and the law administers. One may recall, for example, Hamlet's famous comment on Horatio's incredulity:

> There are more things in heaven and earth, Horatio,
> Than are dreamt of in your philosophy.
>
> (1.5.174–75)

Hippolyta declares:

> But all the story of the night told over,
> And all their minds transfigur'd so together,
> More witnesseth than fancy's images,
> And grows to something of great constancy;
> But howsoever, strange and admirable.
>
> (5.1.23–27)

The "something of great constancy" is not only the miracle of poetry, which has created for the spectator an illusion that is truer than reality itself, but also that fleeting moment of carefree young love which makes it possible to live in a sort of Paradise Lost, with its own ineluctable laws, and which, when once experienced, can be looked back upon with skeptical eye and even mocked—as, indeed, happens in the play—not only by Theseus, as might be expected, but also by the four lovers themselves, now that they have returned to the *polis*. Even at this short distance, they are able to laugh not only at what befell them at a particular moment in their lives but also at the tragedy of Pyramus and Thisbe, which, it is true, is clumsily performed and therefore provokes laughter, but which is also—apart from the tragic ending—their own story.

The possibilities of oxymoronic inversion are all exploited in this curious Shakespearean fantasy. The imperfect performance of the Ovidian tale is not only—as I have already said—an amusing metaphor of the common rudimental failings of Elizabethan acting and settings; it also affords an opportunity to say that all theater invites the spectator to *believe,* for just a moment, the world of enchantment, and thus to *enter,* for just a moment, the sphere of fantasy described with such alluring metaphors in the forest scenes. We are speaking, in other words, of the same appeal Coleridge would later address to the reader of poetry, whose capacity to appreciate that art's distinctive message depends on what he termed the "suspension of disbelief."

Note

Abstracted from *Shakespeare e il paradigma della specularità* (Pisa: Pacini, 1976). Quotations are from *A Midsummer Night's Dream,* ed. H. F. Brooks (London: Methuen, 1979). Other references to Shakespeare's plays are taken from the relevant New Arden editions.

Bonds of Love and Death in *The Merchant of Venice*
ALESSANDRO SERPIERI

Venice is the setting of two of Shakespeare's most complex and "modern" plays, *The Merchant of Venice* (1596–97) and *Othello* (1604). This setting, it is true, he found in the sources: respectively, the first novella of the fourth day in the collection *Il Pecorone* by Ser Giovanni Fiorentino (written in the second half of the fifteenth century but not published until 1558), and the seventh novella in the third decade of the *Hecatommithi* by Gian Battista Giraldi Cinthio (published in 1565). But Shakespeare had to collect considerable background information—over and above what he found in his sources—to be able to re-create so vividly the historical and social atmosphere of Venetian society. It is indeed highly likely that he took great pains in his reading of the sources, in view of the fact (a most singular coincidence) that in Shakespeare's day neither of the stories had been translated into English, both being available only in the original Italian. His Venetian plays must have been worth all the trouble for him.

Venice interested Shakespeare early in his career; he refers to the city in *The Taming of the Shrew* (1592-93) and *Love's Labour's Lost* (1594–95). It is in *The Merchant*, however, that Venice is taken as a specific, well-defined place of dramatic action, one that could not be set elsewhere (as the tale of the shrew or that of Romeo and Juliet might well have been, just to keep within the range of the "Veneto plays"). Venice is a marked historical, geographical, and cultural referent because, despite its incipient decline—already perceptible in the late sixteenth century—it represented for all Europe the republic of great traditions, the western gate to the East, the crossroads of commerce and adventure, the splendid seat of extraordinary wealth and fertile cosmopolitan culture: Italian, but also German, English, Fleming, Jewish, and Oriental.

A place that it was indeed impossible not to be informed about, thanks to the reports—some only oral—of the many travelers who especially for reasons of trade and commerce visited the city every year, and to the more erudite documentation that could be obtained from the various classical and contemporary works published in the numerous Venetian printing shops.[1] A place which for Englishmen at the end of the sixteenth century—that is, at the beginning of the first great epoch of transatlantic colonial expansion which Queen Elizabeth so staunchly supported, became a transposed image of mercantile London, the gate to the West which, because of the importance of its commerce (and, consequently, its political and military power), was soon to take the place of the declining gate to the East.

Venice, for Elizabethan dramatists, was thus a favored place for representing contemporary tensions. We may recall the words of W. M. Merchant, in his Penguin edition of *The Merchant:* "Venice . . . the hub of Italian commerce and one of the most potent centres of the arts, was a dramatic setting to which Shakespeare and his fellow dramatists were frequently to return, its glories and its corrupt decadence establishing tensions of which *The Merchant of Venice* and *Othello* were to make dramatic use."[2] I do not, however, intend to dwell on these summary historical considerations, well known as they are, which serve me merely to stress the topicality—for Shakespeare and his audience—of the Venetian setting of two plays that presented tales of love and death against the background of a tumultuous cosmopolitan society impregnated with countless signs of *discrimination* (racial, ethnic, and religious), and with the more secret phantasms of *projection* (psychological and ideological).

As W. H. Auden pointed out in a perceptive essay published in 1963, Venice was a state whose wealth came from trade, and thus from the accumulation of capital, and not from landed property, as was the case in the feudal and early Renaissance England portrayed by Shakespeare in his history plays. Venice was a mercantile state, therefore international and cosmopolitan, in which the various communities, as Auden says, "must tolerate each other's existence because both are indispensable to the proper *functioning* of society, and this *toleration* is enforced by the laws of the Venetian state."[3] Its *toleration* constituted the pact on which international and protocapitalistic order was based. But this statutory and therefore formally unbreakable *toleration* (to which clear references are to be found at 3.3.26–31 and 4.1.214–18)[4] coexists with the ideological and psychological *intoleration* that is more or less dissimulated in the great deceit, and self-deceit, of bourgeois society. This is the dramatic historical *contract,* or *bond,* against which, in my opinion, the emblematic story of the bond between the merchant Antonio and the usurer Shylock has to be seen.

The action is divided between Venice and Belmont. The great historical city is opposed to a world of fable, apparently feudal, exclusive, noble, rich in ancient and not capitalistic wealth, harmonious and musical, the realm of the fair Portia and her *romance*. This romance revolves around the adventure of a marriage that is to be decided by Chance or Destiny, by the choice of the correct casket of the three (of gold, silver, and lead) that are presented to her suitors in accordance with the wishes of the Mistress of Belmont's late father. The topological and structural bipolarity would appear to indicate a clear semantic and ideological opposition of two stage worlds: the ancient, like a fairy tale and therefore positive, and the modern, dramatic, crossed by tensions and contradictions. But a careful textual reading of the play complicates this bipolarity.

In a stimulating essay written in 1951, Harold C. Goddard sees Venice and Belmont as spaces that rotate around the same principle of pleasure, derived from wealth and luxury, music and "romance," the symbol of which, albeit with different values, is gold. In both spaces, without explanation, sadness or melancholy thrives, as testified in a parallelism that cannot be fortuitous by the opening lines of the first two scenes set in the two apparently opposite worlds, Venice and Belmont: Antonio's words, "In sooth I know not why I am so sad" (1.1.1); and Portia's, "By my troth Nerissa, my little body is aweary of this great world" (1.2.1–2). Both worlds are both rich and alienated. Shylock has the ill fortune to serve as a scapegoat especially for Venice's bad conscience: "Shylock is a representative of both the things of which we have been speaking: of money, because he is himself a money-lender, and of exclusion, because he is the excluded thing," notes Goddard, who adds: "Therefore the Venetian world makes him their scapegoat. They project on him what they have dismissed from their own consciousness as too disturbing. They hate him because he reminds them of their own unconfessed evil qualities."[5] Hatred leads to hatred, so that Shylock, in turn, loathes and persecutes Antonio beyond the rational motivations which he does indeed have. The two antagonists are figures of the same projective intolerance, for if Antonio damns the Jew, the latter, in the name of his "nation"—persecuted but convinced of the authenticity of its Old Testament role as an elected race—in his turn damns the Christian "infidel." In 4.1.35 and following, Shylock publicly indicates the unfathomability of his hatred for Antonio, using a series of examples of unconscious reactions (like that of men who cannot bear the sight of a gaping pig, or go mad if they behold a cat, or of others who cannot contain their urine when they hear the bagpipes), and declares: "So can I give no reason, nor I will not, / More than a lodg'd hate, and a certain loathing / I bear Antonio" (59–61).

The clash between the two is a clash of ideological projections. Goddard again notes: "Unless all signs fail, Antonio, like Shylock, is a victim of force far below the threshold of consciousness . . . Antonio abhors Shylock because he catches his own reflection in his face."[6] The conclusions of my study of *Othello* lead me to agree with these points in Goddard's essay on *The Merchant*.[7] His reading of Portia, mistress of the apparently ideal realm of Belmonte, also appears to me to be textually acceptable: she is not exactly what she seems, since she mocks her suitors pitilessly, discriminates against the Prince of Morocco with evident racism, likes to be in the limelight, and finds her greatest stage in the trial scene.

It is certain, as most critics have pointed out, that the characters in this play can be interpreted in widely different ways. They are complex because the relations between them are complex, placing them at different moments in perspectives that may make them seem positive or negative. The fourth main character, Bassanio, is indubitably ambiguous. He presents himself from the beginning as the predestined winner of the hand of the Mistress of Belmont, but the nobility of his search, which he immediately places in the mythical sign of the quest for the golden fleece, is overlaid with concepts, figures of speech, and expressions of a commercial and capitalistic nature. One may note the first hint of this in his words to Antonio (a hint which comes just after his embarrassed reasoning about his debts to his friend, which can probably be paid off thanks to yet another debt to finance his expedition to Belmont): "In Belmont is a lady richly left, / And she is fair" (1.1.161–62). The conquest of the fair heiress is also strongly marked by expressions having a commercial significance; compare "by your leave, / I come by note to give, and to receive," "stand I even so, / As doubtful whether what I see be true, / Until confirm'd, sign'd, ratified by you" (3.2.139–40, 146–48). Portia replies to him using the same register, in tones that sometimes seem ironical: "I would be trebled twenty times myself, / A thousand times more fair, ten thousand times more rich, / That only to stand high in your account / I might in virtues, beauties, livings, friends / Exceed account: but the full sum of me / Is sum of something: which to term in gross" (3.2.153–

58); or again, more bluntly, "since you are dear bought, I will love you dear" (3.2.312).

All are dominated, more or less explicitly, by the power of money. Lorenzo is—he flees with Shylock's daughter, who steals her father's ducats and jewels when she leaves his roof. So, too, are the minor characters who rotate around the wealth of the "prince of merchants." So, too, deep down, is Launcelot, the servant-clown, who abandons the miserly Jew to enter service with the more munificent and free-spending Bassanio "who indeed gives rare new liveries" (2.2.104–105). Shylock incarnates the evil aspect of the power of money, as has been pointed out by, among others, L. C. Barber (1959), according to whom, as also to Goddard, the Jew is the scapegoat of an entire civilization and therefore the target of an anthropological and historical *projection:* "his role is like that of the scapegoat in many of the primitive rituals which Frazer has made familiar, a figure in whom the evils potential in a social organization are embodied, recognized and enjoyed during a period of licence, and then in due course abused, ridiculed and expelled."[8]

Gold is the symbol, albeit with different values, of both Venice and Belmont, two worlds in formal and semantic opposition yet linked by the transfer not only of characters but also of lexical and ideological registers. Melchiori perceptively points out: "In the context of a society which prizes economic values above all others, the money-lender and the spendthrift are equally guilty, and the distinction between Venice and Belmont is annulled."[9]

The unity of this complex play does not therefore appear to lie in a limpid opposition between two stage worlds, of which the second—the world of the past, of static feudal wealth with the ideal superstructures of harmony, music, circularity and cyclicity of its representation—cannot be a point of strength in the reconstitution of order, in the healing of the historical wound that marks the modern world. If the moneylender is punished, the spendthrift will become the new lord of Belmont, with all his ambiguity and false ideological conscience (that false conscience which, when he is choosing between the caskets—as has been pointed out by many critics—makes him refuse with transparent dramatic irony both the symbol of gold, the real value of which has led him into the affair: "Therefore thou gaudy gold, / Hard food for Midas, I will none of thee," and the symbol of silver: "thou pale and common drudge / 'Tween man and man," 3.2.101–104).

The unity, the cohesion of the work must therefore be sought elsewhere. Graham Midgley identifies it in the theme of solitude.[10] In his opinion, the opposition on which the play is based is not the opposition between Shylock's world and that of love and "romance" but rather the opposition between Shylock and Antonio: "As Shylock is to Venetian society, so is Antonio to the world of love and marriage. The relationship of these two to these two worlds is the same, the relationship of an outsider. The play is, in effect, a twin study in loneliness." If Shylock is an outsider in a Christian society, so too is Antonio (a reading proposed by a number of critics), "because he is an unconscious homosexual in a predominantly, and indeed, blatantly heterosexual society." Here lies the play's thematic and structural unity: "The parallel between Shylock and Antonio is the framework of the play."[11]

It may be, however, that the unity of this play is problematic because it oversteps the constraints and rules of both the comic and the tragic subgenres, making way for an open or mixed structure, which is a symbol of an open or mixed historical model. This appears to be Giorgio Melchiori's suspicion when he writes:

> *The Merchant of Venice* is an extremely complex and subtle play, and for this reason it eludes all traditional classification; its complexity and ambiguity were not perhaps a deliberate choice by the author but are linked to the historical moment in which the work originated and to the social environment to which it is addressed.[12]

I would add that it is also linked to the representation of a world that is actual and not remote—Venice—and to existential and social problems that are unsolved and indeed insoluble in their more or less explicit ideological tensions, in their hidden projections and in the precarious formal recompositions of *historically* dramatic contents.

The secret of the ambiguity of the text lies perhaps in this discrepancy between forms of expression and forms of content, an ambiguity that has been perceived by directors and artists alike, in innumerable performances over the centuries, and by critics of the play. If, indeed, in the forms of expression (the metrical-rhythmical, rhetorical, stylistic, and structural level with regard to the actual form of the play as a comedy), this play more often than not "enchants," in the forms of content, and in particular in the all-pervading monetary-mercantile-judiciary figures of speech (which characterize not only the prose of the merchants, moneylenders, and clowns but also the verse of the "gentle folk"), it brings into question and possibly even completely upsets its stylistic and structural enchantments. Shadows of a competitive, ruthless, materialistic world thus loom over the formal registers and the structural opposition that would seem to be a prelude to the final victory of the harmony of the "romance," the inspiration of the Neoplatonic academy, the music of the spheres, and the resolution of all the threads of the story in full-blown comedy style.

The play seeks unity in its circular structure. As Sigurd Burckhardt observed in 1962, "the plot is circular: bound in such a way that the instrument of destruction, the bond, turns out to be the source of deliverance. Portia, won through the bond, wins Antonio's release from it."[13] But it is a circularity that is sought for, or imposed, but not achieved, as Burckhardt instead concludes: "*The Merchant* is a play about circularity and circulation; it asks how the vicious circle of the bond's law can be transformed into the ring of love. . . . The ring is the bond transformed, the gentle bond."[14] This may, indeed, have been Shakespeare's intention; but the final serenity at Belmont in the last act does not resolve all the unsettled scores, and manifests—more or less obliquely—the tensions of a malaise that can no longer be placated.

This malaise invests the characters and their relationships. The classic form of tragedy would be impossible in the representation of the new bourgeois mercantile world, and the drama of the Jew and the merchant must therefore end in a comic pact. Yet, new and disturbing tragic modalities become visible in the comic genre: (a) the tragic as a feeling of malaise in social relationships, in the interplay of the various coexisting communities, with effects of alienation and exclusion, both passive (suffered by the person) and active (projected by one person on to another); (b) the tragic as a vague and invincible foreboding of the infiniteness of sense and desire, and of the unpredictability of time (a foreboding integral to the history of capitalism and to post-Reformation religiosity). The conventions and perspective of the day prevented direct attribution to the tragic of the radical disturbances of the bourgeois world that was represented (which would, however, be possible in a later age, in the eighteenth- and nineteenth-century novel, as well as in the theater, especially in the late nineteenth and early twentieth centuries), and tended to resolve its peripeteiae structurally and formally in the *comic pact*.

Yet, as we know, the fundamental pact is of another kind, indicated by the term *bond*—at once both obligation and contract—which dominates the entire play, spreading stealthily from the main bond, that of the pound of flesh, to nearly all the relationships this involves.

Let us therefore attempt to read the play in the light of the category of the bond, which is inscribed naturally in the great historical bond of Venetian civilization as a cosmopolitan center of commerce and trade. The scenes of the two stage worlds, Venice and Belmont, appear to be at opposite ends of the axis: market and usury (capitalism) versus property (feudalism), while at the same time they possess kindred qualificative functions: wealth, pomp and ceremony, sadness and melancholy. The principal predicative function, in both places, is that of the bond; in both places, the characters meet, confront each other and associate, forming bonds which they keep, or entering into new bonds. Let us schematically scan the whole play and consider the various bonds agreed upon, which, collectively, are tantamount to the plot of the play.

Antonio's initial sadness—as his friends, Solanio and Salerio, surmise—appears to be due to anxiety about his commercial bonds (his "ventures") or to matters of love. Antonio rejects both explanations: the first, by arguing that on the contrary his solidity as a rich merchant protects him from ruin in partial failures or misadventures; the second, by a somewhat more embarrassed "Fie, fie!" which may denote a process of repression. We shall soon discover, from a number of clues, that the friendship between Antonio and Bassanio is, in its own way, a form of love (Antonio himself will later say as much when he invites his friend to have the newly wed Portia judge "Whether Bassanio had not once a love," 4.1.273), a homosexual love; a bond which Bassanio has therefore shown he wishes to break by proceeding to Belmont to try his luck with the caskets in order to win the fair heiress's hand and resolve his debts by forming a new bond.

At Belmont we find Portia, who is also a prey to melancholy, weary of this "great world," but—as her waiting-woman Nerissa at once points out—she is afflicted by the sickness of abundance, by the ennui of inherited wealth, and not, like Antonio, by scruples of conscience at his economically privileged condition. Yet, like Antonio, Portia is also sad—for reasons of the heart, for reasons of love. She is tied by a bond prescribed by her late father, a bond that is typical of the romance, in which Destiny plays the largest part: she is to have no say in the choice of her husband, as she must accept the suitor who selects the correct casket out of three (one of gold, one of silver, one of lead). The suitors, to gain the right to face the test, also have to accept the constraints of a bond: if they fail, they must not reveal their choice nor ever seek a maiden's hand in marriage.

The situation in Venice develops as we all know: finding himself momentarily without ready money, Antonio asks the moneylender

Shylock for a loan with which to finance Bassanio's journey to Belmont. The bond stipulated between the two sets the forfeit if Antonio should fail to repay the loan: a pound of his flesh will be cut from his breast and given to Shylock. Let us call this *bond A*. It is sealed by Antonio out of love for his friend, who nevertheless leaves him, and by Shylock as an act of retaliation and with the hatred of the outcast. It is a bond of death based on money as a commodity and on the body as a commodity: on the two great mystifications of the new world, the world of the accumulation of capital and usury, and the world of bodies, of slaves, as a commodity, and of bourgeois marriage bonds in which bodies can only be a commodity. Money and love meet dangerously. The money Bassanio borrows from Shylock, with the guarantee of the "prince of merchants," will serve him to win the love of the as yet unknown Portia; but, once that love is won, it will, in turn, serve to make money. If Shylock desires to make money out of money, Bassanio desires to make money out of love. Shylock, however, is the "villain," while Bassanio is presented as the "romantic" hero, the hero of the romance on the way to conquest. The bonds are made secretly, just as Antonio and Shylock meet, beyond whatever good reasons that each may have: Antonio manifests his generosity, which, however, is based on mercantile enterprise, and condemns Judaean usury; while Shylock invokes his holy texts, and repays Christian hatred with his Jewish hatred.

In the meantime, also in Venice, two other bonds are broken and reconstituted. The servant bond between Launcelot and his master Shylock is broken, to be replaced by the new bond between Launcelot and Bassanio, and the family bond—which is also racial and religious—between Jessica and her father is broken, with the formation of the new marriage bond between Jessica and Lorenzo, a bond sealed by the daughter's theft of her father's ducats. Shylock suffers a twofold betrayal. Thus begins the process of isolating the Jew, one of the contracting parties in the main bond, *bond A;* but the isolation of the other contracting party, Antonio, is now also foreshadowed.

All the sequences related to bonds, apart from the main bond, are concluded by sequences of disjunction, with the transfer to Belmont, at different moments, of the Venetian characters as they become involved in new bonds: Bassanio and Gratiano, who find their wives Portia and Nerissa there; Launcelot, who follows his new master; and then Jessica and Lorenzo. Bassanio's choice of the correct casket—a performative sequence—seals the stipulation of the marriage bond with Portia, a bond symbolized by the ring.

Let us call this *bond B*. This is a contract of love versus the death bond *A;* and yet, like the death bond, it is pervaded with economic considerations.

At this point, news comes from Venice that *bond A* is at a critical juncture: all Antonio's ships are thought to be wrecked, Antonio cannot pay his debt in time, and Shylock claims his pound of flesh. *Bond B*, enacted only by virtue of *bond A*, is suspended (the wedding is celebrated but not consummated). This is followed by another act of disjunction that brings back to Venice not only most of the Venetians who have come to Belmont but also Portia and her waiting-woman, Nerissa, disguised as lawyer and scribe.

In the court scene we have the second performative sequence of the play. In the first, Bassanio acted to resolve the enigma posed by Destiny (around which the world of romance revolves), while now, in a precise interplay of symmetries and predicative exchanges, it is the heiress of the romance, Portia, who must resolve the enigma of the Law (around which the bourgeois world revolves). The Law is the law of Venice, its particular statute (to which reference has already been made). But Portia introduces biblical considerations. It has been observed that, against the Old Testament principle of rigorous justice on the basis of the inflexibility of the Law, she sets the New Testament principle of clemency and mercy. This appears to be the case in the first part of the scene, when Portia endeavors to persuade Shylock to desist from his deathly legalism. But when, owing to the formalism of the law, Shylock acknowledges his defeat and is ready to resolve the whole matter by appropriating the sum loaned *without usury,* it is Portia who objects, demanding strict application of the law. If before she had sought Shylock's clemency, now it is she who appears to lack clemency. The destructive relationship of *bond A* has contaminated everyone. Although the Duke's verdict is intended to strike Shylock heavily in his property and goods, Antonio, with apparent clemency, insists that Shylock shall accept, under pain of death, his forced inclusion (or conversion?—it is a forced conversion, another ruthless bond: "that for this favour / he presently become a Christian," 4.1.382–83) in the Christian community, thus depriving the Jew of the most important thing left to him, his religion and culture. This is *bond C*, which Shylock is obliged to accept (like the many Sephardic Jews expelled from Spain in 1492, who in order to find refuge in other countries were compelled to feign belief in Christianity, to be Marranos). It is a bond which would appear to be a bond of Christian love but which, in fact, is clearly a violent bond of coercion of the outsider: yet another bond of "death," then, produced by the false conscience of European ethnocentrism, by its many tragic acts of intolerance occurring against a background of convenient bourgeois-capitalist tolerance which, so long as it was not harmed or disturbed, complacently adopted the *functional* Jew and the *functional* Moor alike.

Now comes another moment of disjunction, with the return to Belmont of all the Venetian characters. But before they arrive, the scene opens with the moonlight night, in the peace and quiet of which Lorenzo and Jessica seem to give a positive interpretation to the themes of love and harmony, safe from the ruthless logic of the *bond*. Yet their evocations of couples of mythical lovers serve only to stress critical and tragic points of *B*-type contracts (Troilus and Cressida, Aeneas and Dido), tragic error (Pyramus and Thisbe), sortilege (Medea and Jason), and theft and flight (Jessica and Lorenzo themselves). As to Lorenzo's celebrated comment on the music and harmony of the spheres, in which the human drama of mortal change is thought to be conciliated (although it is a conciliation which in the view of the Neoplatonic academies could not occur because of the encumbrance of corruptible flesh), it proves to be, on close examination, no more than nostalgia for the Edenic Bond, for the unattainable fullness of Being; the comment is therefore located *beyond* the action, beyond *this* dramatic action and any other real or fictitious action.

Thus, no pacification or resolution of the conflicts is provided, but rather an implicit re-proposal of the open human drama (with the figure of the ellipse or spiral, and not of the circle, as already suggested). The critical point of *bond B* follows in the quarrel of the lovers due to the incident of the rings. Infidelity, if proved, would lead to breakdown. But then, just as Portia saved Antonio at the critical point of *bond A*, Antonio comes to rescue Portia at the same point. He removes any possibility of real disturbance (the disturbance of *his* relationship with Bassanio) to *bond B*, reofficiating it with the guarantee of *his own* exclusion. Note his words: "I dare be bound again, / My soul upon the forfeit, that your lord / Will never more break faith advisedly . . . Here Lord Bassanio, swear to keep this ring" (5.1.251–54 and 256). He remarries them. This is his new bond, which we may call *bond D*, to which, significantly, he commits his soul.

Antonio's *bond D* and Shylock's *bond C* correspond, albeit secretly. The Jew was obliged to suffer an ironic-tragic inclusion (exclusion) in the Christians' community, while now the homosexual Antonio has to accept his own ironic—and, in its way, tragic—inclusion (exclusion) in the lovers' community. Shylock is deprived not so much of his goods but of his culture, and therefore of his human relationships; Antonio is deprived of his love, and of his relationships. The far from comic irony of the play is that, at the end, the two parties contracting the first bond *A*, which triggered the whole story, remain excluded, with no bond. Their function is no longer pertinent to the values of a mercantile-bourgeois society in its positive self-representation, which requires the repression of usury (which under another name, interest, is essential to capitalism) as also of platonic homosexuality, which disturbs the marriage bond (which becomes a relationship of private property and, in many cases, the fusion of economic fortunes).

In the end, success goes—but at a cost Shakespeare gives us secret but unmistakable signs of—to the new bond, symbolized by the union of Bassanio and Portia, which is the historical bond between the new mercantile bourgeoisie and the surviving feudal structure, between Venice and Belmont, a bond that is also a metaphor of the turbulent social and structural transformation of Elizabethan England. The anxiety pervading *The Merchant of Venice,* its melancholy, and its subterraneous projection are hints of a modern tragedy which this "strange" play (and "strange" is possibly the epithet most frequently used by critics to define it), this comedy that brings tears to the eyes (witness theatrical performances over the centuries), creates in extraordinary fashion with its interplay of light and shade.

Notes

An earlier Italian version of this article appeared in *Shakespeare a Verona e nel Veneto,* ed. Agostino Lombardo (Verona: Grafiche Fiorini, 1987).

1. Venice was considered the community of travelers par excellence, "a site of otherness," due to the fact that "The frictions present in any society between brothers and others are particularly enhanced in a community of travellers" (Avraham Oz, "Dobbin on the Rialto: Venice and the Division of Identity," in *Shakespeare's Italy: Functions of Italian Locations in Renaissance Drama,* ed. Michele Marrapodi, A. J. Hoenselaars, Marcello Cappuzzo, and Lino Falzon Santucci (Manchester: Manchester University Press, 1993), 192–93.

2. *The Merchant of Venice,* ed. W. Moelwyn Merchant (Harmondsworth: Penguin, 1967), 38.

3. W. H. Auden, "Brothers and Others" (1963), in *The Merchant of Venice: A Casebook,* ed. John Wilders (London: Macmillan, 1980), 226; emphasis added.

4. Line references to the play are from the Arden edition, ed. John Russell Brown (London: Methuen, 1966).

5. Goddard, "The Three Caskets" (1951), in *The Merchant of Venice: A Casebook,* 144.

6. Ibid., 148.
7. Serpieri, *L'eros negato* (Milan: Il Formichiere, 1978).
8. Barber, "The Merchants and the Jew of Venice" (1959), in *The Merchant of Venice: A Casebook*, 177.
9. Melchiori, *Le commedie romantiche* (Milan: Mondadori, 1982), 10.
10. Midgley, "*The Merchant of Venice: A Reconsideration*" (1960), in *The Merchant of Venice: A Casebook*.
11. Ibid., 195, 199, and 204.
12. Melchiori, *Le commedie romantiche*, 8.
13. Burckhardt, *The Merchant of Venice:* The Gentle Bond," in *The Merchant of Venice: A Casebook*, 211–12.
14. Ibid., 222.

The Interdiction of Eroticism in Shakespeare's Histories
FERNANDO FERRARA

Eros epitomizes the free and joyous satisfaction of human instincts, desires, and impulses. In some moments of history, eros is openly displayed; in others, it is considered something alien, while some cultures restrict it to the extraneous and chaotic world beyond culture, that of uncultivated naturality. "Happiness," said Freud, "is not a cultural value," a statement that is symptomatic of an age that sees culture as the assertion of the superego.[1] It is aptly inscribed in that civilization of renunciation and deferment which ironically produced the *Declaration of Independence,* in which the "pursuit of happiness" is notoriously and mistakenly included among the "inalienable rights of man." Today, after Freud, Marcuse, and Reich, it is a commonplace to say that Western civilization—which sets working hours that leave no place to leisure, demands the discipline of monogamous reproduction and imposes the methodical respect of law and order—in fact, determines deviations and the continual repression of the libido, of eros.[2]

If we wish to understand how all this came about, we can follow a number of paths. In his essay, "Blind Cupid," Edwin Panofsky proposes a path that, to me, seems particularly interesting. At a certain point along this path, in the transition phase between the Middle Ages and the Renaissance, the image of the god Eros gradually became degraded and corrupted until Love was represented as a blindfold figure. The blindfold which at a particular moment in the evolution of iconographic tradition deprives Eros of his sight was the beginning of a procedure of demonization of instinctuality and the subconscious which in the end led to the repression of erotic impulses.

> To the modern beholder the bandage over Cupid's eyes means, if anything, a playful allusion to the irrational and often somewhat puzzling character of amorous sensations and selections. According to the

standards of traditional iconography, however, the blindness of Cupid puts him definitely on the wrong side of the moral world.

To illustrate this development, Panofsky cites the example of John of Gaunt (*Richard II,* 1.3). Discussing the significance of blindfolded eyes, he continues:

> Thus Blind Cupid started his career in rather terrifying company: he belonged to Night, Synagogue, Infidelity, Death and Fortune (the classical *caeca fortuna*) who—we do not know exactly when—had also joined the group of blindfold personifications. Within this group, he was especially associated to Fortune and Death, because these three were blind both in an intransitive and in a transitive sense.[3]

The figure of a blind Eros who blinds others can be found in *Romeo and Juliet, Much Ado About Nothing, King Lear, The Two Gentlemen of Verona, Midsummer Night's Dream* and *The Tempest,* as well as in the *Sonnets.* It is no coincidence that this figure—which we may consider demonized—is opposed, in Shakespeare's verse, to the courtly image of the divine child (the little Love-god . . .) with his inextinguishable torch ("heart inflaming brand") exactly as found in the *Palatine Anthology.* To find this archetype we need only read the last two of Shakespeare's sonnets, 153 and 154.[4]

The great post-feudal civilization—with its concepts of the national state, technical progress, and economic success, a civilization founded on the transcendant values of Christianity which were more or less obliged to coexist with the "truths" of science—tended by its very nature to abolish or imprison eros. In relation to this phenomenon, we will consider here, above all, the initial moment of the exclusion of eros from matters of the *res publica* and from the power of the king which symbolize the new national state.

Medieval kings were seen as "demigods" endowed with mystic powers, and their persons were hereditarily impregnated with divinity. "From them the people expected victory in war and fecundity in peace," says M. Bloch.[5] The fecundity of the king was manifested not only in abundance of crops and fertility of flocks and herds but also in that "fullness of being" that attributed to the king an erotic nature and exceptional reproductive capacities.[6]

The repression of eros from sacred regality, the abolition of eroticism from the management of matters of state, is the implicit datum present in the political doctrines elaborated in the Renaissance and in Shakespeare's histories of the English kings. In accord with the mutations of Elizabethan mentality, this process of interdiction assumes different forms in the various phases of Shakespeare's history plays.

In the archaic histories (among which I include the polyptych on the union of the two noble Houses of Lancaster and York, plus *Edward III* and *King John*), the interdiction of eros manifests itself in the form of ablation, reduction, or anti-exemplum and appears to be fundamentally motivated by Puritan ethical and religious principles.

In the modern histories (among which I include *Richard II* and the three plays devoted to Henry V, first as prince and then as king), the interdiction of the erotic takes the form of abasement and seems to be founded on criteria of the incompatibility—due to rank and status—between eros and power.

In the mythical histories (whose most significant expression is to be found in *Henry VIII*), the interdiction of eros, which finds its expression in sublimation, may be ascribed to changes in the epistemological system which inclined toward hermetic symbolism and Neoplatonic idealism.

The Shakespearean text thus contains and expresses the terms of a long-fought conflict that is about to reach its extreme consequences: an epistemological contest in which the natural urges of the unconscious confront the cultural repressions of a self-confident and demanding superego; a conflict about eros which is part of the transition from one epoch to another—that is, part of the laborious affirmation of the modern mentality of the western world. Only if we bear this in mind can we fully appreciate the spite of Sir Toby Belch when he attacks Malvolio and, with a mixture of rancor and melancholy, shouts at him:

> Dost thou think, because thou art virtuous, there shall
> be no more cakes and ale?[7] (*Twelfth Night,* 2.3.114–15)

Only by reading this sentence as a hypostatization of a conflict between the superego and the unconscious is it possible to understand its true meaning, just as the same criterion helps us understand the historical anguish of the sovereign who, because of the power of his body politic, is willing to renounce the vitality and the exuberance of his physical body ("I know thee not, old man," *Henry V,* 5.5.52).

Henry's absolute repudiation of Falstaff is, in fact, the repression of eros by a culture now imbued with the values of the newly emerging social classes. It implies the interdiction imposed on eros in the discourse on the history of England, a discourse that reaches its acme in *Henry V,* where it finds its epitomization (in the second scene of the first act, history is traced back to Charlemagne)[8] and its regulation a posteriori (the six choruses that punctuate the play establish rules and conventions for this kind of theater).[9]

The conflict between the impulses of the libido and the repression imposed by the new conscience comes into the open and is explicitly represented in the Shakespearean macrotext, both in its most intimate and secret aspect as a drama of the individual conscience (eros denied, as Alessandro Serpieri put it, in the tragedies and tragicomedies)[10] and in its more outward and explicit aspect as a social *agon* (eros rebelling in the comedies and certain atypical plays with a "classical" subject).[11] As we have seen, in the histories, the interdiction of eros prevails.

The histories of Shakespeare and his contemporaries contain plenty of "worthy knights" and "clatter of arms," but there is a dearth of "good women" and "steadfast loves." Nor is it sufficient to plead the restrictions of the rules that governed the writing of this kind of play. The question is not so simple: also because the *exemplaria,* the Greek and Latin classics and the Bible which the singers of national history had at their elbow, did not omit from their tales intriguing and plausible blends of valor and love, of eros and *thanatos.*

These authoritative and respected models proposed a reflection on history in which eros played no mean role in the determination of the destiny of peoples and political leaders: from Samson and Delilah to Antony and Cleopatra, from the chaste Susannah to the violated Lucrece (not to mention the tales of mythology so vividly illuminated by the flame—now bright, now smoldering—of the most violent of erotic passions, the greatest of all being the legend of the War of Troy, which blazed up because of Helen's forbidden love and burned itself out amid the decadent passions of the Achaeans and finally in the demoniac eros of the Atreids).

A fair number of Elizabethan playwrights, Shakespeare included, did, in fact, pick up these hints. Shakespeare, in between his theatrical creations, was practicing erotic writing—in his extremely sensual epyllia dedicated to Southampton, recalling the noble and refined artfulness of the great Marlowe, who had narrated the tale of the two lovers of the Hellespont and of the cunning traps laid by Neptune for the young Leander.

But, returning to the theater, to give an example of the potential qualities of erotic themes in Elizabethan drama, we need only consider the audacious peepshow created by George Peele—who, like all the others, also wrote a number of prim and proper histories—when he saw in the story of David an opportunity for eroticism which had the additional advantage of enabling him to put to good use the features of the Elizabethan stage: he thus placed the king on the upper stage and exhibited in the inner stage the female nude scene of Bathsheba at her bath. His contemporary, George Chapman, opted for the same situation (changing names and places) in his *Ovid's Banquet of Sense,* which presents the full analytical array of Elizabethan erotic sensualism. "The Argument" of this erotic induction, which Chapman places as a foreword to his verse, could be used as a kind of stage direction for Peele's theatrical tableau in order to justify, in this respect, the complex and unusual features of the eros that was repressed from the histories of the English kings:

> Ovid, newly enamoured of Julia, daughter to Octavius Augustus Caesar, after by him called Corinna, secretly conveyed himself into a garden of the Emperor's court, in an arbour whereof Corinna was bathing, playing upon her lute and singing; which Ovid overhearing was exceedingly pleased with the sweetness of her voice and to himself uttered *Auditus.* the comfort he conceived in his sense of Hearing.
>
> Then the odours she used in her bath breathing a rich savour, he expressed the joy he felt in his sense *Olfactus.* of Smelling.
>
> Thus growing more deeply enamoured in great contentment with himself he ventures to see her in the pride of her nakedness; which doing by stealth, he *Visus.* discovered the comfort he conceived in Seeing, and the glory of her beauty.
>
> Not yet satisfied, he useth all his art to make known his being there without her offence; or, being necessarily offended to appease her, which done he entreats a kiss, to serve for satisfaction of his *Gustus.* Taste, which he obtains.
>
> *Tactus.* Then proceeds he to entreaty for the fifth sense, and there is interrupted.[12]

David is invited by Peele to an identical—and, likewise, interrupted—banquet of the senses, in the opening scene of his religious historical play, *David and Bethsabe.* The stage direction reads:

> [The Prologue] He drawes the courtaine, and discovers Bethsabe with her maid bathing over a spring: she sings, and David sits above viewing her.

The scene described by Chapman is repeated and David—who is observing the naked charms of the fair wife of Uriah, his general, engaged far away in the siege of Rabbah—seems to reproduce the passionate outpourings of Ovid, fascinated by the seductive beauty of his beloved:

> What tunes, what words, what looks, what wonders pierce
> My soule incensèd with a suddain fire? (lines 49–50)[13]

The foregoing remarks were necessary before we could proceed to consider the interdiction of eroticism in the histories, in order to appreciate to the fullest extent the quality of this censure. The obliteration of this essential component of contemporary theater ("For what's a play without a woman in it?,[14] Kyd had declared through the mouth of Hieronimo) can be fully assessed only if we bear in mind these ostentations of eros and all the manifestations of this fundamental impulse that can be found teeming in other areas of the Shakespearean world.

I

In the first chapter of his *Arcadia puritana,* Franco Marenco cites a letter by John Jewel, who roundly criticizes princes, "qui sedent otiosi et indulgent voluptatibus." It is true, as Marenco points out, that "the attack is directed not so much at voluptuousness as at absentee rulers"[15]; yet one gains the impression that already in the year 1562 there was criticism of the inauspicious "dissipation" of those in power, a criticism that is still influential in Puritan America today, where more than one candidate has found the road to the presidency barred by his involvement in erotic scandals.

The interdiction of eros in the archaic histories of the English kings, far from suggesting the deliberate adoption of an expressly Puritan ethical and religious rigor,[16] seems, rather, to testify to the formation of a cultural taboo which, in a more general way, became part of the English mentality and declared the incompatibility between power and eroticism on the grounds of the conflict between the concept of "dissipation"—related to eros—and what must be its counterpart in those responsible for matters of state: the sublimation of instinctive impulses.

One of the most striking examples of the interdiction of eros is to be found in *King John,* which celebrates the spirit of the English nation in the disquieting and striking figure of the "Bastard of Faulconbridge" (who is, in fact, the natural son of Richard Coeur de Lion). The erotic tale of the great warrior king's adulterous affair (to a large extent, the same story as that of David and Bathsheba) is dismissed in three lines pronounced by Lady Faulconbridge who, narrating the antefact, provides with cold and discouraging brevity her own succinct version of a love story that might itself have been the subject of a poem or a tragedy:

> King Richard Cœur-de-Lion was thy father:
> By long and vehement suit I was seduc'd
> To make room for him in my husband's bed.
> (1.1.253–55)

The lucidly informative and highly economical nature of the declaration of this adulterous lady represses the typical qualities of eros, which G. Bataille defines as "frenzy, dizziness and loss of consciousness"; these "majestic and inauspicious" elements, fired by an almost religious passion, are replaced by the discipline of a rational narration that destroys all the erotic aspects of the experience.[17]

This experience—of the seducing or seduced king or leader—is often repeated in Shakespearean or pseudo-Shakespearean archaic histories. In this regard, I would draw attention to the first two acts of *Edward III*, where, at least at the beginning, the erotic experience is made to seem not transgression and profanation but fullness of the exuberance of life, which was, at one time, a prerogative of the king.

The meeting between Edward and the Countess of Salisbury is a joyous and lighthearted episode, as every erotic relationship always is in its initial phase. "Venus is the goddess of beauty, the mother of love, the queen of laughter and happiness," said the ancients; and so is this homely Venus, somewhat provincial perhaps but no mediocrity; straightforward and genuine, just a little too unaware of the impetuous strength of her charm.

The portrait that King Edward draws of her reflects the sovereign's passionate infatuation as well as the originality and unpretentious intellectuality of the eros she represents:

> She is grown more fairer far since I came hither;
> Her voice more silvery every word than other,
> Her wit more fluent: what a strange discourse
> Unfolded she of David and his Scots!
> "Even thus," quoth she, "he spake,"—and then spoke broad
> With epithets and accents of the Scot.
> (2.1.25–30)

It is to no purpose to say that the "set speech" is a typical form, the only kind of speech to respect the rules of decorum in these proto-histories,[18] for it is precisely the authenticity of the individualizing observation (which here with happy intuition sets off an unusual but authentic aspect of feminine charm: the capacity for imitation that makes the speech quick-witted and striking), this observation that transgresses all the rules laid down by the masters of rhetoric, that convinces us of the genuineness of the passion, albeit illicit, of the enamored king.

It is indeed a pity, at the end of the second act (after the erotic episode), that this merry countess, in order to honor the interdiction of eros, should assume the haughty, fatal tones of the violated Lucrece and proffer the king a brace of daggers which she sardonically calls "my wedding knives": one to be used to kill the queen, the other to kill her husband the earl, who—according to the rules of courtly love—is imprisoned in the heart of his lady, no longer bright and bubbling. She declares somewhat paradoxically that she is willing to yield so long as her wedding bed is rid of all previous nuptial encumbrances, and the menacing instruments of death, together with her murderous request, provoke Edward's repentance. The king, thwarted in love, returns to arms and prepares to win the first phase of the Wars of France.

Although it is he who is the tempter, Edward III—warrior king and blameless knight—thus overcomes in this episode a crucial moment of his initiation: the erotic trap represented by the Countess of Salisbury. Only he who has passed unharmed through the Bower of Bliss (the reference is to Spenser, not Bosch) may be considered a "parfit knight." Dominion in the territory of war and power, in the reign of *thanatos,* may be achieved only after eros has been suppressed.

This is the rule of the Puritan knight (the "knights of old," with all their authenticity, were of quite a different mettle), the rule respected by Talbot. In *Henry VI,* Part I, this spotless warrior repeats the deeds of St. George, patron saint of England, who killed the dragon (i.e., instinct, the unconscious, eros). Talbot does not become entangled in the golden snare set for him by another countess, the shameless Countess of Auvergne, who with her arts lures him to her castle in order to destroy him. She believes she has him in her power, but she has only the shadow, not the substance. At a blast of Talbot's horn the great general's "true substance" appears—a band of his soldiers, the warriors of England: "These are his substance, sinews, arms, and strength" (2.3.62).

The countess begs pity and the generous Talbot, who now truly possesses her, surrounded as she is by his men-at-arms, ambiguously alludes—dangerously approaching the bounds of forbidden eros—to the rights of the conqueror, the transgressive sacrifice, the eversive orgy:

> What you have done hath not offended me;
> Nor other satisfaction do I crave,
> But only, with your patience, that we may
> Taste of your wine and see what cates you have.
> (2.3.75–78)

Only an aggressive reading can see through the reticence of a text intended to repress the idea of an erotic orgy, but replaces it with the venial sin of alimentary excess. The deliberate interdiction does not annul the erotic thrill clearly detectable in the double entendres "satisfaction" and "cates," the latter of which in Shakespeare's time was often used to indicate "female graces," those parts of the female nude figure (extolled in the numerous *blazons du corps féminin* imported from the more openminded culture of France) which polarized the attention of the erotic impulses of the male world. Moreover, the doctrine of the "dual body" which Talbot adopts (declaring himself to be formed of his physical body—which is empty appearance—and the body politic—his army) already shows that post-medieval cracking of the psyche that was to culminate in the self divided by the Oedipal eros of Hamlet.

It is interesting to follow the widening of this crack, which schizophrenically splits the mind, in the development of the first tetralogy of Shakespeare's histories, observing the impulses induced by the few and singular female figures appearing in them. Here we will consider Joan of Arc (a typically medieval figure, a demoniac witch who uses eros to corrupt honor and valor), Margaret of Anjou (who like a phoenix is born, so to speak, from the ashes of the diabolic Maid of Orleans, but with the Senecan features of Medea, as a manneristic figuration of a new consciousness alternately or simultaneously dominated by erotic or by murderous impulses), Elizabeth Woodville (great-grandmother of Elizabeth the Great and thus a new Bathsheba who, though finding herself "breaking her truth to the ashes" of her first husband, lives among the sprigs of the House of York as an unwilling seductress, a queen for a day, but above all a victim), and Anne Neville (the heartbroken, tearful widow of the Prince of Wales, a tragic version of the more celebrated widow of Ephesus).

From these figures, be they demoniac or merely incautious, springs an eros bringing corruption or death, an eros that presents itself on stage in ambiguous or mystifying forms which induce the powerful to yield, amid the sarcastic comments and vulgar ironies of the onlookers: the Duke of Alençon, bored by the interminable loving whispers between the Dauphin and the Maid of Orleans, remarks:

> Doubtless he shrives this woman to her smock;
> Else ne'er could he so long protract his speech.
> *(1 Henry VI,* 1.2.119–20)

With an almost identical expression, Richard of Gloucester reveals his impatience and scorn at the blandishments addressed by his brother, Edward, to the fair Elizabeth, the far from inconsolable widow who has ensnared him: "The ghostly father now hath done his shrift" (*3 Henry VI,* 3.2.107). Richard's remark, which is apparently a mere vulgarity, contains resentment and spite at his own refusal to love (which he passes off as an impossibility) and at seeing power in the hands of one incapable of using it. This resentment lays bare Richard's ultimate deformity, the deformity of eros known as sadism.

The line of argument that he twice proposes (first, in the frequently quoted monologue that follows immediately in this second scene of the third act of *3 Henry VI,* and, later on, again in the soliloquy that serves as a prologue to *Richard III*) is well known, yet nonetheless often misinterpreted. It is his notorious deformity which, denying him love, is supposed to drive him toward the conquest of power and the crown; yet this deformity is directly invoked by Richard as the matrix of his murderous thirst for power:

> . . . since this earth affords no joy to me
> But to command, to check, to o'erbear such
> As are of better person than myself,
> I'll make my heaven to dream upon the crown.
> *(3 Henry VI,* 3.2.165–68)

This captious justification has been accepted as a revelation of his contorted psyche, of the mental sickness, that is the cause of the death impulse that characterizes the tyrant. But, if that is our interpretation, we merely fall into one of the many traps that the Machiavellian Duke of Gloucester lays for the other characters in the play, for himself, and for his critics.

In reality, his deformity is a symptom, not a cause: it is the symptom of his nature as a "sovereign character," defined by absolute solitude, by isolation, the solitude which, at Bosworth, Richard recognizes as a malediction at the hour of the ghosts: at midnight. "Richard loves Richard; that is, I and I" (*Richard III*, 5.3.184).

Richard is a sadist, a man whose distorted sexuality is different from the desire of all others. It does not require companions of pleasure, since there can be only victims of his pleasure: he is alone.

All things considered, Richard of Gloucester matches very well the description made by Maurice Blanchot of Sade's immoralism which is "founded on the essential basis of absolute solitude. Thus said Sade many a time and in many a way; nature makes us alone . . . the only rule of behaviour is therefore to prefer that which makes us happy and to hold to no account that our preference may cause harm to others; . . . the greatest pain of others always counts less than the least of our pleasures."[19]

Richard's sadism was indeed foreshadowed in the malefic figure of Margaret of Anjou, who seduces Suffolk—King Henry VI's go-between—and is seduced by him in *The First Part of Henry VI*, who, in *The Second Part*, comes on stage clasping Suffolk's decapitated head to her breast, and who rejoices in her torture of the Duke of York, showing him a handkerchief stained with the blood of his son, Rutland, and, in *The Third Part*, finally stabbing him to death.

Richard's sadism comes out especially in the famous episode of the wooing of Lady Anne. During the funeral procession of King Henry VI, murdered by Gloucester, the widow of Edward, also murdered by the monstrous Duke, unexpectedly yields to his perverse courting, to his cunning torture masked as amorous vows.

In the end, Richard exults not so much because he has obtained the object of his desire but because he has violated his reluctant victim beyond all imagination. The only comment pronounced by the sadistic Duke, apart from scorn for Anne, is: "I am crept in favour with myself" (1.2.263). In his solitude as a "sovereign personage," he asserts his perverse singularity by means of total negation:

> What! I that kill'd her husband and his father,
> To take her in her heart's extremest hate,
> . . . .
> And yet to win her, all the world to nothing!
>
> (1.2.235–42)

In the archaic plays about kings of England, the interdiction of eros is propounded by a mentality that sees in the idea of pleasure a harmful dissipation, a shameful waste capable of overwhelming justice, strength, and temperance: "expense of spirit in a waste of shame", (Sonnet 129, 1), which, in the Governour, undermined the virtues indispensable for ruling the state.[20]

Eros is denied, either by suppression or by exhibiting the public triumph of those who overcome its temptations, or by presenting the fatal consequences to those in power who succumb to it. In the last play of this series, *Richard III,* an even deeper and more devastating observation is put forward: the interdiction of eros is not produced by a moral law dictated by the ethics of the people and imposed on their leaders. The interdiction of eros is a symptom, the symptom of the perverse and solitary nature of the tyrant, for whom there *is* no pleasure that is not derived from the domination, subjection, torment, and suffering of his victims. Even amorous conquest—in this aberrant dimension—assumes the form of the torture and ruthless humiliation of the object of desire.

II

In the modern plays about the kings of England, the interdiction of eros manifests itself as the spatial segregation of the erotic and as its degradation in society's scale of values. Eros, reduced to the sordid level of whoredom and grafted on to the stock of vulgar excess, is portrayed as a disruptive secretion of the lowest physical order that accumulates and thrives in places of crime and social perdition.

Interdiction is based on recognized social rules and established cultural practices. The world dominated by eros and sensuality borders on the perverse, sick world described by Philip Stubbes in his *Anatomie of Abuses;* eros is included among the "originals of all uncleanness and impuritie" discussed in the book and is relegated to brothels in quarters of ill repute: eros, stripped of all its fascination, is proffered as an infamy, a sore on the sick body of the state.

In the archaic plays, the threads of erotic discourse that succeeded in passing through the screen of interdiction were interwoven with the deeds of kings and heroes, and borne by ladies of rank, queens, and noble maids. In the world of the last Plantagenets, eros very explicitly passes to Nell Quickly (a hostess and bawd) and Doll Tearsheet (a brothel whore). Eros is experienced and expressed by the outcasts and rejects of society, by the creatures of the low and infamous world that frequent the taverns and tramp the streets in disreputable parts of towns and in the no less dangerous suburbs.

This is the land where Falstaff is king: a disgraced knight, a man-at-arms overcome by sensuality, reduced to mere body, exuberant in his decadent physicality, a deposed king in the Land of Cockaigne, a parody of regality, king of the carnival, Lord of Misrule. In his own way, he is practically a god. And yet, despite his excellence in all that is low and sensual, Falstaff still clings to the degenerate remains of his decomposed dignity, of his besmirched but not forgotten valor.

As a parodist of the king—the father of Hal's political body—Falstaff, the putative father of Hal's physical body, of the erotic body which, in the end, will be denied, describes himself, seeking to save both truth and vain desire:

> A good portly man, i'faith, and a corpulent: of a cheerful look, a pleasing eye and a most noble carriage . . . If that man should be lewdly given, he deceiveth me; for, Harry, I see virtue in his looks.
> (*1 Henry IV*, 2.4.416–22)

The most clamorous and disturbing exhibition of eros that takes place in the hidden world of the tavern is, in Prince Hal's words, "Saturn and Venus . . . in conjunction" (*2 Henry IV*, 2.4.261): the impotent lust of old Falstaff and the venial and affectionately condescending sex of Doll Tearsheet. The scene might have been painful, pathetic even, were it not that even on this incongruous occasion Falstaff exhibits more than ever his invincible regal and godlike manner: after the sterile orgy with his Bacchante, he leaves the stage in grand style, like Dionysus in the mountains of Thrace:

> Pay the musicians, sirrah. Farewell, hostess, farewell, Doll. You see, my good wenches, how men of merit are sought after. . . . Farewell, good wenches: if I be not sent away post, I will see you again ere I go.
> (*2 Henry IV*, 2.4.370–75)

As the Lord of Misrule, as an adoptive father, as a god of sensuality, Falstaff must be sacrificed. The moment Harry, the new king, the new god of rigor and abstinence, accedes to the world of law and order that is watched over by the Lord Chief Justice, he immolates Falstaff on the altar of his newly attained kingship. One stroke of the sword ("I know thee not, old man") puts paid to an age of brilliance, a merry and lively era of the history of England. Possibly that is why Falstaff on his deathbed, as he is about to go (as Mistress Quickly puts it) "to Arthur's bosom," babbled of green fields (in Theobald's famous emendation) and died calling for sack and women.

While the death of Pan (killed by the new Christian religiousness) is accompanied by the cosmic lament of the nymphs of the rivers and woods, the death of this god of the sensual eros of Merry England is hailed by the pathetic weeping of the faithful hostess, who cannot forget the protective numen of her brothel.

Now is the triumphal moment of conjugal love, in which eros is denied by the misogynism of the heroes of abstinence and deferment, preoccupied as they are by the outcome of their power struggles. Such is the mythical Percy, a man of ambition tormented by anxiety and made impotent by an alienation that denies him both pleasure and rest; so, at least, his wife depicts him, in tones not devoid of resentful disappointment:

> O my good lord, why are you thus alone?
> For what offence have I this fortnight been
> A banish'd woman from my Harry's bed?
> Tell me, sweet lord, what is't that takes from thee
> Thy stomach, pleasure, and thy golden sleep?
> (*1 Henry IV*, 2.3.38–42)

After Falstaff's death, all devote themselves to the tepid, regulated, and legalized joys of matrimony, even the vociferous Pistol, the first of Falstaff's cronies, who presents himself (*Henry V*, 2.1) with his wife Nell (Mistress Quickly, who has understood which way the wind is blowing and is seeking to regularize her position). Just like Percy, so Pistol as well deserts his wife for the battlefield; this comic hero does not, however, know whether he has married the hostess Nell or Doll, whose death—of syphilis, what else?—he laments in V.1.

The new king also prepares for matrimony—more to unite the bodies politic of England and France than out of any physical impulse of his body or Princess Katharine's. To his declarations, the princess, who has little English, replies "Pardonnez-moi, I cannot tell wat is 'like me'" (*Henry V*, 5.2.108), possibly saying more than she actually means; for, in this dialogue, neither knows what "to love" means. Henry does his best with military metaphors, whose secondary meanings are indecent rather than erotic ("I should quickly leap into a wife," 5.2.141–42). During this laborious wooing—which requires the services of a simultaneous interpreter—

Henry cannot refrain from alluding to the bellicose progeny that will be fathered by his warrior loins: "I get thee with scambling, and thou must therefore needs prove a good soldier-breeder" (5.2.213–15). This declaration casts a menacing and ironic shadow over the prospective union, menacing because the wars of France will blaze up once again, ironic because Henry VI—the degenerate son of Henry and Katharine, born for reasons of state, not eros— is destined with his fainthearted holiness to bring the English dominion on the Continent to an end.

A separate word is required for *Richard II,* the first of the modern plays on the kings of England, a work that preserves significant links with the world of the archaic histories, apart from possessing its own peculiar dimension. Beneath the surface of this play is a strong tension that seems to be derived from the desire to express a transgressive eros beyond the impediments raised by a barrier of interdiction that is substantially insurmountable.

The analogy with certain less cryptic allusions in Marlowe's *Edward II* suggests that we should make a more oblique interpretation of this text in which, in light of the striking epiphany of the celebrated looking-glass scene, we can read the episode of narcissism characterized by a first phase, during which psychosis divests itself of external objects as if they were the objectives of the libido: "All pomp and majesty I do forswear; / My manors, rents, revenues, I forgo" (4.1.211-12), and a second phase, in which the narcissist reinvests his ego as an object of desire and reaches a state of libidinous autarchy which borders on autoerotism and is a prelude to homosexuality[21] ("My brain I'll prove the female to my soul, / My soul the father, and these two beget / A generation of still-breeding thoughts . . ." (5.5.6–8).

III

Interdictions deriving from the acceptance of an ideology or even the adoption of a new epistemological system are the most drastic and implacable. In the early phase of the reign of James I, Shakespeare's plays absorb and project a number of elements that can be related to the ideology of the absolute sovereign elaborated by the new ruler and his court and to the new epistemological system, with its Platonic and hermetic elements, which thinkers, scientists, politicians, magicians, and alchemists were laboriously producing. "Prospero is both magician and scientist," says Agostino Lombardo, "and this dual quality is such that his scenic action is the image of a delicate and decisive moment in the history of science and ideas."[22] These strong conceptual urges permeate the last plays and, among other things, modify the representation of eros. The natural psychophysical impulse is transfigured in an abstract and falsified idealization that leads to the ultimate degeneration of eroticism: its sublimation.

We thus reach the threshold of what will be the dilemma of heroic theater: love versus honor, an opposition that will reduce the substantial problem to a formal apparatus, finally defeating eros.

The last great opportunity for eros in the matter of the histories of the kings of England might have been offered by the person of Henry VIII, no less vital and sensual than Falstaff, no less transgressive than his forefather Richard Coeur de Lion (father of the bastard of the Faulconbridges), no less passionate than Henry III or Edward IV, no less cynical and sadistic than Richard III. His many wives seemed to guarantee variety and diversity in the realm of eros: it would have been sufficient, as the prologue of Shakespeare's play promises, to tell "that only true we now intend" (*Henry VIII, Prol.* 21).

Henry VIII, however, was destined to another fate. His figure, which became mythical, reflected the absolute power of James I. The first part of his reign foreshadowed the fundamental myths of the new dynasty: the myth of continuity between the Tudor and the Stuart kings and the myth of the political and religious union that James proposed as the guarantee of his new imperial vision, which aimed not only at the foundation of the United Kingdom of New Britain (as in the mythical age of Brut, the exile from Troy) but also at a hegemony of the Stuarts in northern Europe.

In this context, Henry's impetuous eroticism and overly exuberant vitality, which had found full expression in Holbein's celebrated painting, could not be allowed to exist. The only trace remaining, despite the interdictions imposed by reasons of state and ideology, is to be found in two pronouncements which contain bland allusions to the sudden erotic explosion caused by Anne Boleyn and play on the alleged torments of the king's conscience.

Chamberlain.	It seems the marriage with his brother's wife Has crept too near his conscience.
Suffolk.	(*Aside*) No, his conscience Has crept too near another lady.

(2.2.16–18)

The Second Gentleman's exclamation is more spontaneous and not at all malicious when he sees the beautiful Anne in the coronation procession:

> Our king has all the Indies in his arms,
> And more, and richer, when he strains that lady;
> I cannot blame his conscience.
> (4.1.45–47)

A trifling remark if we consider the possibilities offered by this great transgressive passion to any writer desirous of describing its erotic component.

The two queens, on the other hand, quickly take on the hieratic role of symbolic figures epitomizing the traditional virtues of the old religion (Katherine of Aragon) and the regenerated virtues of the new reformed religion (the "Lutheran" Anne Boleyn). Both are ceremonially sanctified on stage and assist the king in the performance of his mission of ecumenical unity.

The slightest of traces of erotic seduction remain within them; but every residue is consumed and sublimated in the beatifying light of the figure of the imperial majesty of Henry VIII, which Shakespeare seems to have derived from Skelton's *Magnificence* and Bale's *King Johan,* two works known to have been inspired by the figure of the instigator of the Anglican reformation.[23]

The intention of the play is the deification of Henry VIII, who has perceptively been described as "not a generically divine king but a specific divinity protecting the British nation."

"I am the husband," James I had declared, "and the whole isle is my wife." Sharing this vision, Shakespeare was obliged to renounce once and for all any representation of eros, for this relationship has nothing to do with human desires and impulses: the union of Great Britain with its king involved no erotic ferments.[24]

If *Henry VIII* is really by Shakespeare and if the theme of the play is the exaltation of the new monarchy, of the union between king and state, and of the mission of peace of the British nation, then it is right that the passions kindled by Cupid should be extinguished. If there is any love in the story of Henry VIII, it is a measured and sacred love such as that of Katherine, whose pure angelic nature is extolled in the following terms by the Duke of Norfolk: "Of her that loves him with that excellence / That angels love good men with" (2.2.33–34).

I now conclude, returning (with acknowledgment to Panofsky) to the icons of eros. The most eloquent, the last of those adopted to illustrate the essay on *Blind Cupid,* reproduces an admirable painting by Lucas Cranach the Elder, which is a splendid illustration of the final episode of the story we have traced out, the last phase of the interdiction of eros, which in *Henry VIII* manifests itself through the sublimation and sanctification of love:

> A picture of his [Lucas Cranach the Elder's], preserved in the Pennsylvanian Museum of Art, shows a little Cupid removing the bandage from his eyes with his own hand and thus transforming himself into a personification of "seeing" love. To do this he bases himself most literally on Plato, for he stands on an imposing volume inscribed *Platonis opera,* from which he seems to be "taking off" for more elevated spheres.[25]

Notes

An earlier Italian version of this article appeared in *L'Eros in Shakespeare,* ed. A. Serpieri and K. Elam (Parma: Pratiche Editrice, 1988).

1. Quoted in H. Marcuse, *Eros and Civilization* (Boston: Beacon Press, 1966), 23.
2. Compare Marcuse, *Eros and Civilization;* and W. Reich, *The Function of the Orgasm* (New York: Farrar Strauss & Giroux, 1943), the "classic" English translation.
3. Panofsky, *Studies in Iconology* (New York: Harper & Row, 1972), 109 and 112.
4. Benvenuto Cellini, *Vita e arte nei sonetti di Shakespeare* (Rome: Tumminelli, 1943); Cellini also mentions Watson and Sidney as possible models.
5. Bloch, *Les rois thaumaturges* (Paris: Leclerc, 1961), 79.
6. For a specific treatment of regality in Shakespeare's histories, see also R. Ciocca's study, *Il cerchio d'oro: i re sacri nel teatro shakespeariano* (Rome: Officina, 1987).
7. Malvolio is notoriously one of the most successful "Puritan" caricatures in all Shakespeare's theater. All quotations from Shakespeare's works refer to the New Arden Edition.
8. Compare *Henry V,* 1.2.33–114.
9. The most notable cases are in 4, *Chorus,* 44–45 and 5, *Chorus,* 15–45. The metatheatrical function of the choruses in *Henry V* has been amply discussed: see, for example, J. H. Walter in his "Introduction," in *Henry V* (London: Methuen, 1954), xliii and passim.
10. In these plays, to generalize an opinion expressed by Serpieri with regard to *Othello,* "the tension, provoked by the violent censure of the Puritan superego, is discharged in the obscure zone between the ego and the id, where ghosts are born"; *"Otello": l'Eros negato* (Milan: Il Formichiere, 1978), 219.
11. I refer, in particular, to *Troilus and Cressida* and *Timon of Athens.*
12. Chapman, *The Works of George Chapman: Poems and Minor Translations,* ed. A. C. Swinburne (London: Chatto and Windus, 1875).

13. *David and Bethsabe,* ed. Elmer Blistein, in *Dramatic Works of George Peele,* gen. ed., C. T. Prouty, 3 vols. (New Haven: Yale University Press, 1952–1970), 3 (1970).
14. *The Spanish Tragedy,* ed. J. R. Mulryne (London: E. Benn, 1970), 4.1.97.
15. Marenco, *Arcadia puritana* (Bari: Adriatica, 1968), 38.
16. For this reason, it seems appropriate to quote Jewel, a stout opponent of all forms of extremism.
17. Bataille, *L'érotisme* (Paris: Gallimard, 1957), 107.
18. Compare F. Ferrara and D. Cuccurullo, "Sostanze mitiche e forme rituali del teatro dei re inglesi," in *Anglistica, AION,* 30 (1987), par. 2, passim.
19. Blanchot, *Lautréamont et Sade* (Paris: Ed. de Minuit, 1949), 220.
20. Jewel's opinion quoted in Marenco, *Arcadia puritana,* p. 38; Shakespeare's Sonnet 129 expresses a similar outlook.
21. Compare S. Freud, *Introduzione al narcisismo* (Turin: Boringhieri, 1976).
22. Lombardo, Introduction to *La Tempesta,* in *Tutto Shakespeare,* I ciclo (Rome: RAI, 1984), 39.
23. King John, according to patriotic tradition the first to assert the autonomy of the crown of England from the Church of Rome, was seen by the Elizabethans as a precursor of Henry VIII, who, with the Reformation, achieved this autonomy.
24. Stubbes, *The Anatomy of Abuses,* ed. F. J. Furnivall (London: The New Shakespeare Society, 1877–79). An entire chapter of the book (pp. 63–84) includes "A particular description of the Abuses of Women."
25. Panofsky, *Studies in Iconology,* 128.

Shakespeare's Discursive Strategies and Their Definitions of Subjectivity

ANGELA LOCATELLI

Introduction

Recent critical debate generally favors the view that both subjectivity and ethics are a matter of cultural strategies.[1] This allows me to try and sketch a profile of the Elizabethan subject as it seems to be articulated within the culture, and then to verify such a "contextual" definition of subjectivity in terms of Shakespearean textual discourse.[2]

What is always implicit in such discourse, and in its rhetorical and dramatic devices, is an ethical and ideological evaluation involving the choice of either stressing or concealing certain "events," and their interpretations. My aim is to come to terms with, and make more explicit, some of the more or less concealed assumptions in the plays.

From Self to "Persona": The Articulation of Early Modern Subjectivity

When the Prince of Denmark procrastinates his revenge and starts philosophizing instead, we realize that a new kind of dramaturgy is taking the stage: the "theater of the word" is replacing the classical theater of action. This is "what happens" in the long four acts, and part of the fifth, of a tragedy, in which "nothing happens." In *Hamlet*, thought and language are dramatized throughout, and not only in the soliloquies. This means that in this new kind of drama the role and function of character needs a completely new, non-Aristotelian definition. The character's position as agent is, in fact, drastically weakened. Consciousness—or, as Hamlet says, "conscience"—is the basis for the new subject of ethics, and the epistemic shift is by no means negligible.

The specific features of classical Greek drama induced Aristotle in the *Poetics* to subordinate character to action and to conceive of ethics in terms of action as well. The drama of the sixteenth and seventeenth centuries, however, both mirrors and produces a widely different sense of action, of character, of ethics, and of the theater itself, which clearly "calls in doubt" the canonical Aristotelian model.

Pico's emphasis on self-knowledge as a value in itself, together with Erasmus' view of the "double nature" of "Man" in the *Enchiridion,* and the "new" psychological dimension of Montaigne's *Essais*[3] are among the most forceful philosophical antecedents to both Hamlet's glory and dejection, as is displayed in the often quoted passage "What piece of work is a man!" (2.2.303–10). After Pico's, Erasmus' and Montaigne's subtle speculation, the subject acquires a new status, one which implies that identity coincides with both the freedom and the burden of "Man's" choice to be either a beast or an angel—being virtually both.

I am well aware that, in the Elizabethan age, women were not subjects, at least not in the sense men were.[4] But, to return to Hamlet, the cowardice of conscience to which he alludes in his famous "To be or not to be" soliloquy (3.1.56–90) also testifies to the fragmentation and protean mutability of Renaissance self, which, if on the one hand it is the energetic and confident beginning of "modern times," on the other hand bears witness to a loss of certainty in a cosmic order and to a loss of fixed meanings, including the erosion of traditional definitions of identity. Hamlet's soliloquies and Pico's works, so different in style and purpose, are remarkably close in their collapsing of medieval hierarchies and in their displacing of what Jurij M. Lotman, in his theory of culture, has called the "symbolic order."[5] Humanist discourse gradually shifts toward a more or less agonized opening onto a "syntagmatic order," where meanings are not "given" but must be "articulated." The "questionable shape" of Hamlet's ghost could indeed be taken as the emblem of the new subject, of the age we now call "early modern."

Stephen Greenblatt has reminded us of the disquieting gap within the subject between the virtual freedom of becoming "arbiter fortunae sue" and the grim reality of social, historical, and cultural forces that drastically reduce such potential.[6] His emphasis on the "shaping power" of self-fashioning has often been stressed, at the expense of his more subdued statement on the abyss that surrounds the artificiality of a self-fashioned identity, however brilliant, famous, or powerful.

Jonathan Dollimore's note of satisfaction for the dawning of a nonessentialist definition of subject in the sixteenth and seventeenth centuries (a satisfaction shared by many in our mass culture) should be balanced against his own awareness that a "decentering" of identity was a source of great bewilderment, confusion, and pain to all parties involved, at the time, in the process of self-definition.[7] As Dollimore puts it: "instead of integrating (ultimately) with a teleological design created and sustained by God, man grows to consciousness in a universe which thwarts his deepest needs."[8]

Elizabethan uneasiness often took the form of a harsh epistemic dualism at the very core of man's vision of himself and the world. This split reverberates in the endless paradigm of oppositions widespread in Elizabethan culture, involving the dichotomies of body/soul, male/female, reason/passion, fate/freedom, fortune/virtue, authority/power, logic/rhetoric, and the many other divisions and subdivisions deriving from them.[9]

When humanism displaces scholasticism and the relics of its Aristotelian "theoria," and moves toward the creation of a distinctively nontheoretical new knowledge,[10] the definition of subjectivity is part and parcel, if not the cornerstone, of this epistemic revolution. However, Aristotle's *Nichomachean Ethics,* together with Cicero's *De Officiis,* still hold a prominent position in both the ethical and the rhetorical discourse of the age.[11] Both classical texts—together with innumerable "conduct books," sermons and homilies, including the well-known *A Mirror for Magistrates,* Sir Thomas Elyot's *The Boke Named the Governour,* and Thomas Wilson's *Rhetorique*—aimed at promoting a sort of layman's morality, based on recognition of the duties of public office, to which all virtues were directed. The cult of "exempla" can be seen as the key to the Elizabethan process of self-fashioning. It is as if simply to live were not enough for the Elizabethan subject; for him, fame was a sort of verification of existence. The Elizabethans' desire to inscribe personal actions into the script of history, by becoming one of its illustrious "exempla," was perhaps their main way of dealing with the anxiety of oblivion. Moving from self to "persona" was their chosen destiny, and "imitatio" the main road to their goal. "Imitatio," "copia," and "exemplum" are clearly responsible for the wealth and sophistication of Elizabethan literature, as well as its definition of subjectivity; but, after all, they are an implicit admission of the lack of value of one's own life per se, as well as one's contemporary history, and suggest the transference of such value to a prized and normative past from which value and meaning had to be projected into contemporary life.

In the Elizabethan age, self-description was coterminous with subjectivity, and yet the self was perceived as incomplete, unfinished, undefined, unless "duplicating" a certain model, usually, as we have seen, the illustrious cases of statesmen, artists, saints, and so on. It is no wonder, then, that the appeal of the theater was so strong in an age that conceived of identity as imitation. The theater was a mimesis of life in a very strict sense, since, for privileged Elizabethans, both were sites of impersonation. The life of both the "dramatis personae" and of "real" persons was sustained by an identical mimetic strategy. John Buxton has drawn our attention to a typically Elizabethan ability, in this respect:

> The power of seeing their own personality from the outside, as others saw it, made them such fine dramatists, freeing their imaginations from those limits of self that make almost all Romantic drama still-born.[12]

Thus, Shakespeare's Caesar, for example, was not only a fictional tyrant, he was also the model for a (virtually) historical one. On the other hand, the meticulous and passionate care that Elizabeth I and James I took in fashioning their own public image highlights the strong link between rhetoric, politics, and ethics in any culture, "via" the pervasive social process of representation. Feminist studies and cultural materialism have appropriated Antonio Gramsci's observations on "subalternity,"[13] and Michel Foucault's lesson on the historical significance of the body and writing,[14] and subsequently have shown that visibility and voice are indeed essential elements in any socially defined subjectivity. The morally relevant question remains: "*Whose* voice? Speaking *of whom?*" If ideology is—as it always is—the justification of (somebody's) power, through political strategies which promote specific assent or dissent, representation is the key to the entire process.

This is a problem I will soon be dealing with when talking about the apparently "technical" device of dramatic enunciation, a device which, on the contrary, I find crucial to our understanding of "who" is speaking, and "of whom," in any text.

Shakespeare's "Double Voice" and the Indeterminacy of Reading

Given that the Shakespearean "subject of ethics" is shaped by precise cultural and textual strategies, it follows that our understanding of such a subject must deal with the shaping forces of the Shakespearean "voice" in the texts. Sometimes actions in Shakespearean drama seem to be valued very differently, despite their similarity, according to the gender and status of the performer of the action. Far from being a relativistic approach to ethics, this, on the contrary, is clearly an essentialist position, one that endows kings with certain attributes and women with others, and that "makes sense" of their actions according to the connotations already socially and culturally ascribed to them. Yet, this "move" seems to be part of a wider dramatic strategy, implying that Shakespeare "has to" start out from essentialist positions in order to subvert them. In other words, Shakespeare does not "make sense" unequivocally, even when referring to relatively stable social protocols and practices. In this light, it is not surprising that the ideology of enunciation in the plays tends to foreground moral and logical contradictions, as well as erase and disavow them.

It would be a crude oversimplification to say that Shakespeare is *exclusively* expressing a conservative political standing, in line with the "Tudor myth," in the Histories, or an anti-democratic position in the Roman Plays, a racist outlook in *The Merchant of Venice* and *The Tempest,* and a misogynous perspective in the Comedies. Shakespeare is *also* expressing these attitudes, and there are unmistakable signs of his being terrified, and therefore biased, when depicting the "people" as a seditious and fickle "mob," Caliban as a strange "animal," the Jew as a threatening economic rival (and partner), and the woman as an irresistible but lewd, capricious, nagging, and "morally inferior" being.

Much time and energy have been devoted to demonstrating that Shakespeare, if he ever existed, was misogynous, and/or that he supported tyrants; equal time and energy have been spent showing that he problematized patriarchy and undermined authority.

This gives Shakespearean drama a special flavor and corroborates the impression that the plays "give with one hand what they take away with the other." This effect, which I would call the plays' "double enunciation," contributes to provoking a verdict of interpretive indeterminacy from a large part of contemporary criticism.

"Double enunciation" seems to explain why Shakespeare, like all great art, is political but not doctrinaire. By *political,* I mean that Shakespearean drama can illustrate controversial issues and represent conflicts of interest in detail, and from different angles, while eschewing black-and-white statements. The controversy over just about any issue of race, gender, religion, and politics found in the canon can, and probably will, continue to go on "forever," because the essence of political theater is to promote debate while that of doctrinaire theater is to quench it (incidentally, this seems one of the reasons for inserting Shakespeare in academic curricula).

If, in the past, and above all in the nineteenth century, interpretation sought, and found in the Shakespearean canon, ground for the belief in, and production of, a sure "central meaning" through identification with the protagonists, we nowadays seek another kind of significance, in the same texts and in their contexts. We have clearly shifted focus, from characters as "real people," to language, to questions of rhetoric and "genre," a shift which permits, among other things, our recognition of the fact that tragedy has a polysemic dimension lacking in melodrama.[15] If the nineteenth century displayed a prevalent critical interest in character rather than action (which had been Aristotle's perspective on drama), our century's crucial critical move is from character to language. Another of its immediate consequences is due emphasis on Shakespeare's rhetorical ability. Shakespeare's mastery of rhetoric has relevant ethical implications in the plays, first of all, because rhetoric has taken Shakespeare far beyond "plain talk" (a favorite mode of speech among doctrinaires), and beyond the reductive logic of either/or when entering disputes. Rhetoric no doubt strengthened Shakespeare's perception of drama as controversy, as a fight between rival positions, each of which must be convincingly voiced; and rhetoric certainly helped provide the greatest dramatist of the age with more than a touch of the ability to impersonate—that is, fully enter the fictional mind and desire of different, even opposite—"dramatis personae."

René Girard's brilliant reading of Bottom as the archetypal actor, because the most veracious impersonator among Shakespearean characters,[16] confirms the protean nature of the self-fashioned Elizabethan subject, while shedding a new light on the crucial "mimetic" desire and cultural strategy of an age which, as we have said, conceived of subjectivity in terms of impersonation and of drama as a perfect, but certainly not photographic, mimesis of life.

What is relevant in the definition of the subject of ethics, however, is that, precisely while dramatizing contending and controversial positions—and, therefore, to some extent, problematizing each and all of them—the dramatist or, more precisely, the watermark of his "presence"—i.e., dramatic enunciation—still passes judgments and makes ideological alignments "over the heads" of the different positions he represents. In this respect, I think it essential to draw a distinction between the utterances of single characters and the global enunciation of each play. In Shakespeare's case, the dramatist's alignments must not be sought solely or mostly at the level of character, because characters are but one level of a much more complex message: i.e., the play in its totality, including character, action, dialogue, symbols, icons, allusions, and understatements and including, beyond all this, the cultural codes a play mirrors and, at the same, re-creates.[17] Characters will always offer the indeterminacy of reading, as well as "problematizing" issues, because they are always involved in disputes. That is their quintessential dramatic function, whether they are "types" and silhouettes (in which case, they tend to promote an allegorical reading of themselves and of the play) or psychologically "well-rounded" (which has favored a "Romantic" identificatory reading).

"Double Enunciation" in *Julius Caesar, The Merchant of Venice* and . . . other controversies

I have said that, in drama, enunciation greatly differs from linguistic utterances per se (that is, from what individual characters say on the stage), that enunciation is largely responsible for the attribution of "value" to both characters and actions. This happens because enunciation produces either a disparaging or a glorifying attitude toward single characters, and either foregrounds or conceals crucial ideological assumptions in the plays. Enunciation often meta-comments dramatic situations, thus "guiding" and directing readers, as much as it shapes characters. Sometimes this procedure even reverses the meaning of the entire previous dramatic action. Katharina's final speech in *The Taming of the Shrew* (5.2.137–80) is indicative of the entire strategy. In this speech, Katharina's "new self" is the negation of all that she was, and of all that happened before, unless it is ironical—which, of course, would open up the possibility of a formidable blow to patriarchal ideology for the times when it was written. We are left in doubt as to the irony of a husband's attributes ("lord," "king," "governor"), and as to the theatricality of Katharina's gesture of submission. If the speech is not ironical, however, it must sound like a grim and inevitable defeat. This speech is the end not only of a fierce character but also of the possibility of articulating an anti-patriarchal discourse, a possibility the dramatist may reject in favor of the triumphantly misogynous and socially expected "happy ending." We seem to have a familiar instance of Shakespearean "double enunciation"—that is, the dramatization of contradiction and conflict, as well as the resolution that best confirms the status quo.

Enunciation draws characters along specific lines and not others. Sometimes it returns on its own pronouncements in order to revise them and to modify connotations and attributes. This is often done, for example, by having one character tell us how to "read" another: Lavinia and Desdemona are "interpreted" even before expressing their own feelings. The "spying plots" in *Hamlet* confirm the habit of "reading" someone's mind through his or her actions.[18] Polonius's erroneous judgments on Hamlet's madness and Ophelia's role in it miss the point but well illustrate the technique: Claudius and the Queen "believe" him and endorse his "reading." They also appoint more "readers": Rosencrantz and Guildenstern. But they are, in turn, "read" by the more sagacious Hamlet, who tells the audience (the last "readers," spies, and eavesdroppers, in the interpretive chain) how to read the Court: to notice their falsity versus Hamlet's own sincerity. Hamlet's punning on the word *seems* (1.2.75–85), his distinction between the Court's "show" of grief, and his own inner feelings are important in this respect. They are clearly directed to the audience as much as they are to Hamlet's mother.

I will now explore dramatic enunciation more closely in two morally significant works, *Julius Caesar* and *The Merchant of Venice*. I have chosen them because "double enunciation," as I define it above, is here discernible in the apparently balanced voicing of conflicting positions, one of which is, however, favored a priori.

Julius Caesar is a masterpiece of dramatic and forensic rhetoric, where we can verify Shakespeare's ability in representing ideological conflict, but also the crafty devices of enunciation in both keeping historical "truth" and reinterpreting it in Tudor-Stuart terms. Robert Y. Turner has rightly called our attention to Clifford and Cade, in *2 Henry VI,* as "the forerunners of Antony and Brutus."[19] The similarity should be appreciated in political as well as stylistic terms (the respective use of poetry and prose). Clifford's royalist sentiments anticipate Antony's celebration of Caesar's symbolical and political authority. We can add that, from the point of view of dramatic enunciation, there is also a similar perlocutory purpose in the two plays: the aim, with reference to one of the hottest political controversies of the times, is to persuade the audience to side with the king and against parliamentary rule; more generally, it is a defense of "illuminated despotism" against the threat of civil war and revolution. Isn't this also the controversial ideology of the Histories, in which conflicts and inconsistencies are indeed dramatized, but almost, one feels, in order to empty out the potential of the revolutionary party?

I find it significant that in *Julius Caesar,* Brutus' anti-authoritarian position is grossly misunderstood by the people, who end up wanting him "to be Caesar." They completely pervert, or at best ignore, his deepest aspirations against tyranny, an institution he abhors so much that he is ready to sacrifice himself to avoid it, in the way that he had, for the same reason, "sacrificed Caesar" (3.2.51–52). In his desire to "awake the senses" of his listeners, and in his appeal to "judgment," Brutus sounds exactly like a "philosopher." His conflict with Antony echoes the Elizabethan controversy between logic and rhetoric, a controversy that was also political, because imbued with ideological overtones.[20] When looking at Brutus' attributes and mode of speech, we may recall Sidney's mistrust of philosophy, because, as he writes in *Am Apologie for Poetrie,* philosophy "teacheth *occidendos esse.*"[21] If history had, in Brutus' case, confirmed Sidney's worst fears of sedition in killing the "tyrant Caesar," it is interesting to look at what Shakespeare makes of both Plutarch's *fabula* and Sidney's comments. Sidney, like Ascham before him and a host of contemporary rhetoricians, maintained that only a good man could be a good orator; in this light, rebel Brutus' rhetorical and political failure had to become synonyms. In fact, Shakespeare builds a subtle and inevitable defeat for his "republican" hero. His downfall is promoted through several dramatic devices. One of them is the fact that Brutus leaves the stage (the public assembly) when introducing Antony. This obviously prevents all possibility of debate with the next speaker. By erasing the likelihood of the emergence of contradictions in the final speeches of the two protagonists, whose ideological rivalry has given the play its main thrust, dramatic enunciation carefully avoids a true dialectic between Antony and Brutus, who cannot respond to his rival's sarcastic refrain, "Brutus is an honorable man."

Moreover, before Antonio's crucial speech, we see the crowd give their consent to the last speaker: they side with Pompey, after Marullo's speech; then they change their mind and favor Brutus. Inevitably, they will side with Antony, provided he speaks last, which he does, since he "has to win." This, of course, also confirms the anti-democratic ideology of the play's enunciation, which depicts "the mob" as amorphous, easily mystified, and unimaginative.

Julius Caesar is founded on the central Aristotelian distinction between the violence of weapons and the violence of the word. Brutus' rhetoric is made to fail in Shakespeare because Brutus was a murderer in Plutarch (and probably, but this remains questionable, because Shakespeare feared regicide as much as Sidney did). Thomas Wilson's authority proclaimed that words can bend and bind the listener's "conscience" with their power of seductiveness, and that persuasion can achieve more than bloodshed itself: "Good was that Oratour whiche coulde do so muche: and wise was that king which would use such a meane. . . . If profite may perswade, what greater gayne can we have, than *withoute bloudshed* to achieve a conquest?"[22] We should not ignore the fact that Wilson's opinion proves so important in the Shakespearean canon, on more than one occasion, both in upholding the "peaceful" and political uses of rhetoric and as a direct reference to the debate on usury, as we shall now see.

A general ambiguity pervades *The Merchant of Venice,* which critics have generally noticed.[23] A. D. Moody, among others, has rightly pointed out that: "The play does not celebrate the Christian virtues so much as expose their absence."[24] What I wish to illustrate here is that this ambiguity is to be found both at the level of the characters' utterances and, even more important, at the "framing" level of dramatic enunciation.

In this comedy we find many examples of significant gaps between "saying" and "doing": words often proclaim what actions fail to achieve, or actions determine what words deny. The comedy's driving force seems to be a sharp dialectic between the main characters who enter a dispute on the theme of usury, while, at the same time, entering a risky money-lending contract. None of the protagonists is ever fully sincere about his or her own motives and intentions. The first dispute (1.3) is rhetorically interesting since it closely echoes contemporary works on this theme: Thomas Wilson's *Discourse upon Usury* (1572) and M. Mosse's *Arraignment and Conviction of Usury* (1595). Based on well-known Aristotelian, biblical, and political arguments, these works reflect some of the social and political concerns of the age. The role of the aristocracy vis-à-vis the transition from a feudal economy to a proto-capitalistic system, in which moneylending was the central transforming force, is a crucial preoccupation of this comedy's enunciation. In fact, the contract between Antonio and Shylock is the occasion on which the two protagonists immediately appear as both rivals and partners, inaugurating a series of interesting ideological aporias in this text.

The two protagonists converge in a ritualized exchange, which is, in fact, a pseudo-exchange, given the duplicity and reciprocal mistrust of both parties. The object of their pact is money, but is also the famous "pound of flesh."[25] This unusual "token" of exchange has several textual and extra-textual meanings: on the basis of ancient Roman law, by which a man could either be dismembered or sold as a slave to pay his debts, the "pound of flesh" represents a legally "acceptable" counterpart for failing to keep the contract. In a Freudian and symbolical reading, the pound of flesh represents Antonio's virility which he gambles against the sterility of money. Given the ambiguities that mark the "pound of flesh," we should return to the duplicity of the partners, who seem to reach an agreement but whose contract is strongly undermined by their rivalry and mistrust, as the metalinguistically relevant opposition "*Fair terms / Villain mind*" suggests.

Antonio and Shylock do not listen to each other. Each one starts out from his own presuppositions, which drastically diverge from those of the other; and each one clings to them stubbornly and blindly. The semantic gap begins with the fact that they discuss *the same theme*, usury, thus creating the illusion of a communicative exchange; but they do so from irreconcilable angles, and therefore empty the exchange of its true communicative significance. The irreconcilable angles consist in the fact that Antonio discusses the *legitimacy* of usury, adopting an "abstract," moral, and legalistic approach; while Shylock discusses its *usefulness* and its profitableness according to a purely practical criterion. Epistemically, we have a collision between a theoretical and a pragmatic approach; such a clash in point of view cannot but produce a pseudo-reality which is even more "false," since none of the two parties can meta-comment its nature.

Not surprisingly, Laban's parable and his "well won thrift" do not convince Antonio, but Shylock's practical "ratio" is taken to its logical and yet unpleasant extreme when he equates "good" with "sufficient," and when he sarcastically calls Antonio a "prodigal." How diametrically their positions diverge is also visible in the qualification of "prodigal Christian," an insult in the context of Shylock's logic but a compliment in Antonio's.

In "Shakespearean inscriptions: The voicing of power," Jonathan Goldberg warns against sentimentalizing Shylock, who is "ravenously greedy," as his refrain "three thousand ducats" demonstrates.[26] In the play, Shylock is certainly "sinning." He is unscrupulous, mean-spirited, and violent. A nonsentimental reading will also show Shylock's bad faith in hiding his blood thirst and desire for revenge under the famous "Hath not a Jew eyes?" speech (3.1.47-66). This is not, in fact, a humanitarian plea, but an excuse for vengeance, a justification for his desire to "bait fish" with Antonio's flesh.

At this point, however, we must also recognize that the role of dramatic enunciation has already produced massive effects. Characterization is ruled by the idealization of Antonio and the debasement of Shylock, which explains the impossibility of sentimentalizing the Jew if we remain at the level of the characters' ethics.

If we move beyond the characters toward the play's ideology, and include enunciation in our reading, we find that things are completely different. At this level, Shylock is truly "sinned against," by the crafty and biased enunciation that foregrounds his "extreame crueltie" from the very title of the comedy, and throughout, in his words and deeds.[27]

Antonio's bad faith, on the other hand, is both visible and concealed in his posture of "ennui" (1.1.1–7), in his pseudo-stoic attitude to "the world," in his pretentious nobility of mind when extolling the virtues of male friendship, and, above all, in his acceptance of the usury he deprecates. Dramatic enunciation covers up Antonio's contradictions and foregrounds his loud proclamations of morality. Antonio is thus inscribed in a medieval chivalric code where his passivity and theoretical bent are cherished as the equivalent of true nobility.

Moreover, and from the point of view of the play's reception, the epistemic divarication we have outlined in Antonio and Shylock's dialogue forbids a reasoned "taking sides" with either one of the contenders. In fact, historically, the play has generally been received "emotionally," with complete disregard for its logical contradictions. If we needed "proof" of Shakespeare's oratorial ability and power of persuasion, we can see it in the fact that the rhetorical appeal of the play has decisively won over the logic of its argument.

Similarly, dramatic enunciation highlights Portia's plea for mercy, in the trial scene, instead of her plain lack of it, when she is in a position to practice what she preaches.

In the essay already mentioned,[28] Jonathan Goldberg proposes a subtle, but not entirely convincing, reading of the character of Portia and of her court appearance. Goldberg wants to reject the idea that "Shakespeare is inevitably expressing the positions of a patriarchal culture." I agree with his thesis because, as I have said, semantic inevitability would make Shakespeare's plays doctrinaire, rather than political, and I do not think Shakespearean drama is doctrinaire. However, I find it hard to share Goldberg's specific argument and conclusions on the character of Portia and her bearing on *The Merchant of Venice,* when he writes:

> My argument, in brief, is that the play fully problematizes the notion of the law and that Portia has a voice *within* the law; not that it constricts and denies her, not that she must submit to the father, but that she *becomes* the father precisely because the law is not the father's, and not exclusively a male territory. The law Portia enacts knows no kind; it is the law of genre. (pp. 120-21)

He also says:

> Portia arrives in the court of law to function in place of the learned Bellario in offering an opinion on the legality of Shylock's proceedings against Antonio—and he adds—: In order to assume the authority of Bellario, Portia must arrive clothed inwardly and outwardly as a man. (p. 121)

There seems to be a contradiction here between the statement about "the law not being exclusively a male territory" and not being the father's law, and Goldberg's own emphasis, which I find brilliantly perceptive but, unfortunately, undeveloped in his discussion, of the fact that Portia "functions *in place of*" Bellario and in a man's attire and frame of mind. The voice Portia supposedly "has within the law" is not her own, and therefore the law is far from being neutral. At the level of rhetoric, we are experiencing exactly the opposite of "prosopopeia." In fact, Portia does not foreground "her" "self," but is a pawn in a man's game, and in a man's world that includes her father and his legacy, Bassanio and his privileges as husband, Antonio as her husband's best friend, and, last but not least, Bellario, the voice of the law. It is indeed true that "the letter from Bellario serves as her credentials," a fact clearly stressed in the dramatic enunciation as much as it repeatedly insists on Portia's appearance as a man, and ultimately as a substitute, thus foregrounding the masculinity of the law. Portia is almost a "pure sign," that is, something that stands in place of something else, and therefore not an autonomous subject. Her referentiality is erased and her symbolical value is heightened, within an order of discourse that is alien to her, within the "will" and "name of the father." What we see in her court role is the substitution of a speaker (Bellario) with another, who speaks on his behalf, in his name, and in his clothes. Portia is a vitally necessary element in Antonio's world, and this is indeed one of the greatest contradictions of a patriarchal universe, and another of the aporias of enunciation. Far from being "silent," like Cordelia, Portia is eloquent in the trial; in the scene of the three caskets, she is praised for her knowledge of the law, as much as the audience is expected to praise her for her "pale" and "silent" obedience to her father's will.

This is a case in which the "double standard" of enunciation reaches a climax: we have the illusion of subjectivity (hosts of critics have delighted in Portia as an "active" heroine) while the dissolution of the (female) subject is carried out almost completely. Who is playing this trick on us? Neither Portia nor Bellario, but a crafty dramatic enunciation, which is exploiting the gaps between the "reality" of the actor on the stage and the role(s) it impersonates, between the woman's presence and her negation in the discourses of subjectivity, starting with the iconic denial of her disguise.[29] And yet a hasty, and perhaps well-meaning, interpretation has induced generations of readers to believe in Portia's dynamic subjectivity. Like several other institutions and political positions (usury, marriage, the aristocracy), patriarchy is "problematized" in *The Merchant of Venice* because of the crucial "difference" Portia's court appearance makes in a masculine universe, as well as because her role, as daughter and wife, is explicitly confronted with Jessica's.

Jessica creates a "double bind" for the audience. They are expected to approve of her love for a Christian while at the same time condemning her treason of her father. Significantly, from the point of view of the play's enunciation, her virtues are faults in Shylock's eyes. She is romantic, generous, and open; he is literal, pragmatic, and mean. Their points of view are irreconcilable, which means that the audience cannot side with both, even if seeing the "reasons" of each. Patriarchy is problematized, but not because the law in the *Merchant of Venice* is not "the law of the father." It is problematized because of the series of semantic aporias I have pointed out, aporias which spread out from single dramatic utterances and spill into the level of enunciation.

The play's ideology is articulated in such a subtle, complex way that we are led to believe that the two parties involved in the controversy (Shylock and Antonio, Portia and Jessica) are given an equal chance, when they are not. I am thinking, of course, of the famous trial scene in Act 4, which clearly shows how *The Merchant of Venice,* like most Shakespearean drama, is imbued with an extraordinary perceptiveness of duplicity, in words and deeds.[30]

I wish to conclude with a few remarks on the transference of "Shakespearean duplicity" from text to reader. A play like *Othello* best illustrates my meaning. Jane Adamson has shown[31] that criticism which concerns itself with the issue of Othello's guilt tends to split into two parties: one of those who, despite Desdemona's murder, still see Othello as a "Noble Hero" (among them is A. C. Bradley), the other, the party of those who, like F. R. Leavis, see Othello as the supreme villain, together with Iago. I believe that both of these widely different opinions paradoxically stem from the same approach to the issue of ethics in the play. The two radically differing moral judgments derive from an identical interpretive position, which accepts the protagonist's dilemma, behavior and "tragic fault," as the ultimate locus of the play's moral significance. Both interpretations express a moral judgment from the standpoint of the protagonist's choice, at the expense of the play's *tragic* quality. By so doing, they turn Othello into melodrama. It goes without saying that many of the "Romantic" and "Victorian" readings of Shakespeare are in this line. But, while objecting to the moral indifference of deconstruction (which is not as neutral as it wishes to believe), we can still try to be moral, while not being "Victorian" in our interpretive attitude. We can, for example, move a little further from the single character's single speech toward a more global (but obviously never complete or "final") view of the plays. Very briefly, let us ask: "Is Cordelia's unresponsive shrinking from her father's 'incestuous' and senile claims more 'unnatural' than his expectations?" Yet, readings of this tragedy prevalently "side with him," making *his* point of view absolutely relevant. Is Hippolyta's deceit in *A Midsummer Night's Dream* an excessive and/or immoral response to the behavior of someone who "woo'd her with the sword" and "won her love doing her injuries"? A similar situation (and the same dilemma) is magnified, of course, for Lady Anne in *Richard III;* yet some critics have failed (or defensively refused) to see the feigning in her protestations of love for the murderous king, who angers and revolts her. Is Tamora's revenge in *Titus Andronicus* more cruel than Richard III's behavior in the Histories? And yet, critics have often been so blinded by what they perceive as the unequivocal ideological assumptions of both plays that they have spent immense skill and effort in finding excuses for Richard but never attempted to find any for her. Dramatic enunciation has a complexity that allows for "cracks" and defacements in the picture; yet critics have often been too afraid of "the figure in the carpet," and rightly so, when finding it would have been the end of their complacent, doctrinaire understanding.

Many critics and readers simply do not (want to) pay sufficient attention to the complexity of dramatic enunciation, which, while making its appeal to the "obvious" stock responses in our culture, is also undermining them, forcing us to ask questions on ethics and character that may be both disturbing and liberating.

While looking for the play's ideology, interpretive uncertainty can, of course, remain; and it often does, as we have seen, but the contradictions of confrontation (within the play, and when the play is in progress) cannot be equated with what remains problematic in interpretation, with its irreducible residue. The indeterminacy of textual meanings should be proclaimed after a certain depth of analysis and in the context of conscious and self-reflexive methodological specifications on the part of the interpretant, lest we fall back on a variant of the "idealistic" approach criticism has problematized and eroded since early structuralism.

If we cannot invite Hamlet to dinner or know "How many children had Lady Macbeth?" it is simply because we have changed our questions about characters, texts, and reading. Having changed our questions and, together with them, our definitions of subjectivity, we have, of course, another problem to deal with. "What is the ideology of our own criticism? Whose interests are defended in our narratives of decentering?" But this is, of course, something to be discussed on a future occasion.

Notes

1. The major works of Jaques Lacan, Emile Benveniste, Roland Barthes, Michel Foucault, Jaques Derrida, and Milton Singer have decisively contributed to our understanding of subjectivity in terms of cultural and discursive strategy.

Specifically, on the issues of "subject" and "ethics" in recent critical debate, see also, Richard Eldrige, *On Moral Personhood: Philosophy, Literature, Criticism, and Self-Understanding* (Chicago: University of Chicago Press, 1989); *The Self: Interdisciplinary Approaches,* ed. Jaine Strauss and George R. Goethals (New York and Berlin: Springer-Verlag, 1991).

2. I found the following works relevant to the topic of "Shakespeare, Ethics, and Subjectivity": Stephen Greenblatt, *Renaissance Self-Fashioning: From More to Shakespeare,* (Chicago: University of Chicago Press, 1980); Stephen Greenblatt, *Learning to Curse: Essays in Early Modern Culture* (New York and London: Routledge, 1990); *Representing Shakespeare: New Psychoanalytic Essays,* ed. Murray M. Schwartz and Coppélia Kahn (Baltimore: Johns Hopkins University Press, 1980); Catherine Belsey, *The Subject of Tragedy: Identity and Difference in Renaissance Drama* (London: Routledge, 1985, 1991); Jonathan Dollimore, *Radical Tragedy: Religion, Ideology and Power in the Drama of Shakespeare and his Contemporaries* (New York: Harvester Wheatsheaf, 1984, 1989); Jonathan Dollimore, "King Lear (c. 1605–06) and Essentialist Humanism," in *Shakespearean Tragedy,* ed. John Drakakis (London: Longman, 1992), 194–

207; *Shakespeare and the Question of Theory,* ed. Geoffrey Hartman and Patricia Parker (New York: Methuen, 1985); S. C. Boorman, *Human Conflict in Shakespeare* (London: Routledge & Kegan Paul, 1987); Christy Desmet, *Reading Shakespeare's Characters: Rhetoric, Ethics, and Identity* (Amherst: University of Massachusetts Press, 1992).

3. Giovanni Pico della Mirandola, *Oration on the Dignity of Man,* trans. Elizabeth Livermore Forbes, in *The Renaissance Philosophy of Man,* ed. Ernst Cassirer et al. (Chicago: University of Chicago Press, 1948), 224–25; Desiderius Erasmus, *Enchiridion,* trans. and ed. Raymond Himelick (Bloomington: Indiana University Press, 1963); Michel Eyquem de Montaigne, *Les Essais,* ed. Maurice Rat (Paris: Garnier, 1942).

4. As Catherine Belsey tells us:

"The subject of liberal humanism claims to be the unified, autonomous author of his or her own choices (moral, electoral and consumer), and the source and origin of speech. Women in Britain for most of the sixteenth and seventeenth centuries were not fully any of these things. Able to speak, . . . they were none the less enjoined to silence, discouraged from any form of speech which was not an act of submission to the authority of their fathers or husbands. . . . They speak with equal conviction from incompatible subject-positions, displaying a discontinuity of being, an 'inconstancy' which is seen as characteristically feminine. Legally the position of women was inherently discontinuous, their rights fluctuating with their marital status. From the discourses defining power relations in the state women were simply absent; in the definitions of power relations within the family their position was inconsistent and to some degree contradictory."

Belsey, *Subject of Tragedy,* 149. The bibliography on feminist studies of Shakespeare is simply too vast even to start listing. The following works are mentioned because they have had a conscious impact on the writing of this essay: Coppélia Kahn, *Man's Estate: Masculine Identity in Shakespeare* (Berkeley: University of California Press, 1981); Elaine Showalter, "Representing Ophelia: Women, Madness and the Responsibilities of Feminist Criticism," in *Shakespeare and the Question of Theory,* 77–94; *Rewriting the Renaissance: The Discourses of Sexual Difference in Early Modern Europe,* ed. Margaret W. Ferguson, Maureen Quilligan, and Nancy J. Vickers (Chicago: University of Chicago Press, 1986); *The Matter of Difference: Materialist Feminist Criticism of Shakespeare,* ed. Valerie Wayne (New York: Harvester Wheatshaft, 1991); Sara Eton, "Defacing the Feminine in Renaissance Tragedy," in *The Matter of Difference,* 181–98; Janet Adelman, *Suffocating Mothers: Fantasies of Maternal Origin in Shakespeare, from "Hamlet" to "The Tempest"* (New York: Routledge, 1992).

5. Lotman, "Il problema del segno e del sistema segnico della cultura russa prima del XX secolo," *Ricerche Semiotiche,* ed. Jurij M. Lotman and Boris A. Uspenskij (Turin: Einaudi, 1973), 44–46.

6. Greenblatt, *Renaissance Self-Fashioning.*

7. Dollimore, *Radical Tragedy.*

8. Dollimore, "King Lear," 195.

9. I have dealt with the Elizabethan epistemic dualism in "Doubles and Doubling as Shakespearian Difference," *Saikoanaritikaru Eibungaku Ronso, Psychoanalytical Study of English and Literature,* 5 (Tokyo, 1992): 20–36.

10. Victoria Kahn, "Humanism and the Resistance to Theory," in *Literary Theory/Renaissance Texts,* ed. Patricia Parker and David Quint (Baltimore: Johns Hopkins University Press, 1986), 373–96.

11. S. C. Boorman, *Human Conflict in Shakespeare* (London: Routledge & Kegan Paul, 1987), 7–8. Boorman reminds us that Cicero's *De Officiis* was first

published in English in 1534, in R. Whytinton's translation, which was followed by N. Grimalde's successful editions and re-editions from 1553 to 1600. Aristotle's *Ethics,* available in Latin in 1479, was "paraphrased in English, from an Italian version, in an edition of 1547."

12. Buxton, *Sir Philip Sidney and the English Renaissance* (London: Macmillan, 1954), 23.

13. Gramsci, *Selections from Prison Notebooks,* ed. and trans. Quintin Hoare and Geoffrey Nowell Smith (London: Lawrence & Wishart, 1971).

14. Foucault, *Language, Counter-Memory, Practice* (Ithaca: Cornell University Press, 1977); Michel Foucault, *The Order of Things: An Archaeology of the Human Sciences* (London: Tavistock, 1970); Michel Foucault, *The Archaeology of Knowledge* (London: Tavistock, 1974).

15. Angela Locatelli, "La melodrammaticità di *Othello* nel testo e in alcune varianti di fruizione," in *Forme del Melodrammatico: Parole e musica (1700–1800), Contributi per la Storia di un genere,* ed. Bruno Gallo (Milan: Guerini e Associati, 1988), 329–38.

16. Girard, "Bottom's One-Man Show," in *The Current in Criticism: Essays on the Present and Future of Literary Theory,* ed. Clayton Koelb and Virgil Lokke (West Lafayette, Ind.: Purdue University Press, 1987), 99–122; René Girard, *Violence and the Sacred* (Baltimore: Johns Hopkins University Press, 1978); René Girard, "The Politics of Desire in *Troilus and Cressida,*" in *Shakespeare and the Question of Theory,* 188–209.

17. L. C. Knights, "The Question of Character in Shakespeare," in *Approaches to Shakespeare,* ed. Norman Rabkin (New York: McGraw-Hill, 1964), 47–65. In his challenging reassessment of A. C. Bradley's views, Knights rightly insists: "Shakespeare . . . works not through realistic portrayal but through poetry—that is through symbolism and suggestion"; ibid., p. 54. Knights invites us to see that "What is relevant for us is not an assumed hinterland of motives, but simply the particular 'address to the world' that is embodied, with different degrees of explicitness, in the different characters"; ibid., 55-56.

18. The idea of "spying plots" in *Hamlet* is mentioned in Marcello Pagnini's pioneering article, "Per una semiologia del teatro classico," *Strumenti critici* (June 1970): 121–40.

19. Turner, *Shakespeare's Apprenticeship* (Chicago: University of Chicago Press, 1974).

20. Angela Locatelli, "'Wisdom' and 'Eloquence': Note sull'episteme della retorica inglese del XVI e XVII secolo," in *La Fortuna della Retorica,* ed. Giuseppe G. Castorina and Vittoriana Villa (Chieti: Metis, 1993), 91–98; Angela Locatelli, "The Image of the English Language in the Elizabethan Controversy on Rhyme," *Quaderni del Dipartimento di Linguistica e Letterature Comparate* 5 (1989), 43–49.

21. Sidney, *An Apologie for Poetrie* (1588–89), ed. Geoffrey Sheperd (Manchester: Manchester University Press, 1973).

22. Wilson, *The Arte of Rhetorique* (1553/1560), ed. Thomas J. Derrick (New York: Garland Publishing, 1982), 25.

23. H. B. Charlton, *Shakespearian Comedy* (London: Methuen, 1938, 1966); Frank Kermode, "The Mature Comedies," in *Early Shakespeare* (London: Stratford Upon Avon Studies, 1961); Leslie Fiedler, *The Stranger in Shakespeare* (New York: Stein & Day, 1972); Alexander Leggatt, *Shakespeare's Comedy of Love* (London, 1974); Lawrence Danson, *The Harmonies of* The Merchant of Venice, (New Haven: Yale University Press, 1978); Leonard Tennenhouse, "The Counter-

feit Order of *The Merchant of Venice,* in *Representing Shakespeare: New Psychoanalytic Essays,* ed. Schwartz and Kahn (Baltimore: Johns Hopkins University Press, 1980), 54–69; Carol Leventen, "Patrimony and Patriarchy in *The Merchant of Venice,*" in *The Matter of Difference: Materialist Feminist Criticism of Shakespeare* (New York: Harvester Wheatshaft, 1981), 59–79.

24. Moody, *Shakespeare:* The Merchant of Venice, *Studies in English Literature,* 21 (1964).

25. Textually, the *pound of flesh* is repeatedly related to Shylock's desires and motives, as we can see in the following passages:

> —Act 1, scene 3, 41–42: "If I can catch him once upon the hip,/ I will feed fat the ancient grudge I bear him." This is but one of several instances of literalization of metaphor in Shylock's speech, a speech which is always marked by a deep distrust of words and faith in "facts."
> —The idea returns in Act 2, scene 5, lines 14–15: "But yet I'll go in hate to feed upon / The prodigal Christian." The banquet here, far from being a communion, recalls and repeats the ambiguous dealings of the original contract.
> —Act 1, scene 3, lines 161–163: "A pound of man's flesh taken from a man / is not so estimable, profitable neither / as flesh of muttons, beefs or goats." These lines clearly foreground Shylock's attempt to debase his rival, by unfavorably comparing him with animals. A similar obsession with Antonio's "flesh" is present in Act 4, scene 1, lines 40-43: "I rather choose to have / A weight of carrion flesh, than to receive / Three thousand ducats." Here, Antonio is defined as sexually corrupt, lewd ("carrion flesh"), and therefore as morally base. Shylock is perhaps also suggesting that he will be the surgeon who cuts off the infected organ in Antonio's sick body. The overtones of castration also suggest a sado-masochist "relationship."

26. Goldberg, "Shakespearean Inscriptions: The Voicing of Power," in *Shakespeare and the Question of Theory,* 116–37.

27. The "extended" title of the quarto dated 1600 reads:"The most excellent/ Historie of the *Merchant of Venice.* / With the *extreame crueltie* of Shylocke the Iewe / towards the sayd Merchant, in cutting a iust pound / of his flesh: and the obtaining of *Portia* / by the choyse of three chests / . . .," in the Arden edition of *The Merchant of Venice* (London: Methuen, 1971), xi.

28. Goldberg, *Shakespearean Inscriptions,* 120–21.

29. Lisa Jardine, *Still Harping on Daughters* (New York: Columbia University Press, 1983, 1989); Catherine Belsey, "Disrupting Sexual Difference: Meaning and Gender in the Comedies," in *Alternative Shakespeares,* ed. John Drakakis (London: Methuen, 1985).

30. Since, for reasons of brevity, I cannot analyze this scene in detail, I refer the reader to "Dialettica e ideologia in *The Merchant of Venice,*" in my *L'Eloquenza e gli Incantesimi: Interpretazioni Shakespeariane* (Milan: Guerini e Associati, 1988), 73–88.

31. Adamson, *Othello: Some Problems of Judgment and Feeling* (Cambridge: Cambridge University Press, 1980).

Part Two
Theme and Culture

In a Time of Unrest: A Role for the Theater In *Measure for Measure*
VITO AMORUSO

Of all the "problem plays," *Measure for Measure* is not only one of the most evidently complex and contradictory in its formal structure but also the play that has most divided a long critical tradition on nearly every point of its complex nature.

I should therefore clarify from the outset what, to my mind, cannot in any way represent a starting point: the allegorical, religious reading (from Wilson Knight to Roy Battenhouse)[1] which sees the work as a thesis play exemplifying the morality of the Gospels, and in particular Atonement, repentance, and the humble Christian acceptance of the will of God, incarnated in the central omniscient figure of the Duke.

It cannot be a starting point, for two simple and obvious reasons. The first concerns the texture and, above all, the actual course of the scenic action. Even granting, for the sake of argument, that this was Shakespeare's dramaturgic intention, *Measure for Measure* registers not only its abstract, rhetorical, and juxtaposed nature with regard to the impervious course of reality but its denial and overturning as well, so that the very person who should have been its driving image, the emblematic "figure" of those values, ends up reducing this ideal code to selfish empirics.

The second reason is, broadly speaking, cultural: no philological analogy that can be traced will ever be able to reduce Shakespeare's overall point of view to a simple, orthodox Christian transcription of the morality of the Gospels.

As has been variously shown, this text, among others, contains a number of more marked and more convincing humanistic Renaissance referents (for example, Seneca, with *De Clementia,* or Cicero, with *De Officiis, auctores*, who in relation to the art of good government or the role of the sovereign are explicitly mentioned by Sir Thomas Elyot and by James I himself, in *Basilicon Doron*).

It might, on the contrary, be possible to affirm that one of the dramatic results of *Measure for Measure* is precisely that it unequivocally confirms the gap that has irreparably opened up between ideals and reality, along with the impossibility of confining everything to the "rationale" of a unitary culture framework.

Even the exact contrary of the edifying and spiritualistic reading of *Measure for Measure* does not provide an exhaustive interpretation. This interpretation degrades the tragic and potentially destructive tension that pervades the text (especially in the first two acts) to the code convention of staging,[2] and thus to a dramaturgic intention which is confined to a manipulatory and parodistic purpose, within the "device" of comic tradition (as W. W. Lawrence was the first to suggest).[3]

Indeed, the text describes, first and foremost, an *iter,* whereas the comic solution, the parodistic reversal of fortune, the artifice of stage and roles (primarily, the Duke as a disguised ruler) are merely a final, abrupt outcome, rather than a planned purpose. They also present, to my mind, an unmistakable trace of compulsion, of forced choice, necessary but bitter.

One could also consider the historical conditions, the relation between artist and court. The considerable degree of critical freedom allowed (witness, above all, the flourishing of all kinds of texts laden with topical meaning in the Elizabethan age, though to a considerably lesser extent after James I came to the throne) permitted no direct questioning, however allusive, of the figure of the sovereign.

To appreciate the true nature of the play, one need answer a simple, though often eluded, question. As W. Empson pointed out in one of the few illuminating studies on *Measure for Measure,*[4] this question asks what is likely to have drawn Shakespeare's attention to the theme, as he found it in the sources (G. B. Giraldi Cinthio and Whetstone).

In my view, there is no doubt that the theme of the Duke—who temporarily renounces his dukedom, who rules by proxy and *in absentia,* thereby deliberately provoking a centrifugal disgregation of the structure of civilized society—attracted Shakespeare at this particular moment precisely because of its immediately and explicitly "political" nature. Besides, this reflects a consolidated English humanistic cultural tradition, as well as a long-standing preoccupation with the nature, credibility, and hold of the House of Tudor and its rapport with the complex reality of Elizabethan England (one need only recall the critical reading of English history provided by the history plays).

What I call the political nature of the theme does not, however, imply only the broad, general sense of a play of ideas, centered on the proper, balanced, "measured" relationship that must exist between authorities and subjects, between governor and governed—in other words, between state and society—for, in this sense, we should take for granted an identity between the idea of state and society represented in *Measure for Measure* and what lies outside: the real English society of those years, which instead, in its totality and generality, is no longer included here.

The political theme of the play may, instead, aim at recapturing within a theatrical microcosm a zone of reality that now threatens to be conflictually different.

What interests Shakespeare is that, with rational passion, this theme offered him a dramatically critical analysis, from the viewpoint of a courtier's ideology, of an institutional crisis that was no longer latent, of a dangerous loss of identity of the role and nature of the ruling class.

The audience he chose to address is this, and no other. It is, per se, a political—and, therefore, subjective—choice. Thus, it necessarily requires the maximum of ideal adhesion and, at one point, also the maximum of lucid, impassionate distance.

Beyond the urgency of the moment, Shakespeare strives to investigate the origins of a crisis of hegemony that goes far beyond a specific political context. To realize it, he must reject that mirror image of the theater, which has usually been found in Hamlet's famous precept. All is reduced to a courtly context, to its varied degrees of representativity and functions, so that even its "scene"—that is, the actual staging—is represented by a center that degrades and ramifies, from high to low.

Obviously, this does not prevent the powerful and sometimes burning tensions of the historical moment from constituting the alarming background without which the lacerating contradictions that explode within the play would not appear to be as they are.

It is not necessary here to reconsider all the reasons that made the years immediately before and after 1603 a crucial turning point, a period generally considered a moment of final passing, when it was difficult and increasingly unpopular to adopt any humanistically or classically intermediate or moderate position. The very concept of compromise, in the cultural and political sense, was out of the question for both fronts—the monarchy and the Puritan London citizenry, of whom even the most moderate identified themselves less and less with that state.

I would like to recall just one of these factors because of its direct relevance to a reading of *Measure for Measure,* and which—in the framework of a debate that is only formally religious and moralistic—directly invests the function of an artist like Shakespeare.

I am referring to the growing Puritan hostility toward the theater, which in those years was already ceasing to be in some way a mouthpiece of these requirements and thus a place of compromise and debate on a complex cultural and political reality.

This is shown by the activity of Anthony Munday (*Sir John Oldcastle, Sir Thomas More*) and in particular by a very popular play about Robin Hood (*The Downfall of Robert Earl of Huntington,* 1598–1601), written for the Admiral's Men, which, behind a legendary heroic story, justifies the choice of exile in order to deny obedience to oppression and thereby the legal representativeness of the institutions of the state.

This climate of radicalization came, moreover, at a time of grave economic and social tension. I am referring to the triennium 1595–1598 and to the recurrent "rebellions" throughout the Tudor period: the famous Essex rebellion in 1600 (the dying gasp of feudal-type conflict), but also—apart from the extremes of Puritan radicalism—to the entire range of social discontent which, albeit among a minority, was beginning to express aspirations to egalitarianism and revolt, which the Levellers' program of 1640 was eventually to appropriate, as Christopher Hill stated in 1972 in *The World Upside Down*.

This alarming reality is always in the background—never directly referred to, explicitly kept outside the borders of the "body politic," and yet evoked in its absence by the silence that precisely in the theater descends upon its ominous quality of radical antagonism: if it is occasionally present, it is, so to speak, as a by-product of this exclusion—that is, as "mob," "misrule," a degraded reality, a low, instinctive naturality.

The terms of this bitter, general contradiction could be analyzed by Shakespeare *only* from the point of view of the court and its ideology, although its incumbent crisis is decidedly acknowledged by him. This is why the theatrical medium acquires a formal structure that is the exact counterpart of a multiplication of centers, a madreporic proliferation of realities and diasporas, of centrifugal islands of values.

What was required, therefore, was a theatrical genre that could be both mirror and locus of a possible and dramatically urgent recomposition, a metaphorically all-inclusive expression of a critical reality, of a sense of malaise and dark foreboding, of those "mixed feelings" that constitute the new note—strident and bitter in its suspended uncertainty—presented by *Measure for Measure*.

As James Lever points out in the Arden edition (from which all the following quotations are taken), this genre is tragicomedy, as theorized by G. B. Guarini in *Compendio della poesia tragicomica* (1601): because in its "favola verisimile, ma non vera," in its "nodo finto," and above all in its "rivolgimento felice," tragicomedy perfectly expressed a need for equilibrium which, through the order of the theater, might possibly become a norm representative of an order beyond the theater. A need, however, not an actual reality; the proposal of an achievement, not its realization. The entire significance of the divided and divergent dramatic discourse of *Measure for Measure* lies precisely in this gap between aim and achievement. In its extreme and paradoxical form, in the intense, frantic "comic" finale, this gap reaffirms, with great ideal and dramaturgic coherence, all the tragic rationality of the conflict and keeps it intact in the final apparent reversal.

So drastic is the asperity of this conflict that it is introduced with uncommon exemplificatory clarity at the very beginning, when the curtain rises: not only in the choice announced by Duke Vincentio but also in the way this is worded, as a sudden and unmotivated "absence," which another, Angelo first and foremost, must "supply," to represent, by proxy as if he really embodied Power, the institutions, the "properties of government," and "Common Justice."

This power of proxy, however, is purely nominal and "feigned." It is a tactical device and rhetorical expedient; for the duke conceals his demiurgically real, central role which (as we see in the unfolding of the action) he programmatically reserves to himself. Moreover, the power of proxy is, from the very start, tragically ambiguous and contradictory.

A void is created at the center of institutional reality. A point of reference is annulled, which the duke seeks variously to fill in terms of splitting between form and reality.

When the duke explains to Angelo the reason why he is the one to have been chosen ("There is a kind of character in thy life / That to th' observer doth thy history / Fully unfold" 1.1.27–29), he insists, as he has already done with Escalus, on the juridical and moral necessity of this "unfolding," on the syntony or consistency between virtue and action, that is, on the imperative nature of a moral duty and its necessary operativity ("Heaven doth with us as we with torches do, / Not light them for themselves," 1.1.32–33). There is clear irony in his asking others to "go forth," showing the light of a consistency he has denied first, creating the shadow of his absence, stealing away behind an empty mask.

Even at this early point, and with a bitter connotation of tragic irrationality, the man who represents power is, absent as he is, that "old fantastical duke of dark corners" (4.3.156) of whom Lucio will speak at a much later stage. He already embodies what the course of action will congeal in the puppet-like artifice of convention: a peculiar capacity to relativistically degrade values to names, to separate them from behaviors, so that the criterion of double and multiple nominal truth is upgraded to ideology.

Of course, the duke's metaphors run contrariwise. They are, so to speak, monovalent and one-way, in the sense that they are intended, with utterly rhetorical insistence, to describe an equation and ultimately a tautology. They seek to draw a specular measuring line between what one is and what one does, with extra stress on right action, both in private and in public, in government and in morality.

What the duke says, however, differs from what occurs as a consequence. In the exercise of justice, as in the interpretation of the law and thus of the relationship with society, Escalus and Angelo are two pans in an unbalanced scale. The tolerance of the former—a mixture of compliance and shrewd, realistic obedience to the customary tradition of common law—is the exact opposite of Angelo's absolute rigor and Puritan furor. What is worse, the real effect of the split is the pure mechanism of arbitrium, the divisive violence that follows, as in a geometric equation, both in the relationship between the state and its citizens and, within each citizen, between private and public, norm and deviation. In the end, it threatens to enforce this separation, this reversibility, ominously as *the* new law.

As on a chessboard that has lost its pattern, the rules of the game, the sense of a dialectic and a connective relationship, are drastically upset. Each character is situated at the extreme point of his latent inclinations, stalemated yet obliged to move. In this generalized diaspora, in this stiffening of roles and functions, measurelessness reigns supreme—or, rather, the constellation of many measures—a culture and a reality, so to speak—of the island and the fragment.

All this, moreover, goes on in an atmosphere (of which all are darkly aware) of ambiguity, falsehood, and treachery: "in th' ambush of my name," (1.3.41) in the duke's words, an expression that is all the more menacing, the more the duke strives to connote it only in a neutral, almost technical sense.

Therefore, it is only natural that the images so insisted upon regarding external appearance—"figure," "character," "stamp," "coin"—are matched by the precise reversal of the medal: empty sacral solemnity is countered by the equally rigid deformation of scurrilous sarcasm or the defamatory licentiousness of Lucio, Pompey, and Mistress Overdone, since it is at the very center of reality that high and low, tragic and comic, are inextricably mixed up.

Claudio, the forced victim of these tensions, echoes this confusion-identity between "liberty" and restraint. Wavering neurotically between despair and rebellion, between a longing for guilt and the impulsive amoralism of "naturality," he embodies the extreme level of the impasse in which all are trapped—that is, not only the pure nominalism of values but also the vague perception and climate of illicit traffic and exchange; of utilitarian leveling by which all the characters are affected; and, above all, that sense of being manipulated from without rather than acting independently, whether moved by ethics or impulse.

Upon close inspection, even the prime motor of the dramatic intrigue, the duke, is himself compelled to translate the ideal "high" representativity of his role into routine ability, to reduce to mere tactics and everyday administration that which has lost all solid credibility: that he represents, indeed, is the ethically founded, absolute legitimation of Power.

Mask and disguise are something more than a stage device. They are of the essence, and for that very reason are a forced, consubstantial choice. Power is not merely a Machiavellian reality (as the vicissitudes of the Bolingbrokes and Prince Henry in the history plays had shown), founded on the restricted base of its brute form; now it is a tactical disintegration, "vulgar" empirics.

It is in one of the greatest tragic moments in *Measure for Measure*—the clash between the incorruptible deputy and the cold, virginal Isabella—that this disintegration is already at work. Both Angelo and Isabella have taken up their stand at the extreme limits of the nominalism of principles; but what is truly relevant is that the scene of a subtle, ambiguous duel over essences is transformed into an all-devouring, individualistic engulfment.

We can see this disintegration, this opaque timbre that reality adopts, a dull background silence amid the clamor—the din, one might say—of that heated, impervious dialectic.

Obviously, this does not mean that at the particular moment (in their fiery vehemence, in the conflict between them) Angelo and Isabella are false, unauthentic, but rather that it is the notion of tragedy which, in them, undergoes a profound yet subtle transformation, a mutation that develops through the splitting—so manifest in them—between values and deeds.

Empson has brilliantly demonstrated the multiplicity of senses that the word *sense* acquires when Angelo collapses after the clash with Isabella. The reversal I mentioned, however, is not produced merely by the fact that here we have two passionate natures that overwhelm each other far beyond the formal reaches of a rationality of principles. What is striking is the absence of a true dialectic or human compromise, precisely because these seem to speak out from beyond the characters, like a stage direction or a director's idea. Consider, for example, the successive steps of Isabella's approach to Angelo, and the way they are guided, urged and stimulated by Lucio's comments, which make Isabella something real and feigned—in other words, an actor, an individual, and a role.

At the very moment when we realize that one of the main characters in the play is beginning—by a process of trial and error, hesitantly yet impetuously—to define herself and her growing awareness, when we see her actively playing her role—a role that both reveals and modifies her—the context of the situation makes the tragic, passionate, magniloquent scale eventually attained by Isabella appear to be surrounded and delimited by an anguishing overabundance of language, an overtone or redundancy of the overall effect of the images. It is almost as if these were not produced and guided by an indignant, emotive disorder of the heart, but rather by the calculated, orderly, and practically self-propelled mechanism of an *ars dictandi*.

The discrepancy between intention and result is certainly accentuated by the fact that the glosses of a prompter such as Lucio, like the comments of an attentive director watching an actor slip into his role ("Ay, well said; That's well said, Thou'rt i' th' right, girl, more o' that; Art advis'd o' that? More of it" 2.2.90, 111, 130, 133), establish on stage a secondary, lateral point of view that transforms the audience into outsiders looking on. Isabella, too, undergoes this peculiar doubling of her role, which confers on her a split identity, a way of creating around her, from this moment on, the margin of a different truth about herself.

Isabella's modes of expression, her vehement, classical metaphors, thus sound like a passion that has been subtly created and *written,* and therefore at once true and feigned, in which we may even discern a casuistic, sophisticated pedantry indirectly produced by certain repetitions, clauses, and alliterations: "Could great men thunder / As Jove himself does, Jove would ne'er be quiet, / For every pelting petty officer / Would use his heaven for thunder; nothing but thunder" (2.2.111–14).

If this is true—if already at this moment the tragic role appears to be corroded from within, incapable of dominating and being *all* the scenic space, if the dignity and the stature of a hero (qualities insistently framed in a Classical-Renaissance code) are flawed in their plastic unitariness—then Isabella is not really contradictory as a character. In fact, in the end, she not only accepts the exchange the duke proposes to her but asks that Angelo be pardoned. She saves Angelo because, according to her, he always meant well, after all, bewitched as he was by her beauty, an affirmation which as we may remember gave rise to Dr. Johnson's unrivaled ironic comment.[5] Isabella descends unashamedly from the dizzy peaks of the tragic absolute to the "middle way" of reality, and without difficulty complies with the empirical and relative hybridated norm that governs her.

The parabola described for Isabella can be traced in all the major characters and is, to a certain extent, the general sign of the dramatic development and structure of *Measure for Measure:* a progressively impoverishing reduction of gestures and passions into acts and words which, as the action proceeds, gradually become more mechanical and vacuous, as if they were moving down an incline, at the same time seemingly both motionless and rapid, on the plane of reality, of all its modest daily traffic.

From Act 4 on, this overall impression is quite clear—that is, after the duke openly returns as a friar and as himself, to take remote control over the show. For now it is indeed a show, a fiction, a comically bitter *mise-en-scène*.

Everything imaginable happens: intrigue, half–truths, facts concealed from one and narrated to another, entries and exits of characters, a shadow of confusion even in the duke's management of affairs. One character, Barnardine, refuses to play the part assigned to him (to die at the appointed time), while others agree to be once again pawns in the game so that a chessboard, or rather its empty shape and design, can somehow be reconstructed and some temporary, precarious, artificial form of order—that of the theatrical machine—can, in some way, cover up the disorder of the ethical and ideal vacuum and propose itself as a sole, last desperate measure, in the absence of any other measure of reference.

The Classical and Renaissance "middle way"—a lofty, solemn level of values—is now the one offered by the theatrical performance, vicariously, that is, as a transient solution. No longer the central median axis of reality, the "middle way" has become a tactical shortcut which leaves the dramatic impasse intact, redesigning it in its own way.

In this light, it seems that, unlike what happens in *Hamlet,* the theatrical experimentalism of *Measure for Measure* is, instead, the result of a coming to terms with a mixed theatrical genre, precisely because "tragicomedy" has shown that a code of values is, indeed, a "favola verosimile" and a "nodo finto," but in a markedly negative and ambiguous sense, since the theatrical machine has proved to be a mirror rather than a probing into reality.

In the general context of the "problem plays," this bitter manipulatory pleasure that levels and remixes the planes of sense and action seems to put an end to a dramaturgical season, and, necessarily, implies a turning point, a search for a different foundation and a different nature of tragic and theatrical space. There is a breakaway, not a continuity with the immediate past. That is because the cultural and ideological compromise that was programmatically involved in the adoption of the tragicomic genre proved in actual fact, *in re,* to be impossible—or, rather, overly faithful and close—to the empirical meanness of a historically circumscribed and determined reality. The implicit threat in *Measure for Measure* is that the theater may become merely an "abstract and chronicle" of the times, an analogical and tautological recording.

At a time of impossible extremes, Shakespearean theater ran the risk of no longer being able to speak in the name of its vital, unifying function of space and image in which the many faces and voices of the Elizabethan social universe could agree on a common perspective with regard to ends and means.

The great tragic season, which unmistakably is announced in the tense, malleable, mimetic yet radical "otherness" of Hamlet, thus begins under the polemic sign of distancing from the chronicle, of an opening up of perspective. From an absolutely tragic point of view, with all its consequent clashes and conflicts deliberately chosen, Shakespeare discovers the critical and destructive force of the negative as an indispensable premise for a search that ultimately aims to weave again—at another level, in another order—the weft of reality. This, it seems, is the profound reason for that almost archetypal backdating that characterizes the stories of Shakespeare's major phase, and particularly the greatest of all, *King Lear,* a backdating which singularly will also remain unaltered in the phase of the romances.

Something of this need of a breakaway, a distancing, is present in *Measure for Measure.* There is a strident note which at times breaks through the texture of words, reaching well beyond the level of the bitter and ambivalent definition of a character or of the specific context; a note that sounds more like something impersonal and extraneous, like a dark worrying premonition; a pure question that bounces back as if unrelated, as if it had no corresponding echo within the dramatic context.

I am referring to the negative association related to "sense" and sexual revulsion, but that is not all. Consider, for example, the exhortation to death pronounced by the duke (who is like an impersonal chorus) in order to persuade Claudio with evangelic meekness to accept and yield to his ordained fate.

The duke speaks like the great orator he is. The instrumentality or tone of artifice and rhetorical and didactic exercise that once again characterizes his way of speech marks out the limit within which his invitation to the "cupio dissolvi" must be seen. It is the same invitation which in the final part of the parabola the "dissolute prisoner," Barnardine, with ironic punctuality, will refuse to accept, when against that "Be absolute for death" (3.1.5), which sounds out in its timeless solemnity on stage, he mockingly counterposes the worthless, minimal fact of his own unreadiness, that tenacious segment of our daily life that abruptly draws us back to the measure of reality.

Even so, it is difficult to escape the sound of this profound, rare, more directly Shakespearean note, one that is almost indefinable in clear philological terms but quite unmistakable, which we suddenly find as if we were listening to a voice already heard, an echo we will meet again. I refer to those celebrated lines, albeit few, that break away from the mesh of syllogisms, the lay reasoning and variations on a theme with which the duke dresses his persuasion: "Thou hast nor youth, nor age, / But as it were an after-dinner's sleep / Dreaming on both" (3.1.32–34).

In this strikingly expressive synthesis, how can we not sense a note of total, overwhelming bitterness, a look from afar that is a mixture of tormented pity and harsh and resentful scorn, a tone of laceration compounded of acceptance and refusal?

In the strength of their expressive *sprezzatura*, in their concise elegance, these lines (which truly come from afar) speak of reality with the same voice as the great tragedies.

But it is just a moment, a hint, nothing more; for, if we look more carefully, these lines appear to be part of (almost suffocated by) the gray, dramatic context in which they are expressed, which gives them a sort of opaque, toneless splendor. Youth, old age, all the uselessly parabolic passage of life, its insubstantial stuff denied through disjunctives as a delusive brief moment, they are vain, like a gloomily and mechanically animal or biological double dream.

A premonition of a new tragic measure, this passage of *Measure for Measure* must be interpreted as a sort of memento or self-critical gloss by Shakespeare, which runs the risk of involving the writer in the desolation of the truth represented but which, at the same time, announces the necessity of a new season, of a time of unrest.

Notes

An earlier Italian version of this article appeared in *Contesti*, 1 (1988).

1. G. Wilson Knight, "*Measure for Measure* and the Gospels," in *The Wheel of Fire* (London, 1930, 1972); Roy W. Battenhouse, "*Measure for Measure* and the Christian Doctrine of Atonement," *PMLA* 61 (1940): 1029–59; N. Coghill, "Comic Form in *Measure for Measure*," *Shakespeare Survey* 8 (1955): 14–27; F. R. Leavis, *The Common Pursuit* (London: Chatto and Windus 1952), 160–72. See also, the objections to this interpretation advanced by Clifford Leech, "The 'Meaning' of *Measure for Measure*," *Shakespeare Survey* 3 (1950). There are also some interesting comments on this heated debate in J. C. Maxwell, "*Measure for Measure*: A Footnote to Criticism," *Downside Review* 65 (1947): 45–59; and in Robert M. Smith, "Interpretations of *Measure for Measure*," *Shakespeare Quarterly* 1 (1950): 208–18.

2. On the staging, and more generally on the theatrical structure of the play, see C. A. Bernthal, "Staging Justice: James I and the Trial Scene of *Measure for Measure*," *Studies in English Literature, 1500–1900* 32:2 (1992): 247–69; A. B. Dawson, "*Measure for Measure*, New Historicism and Theatrical Power," *Shakespeare Quarterly* 39:3 (1988): 328–41; and J. D. Hubert, "The Textual Presence of Staging and Acting in *Measure for Measure*," *New Literary History* 18:3 (1987): 583–96.

3. Cf. Lawrence, *Shakespeare's Problem Comedies* (New York: Macmillan, 1960).

4. Cf. Empson, "Sense in *Measure for Measure*," in *The Structure of Complex Words* (London: Chatto and Windus, 1951).

5. Samuel Johnson's comment concerns Isabella's lines in 5.2.43–45 (I partly think / A due sincerity govern'd his deeds / Till he did look on me.):

"I am afraid our Varlet Poet intended to inculcate, that women think ill of nothing that raises the credit of their beauty, and are ready, however virtuous, to pardon any act which they think incited by their own charms."

(*Johnson on Shakespeare*, ed. Walter Raleigh (London: Oxford University Press, 1908).

Shakespeare's Uncultured Caesar on the Elizabethan Stage

CLAUDIA CORTI

Shakespeare's singular treatment of the figure of Caesar in *Julius Caesar*—an implicitly ironic, sometimes even sarcastic treatment that is without doubt an explicit deflation of the myth—merits particular attention, certainly far more than the superficial, merely stylistic and thematic interest generally shown in the play by traditional criticism, as summed up in George Bernard Shaw's famous remark that Shakespeare intended to "write Caesar down for the mere technical purpose of writing Brutus up." The attention due this particular phenomenon of reductio ad absurdum of a charismatic figure is, I think, cultural and epistemological in character, and therefore, at one and the same time, historical and existential and thus of much wider scope.

It is important, first of all, to consider how the myth of Caesar is exploded morphologically (on the ideational level) and syntactically (on the compositive level).

An accurate and complex research project in which I participated, on the transformational and transcodificatory relationships between Shakespeare's historical and Roman plays and his historiographical sources,[1] shows that Shakespeare, in his dramatic adaptation of *Julius Caesar* from North's translation of Plutarch's *Lives*, was substantially faithful, with a certain measure of elasticity, both to history and to traditional characterizations.[2] He does, however, present us with a clamorous transformation in the eponymous character of Caesar.

The first striking aspect is that in the dramatization of Caesar's life story, Shakespeare completely eliminates all those years (corresponding more or less to the entire period of the hero's prestigious rise to power) when he was performing the extraordinary feats which, to use Montaigne's phrase, "enabled him to become Caesar": not just the brilliant military campaigns but also the advancement of his political career from pontifex to *imperator*, triumvir and eventually dictator for life. Shakespeare selects only the final part of Caesar's life, beginning his dramatization at the moment of the dictator's last Roman triumph (the fifth) after his victory at Munda over the sons of Pompey (45 BC), a triumph which, in fact, was more apparent than real, as it was intrinsically undermined by the already active anti-authoritarian republican revival.

It is true that classical plays—both ancient and Elizabethan, in the broad sense, that is, prior to eighteenth-century "middle-class" plays—conventionally tend to begin with some form of *crisis,* a breaking point, pregnant with potential choice, that is destined to affect the development and consequences of the story (as well as the fabula, the logico-chronological pattern that can be extrapolated from it) which has been selected for adaptation to the stage. It is equally true, however, that Shakespeare's choice hits on precisely the situation that paves the way (historically and dramatically) for Caesar's decline. Of all the many moments of dramaturgic crisis he could have taken from Plutarch's *Lives,* all filled with intense dramatic potential—the hostility of Silla, the trial of Dolabella, the opposition of Cicero, the struggle with Cato, the conspiracy of Catilina, the scandal of P. Clodius which led to the repudiation of Pompea, and, not least, the outbreak of the civil war—Shakespeare selects an occasion marked by the historical and existential signs of the hero's downfall.

The second striking aspect, and one that is even more surprising, is that the characterization of Caesar, owing to a deliberate process of omission or invention, is notably different from that which is provided by the main source, Plutarch's *Lives* of Caesar, Brutus, and Antony. Plutarch's Caesar is sharp, intelligent, versatile, ingenious, cultured, sagacious, and witty—sometimes even at his own expense. Shakespeare, as we shall see, demolishes all Caesar's positive behavioral, mental, and psychological aspects, a phenomenon certain to arouse our curiosity.[3]

We might take into consideration the possible influence of minor, not necessarily historiographic, sources in which Caesar's figure is less positive than it is in Plutarch. For example, a reading of Lucan's *Pharsalia,* a probable secondary source, might account for this clamorous reductio, were it not for the fact that Lucan's consistent process of vilification and deprecation is directed at the character's diabolical authoritarianism (at Pompey's expense).[4] In Shakespeare, Caesar's negative components are of quite a different order and lead to a vastly different series of considerations.

The devaluation of the figure of Caesar is characteristically articulated around conceptual units that have two basic paradigms:

linguistic and rhetorical *verbosity,* and *superstition.* Both paradigms seem to have the task of transmitting to the spectators of the time a paradoxical *lack of culture* in a historical character generally credited as a leading figure in classical culture. The singularity of this feature of the text requires accurate analysis and careful attention.

We must first identify the distinctive traits of the reductio Caesar undergoes, some of which are perceptible directly from the action of the play, while others are assigned to the voices (and therefore to the judgments and ideologic or axiologic positions) of various characters.

I would put first of all Caesar's *démesure,* an overemphasis of manner and language that characterizes Caesar throughout the action of the play and often makes him seem ridiculous. His susceptibility to flattery is part of this embarrassing pomposity, a weakness Decius Brutus puts to good use:

> *Decius.* But when I tell him he hates flatterers,
> He says he does, being then most flattered.
> Let me work;
> For I can give his humour the true bent.[5]
>
> (2.1.207–10)

Decius Brutus is used by Shakespeare to portray another weakness of Caesar's: infantile gullibility, which suggests underlying intellectual inadequacy:

> *Decius.* I can o'ersway him; for he loves to hear
> That unicorns may be betray'd with trees,
> And bears with glasses, elephants with holes,
> Lions with toils . . .
>
> (2.1.203–206)

Verbosity, weakness, and gullibility are then associated with a physical frailty that immediately becomes the symbol of an intellectual frailty which Cassius, Caesar's greatest detractor, is not slow to make known.

In Act 1, scene 2, Cassius recalls two episodes when this presumed god, this false dominator—in other words, this pseudo-Caesar—revealed signs of degrading physical weakness, which in him bear symbolical meaning: after brazenly challenging Cassius to a swimming race in a cold and troubled Tiber, Caesar nearly drowns and owes his life to his rival (1.2.99–114); while during the war in Spain, Caesar, shaking with fever, implores Cassius for some water "As a sick girl" (1.2.118–27).

The first episode is not only a purely Shakespearean invention, it is also the complete reversal of a thematically analogous occurrence encomiastically narrated by both Plutarch and Suetonius (in *Vitae Duodecim Caesarum*): Caesar's long swim in Alexandria harbor to escape the Egyptians, in Plutarch's version holding up various books to keep them dry, and in that of Suetonius drawing his rich coat armor after him by his teeth.

The second episode, also an invention, is the elaboration of a slight suggestion in Plutarch that Caesar suffered from headaches and the falling sickness, the first attack occurring at Cordova; but, while Plutarch hastens to emphasize how courageously the general fought his illness, Shakespeare—through Cassius—transforms Caesar's epilepsy into an element of degradation.

Cassius' scorn and Shakespeare's devaluation of Caesar are concentrated, above all, in the near-drowning incident, as seen in the ironic treatment of an evident Virgilian parallel:

> I, as Æneas, our great ancestor,
> Did from the flames of Troy upon his shoulder
> The old Anchises bear, so from the waves of Tiber
> Did I the tired Caesar.
>
> (1.2.111–14)

This means, in Shakespeare's assessment of Caesar told through the words of Cassius, that despite his heroic and mythical ancestry (Virgilian tradition made him the founder of the Roman nation), despite his charismatic role as first citizen of Rome, Caesar was the heir not of Aeneas but of Anchises: a frail, sick being, an encumbrance for the state, anything but its savior.

It must, however, be borne in mind that Cassius' ironic treatment of the Virgilian parallel hits upon a fundamental point of Roman culture as it was perceived in the English Renaissance. For British humanists, such as George Sandys (who translated the *Metamorphoses*), Arthur Golding (who translated Seneca), and Geoffrey Whitney (who wrote the first emblem book in English), Aeneas' relationship with his father Anchises, signified iconically in the figure of a son saving a father, represented the highest expression of the Roman virtue of *pietas* (the virtuous respect of the gods, the motherland, and the family)—that is, the virtue that was to determine the fortune of the Roman empire. As Sandys wrote, "this pity of Aeneas was rewarded in his posterity with the greatest,

& longest continuing Empire, that ever virtue or fortune afforded."[6] Not to be equal to Aeneas, according to the episteme of the Elizabethans, was tantamount to not possessing the moral and intellectual stature necessary for government.

A further physical defect in Caesar—another original invention of Shakespeare's and this, too, symbolically marked on the cultural plane—is his partial *deafness:* Caesar himself informs us that he is deaf in the left ear (1.2.210).

How are we to interpret this? Inability to hear was an anthropologically important deficiency in the Elizabethans' logocentric, verbalist, and nominalist culture. For British humanists, whether they were neo-Aristotelians or neo-Platonists, conventionalists or naturalists, language was the supreme manifestation of the order of the creation. Words were the instruments of human control over reality; *logos* was that which held, gathered (from *legein*), ordered and coordinated all things. Difficulty in understanding words, thus, was certain to be interpreted as inability to enter into the system of language and thought dominated by *logos,* and therefore as a typically cultural deficiency.[7]

If his physical frailties—and a certain weakness of character, together with certain turns of phrase and expression characterized by hollow hyperbolism—are a *metaphorical* allusion to intellectual inadequacy, two other closely interrelated paradigms are a *direct* measure of Caesar's substantial cultural shortcomings. Here, I refer to two qualities Shakespeare attributes to Caesar: *superstition* and *disregard for divination*. These are conceptual elements of extraordinary importance and semantic significance, which open up new horizons for an understanding of the text.

In the crucial first scene of Act 2, it is Cassius, as usual, who names this eccentricity, of which, significantly, there is not the slightest trace in Plutarch's *Lives*.[8]

After the unnatural prodigies reported to have occurred during the stormy night and described to Cicero by Casca, in 1.3.15–32, Cassius wonders whether Caesar will go to the Capitol that morning (when the conspirators are due to act), as he may be dissuaded from doing so by fear of the omens:

> *Cassius.*   But it is doubtful yet
> Whether Cæsar will come forth to-day or no;
> For he is superstitious grown of late,
> Quite from the main opinion he held once
> Of fantasy, of dreams, and ceremonies.
> It may be these apparent prodigies,

> The unaccustom'd terror of this night,
> And the persuasion of his augurers,
> May hold him from the Capitol to-day.
>
> (2.1.193–201)

Cassius' accusation of superstition explicitly confirms the stage action represented in the *incipit* in the second scene of the first act, when Caesar, on his way to the "holy course" of the Lupercalia, invites his consort, Calphurnia, to stand directly in Antonius' way and asks Antonius to touch her, as he believes in the taumaturgical power of the hero's touch to cure her sterility:[9]

> *Cæsar.* Forget not, in your speed, Antonius,
> To touch Calphurnia; for our elders say,
> The barren, touched in this holy chase,
> Shake off their sterile curse.
>
> (1.2.6–9)

The accusation is repeated in 2.2., in Caesar's dismay at the thunder and lightning in the night, at Calphurnia's terrible dream (she has seen her husband's statue spouting blood), and at the augurs' response that they have found a sacrificial beast without a heart. Although it is true that, in the end, the strategically and instrumentally propitious interpretation of Calphurnia's dream by Decius Brutus[10] persuades Caesar to go to the Capitol (where he is, in fact, killed), it is also true that, before yielding to Decius' flattery, Caesar twice shows his fear by declaring that he will not leave his house (lines 55 and 71).

This stressing of Caesar's superstitiousness, however, would seem to clash with the opposite paradigm of his nonchalance regarding the prediction made by the soothsayer. We all remember the famous warning in the second scene of Act 1 (line 23): "Beware the ides of March"; Caesar, however, is not troubled but simply irritated by this "dreamer" who causes him to waste his time, and he bids him go away. Then, in the *incipit* of Act 3 (when he is about to be killed and encounters the soothsayer again), he even mocks him (line 1): "The ides of March are come," boldly implying that nothing, in fact, has happened (to which the soothsayer makes his famous retort (line 2): "Ay, Cæsar, but not gone").

As we shall see, this contradiction between superstition and disregard of divination is only apparent; their interdependence is comprehensible in terms of referential culture.

We must first understand the partial meanings of the various projections of the figure of Caesar, then proceed to interpret the entire system of belittling paradigms Shakespeare applies to him. With regard to the formal paradigms—rhetorical verbosity, *démesure,* a weakness for flattery—it has to be recognized that the characterization of Caesar derives from a long and rich theatrical tradition of pseudo-Senecan dramas and university plays. According to information provided in Philip Henslowe's famous diary, the figure of Caesar was presented at least ten times in British theaters in 1594 and 1595 alone—that is, not long before *Julius Caesar* is thought to have been written (1599).[11]

This is a dramaturgical and theatrical tradition that reached its climax in William Alexander's *Julius Caesar* in 1604, which was a mélange of plays by the refined university wits of Oxford and Cambridge—among which works we can distinguish, above all, the anonymous *Caesar and Pompey or Caesar's Revenge* (circa 1592) and Richard Eedes' *Caesar Interfectus,* which was performed at Christ College, Oxford, in 1581–82, a play often cited, though not with absolute philological certainty, as the source of Shakespeare's celebrated *Et tu Brute.*

This theatrical tradition embraced corresponding plays in a prestigious French production widely known and appreciated in England: a brief Latin text by Marc-Antoine Muret (Montaigne's tutor) written about 1544, *César* by Jacques Grévin (1558), *Cornélie* by Robert Garnier (1574), and the fortune-favored *Il Cesare* by an Italian, Orlando Pescetti (1594), which was successfully performed in both France and England.

It is precisely in this pseudo-Senecan theatrical tradition (often verbose and too grandiloquent for the stage) that Caesar gradually began to assume the more or less deliberately parodistic manner of a boasting, bombastic, charlatan braggadocio, a *Hercules furens* governed by *furor impius.*[12]

It is curious that Shakespeare chose the emblem of Hercules bearing the terrestrial globe as the sign for the Globe Theatre when it opened in 1599, in the fall of which year the very first "program" included *Julius Caesar.*

However that may be, beyond any possibly fortuitous coincidence, what is interesting is that we can identify a very successful theatrical tradition that may have influenced Shakespeare in his somewhat biased delineation of Caesar's character. Only a parodistic treatment could act as a support for this demythologizing, demystifying stage project.

A well-established theatrical tradition can also be invoked as regards the physical paradigms—constitutional weakness, deafness, and epilepsy. This is the tradition of classical drama based on the theme of *ate:* the infatuation, madness, blindness, or deafness (whether physical or mental) which the gods inflict on those they have resolved to destroy, as superbly expressed in the words Shakespeare puts into Antony's mouth in another Roman play, *Antony and Cleopatra:*

> But when we in our viciousness grow hard—
> O misery on't!—the wise gods seel our eyes,
> In our own filth drop our clear judgements, make us
> Adore our errors, laugh at's while we strut
> To our confusion.
>
> (3.13.111–15)

It is also true that in emblem books and Renaissance collections of proverbs—both plundered by Elizabethan playwrights for their *coups de théâtre*—pride of place seems to be given to the adage, "quem Jupiter vult perdere prius demendat," the commonest form of several analogous proverbs of more distinguished literary origin, but all descending from the following sentence, attributed by Elizabethan scholars to Euripides:

> "Ὅταν ὁ Δαίμων ἀνδρὶ πορσύνη χαχά,
> Τὸν νοῦν ἔβλαψε πρῶτον.

It is almost certain that in this peculiar characterization there is also a reminiscence of Philemon Holland's translation of Suetonius' *Lives of the Twelve Caesars* (probably a secondary source of Shakespeare's play), according to which Caesar, in the last months of his life, "stood not well to health but was ever more crasie," an expression which does not exactly translate but effectively reinterprets and recontextualizes (psychologically and mentally rather than physically) the original expression, "valetudine minus prospera uteretur."

Let us now consider the belittling paradigms of Caesar that are truly and characteristically cultural in nature: his *superstitiousness* and his *indifference to fortune-telling*. In this specific case, there is no direct or indirect source, either in Plutarch (who briefly mentions the encounter with the soothsayer, probably to suggest the political hero's superiority and disenchanted imperturbability) or in Suetonius (who, at most, stresses Caesar's scorn for prodigies) or in any other theatrical tradition, whether ancient or modern, serious or comic. The issue of superstitiousness is therefore a complete invention of Shakespeare's, on which it is worth reflecting.

By attributing to Caesar a timorous, plebeian belief in fantastic prodigies and at the same time total disregard for prophecies, Shakespeare deprives his hero, or at least his presumed hero, of two culturally strong, anthropologically epochal paradigms.

The Elizabethan episteme regarding these two concepts, which are in no way contrary but in fact are closely interrelated in a global conception of Providence, can be summed up in the elementary terms of the following formula: a cultured man does not believe in chance or prodigies, whereas he may believe in fortune-telling (that is, the reverse formula of Shakespeare's Caesar); the reason for this we shall soon see.

The sixteenth- and seventeenth-century concept of Providence, formed in the wider context of a general theory of religious and scientific knowledge—the two maximum systems of contemporary thought—utterly excluded the role of chance, or fate, or miracles, in human experience. Therefore, whatever occurred in the physical world was, for both believer and layman, the consequence of what had happened before and was the cause of what would happen next.

Science could entertain no role of chance in the pattern of nature, for that would have made knowledge difficult, if not impossible. The prime requisite of science was that there had to be absolute *regularity* in the development of natural phenomena, which could be observed, related to generalized models and patterns, and then used to understand the causes of other events and to establish further generalizing relationships.

Conversely, on the religious plane, nothing could be conceived to occur that was beyond the control of divine power, as that would have conflicted with the dogma of God's omnipotence. Throughout the ages, every single event in the reign of physical nature had been foreseen and preordained by God, since the beginning of the world (including such phenomena as famines, floods, and earthquakes, which the Creator sent for the moral exhortation or physical punishment of sinning humanity).[13]

Let us, for example, consider what William Perkins wrote in *An Exposition of the Creede* in 1595 (that is, the same historical context as *Julius Caesar*). God governs things:

> by mooving them that they may attaine to the particular endes for which they were severally ordained. For the qualities and vertues which were placed in the Sunne, Moone, starres, trees, plants, seedes, &c. would lie dead in them and be unprofitable, unles they were not

onely preserved, but also stirred up and quickened by the power of God as oft as he imploies them to any use.

Let us also consider the point of view of a "philosopher of nature," Walter Bailey, whose *A Briefe Discours of Certain Bathes* (1587) launched a resolute attack on the gullibility of those who believed in the miraculous properties of thermal springs:

> We may affirm, that in these our latter daies, God for the most part doth in his actions put naturall meanes as instruments, of which the Philosophers do consider as naturall and inferior causes. For if we shall say that God without any naturall course, supernaturally doth produce all things, we shall subvert all the grounds of Philosophy and spoil nature of all actions. Rather in mine opinion are we to imbrace that saying in Genesis, that God doth cease from newe creation of things, having given to them a nature and power, by the which they stande and fall.

The choices men made, whether freely or under compulsion, fell within the natural and rational pattern ordained either by God or by the order of the universe, as a result of which every choice produced consequences with naturally and logically predictable outcomes. Thus, if random chance happenings were discounted by Elizabethan erudition, so too were any prodigious or miraculous manifestations.

Prodigies and miracles were not accepted by scientists and intellectuals, the university wits who produced contemporary lay culture, since nothing could interrupt the preordained and rationally guaranteed flow of existence. The great Cambridge scientist and scholar Gabriel Harvey offers an illuminating example of the rationalist lay attitude in his comment—contained in a letter to Spenser—regarding an earthquake in 1580. There was no need to talk of miracles, he explained to his literary friend, since God, who is in full control of the reality of the cosmos, could easily "put in execution such Effectes, either ordinarie or extraordinarie, as shall seem most requisite to his eternal Providence." Indeed, he added, "now in these latter dayes, very seldom, or in manner never worketh any thing so myraculously and extraordinarily."[14]

If miracles and prodigies were a source of intellectual embarrassment for men of science, they also created theoretical problems for theologians, who hastened to restrict the field of transcendent phenomena to a limited number of cases. These were justified on the basis of God's omnipotence, which, in certain very special cases, decided to draw attention to itself, intentionally interrupting the constructive pattern of rigorously predicted events. Assuming that God, in His omnipotence, *may* act without the second causes which philosophers granted Him, there remained the problem of establishing how often, and on the basis of what criteria, God acted without second causes. Elizabethan theologians made abundant use of the word "sometimes," as can be seen in a highly significant passage (considering the prestige of the author) in the already mentioned *Exposition of the Creede* by Perkins:

> Sometimes God worketh without means . . . sometimes hee governes according to the usuall coursè and order of nature, as when hee preserves our lives by meat and drinke: yet so, as hee can and doth most freely order all things by meanes either above nature or against nature, as it shall seeme good unto him. As when hee caused the sunne to stand in the firmament (Jos. 10, Isa. 38).

In the Elizabethan episteme, however, the intellectual attitude toward prophecy and divination was quite another thing; for, if all was predicted and preordained—whether by God or by natural order—on the basis of an inexorable mechanism of cause and effect, then it might be admitted that certain links in the causal-consequential chain could in some way be foreknown, possibly through the special powers of exceptional individuals.

This explains—at a time when the foundations were being laid for a preeminently empirical, deductive, and rational "new science"—the enormous credit enjoyed by celebrated prophets, fortune-tellers, and visionaries who were part of a historical, philosophical, and literary tradition of multiple origin, both religious and lay: ample and often heterogeneous collections of "visions" and "prophecies" circulated incessantly throughout Elizabeth's England, bringing together a vast collection of authors and works in which we find the Venerable Bede next to Henry II, Edward the Confessor, and Thomas à Becket, Gerald of Wales, and Chaucer, Friar Bacon and Savonarola, Ignatius Loyola, even James VI of Scotland, the future James I.

It is particularly interesting and pertinent to consider, in view of what we shall now see, that many of these historical and traditional prophecies were used by Elizabeth's Protestant entourage both to justify her right to the throne (against the Catholic Queen Mary) and to uphold the Reformation, many of them having references to the fall of Rome and to the social, political, and religious schism. To give an example, I would recall that a copy of the prophecy made by Paul Grebner, a German Protestant commentator on the

Bible, who foretold the future of Europe along profoundly anti-Catholic lines, was presented to Queen Elizabeth and officially deposited in Trinity College Library at Cambridge (where it may still be consulted). Prophecy, in other words, is put to political use, both to justify any possible resistance to established authority and to support the new regime.[15]

Whatever the case, apart from the political or encomiastic value of these predictions, it is significant that the prophetic, predictive component found everybody in agreement: theologians and scientists, religious scholars and lay scholars—the intellectual élite of the time—all actively committed to founding the new theory of knowledge on extraordinary blends of thought, where the pagan philosophies of Greece and Rome were fused with Christianity, Neoplatonism and the more recent ideas of the Renaissance in continental Europe.

In Shakespeare's Caesar, the themes of superstition and divination allude to two important elements of contemporary sensibility, defining both an existential and a behavioral model which the audience of the time could interpret in one way only: Caesar was simultaneously superstitious and indifferent to divination, simply because he was rough and uncultured.

For, although religious and lay intellectuals rejected superstition and accepted divination, uncultured ordinary people were willing to interpret any extraordinary physical event—an earthquake, the appearance of a comet, or the sudden gushing of a mineral spring—as a miracle, that is, an unpredictable, unknowable departure from cosmic laws.

One need only read the countless popular pamphlets (most of them anonymous) that circulated after the appearance of the comet in 1572, or the earthquake on 6 April 1580, or the abrupt flowing of a spring in Cheshire in 1588, or the disastrous plague in 1593, to understand the excessive perturbation or fanatical dismay with which ordinary people responded to the rational, reassuring explanations of these phenomena by intellectuals of the calibre of Gabriel Harvey, John Downame, or Reginald Scot, all of whom were strongly inclined to relate spectacular and apparently prodigious events to strictly natural causes.[16]

When Shakespeare represented Caesar's trepidation after the storm in the night, Calphurnia's dream, and ordinary people's reports of extraordinary events (a tempest of fire, men in flames walking up and down the streets, birds of night flying by day), he evidently wished to stress the subjection of the presumed hero to absurd beliefs and irrational prejudices. It is no coincidence that

Caesar's fearful superstitiousness has a foil in the imperturbable, detached, and skeptical indifference of Cicero, an intellectual and layman who replies to Casca's terrified and terrifying account with his own calm, measured interpretation:

> Indeed, it is a strange-disposed time:
> But men may construe things, after their fashion,
> Clean from the purpose of the things themselves:
>
> (1.3.33–35)

Conversely, the disregard of Shakespeare's Caesar for the soothsayer's prediction marks a denial of one of the fundamental circuits of the intellectual culture of the age. The prediction concerned the ides of March—that is, a specific day. It should be remembered that in the sensitivity of Elizabethan intellectuals to divination, a large portion of them regarded temporal considerations, in the sense that there was a strong belief in the positive or negative qualities of certain days of the year.

We can, for example, take the testimony of a little paper prepared by Elizabeth's treasurer, Lord Burghley, entitled *Advise to his Son,* in which he mentions "three Mondays of the year" to be avoided for political or diplomatic events: the first Monday in April (considered the anniversary of the death of Abel), the second Monday in August (destruction of Sodom and Gomorrah), and the last Monday in December (birthday of Judas Iscariot), which were thought to correspond to the unpropitious days named by Hippocrates and popularized in the Middle Ages by Isidore of Seville.[17]

All the above data incontrovertibly indicate that Shakespeare intended not only to vilify the figure of Caesar but also to do so in a precise and inequivocable dimension: that of a substantial unculture that inverts the traditional perception of the character.

It is true, as we have seen, that the dequalification had already partially begun in certain pseudo-Senecan plays, but it is even more true that in no previous play had the vilification of Caesar concerned those determinate aspects that particularly seemed to interest Shakespeare—that is, those elements of unculture that were not formal but of considerable conceptual content.

To conclude this analysis, I shall endeavor to interpret the textual data and give meaning to Shakespeare's constructive strategy.

It would appear that two interpretations can be put forward: one historicopolitical, the other more widely historicocultural and epistemic.

The historicopolitical interpretation can be formulated directly and without any great difficulty: Shakespeare reduced the figure of Caesar ad absurdum because he intended to use political means to destroy the myth of Caesarism, taken paradigmatically as a model of authoritarianism. It was a political warning that he presented in the form of a historical *anti-exemplum* to Elizabeth and James, lest they include the Caesarian—and, therefore, authoritarian—model in their construction of the Tudor myth, to which Shakespeare himself had contributed so much, with his great tetralogies of history plays written between 1590 and 1599, from *1 Henry VI* to *Henry V*. The relative dates are significant. *Julius Caesar* can be attributed to the same year as *Henry V,* which portrays the apotheosis of the Tudor myth. Put another way, as Shakespeare celebrated the triumph of Elizabeth through the mythical figure, at the same time, by presenting to her Caesar's *ate,* he alerted the sovereign to the inherent danger of political triumph: the danger of narcissistic and despotic temptation.

The historicocultural and epistemic interpretation is more complex and articulated. Shakespeare was not making only a political statement—the point he was making was fundamentally cultural in nature. By vilifying Caesar, Shakespeare not only undermined Caesarism but also launched a direct attack on Rome, with everything Rome meant for the Elizabethan *Kultur* of Anglican Protestant tradition, to which he himself belonged.

For Anglican intellectuals faithful to Elizabeth, Rome (and, in general, Italy, epitomized in the capital of the ancient empire) stood for barbarity and obscurantism, which to their mind were typical of Roman Catholic culture.[18]

One need only consider, within the world of drama with which we are more directly concerned, the symbolic function of Italian—and, more specifically, Roman—settings in such playwrights as Webster, Marston, Chapman, Tourneur, Ford, and Middleton, which were used to connote intrigue, falsehood, hypocrisy, imbroglio, crime, oppression, and so on. Caesar and Caesarism thus became in Shakespeare symbols of the moral and political degradation induced by a certain type of culture, or, rather, *unculture.*

In this regard, it should be borne in mind that practically all the intelligentsia who rotated around the court, constituting the new *Culture,* were of Protestant or Puritan origin, *Puritan* being meant in its typically Elizabethan sense of a radical, reformist Protestant.[19]

This category included the first translators of the classics, who belonged to a homogeneous group that operated outside the traditional university circles, as also the first scientists: Robert Recorde, for instance, founder of the English school of mathematics; John Dee, possibly the best-known philosopher and scientist of the day, who had been accused of heresy during the reign of Queen Mary; and the Copernican astronomer, Thomas Digges, son of the Leonard Digges who also during Mary's reign had taken part in the rebellion led by Wyatt. Others were William Turner, a Protestant preacher and the pioneer of natural history in England; John Halle, widely known in the early years of Elizabeth's reign, both for his writings on anatomy and for his antipapist poetic writings; Nicholas Udall, one of the first supporters of the Reformation at Oxford, an indefatigable Protestant propagandist and a distinguished translator; William Fulke, the leading scientist in the fight against superstitious credulity; and yet more—William Perkins, Thomas Hood, Edward Wright, and many others so numerous that they cannot all be listed. One name that must, however, be mentioned is that of Sir Thomas Bodley, son of an exile in the days of Queen Mary and a disciple of Calvin and Beza, who founded the Bodleian Library at Oxford specifically as a center of anti-Catholic influence and scientific research. Gresham College in London had also been sponsored since the reign of Henry VIII with the purpose of creating a center of studies that would combat papism. Even the schools founded, financed and controlled by the merchant guilds were cradles of Protestant radicals.[20]

It would therefore appear legitimate to deduce that Shakespeare's treatment of Caesar can be related to a clearly identifiable school of thought and an inequivocal ideological matrix. If this interpretation can be accepted, it suggests a conclusion that can be verified in other Shakespeare plays: that the leading Elizabethan playwright, who defended the Tudor myth and thus Elizabeth's policy with the most effective, evasive, and popular instrument of the time, actively entered into the debate proposed by the Anglican or Protestant intellectuals and the university wits against any Roman Catholic papist revival.

I cannot believe that it is a coincidence that Shakespeare attributed to Caesar, in the absence of any certain, probable, or possible influence of the sources, precisely the defect of *superstitiousness*. It does not seem accidental because superstitiousness was precisely the fundamental paradigm of the Anglo-Protestant argument against the Catholics: from Reginald Scot (*The Discovery of Witchcraft*, 1584) and Samuel Harsnet (*A Discovery of Fraudulent Practises*, 1599—the same year as *Julius Caesar*)—to James Mason (*The Anatomie of Sorcerie*, 1612) and Fernando Texeda (*Miracles*

Unmasked, 1625)—not, of course, forgetting *Daemonologie* (1597) by the future James I, patron and personal friend of Shakespeare (who was born a Catholic but espoused the Protestant cause)—all the anti-Catholic intellectuals directed their attention at unmasking, scorning and ridiculing the miraculistic and superstitious practices of Roman Catholic culture.

If one was superstitious, it meant—according to the Elizabethan intellectual episteme—that one was a papist and a "Roman," in other words, strategically foolish (or falsely ingenuous) and inevitably corrupt and untrustworthy.

If we consider the matter, the identification of Catholicism with witchcraft, the falsity of miracles, the deceitful use of alleged magic arts—all these became a leitmotiv of works not only by well-known, recognized writers (like those just mentioned) but also by anonymous pamphleteers and lesser or virtually unknown essay writers of various Anglican, Protestant, Calvinist, or Puritan extraction who exploited the anti-Catholic polemic for openly political ends.[21]

By making his Caesar not only pompous and bombastic, not just weak and ailing and epileptic, but also *uncultured,* inasmuch as he was superstitious and indifferent to rationally verifiable predictions, Shakespeare was transmitting a political message to the honored Queen and his beloved friend, James, heir to the thrones of England, Scotland, and Ireland; but at the same time, and more importantly, he was informing contemporary and future spectators of a personal ideological and cultural choice that he had made: that of the Anglican philosophical and ethical camp on which Elizabeth's political strategy was based. Let us not forget that, from the reign of Henry VIII to that of James I, all the intellectual supporters of the Tudors (and subsequently of the early Stuarts) applied the prophetic/predictive component, on the one hand, and the denunciation of superstition, on the other, to justify the political and religious Reformation and to legitimate the break with Rome.[22]

The important cultural message was thus inevitably political. By adopting the ideologic and epistemic attitude of anti-Catholic and antipapist Anglican intellectuals, Shakespeare was also adopting the typically Tudor attitude, always wary of any "Roman," and therefore in some way Caesarean, revival.

Notes

An earlier Italian version of this article appeared in *La cultura in Cesare,* ed. D. Poli, vol. 2 (Rome: Il Calamo, 1993).

1. Compare *Nel laboratorio di Shakespeare: dalle fonti ai drammi,* 4 vols. (Parma: Pratiche, 1988).

2. Compare *The Lives of the Noble Grecians and Romans, . . . translated out of Greeke into French by Iames Amyot . . . and out of French into Englishe, by Thomas North,* Imprinted at London by Thomas Vautrollier and Iohn Wight, (1579 [first edition], 1595 [second edition]). The edition of *Plutarch's Lives* used by Shakespeare for the Roman plays was certainly the second, in view of a number of incontrovertible lexical similarities. The second edition, as also the first, can be consulted in the nineteenth-century photolithographic reprint by Leo. Compare F. A. Leo, *Plutarchus: Four Chapters of North's Plutarch* (Berlin—London: Trübner & Co., 1878). The *Lives* constituting the main sources of *Julius Caesar* are: *The Life of Julius Caesar,* pp. 758–91; *The Life of Antonius,* pp. 968–1009; and *The Life of Marcus Brutus,* pp. 1053–78.

3. The aim of the research group was to focus on the *construction* of the plays in relation to the sources. It did not take into consideration the aspects of the characterization of Caesar that are the object of this essay.

4. The sorting of all the sources of the play, rigorously and systematically subdivided into probable, possible, and analogous, was made (as for all Shakespeare's plays) on the basis of G. Bullough's monumental work *Narrative and Dramatic Sources of Shakespeare,* 8 vols. (London: Routledge & Kegan Paul; New York: Columbia University Press, 1964); the Roman plays constitute the material analyzed in the fourth volume, 1964. Lucan's *Pharsalia* had been translated into English in 1589; Christopher Marlowe translated the first book (concerning Caesar); although this translation was not printed until 1600, it is known to have circulated in manuscript form. Shakespeare may, therefore, have known of it when he conceived the idea of a play on Julius Caesar.

5. I quote from the Arden Shakespeare edition, ed. T. S. Dorsch (London: Methuen, 1961).

6. *Ovid's Metamorphoses Englished, mythologized, and represented in figures by George Sandys,* ed. K. K. Hulley and S. T. Vandersall (Lincoln: University of Nebraska Press, 1970), 119.

7. I consider the problems of the Elizabethan debate on language in *Macbeth: la parola e l'immagine* (Pisa: Pacini, 1983), and in an essay, "I modi signandi del Macbeth," *Anglistica* 1:18 (1985): 31–51, to which I refer the reader. Illuminating and documented studies of the linguistic and communicational systems of Shakespeare and his contemporaries can be found in the works of K. Elam, in particular, *Shakespeare's Universe of Discourse* (Cambridge: Cambridge University Press, 1984); and his edition of *La grande festa del linguaggio: Shakespeare e la lingua inglese* (Bologna: Il Mulino, 1986).

8. Plutarch neither mentions nor in any way hints that Caesar was superstitious; he merely states that Calphurnia's fear at her dream of Caesar's assassination and her imploring him not to go to the Senate to persuade Caesar to postpone the session. Suetonius, whom Shakespeare certainly knew, is even more explicit in defining Caesar as being scornful of prodigies—"no religious feare of divine prodigies could ever fray him from any enterprise, or stay him if it were once in hand"—such that he was publicly accused of "impiety" for his refusal to heed the augurs, when their pronouncements did not satisfy his expectations. Compare Suetonius, *The Historie of Twelve Caesars,* trans. Philemon Holland (London, 1606, 1659, and 1680).

9. Shakespeare took the original idea (which he completely transformed for his own purposes) from Plutarch's description of the celebration of the Luper-

calia, when young men of distinguished family and the sons of magistrates ran naked through the streets, striking passersby with leather thongs; young patrician women allowed themselves to be so treated in the ancient belief that in this way they would not suffer pain in childbirth or would conceive more easily.

10. Compare 2.2.83–90:

> This dream is all amiss interpreted;
> It was a vision fair and fortunate:
> Your statue spouting blood in many pipes,
> In which so many smiling Romans bath'd,
> Signifies that from you great Rome shall suck
> Reviving blood, and that great men shall press
> For tinctures, stains, relics, and cognizance.
> This by Calphurnia's dream is signified.

11. Compare F. E. Schelling, *Elizabethan Drama, 1558–1642,* 2 vols. (Boston: Houghton Mifflin, 1908) 2:20–22.

12. Compare H. M. Ayres, "Shakespeare's Julius Caesar in the Light of Some Other Versions," *PMLA* 25:2 (1910): 183–227; and A. La Penna, *La non gloriosa entrata di Cesare nella tragedia moderna,* in *Tersite censurato e altri studi di letteratura fra antico e moderno* (Pisa: Nistri-Lischi, 1991). It should be noted that the fatuous verbosity attributed to Caesar by French playwrights of the Senecan school and by their academic English imitators is a parodistic twisting of the hero's "eloquence," which was acclaimed by both Plutarch and Suetonius.

13. The following are fundamental studies on the Elizabethan view of Providence: P. H. Kocher, *Science and Religion in Elizabethan England* (New York: Octagon Books, 1969), esp. chap. 5; K. V. Thomas, *Religion and the Decline of Magic* (London: Weidenfeld & Nicolson, 1971), esp. chap. 4; P. Rossi, *Francesco Bacone: dalla magia alla scienza* (Turin: Einaudi, 1974), passim; R. S. Westfall, *Science and Religion in Seventeenth-Century England* (New Haven: Yale University Press, 1958); and D. P. Walker, *Spiritual and Demonic Magic from Ficino to Campanella* (London: Studies of the Warburg Institute, 1958).

14. *Letters between Edmund Spenser and Gabriel Harvey,* in *Ancient Critical Essays upon English Poets and Poesy,* ed. Joseph Haslewood (London, 1811–15), 2:51.

15. In this regard the prophecies based on the myth (popularized in the Middle Ages by Geoffrey of Monmouth) constructed around the Trojan origins of the English nation are paradigmatic: Brutus, a descendant of Aeneas, after overcoming the giants that devastated the island, was said to have founded London and given rise to a dynasty that was to last until the days of King Arthur—that is, until the Saxon invasion. The last British king, Cadwalader, on his deathbed, received from an angel a prophetic message containing the promise that one day the Britons would reconquer their ancient kingdom. The triumph of the Tudors was therefore hailed by their apologists as the fulfillment of the prophecy transmitted to the dying Cadwalader.

16. Compare Thomas, *Religion and the Decline of Magic,* 23–28, 78–112; Kocher, *Science and Religion in Elizabethan England,* 110–14.

17. Compare Thomas, *Religion and the Decline of Magic,* 615–23.

18. Compare R. S. Miola, *Shakespeare's Rome* (London: Cambridge University Press, 1983), chap. 4.

19. Compare C. Hill, *Intellectual Origins of the English Revolution* (Oxford: Clarendon Press, 1965), chap. 2.

20. Compare C. Hill, *Society and Puritanism* (London: Secker & Warburg, 1964), passim; and C. Hill, *Intellectual Origins of the English Revolution*, 47–90; C. E. Raven, *English Naturalists from Neckham to Ray* (Cambridge: Cambridge University Press, 1947), 93–133; F. A. Yates, *Giordano Bruno and the Hermetic Tradition* (London: Routledge & Kegan Paul, 1964), 375–89.

21. Compare Thomas, *Religion and the Decline of Magic*, 561–69.

22. Compare G. R. Elton, *Policy and Police: The Enforcement of the Reformation in the Age of Thomas Cromwell* (London: Cambridge University Press, 1972), 46–83. See also, W. Gordon Zeeveld, *Foundations of Tudor Policy* (Cambridge, Mass.: Harvard University Press, 1968), passim.

Shakespeare's History Plays as a "Scene" of the Disappearance of Popular Discourse
LAURA DI MICHELE

When one considers the works that make up the great "theater of kings" with which Shakespeare illustrates and at the same time rewrites English history, one immediately notices the lack of any autonomous and conscious popular discourse capable of modifying the power relationships between the various levels of society represented. Indeed, one can speak of a substantial absence of popular discourse from the dramatic texture of Shakespeare's histories; one could even argue that material and characters related to the people are "expunged" from the text, as if to testify to the fact that Shakespeare—after having allowed them to play a role for a certain length of time—later desired to present the various procedures of ideological and textual hegemonization that deprived popular discourse of its potential subversive strength.

To give an example, in the second part of *Henry VI,* when the artisans of the city of London rise up against the despotic power of the constituted authority, they are degraded to clown-like functions, in accordance with styles and techniques typical of parodistic vilification. Their protest looks like a sort of improvised carnival. Their leader, Jack Cade, becomes an extemporary and histrionic mock king. And their menacing procession—which takes them from Blackheath to Cannon Street, and as far as London Bridge and Smithfield—appears to have all the festive tone of a fairground show. In this way, social tensions are played down and the confines of the bloody drama of an uprising are obliterated in the amusing, grotesque masque of popular entertainment.

It can also happen—as in the case of *King John*—that ordinary people are involved in the idealizing operation of a rise to a higher level, which is, however, generic and devoid of any connotation of class association. They are absorbed and confined—together with everybody else—in the broad, amorphous, reassuring category of "loyal subjects," who then find their ideal sublimation in the person and voice of the bastard, Philip Faulconbridge, who is the expression of both vox populi and vox dei.

The much discussed example in the two parts of *Henry IV* relative to the changing yet predictable relationship between Prince Hal and Sir John Falstaff, a man of the people, offers an opportunity for viewing the operation of a further—and possibly more complex, discursive—practice realized by the constituted authority. This authority hegemonizes the social and textual scene and imposes norms that establish hierarchies between the various discourses that traverse it, making the resultant texts reticent, unwilling to speak or utter the voices that are an integral part of it—unless a capillary investigation is made.

It will, therefore, be clear how important it is to question a text, somehow compelling it to let all its components express themselves freely, including those that have been removed and silenced (that is, constrained to become *latent*).[1] To make a text speak means cooperating in the construction of its overall sense, sharing in the act of attributing meaning to that which is not explicitly stated and even to that which is interdicted.

Viewed from this angle, Shakespeare's historicopolitical theater is a textual and cultural system containing within it a multiplicity of widely differentiated and conflictual discourses. Furthermore, texts of this type of theater institute—in a close dramatic interplay, both tragic and comic—a significant network of relationships through the choice of episodes, characters, and systems of values and through the organization of the actual dramaturgic structure of the political discourse. All this occurs according to a process of textual and ideologic hierarchization which proclaims the hegemonizing priorities and capacities of a discourse—that of regality—with regard to others that pass through its space.

Seen in this light, Shakespeare's histories can legitimately be considered a "theater of the histories of the English nation" rather than a "theater of the history of kings": a theater in which there is an intermingling of dominant voices and alternative voices, lofty tones and humble tones, epic style and comic style, textual explicitness, and latency.

The Histories must, therefore, be carefully questioned in the manner suggested, in order to bring to light what at first sight is concealed, to make evident what "counterinforms on one or more planes—logical, semantic, ideologic and actantial—of discourse."[2] The Histories foreground a complicated network of relationships which may be neglected or not clearly perceived, yet which leaves more or less visible traces, even in apparently insignificant areas of reality. This dynamic of strengths is variously explored by Shakespeare, who succeeds—perhaps even unconsciously—in illuminating the multiplicity of intersections that occur between different points of view and make sense in his culture and society.

It may, therefore, be apposite to attribute to the histories thus seen, in addition to the various other roles they perform, the role which, from the viewpoint of theatrical anthropology, E. Barba identifies as the potential power of a theatrical performance. According to Barba: "Performance can be the representation not of the 'reality' of the surface and colours of history but of its muscles and nerves; of its skeleton, of what one sees only in a history stripped of all its flesh; the power game, the socially centrifugal and centripetal forces, the tension between freedom and organization, between equality and authority."[3] In fact, one might imagine the historicopolitical theater of the histories as the articulatory mechanism "stripped of all its flesh" of the *histories* of many in the *history* of the few, as the compositive model harmonizing dissonant voices and sounds within a textual and ideological texture dominated by the logic of royal power which subjugates, removes, and represses all other logics. It is also true, however, that the texts are permeated by irregularities, splits, and fractures, different levels of discourse variously bound together according to the rules of the different realities that come together, confront each other—sometimes not altogether pacifically—and, in the end, leave the scene.

At this point, considering the marginal and limited presence of popular discourse in plays based on English history, one gets the clear impression—as one proceeds diachronically through the Histories, finally reaching the Roman plays *Julius Caesar* and *Coriolanus*—that popular discourse is struggling to affirm itself, to be louder and more effective in its oppositive force, especially in the two *Henry IV* plays. It is almost as if in the last decades of the sixteenth century the world of the people was finally capable of achieving some sort of official recognition, which ultimately becomes "discourse." As Michel Foucault observes: "I suppose that in every society the production of discourse is controlled, organized and distributed by way of a certain number of procedures whose function is to avert its powers and dangers, to dominate the uncertainty of its outcome, and to eschew its heavy, fearful materiality."[4] It is the "heavy, fearful materiality," both corporal and political, of the mocking Sir John Falstaff—himself also always mocked—that has to be eschewed and dominated, by a process in which discourse is, as it were, called to order—that is, the potential proliferation of alternative discourses is limited and the prohibitions and actions of the law of the state are applied. Prince Hal's behavior is guided by such a manner of practicing power and such a realization of rational and conscious logic.

It is thus the "heavy, fearful materiality" of Falstaff and the popular world he represents that the heir to the throne understands he must know, dominate, and, in the end, reject. Let us consider the Prince's reflections in the scene of *1 Henry IV*, where, alone on stage, he establishes an intense relationship with the audience as if he meant to prepare it for his subsequent reformation, of which he is the supreme and undisputed protagonist.

> I know you all, and will awhile uphold
> The unyok'd humour of your idleness.
> Yet herein will I imitate the sun,
> Who doth permit the base contagious clouds
> To smother up his beauty from the world,
> That, when he please again to be himself,
> Being wanted, he may be more wonder'd at
> By breaking through the foul and ugly mists
> Of vapours that did seem to strangle him.
>
> (1.2.190–98)[5]

We cannot fail to perceive the clear-mindedness of this character, who displays rationality, political perspicacity, the capacity to distinguish between appearance and reality, and a firm will to reveal at the appropriate time that "he is not what he is." This naturally brings to mind Iago's words, "I am not what I am" (*Othello*, 1.1.65), in which he recognizes himself as a perverse simulator: many of Hal's attitudes and behavioral patterns could, indeed, confirm the same impression. However, if we were to consider only his Machiavellian aspect, we should be oversimplifying the functions he performs in the play and his characterization as an up-to-date political stategist, one who is far more modern than the king his father and much more aware of the symbolic quality of the new title of monarch that he is soon to bear. In actual fact, during his apprenticeship—which is both political and theatrical, as his father Henry IV often reminds him—before becoming the rightful King of England, Prince Hal knows he must act with great mastery the various roles that circumstances will present to him. In an absolute sense, it is the role of king that imposes on him the planning and performance of the various aspects that combine to realize his overall political design. From his first soliloquy, he informs his privileged interlocutors, the audience, of this; and the spectators, learning his intentions, are in a position to compare his intentions with his subsequent action. As Hal says:

> So when this loose behaviour I throw off,
> And pay the debt I never promised,
> By how much better than my word I am,
> By so much shall I falsify men's hopes;
> And like bright metal on a sullen ground,
> My reformation, glitt'ring o'er my fault,
> Shall show more goodly, and attract more eyes
> Than that which hath no foil to set it off.
> I'll so offend, to make offence a skill,
> Redeeming time when men think least I will.
>
> (1.2.203–12)

These musings, rich in terms evoking the world of the theater ("throw off," "falsify," "show," "attract," "skill"), are a foretaste of the phase in the play in which Hal divests himself of the habits he has worn hitherto and, forsaking the role of the disobedient ne'er-do-well son, promises the king: "I shall hereafter, my thrice gracious lord, / Be more myself" (3.2.92-93). These words not only relieve the king's profound sorrow at the idea of being unable to count on a son who was capable—as, in contrast, Hotspur appeared to be—of governing the kingdom he was one day to inherit (1.1.77–90) but they also echo almost verbatim the words uttered by Henry IV on another occasion:

> I will from henceforth rather be myself,
> Mighty, and to be fear'd, than my condition.
>
> (1.3.5–6)

Hal's promise sounds like a kind of perfecting of the intention manifested by his father, as if to intimate that the moment of the passage of the signs of power from the sovereign to the heir apparent is near at hand. Hal demonstrates that he realizes the implications of wearing a crown with full responsibility; therefore, he prepares to proceed toward the new role he will be called on to play:

> For God doth know, so shall the world perceive,
> That I have turn'd away my former self.
>
> (*2 Henry IV*, 5.5.57–58)[6]

In the second scene of the third act of *1 Henry IV*, the prince strives to persuade the king that he is up to the task his future position will require of him and that he is able to avenge his slandered honor by defeating Hotspur:

> Do not think so, you shall not find it so;
> And God forgive them that so much have sway'd
> Your Majesty's good thoughts away from me!
> I will redeem all this on Percy's head,
> And in the closing of some glorious day
> Be bold to tell you that I am your son,
> When I will wear a garment all of blood,
> And stain my favours in a bloody mask,
> Which, wash'd away, shall scour my shame with it;
> And that shall be the day, whene'er it lights,
> That this same child of honour and renown,
> This gallant Hotspur, this all-praised knight,
> And your unthought-of Harry chance to meet.
> (3.2.129–41)

The garment and mask dripping with Hotspur's blood inevitably bring to mind the ritual of the sacrifice necessary for Hal's purification and rebirth, for only in this way can he be restored to authentic regality. The prince's words can, however, also be interpreted as an explicit manifestation of his awareness of the functions of theatricalization and ritualization that must accompany him on his way to the crown. A few lines later, Hal says:

> This in the name of God I promise here,
> The which if He be pleas'd I shall perform.
> (3.2.153–54)

The verb *perform* means not only to carry out an action but also to execute an order, to put on a play, to fulfil a plan. That Hal should choose such a term is extremely significant and certainly not due to chance. By this, he shows that he understands that life in society (and, by analogy, in the theater) is punctuated by a continuous series of tensions and movements which take place in time and space and are resolved in a series of uninterrupted transformations and changes of status.

These changes are also produced by rituals; here, at this point of the play, the rituals are merely narrated and some of their symbolic functions can be identified. Later on, the rituals hinted at are actually dramatized, giving rise to a full-scale cultural performance, in which Hal plays his part in a *mise-en-scène* that enacts the promise made to the king his father and gives life to the "rites of violence" that will enable him to redeem himself and assume authority. Over the body of the defeated Hotspur, Hal pronounces the words that seal his oath to the king:

> If thou wert sensible of courtesy
> I should not make so dear a show of zeal;
> But let my favours hide thy mangled face,
> And even in thy behalf I'll thank myself
> For doing these fair rites of tenderness.
>
> (5.4.93–97)

The solemn atmosphere of the ceremony, which Hal concludes with an untriumphal epitaph in honor of the warlike Hotspur, is overshadowed by a presence that clouds the value of the celebration: beside Hotspur's body, the prince suddenly perceives the "heavy, fearful materiality" of the apparently lifeless body of Falstaff. The noble prince pronounces some affectionate words of sorrow (5.4.101–105) which, however, are almost entirely deprived of meaning by his next words:

> Death hath not struck so fat a deer today,
> Though many dearer, in this bloody fray.
> Embowell'd will I see thee by and by,
> Till then in blood by noble Percy lie.
>
> (5.4.106–109)

The series of puns—initiated possibly unconsciously by the term *deer*—recalls the bloody world of hunting and, inevitably, the sharing of roles that is evoked. If Falstaff is a fat deer, Hal is a relentless hunter, an imperturbable spectator of the disemboweling of his prey. The fact is that Falstaff—at least, at this stage of the play—does not remain motionless on the ground waiting to be gutted; he is not dead yet and will indeed arise as a symbolic negation—with all his corpulent comicality—of the heroism incarnated by the noble Hotspur and now appropriated by Hal in the symbolic funeral ceremony celebrated on the battlefield. The cowardly Falstaff then savages Hotspur's body, thus desecrating the ritual Hal has just performed. Once again, it is the "heavy, fearful materiality" of Falstaff's body and voice that opposes Hal: "Embowelled? If thou embowel me today, I'll give you leave to powder me and eat me too tomorrow (5.4.110–11). Yet, Falstaff's words and falsifications, and all his lies, never have any subversive effects; at the end of the episode in which Hal and Lancaster unmask Falstaff's boastings, the prince tells him directly in an aside:

> For my part, if a lie may do thee grace,
> I'll gild it with the happiest terms I have.
>
> (5.4.156–57)

The discovery of Falstaff's pretense persuades Hal that he can wait no longer to display—as he has already done with Falstaff in private—his talents as a man of power who is capable of impressing new order on the political body it is his intention to create.

If we bear in mind these crucial moments in the first part of the events of *Henry IV,* we can perhaps better understand the overall meaning of the remarks with which Hal—now Henry V—inaugurates his reign. He addresses the Lord Chief Justice, his new spiritual guide and adoptive father, instructing him to carry out his sovereign will and his royal word against the desire and unruly words of Falstaff:

> Be it your charge, my lord,
> To see perform'd the tenor of our word.
> Set on.
>
> (*2 Henry IV,* 5.5.70–72)

As the new king starts his reign, the verb *perform* can only mean "carry out an order."

The man who is now speaking is no longer the irresponsible prince led astray by bad company, but the heroic sovereign, a model for all Christianity, one who wilfully dominates the social and theatrical scene and who, as a representative of royal majesty and the incarnation of the power of the law and justice, must formally prevent the utterance of any subversive speeches. Also, in this scene of Falstaff's repudiation (as in that of Hal's reformation), the words pronounced by Hal-Henry V are inspired by a sense of awareness and rationality:

> I know thee not, old man. Fall to thy prayers.
> How ill white hairs becomes a fool and jester!
> I have long dreamt of such a kind of man,
> So surfeit-swell'd, so old, and so profane;
> But being awak'd I do despise my dream.
>
> (*2 Henry IV,* 5.5.47–51)

Such are the new king's first words to Falstaff. He raises his tone, which becomes formal, placing it beyond Falstaff's reach. The king's solemn language gives tangible concreteness to a barrier that has always existed and which now becomes manifest with pitiless logic in its function of exclusion. At this point of the state ritual that is being celebrated, and at the end of the homily urging Falstaff to "reform himself," it is no coincidence that the new monarch orders the Lord Chief Justice to ensure that his former wassailing companion does not invade the symbolic space of his regality or perform any subversive actions contrary to law and order.

Indeed, the king could do no other: he is exposed—as actor and "governour"—to the general view and judgment. It is therefore advisable for him to follow suggestions and norms of behavior of proven efficacy, such as those to be found as early as 1531 in *The Boke Named The Governour,* in which Sir Thomas Elyot warns against the danger of adopting attitudes not in keeping with the privileged position of a statesman:

> . . . by their pre-eminence they sitte, as it were, on a piller on the toppe of a mountaine, where all the people do beholde them, not only in their open affaires, but also in their secrete passetimes, privie daliaunce, or other improfitable or wanton conditions.[7]

As he is fully aware of his position of preeminence and visibility, the king soon learns that he must dominate the scene if he is to control the social and cultural order for which he is, in the ultimate analysis, the person with the greatest responsibilty. His domination of the stage must, however, be constantly exhibited and reiterated, and put to the test: as indeed happens in the dramatic sequence leading up to the exclusion of Falstaff in Shakespeare's play and as happened to Elizabeth on many a public occasion, when one has the impression that the Tudor queen, in many ways, mirrors herself in the exemplary figure of Henry V.

In this regard, it may be interesting to consider briefly two triumphal entries into the city of London: Henry V's, in the second part of *Henry IV,* and Elizabeth's, the day before her coronation. In both cases, the sovereigns proceed through crowded London streets; in both cases, their route takes them to their formal assumption of power in Westminster Abbey. In both cases, the royal personages unexpectedly find themselves in an embarrassing situation that runs the risk both of spoiling the sophisticated self-celebration of royal power and of throwing doubt on the encomiastic intention of the coronation. In the second part of *Henry IV,* Act 5 Scene 5 is set in a London street near Westminster Abbey. The grooms are busy strewing rushes along the procession route (5.5.1–4); the stage direction reads: "Trumpets sound, and the King and his train pass over the stage: after them enter Falstaff, Shallow, Pistol, Bardolph, and the Page": the audience's eye follows the royal train entering the Abbey and lingers on the "Tavern friends." The foul-smelling Falstaff and his humble companions take up their stations, anxiously awaiting Henry's return. At first, Falstaff appears sure of the influence he will have over the new king: "Stand here by me, Master Robert Shallow, I will make the King do you grace. I will leer upon him as a comes by, and do but mark the countenance that he will give me" (5.5.5–8). He then expresses his regret at not having had new liveries made in the king's honor, but immediately finds a justification that is acceptable on the affective plane and in view of the effects this may have on the practical level: "But 'tis no matter, this poor show doth better, this doth infer the zeal I had to see him" (5.5.13–14). At this point, Falstaff exaggerates somewhat, seeking also the support of Shallow who, interrupting Falstaff with his repeated "It doth so," warns the audience of the quality of the meeting that is soon to take place between Hal/Henry V and Falstaff:

Shallow.	It doth so.
Falstaff.	It shows my earnestness of affection—
Shallow.	It doth so.
Falstaff.	My devotion—
Shallow.	It doth, it doth, it doth.
Falstaff.	As it were, to ride day and night, and not to deliberate, not to remember, not to have patience to shift me—
Shallow.	It is best, certain.
Falstaff.	But to stand stained with travel, and sweating with desire to see him, thinking of nothing else, putting all affairs else in oblivion, as if there were nothing else to be done but to see him.

(5.5.15–27)

Falstaff is disappointed when he sees his king, for the figure that appears before him is one quite unknown to him; the sovereign will not even listen to him:

Falstaff.	God save thy Grace, King Hal, my royal Hal!
Pistol.	The heavens thee guard and keep, most royal imp of fame!
Falstaff.	God save thee, my sweet boy!
King.	My Lord Chief Justice, speak to that vain man.
Chief Justice.	Have you your wits? Know you what 'tis you speak?
Falstaff.	My King! My Jove! I speak to thee, my heart!

(5.5.41–46)

Falstaff in vain seeks to speak directly to his one-time boon companion; but the sovereign appears to snub him and turns to his high-ranking intermediary, the Lord Chief Justice, requiring him to silence "that vain man." The joy, the uncontrolled emotions, and the spontaneous familiarity that burst from the words of the irrepressible Sir John are finally checked—not by the Chief Justice's intervention—but by the cold, devastating words of the king. The king himself is directly involved, since Falstaff, deaf to the Chief Justice's injunctions, continues to address the monarch; Henry is finally forced to speak to Falstaff, in the celebrated speech that begins with the declaration of repudiation:

> I know thee not, old man. Fall to thy prayers.
> How ill white hairs becomes a fool and jester!
> (5.5.47–48)

After his initial scorn, the king proceeds to dissuade his former companion from replying, that is, from using language unsuited to the ceremonial occasion:

> Reply not to me with a fool-born jest.
> (5.5.55)

For the one-time Hal, there is no more time for promises and oaths; now it is time for orders ("Make," line 52; "Leave" and "know," line 53; "Reply not," line 55; "Presume not," line 56). Now it is time for exemplary action that requires only Falstaff's silence and his departure from the scene:

> Till then I banish thee, on pain of death,
> As I have done the rest of my misleaders,
> Not to come near our person by ten mile.
> (5.5.63–65)

When Elizabeth passed through the streets of London to be formally recognized as Queen of England in the coronation ceremony at Westminster Abbey, she found herself faced with a situation that was almost as difficult to handle as the one so masterfully dominated by Shakespeare's Henry V. According to the chronicle account of the ceremonial occasion provided by Richard Mulcaster, in *The Passage of our most dread Soveraigne Lady, Quene Elyzabeth, through the citie of London to Westminster . . .* (1559), the City directly challenged the young sovereign, in order to put her to the test and make a message quite clear to her. As Elizabeth approached the penultimate pageant, she desired to know beforehand what would be performed on the stage:

> And it was told Her Grace, that there was placed TIME. "TIME," quoth she, "and TIME hath brought me hither." And so forth the whole matter was opened to Her Grace, as hereafter shall be declared in the description of the pageant. But when in the opening, Her Grace understood that the *Bible* in English, should be delivered unto her by TRUTH (which was therein represented by a child), she thanked the City for that gift, and said that she would oftentimes read over that book; commanding Sir John PARRAT, one of the knights which held up her canopy, to go before, and to receive it: but learning that it should be delivered unto Her Grace, down by a silken lace, she caused him to stay.[8]

The episode is particularly interesting if it is read not just as a manifestation of the specific spectacularity of this kind of "text" which describes the assumption of royal power; that is, if it is read as a signal directed by the City above all to the new queen. The Bible must be received personally by Elizabeth. It is evident that, with such an insidious subject as religion—represented iconographically by the text of the Bible—the City intends to set her a hard question. This the young sovereign succeeds in answering with the consummate skill of a leading actress who is able to improvise the right gestures and words and thus save the show, not in the least overawed by the imposing and significant presence of the guilds of London, which come between herself and the text of the Bible. The Holy Book, so majestically presented by the City, is also the sign of another form of discursive practice that is there before her, present and menacing, in the same historical and temporal space where Elizabeth is about to ascend the throne as monarch of England. The subversive power of the holy text must therefore be neutralized according to a liturgy that is acceptable at one and the same time both to the spectators (including the members of the City guilds) and to the queen. As Mulcaster comments:

> But she, as soon as she had received the book, kissed it; and with both her hands held up the same, and so laid it upon her breast; with great thanks to the City therefore.[9]

Elizabeth has taken control of the situation. She fully occupies the space required for the performance: the danger of social tension has been successfully averted, and it is now possible to celebrate the rite of harmonious communion which symbolically represents the cohesion between the subjects and the crown.

Like Henry V, Elizabeth shows that power is really a matter of hegemony of, and in, cultural performance, which is manifested as a systematic series of impositions of "narrations" and "social metacomments" on the sociocultural system and as a sometimes annoyingly insistent reiteration of their authenticity.

Unlike Elizabeth, Henry V expels from the body of the state the popular classes, personified by Falstaff in the two parts of *Henry IV,* who are mocked and reduced to silence by Hal. The history play thus shows itself to be a genre that removes popular discourse—which is present but as yet ineffective—from its surface texture. In the two *Henry IV* plays, the tension between royal power and the transgressive power of the popular classes incarnated by Sir John Falstaff is resolved in Prince Hal's undisputed victory and the gross knight's exile from court. In *Henry V,* the process of destruction, and the subsequent disappearance from the scene of Falstaff's cumbersome body (with the "heavy, fearful materiality" of sensuality present in his person), is rapidly performed between the first and the third scene of the second act. First, we hear from the faithful Boy that Falstaff is "very sick, and would to bed" (2.1.82–83), and immediately afterwards the Hostess informs us that "The king has killed his heart" (2.1.88), thus identifying the cause of Falstaff's severe illness. This explanation is further explored a few lines later by the shabby band of tavern cronies, when the responsibility for Falstaff's slow wasting away is laid upon the sovereign's head:

Hostess.	As ever you come of women, come in quickly to Sir John. Ah, poor heart! he is so shak'd of a burning quotidian tertian, that it is most lamentable to behold. Sweet men, come to him.
Nym.	The king hath run bad humours on the knight; that's the even of it.
Pistol.	Nym, thou hast spoke the right; His heart is fracted and corroborate.
Nym.	The king is a good king: but it must be as it may; he passes some humours and careers.
Pistol.	Let us condole the knight; for, lambkins, we will live.

(2.2.117–27)[10]

The sovereign's behavior is, in fact, justified and seen as necessary by Nym, who calls Henry a good king, a king capable of imposing the authority he represents by the exercise of power, even if it means sacrificing the life of a friend.[11] In the scene that follows—apparently unrelated to the one we have just seen—the king continues to prove a good king, caught as he is in the dramatic moment of the trial for high treason of the nobles Cambridge, Scroop, and Gray (2.2): the whole scene, punctuated by Henry's lengthy homiletic harangues against the three "English monsters" (2.2.85), comes across as a further elaboration of the cardinal virtues (prudence, temperance, and justice) which—as already seen in his repudiation of Falstaff—are now the indispensable guides of this good king, who sets himself as an exemplary model to all Christendom. The Chorus at the beginning of Act II defines him (line 6) as "the mirror of all Christian kings." The episode of the plot, with its discovery and the death of its perpetrators, completely redeems Hal's "guilt" with regard to Falstaff. It is inevitable—in this process of the elevation of Hal from prince to sovereign—that the next scene (3.3) should make no mention of the heartless king's responsibility for the death of the heartbroken Falstaff. In this scene—set in a London street, appropriately "before a Tavern"—some true friends (the Hostess, Nym, Pistol, and Bardolph) pronounce the funeral oration and celebrate the adventures, mainly involving sack and women, of Falstaff's unruly life. It falls to the Hostess to recall his final moments:

> ... a' parted even just between twelve and one, even at the turning o' the tide: for after I saw him fumble with the sheets and play with flowers and smile upon his fingers' end, I knew there was but one way; for his nose was as sharp as a pen, and a' babbled of green fields.
> (2.3.12–17)

Thus we hear of the slurred babbling of a Falstaff who has come to the valley of the shadow of death (the "green pasture" of Psalm 23) and is unable to utter meaningful sounds and words. Only the term *God*—repeated three or four times, the Hostess tells us (2.3.20–21)—appears to have been pronounced fully consciously; then his body is cold and emanates a message of death:

> So a' bade me lay more clothes on his feet: I put my hand into the bed and felt them, and they were as cold as any stone; then I felt to his knees, and so upward, and upward, and all was as cold as any stone.
> (3.3.23–27)

Despite the clearly melodramatic presentation, the scene of Falstaff's death should make us reflect on the various aspects that mark the departure from the stage of the "heavy, fearful, materiality" of the massive body and thundering voice of Sir John Falstaff. Both body and voice have become feeble, stripped of all the vigor that enlivened them throughout the episodes of *Henry IV* and *Henry V*. As he loses his corpulence and power of speech, Falstaff has to renounce every possibility of resisting the power of the royal authority, which, with its strong presence, hegemonizes the entire textual and ideological space of the Histories.

The process of Falstaff's gradual weakening actually begins in the first part of *Henry IV*, as is particularly evident in the delightful episode of the "play extempore" (2.4), when Falstaff is prevented from finishing the performance just when, in the role of Prince Hal, he is about to conclude the harangue in his own favor: "Out, ye rogue! Play out the play! I have much to say in the behalf of that Falstaff" (2.4.478–79). Falstaff's subversive force is further weakened in the second part of *Henry IV*, when the prince blames Falstaff and his Eastcheap companions for preventing him from showing feelings of filial sorrow at his father's serious illness:

Prince. Marry, I tell thee it is not meet that I should be sad now my father is sick; albeit I could tell to thee, as to one it pleases me for a fault of a better to call my friend, I could be sad, and sad indeed too.

Poins. Very hardly, upon such a subject.

Prince. By this hand, thou thinkest me as far in the devil's book as thou and Falstaff, for obduracy and persistency. Let the end try the man. But I tell thee, my heart bleeds inwardly that my father is so sick; and keeping such vile company as thou art hath in reason taken from me all ostentation of sorrow.
(2.2.38–48)

Later in the same scene, the prince becomes indignant with Falstaff, who has irreverently dared to send him a letter in which—despite the parody of the formality of epistolary style (122–25) and the Puritan-type idiomatic expressions ("by yea and no," 124), but with all the effrontery of the *miles gloriosus* (125–27)—he places himself dangerously above his proper rank. It is also for this reason that Hal resolves to punish him. Once again (for the last time, in fact) the prince organizes a jest at his expense with the complicity of the secondary characters Poins, Bardolph, and Falstaff's own page. For the occasion the prince will dress as a tavern "drawer," thus inverting the social hierarchy that Falstaff had also ignored in his letter. Hal comments:

> From a god to a bull? A heavy descension! It was Jove's case. From a prince to a prentice? A low transformation, that shall be mine, for in everything the purpose must weigh with the folly.
> (2.2.166–69)

In Act 2, scene 4, when the jest takes place, the prince has distanced himself from the old company of the Boar's Head Tavern and can therefore betake himself without further ado to Westminster, where he must attend to his duties as heir to the throne. Taking his leave from Falstaff and the idle tavern drinkers, Hal observes:

> By heaven, Poins, I feel me much to blame,
> So idly to profane the precious time,
> When tempest of commotion, like the south
> Borne with black vapour, doth begin to melt
> And drop upon our bare unarmed heads.
> Give me my sword and cloak. Falstaff, good night.
> (2.4.358–63)

This good night addressed to Falstaff is, in fact, a farewell; for it is the last time the two characters meet in the friendly, joyous, animated world of the tavern, a world where the two characters were, so to speak, of "equal" stature, each capable of preparing with "equal" inventive spirit jokes and jests that seemed to invert roles and situations. When the two characters next find themselves face to face, not only has much time passed (the scene is in Act 5) but the meeting takes place in a territory unfamiliar to Falstaff, for the court is the uncontested reign of Hal and, at court, Hal—now Henry V—is bound to declare publicly (and to Falstaff, above all) that social differences must be observed; at court, Hal will also put into practice the skills he has learned from the king his father ("cold blood") and those he has picked up from the humble world of his subjects ("fertile sherris"). It is ironic that Falstaff himself, in his celebrated praise of sack (4.3.84–123), notes and desires this conciliation, although he is about to lose his "son" Hal, in his own hypothetical children:

> . . . and this valour comes of sherris. So that skill in the weapon is nothing without sack, for that sets it a-work, and learning a mere hoard of gold kept by a devil, till sack commences it and sets it in act and

use. Hereof comes it that Prince Harry is valiant; for the cold blood he did naturally inherit of his father he hath like lean, sterile, and bare land manured, husbanded, and tilled, with excellent endeavour of drinking good and good store of fertile sherris, that he is become very hot and valiant. If I had a thousand sons, the first human principle I would teach them should be to forswear thin potations, and to addict themselves to sack.

(4.3.111–23)

When Hal ascends the throne, not only does he show that he knows how to put Falstaff's observations to good use, he sanctions his uncontested superiority, which enables him to prevent his reign (and his dramatic text) from degenerating into the linguistic Babel announced by the slanderer Rumour in the Induction to *2 Henry IV* (1–10) and constructed on the calumnies of Falstaff, who, from several points of view, is, in fact, Rumour's echo. It strikes the imagination that, iconographically, Rumour is represented with a costume painted full of tongues (but not of tongues and eyes, as was the tradition[12]) and that Falstaff appears emblematically and dramatically as an incarnation of Rumour when he slanders the king (1.2.102–103), when he pours discredit on Prince Hal entering the tavern in disguise (2.4.250–52), and when he describes himself to Colville of the Dale as a famous knight who has "a whole school of tongues in this belly of mine" (4.3.18). It equally strikes the imagination that Prince Hal should defend himself from Warwick in the following terms:

> The Prince but studies his companions
> Like a strange tongue, wherein, to gain the language,
> 'Tis needful that the most immodest word
> Be look'd upon and learnt; which once attain'd,
> Your Highness knows, comes to no further use
> But to be known and hated. So, like gross terms,
> The Prince will, in the perfectness of time,
> Cast off his followers, and their memory
> Shall as a pattern or a measure live
> By which his Grace must mete the lives of others,
> Turning past evils to advantages.

(4.4.68–78)

The world of language is metaphorically evoked to indicate Hal's need to become a polyglot king capable of translating the various idiolects—which run the risk of generating general chaos—into a harmonious and harmonizing language, an expression of the simultaneous will to communicate and to listen, intended—for all the characters—to establish significant relationships that interweave to give life to a dramatic unity analogous to the social unity that the true art of the governor must achieve.¹³ In *Henry V,* Exeter observes:

> For government, though high and low and lower,
> Put into parts, doth keep in one consent,
> Congreeing in a full and natural close,
> Like music.
>
> (1.2.180–83)

In a polyphonic kingdom such as that dominated by Henry V, there is no room for popular styles, languages, attitudes, and poses that escape the vigilant eye of power. However, to appreciate fully the political system proposed by the heroic sovereign, it is necessary to recall for a brief moment the presence in the recent history of the new monarchy of figures like Falstaff, figures whose disruptive strength and extraordinary charm are derived from the way they become fools and jesters. But this presence had to remain a fleeting presence, just like that of the fools and jesters who brightened a large part of court life, the popular theater, and comic drama in the Elizabethan age. It is appropriate here to recall the new king's precise words to Falstaff in the repudiation scene:

> I know thee not, old man. Fall to thy prayers.
> How ill white hairs becomes a fool and jester!
>
> (*2 Henry IV,* 5.5.47–48)

A few lines later Hal commands Falstaff: "Reply not to me with a fool-born jest" (5.5.55). Hal does nothing but remind Falstaff and the audience that the stout old man is merely an amateur actor who can and must do nothing against the arts of the professional actor—the expert in all arts, in all the tricks of acting. Falstaff's ingenuous, amusing, sometimes even mocking way of acting is quite ineffective against Hal's sharp perspicacity. Falstaff may be capable of showing a mastery worthy of Dick Tarlton in organizing improvised theatrical actions and inventing comic hoaxes at Hal's expense; but Hal soon proves himself even more skillful than Falstaff in the creation of jests and hoaxes that are sometimes cruel to Hal's own clown, Falstaff.

For we also see that this theatrical dimension—which connotes the popular world of Falstaff—is incorporated and defeated by Hal's masterful performance. Improvised theatrical action is not something to be encouraged, since it is indecorous and dangerous:

this is shown by the celebrated scene of the play-within-the-play in *1 Henry IV,* at which point Falstaff still enjoys the crown prince's favors and can cross with impunity the border between licit and illicit, just like Dick Tarlton of the Queen's Men. Tarlton moved with impunity between the world of the popular theater and theater-taverns (he and his company were licensed to perform at two taverns, The Bell and The Bull) and that of the Banqueting Hall, often provoking not only hilarity and amusement but also embarrassment and concern. The Lord Mayor, of course, had the power to prohibit such performances, which were most popular precisely when improvised. In 1574, for example, an ordinance forbade tavern-keepers to "suffer to be interlaced, added, mingled or uttered in any such play, interlude, comedy, tragedy or show any other matter than such as shall be first perused and allowed."[14]

Tarlton, however, had royal protection, just like Falstaff. The new norms governing theater censorship were ineffective when Henry Tilney, Master of the Revels, obtained permission to impose the emendments necessary to make theatrical texts legally acceptable (1581). But his jests and his collusion with the audience could give rise to unexpected reactions, a source of possible danger due to the atmosphere of intimate participation which Tarlton—like Falstaff and unlike Hal—expected from the spectators. There can be no doubt that in the scene performed in the Eastcheap Tavern, the fat blusterer wears Tarlton's "mantle" and like him behaves like a "tavern fool or table-side jester."[15] In the low world of Eastcheap, in the Boar's Head Tavern run by the ill-famed Mistress Quickly—a tavern which, in many ways, recalls the Christopher Tavern frequented by Shakespeare's clown, Will Kemp and enlivened by one Emma Ball, a lady of dubious reputation—Prince Hal accepts the suggestion/supplication of Falstaff whose "play extempore" promises merry fun for one and all. Falstaff's words are: "What, shall we be merry, shall we have a play extempore? (2.4.275–76). "Extemporal wit," it will be remembered, is what the Elizabethans expected from Tarlton and from Will Kemp, who may have played the part of Falstaff in performances of Shakespeare's play;[16] and Falstaff seems to possess many of Kemp's theatrical skills.[17]

Let us examine the development of the play-within-the-play scene. The suggestion put forward by Falstaff, who is eager to unleash his energy in a theatrical improvisation, is left unanswered. Falstaff does not give up, however:

> Well, thou wilt be horribly chid tomorrow when thou comest to thy father; if thou love me practise an answer.
> (2.4.368–70)

Eventually, Hal deigns to obey, as it were, and immediately pronounces directives for Falstaff:

> Do thou stand for my father and examine me upon the particulars of my life.
> (2.4.371–72)

To which Falstaff rejoins:

> Shall I? Content! This chair shall be my state, this dagger my sceptre, and this cushion my crown.
> (2.4.373–74)

The prince gives him not a moment's pause; and, while he does in fact cooperate with Falstaff almost on equal terms in the invention of the situation and the sceneplay, it is also true that he proceeds by means of a cruel game of mixed comedy and sarcasm intended to make use of Falstaff but also to humiliate him:

> Thy state is taken for a joint-stool, thy golden sceptre for a leaden dagger, and thy precious rich crown for a pitiful bald crown.
> (2.4.375–77)

These words of Hal's put Falstaff back at his social level, which is that of the clown, of the artisan apprentice, not that of the gentleman, as indeed his very name proclaims: "False staff."[18]

The climax of the play-within-the-play, which marks the decisive turning point in the sharp, irreversible separation of the two symbolic bodies of subjects and king, comes in Falstaff's speech when he plays the part of Henry IV:

> *Falstaff.* This pitch (as ancient writers do report) doth defile, so doth the company thou keepest: for, Harry, now I do not speak to thee in drink, but in tears; not in pleasure, but in passion; not in words only, but in woes also. And yet there is a virtuous man whom I have often noted in thy company, but I know not his name.
> (2.4.408-14)

And so the jest begins. The audience prepares to enjoy the jokes and ribaldry alluded to by the feigned Henry IV, who—almost forgetting his real rank, and accepting that incarnated in the character of Falstaff and the Shakespearean clown—pronounces his "And yet . . ." and then his crafty "and now I remember me, his name is Falstaff" (2.4.419–20). The prince, playing his part, is disturbed by the preponderant role that seems to have fallen to the lot of his fat, immoral drinking companion. He is annoyed by the benevolence which the king his father, in the words pronounced by Falstaff/Henry IV, shows to Falstaff rather than to himself: ". . . there is virtue in that Falstaff; him keep with, the rest banish. And tell me now, thou naughty varlet, tell me where hast thou been this month?" (2.4.424–26). The prince now berates Falstaff, the actor, who is unable to behave as might be expected in his kingly role: "Dost thou speak like a king? Do thou stand for me, and I'll play my father" (2.4.427–28). Both characters cleverly enter into the role which they are soon to abandon; here, however, the prince is quick to pick up Falstaff's speech, taking from him the role which he has played up to now and which runs the risk of depriving Hal of the leading role.

> *Falstaff.* Depose me? If thou dost it half so gravely, so majestically, both in word and matter, hang me up by the heels for a rabbit-sucker, or a poulter's hare.
>
> (2.4.429–31)

Improvisation, which was about to get the upper hand of the character/actor Hal, must be submitted to authoritative control. For a moment, the barrier of theatrical fiction has to be removed; it is then restored by Hal, who now totally dominates the scene, upsetting the portrait which a few moments before Falstaff had drawn of him and showing that the *mise-en-scène* of the spectacle of power is subject to his law. The order of acting imposed by Hal restores the order threatened by the carnival-type transgressions of temporary Lord of Misrule, Sir John Falstaff. The prince, now in the role of the king his father, no longer plays along with Falstaff; he creates a play of his own invention which will not become reality until the end of the second part of *Henry IV*. Now Hal/Henry IV shifts the figure of Falstaff to a world that befits him, a world remote from the world of regality to which he can have no access except on a temporary basis, in jest, to play the part of a clown, a fool, or the Vice. Falstaff is now described as an evil villain, an attractive figure possibly but one that must be *deposed* and *denied,* as required by the tradition of the Moralities and Interludes to which the Vice—and, consequently, Falstaff—belongs:[19] Falstaff is defined, in terms of that popular tradition, as "devil" / "vice" / "iniquity" / "ruffian" / and "Satan" (2.4.441–57). The comic crescendo cannot but recall the association between the world of the

Eastcheap tavern and the subterranean world of Hell. As D. Wiles aptly points out:

> The tavern is a prelude to Hell. Falstaff speaks of the damnation of Dives (1.2.34), and Pistol swears he will see Doll damned (2.4.153). Falstaff catalogues the damned souls: Bardolph's face is Lucifer's kitchen; the devil attends on the boy; the pox-ridden Doll is "in hell already, and burns poor souls"; the Hostess will probably howl for breaking Lent (2.4.329-73).[20]

Falstaff knows that once he is obliged to return to his infernal world, once he is presented as a bad counsellor, a bad angel who leads Hal astray, he will have to leave the stage—both theatrically and politically. This is what he strives to resist; but the defense he puts together—in Hal's clothing—proves quite useless, destined to failure even before it starts:

> If to be old and merry be a sin, then many an old host that I know is damned: if to be fat be to be hated, then Pharaoh's lean kine are to be loved. No, my good lord; banish Peto, banish Bardolph, banish Poins—but for sweet Jack Falstaff, kind Jack Falstaff, true Jack Falstaff, valiant Jack Falstaff, and therefore more valiant, being as he is old Jack Falstaff, banish not him thy Harry's company, banish not him thy Harry's company, banish plump Jack, and banish all the world.
>
> (2.4.465-74)

The prince punctually promises: "I do, I will" (2.4.475). And punctually, in the second part of *Henry IV,* the promise of theatrical fiction becomes reality. However, before reaching this final stage, Falstaff undergoes a further "injustice," owing to which he is caused to disappear even before his death, which is related in *Henry V*. The epilogue of *2 Henry IV*, which comes after Falstaff's repudiation and after his arrest by the Lord Chief Justice, promises a sequel to Falstaff's adventures:

> . . . where, for anything I know, Falstaff shall die of a sweat, unless already a be killed with your hard opinions; for Oldcastle died martyr, and this is not the man. My tongue is weary; when my legs are too, I will bid you good night.
>
> (Epilogue, 29-33)

This Falstaff, Shakespeare would appear to be suggesting, has nothing subversive about him that might compare him to that awkward character, the symbol of Lollard heresy, the forerunner of the Puritans and the protagonist of *The Life of Sir John Oldcastle,* an anonymous theatrical text that was censured around 1600. *This* Falstaff was transformed into a pathetic Old Lad of the Castle and then into the character of the timid Sir John Falstolfe in the first part of *Henry VI*. *This* Falstaff, as the epilogue to *2 Henry IV* reminds us, takes upon himself the impertinent popular characteristics which—typical of the clown—preclude his participation in Henry V's royal procession and prevent his access to the world of power. Falstaff's place seems to be that of the jig: capering and singing, improvising, seeking close rapport with the audience:

> Here I promised you I would be, and here I commit my body to your mercies. Bate me some, and I will pay you some, and, as most debtors do, promise you infinitely: and so I kneel down before you—but, indeed to pray for the Queen.
> If my tongue cannot entreat you to acquit me, will you command me to use my legs?
>
> (Epilogue, 13–19)

This figure's role and face greatly resemble those of Will Kemp, who was always ready for a dance and a song, a witty retort, a jest, so long as these did not interfere with the preordained structure of the epic plot of the history play. Falstaff, excluded from the text by the action of repudiation over which Hal publicly presides in his new monarchic function, briefly reappears in the final speech pronounced by the Epilogue: he bends his knee, it is true, before royal authority, but he asks the audience to intercede on his behalf to free him from the sentence that has been meted out to him.

Notes

An earlier Italian version of this article appeared in *Anglistica,* 30, 1–2 (1987).

1. J. Starobinski, *L'occhio vivente* (Turin: Einaudi, 1975), 315–16.
2. Alessandro Serpieri, *Retorica e Immaginario* (Parma: Pratiche, 1986), 22.
3. Barba, *La corsa dei contrari* (Milan: Feltrinelli, 1981), 65.
4. Foucault, *L'ordine del discorso* (Turin: Einaudi, 1972), 9.
5. William Shakespeare, *The First Part of Henry IV,* ed. A. R. Humphreys, The Arden Shakespeare (London: Methuen, 1960).
6. Shakespeare, *The Second Part of Henry IV,* ed. A. R. Humphreys, The Arden Shakespeare (London: Methuen, 1966).
7. T. Elyot, *The Boke Named The Governour* (1571), ed. F. T. Watson (London: Dent, 1907), 119.
8. Mulcaster, *The Passage of our most dread Sovereigne Lady, Queen Elizabeth, through the Citie of London to Westminster, the day before her coronation* (1559), in *An English Garner,* ed. E. Arber (Birmingham: E. Arber, 1882), 4:232.

9. Ibid., 235.
10. *King Henry V,* ed. J. H. Walter (London: Methuen, 1964).
11. J. F. Danby, *Shakespeare's Doctrine of Nature* (London: Faber & Faber, 1961), 95.
12. *Second Part of Henry IV,* 4.
13. See J. A. Porter, *The Drama of Speech Acts: Shakespeare's Lancastrian Tetralogy* (Berkeley: University of California Press, 1979).
14. E. K. Chambers, *The Elizabethan Stage* (Oxford: Clarendon Press, 1923), 4: 274.
15. D. Wiles, *Shakespeare's Clown* (Cambridge: Cambridge University Press, 1987), 15. For a very interesting treatment of Falstaff, see further, F. Ferrara, *Il teatro dei re. Saggio sui drammi storico-politici di Shakespeare* (Bari: Adriatica, 1995), 196–98, 201–13; and P. Pugliatti, *Shakespeare the Historian* (London: Macmillan, 1996).
16. J. D. Wilson, *The Fortunes of Falstaff* (1943; New York: Macmillan, 1964), 39.
17. Wiles, *Shakespeare's Clown,* 128–29.
18. Ibid., 121–22.
19. R. Weimann, *Shakespeare and the Popular Tradition in the Theater* (Baltimore: Johns Hopkins University Press, 1978). See also, B. Everett, "The Fatness of Falstaff," *London Review of Books* (16 August 1990): 18–22; and D. Womersley, "Why Is Falstaff Fat?" *Review of English Studies,* NS 47, 185 (1996), 1–22.
20. Wiles, *Shakespeare's Clown,* 124–25.

"Now I play a merchant's part": The Space of the Merchant in Shakespeare's Early Comedies

MARIANGELA TEMPERA

Absent Authority and the Rise of the Merchants

The playing of a role, the essence of the actor's profession, is a theme that is constantly explored in Shakespeare's theater. Indeed, it may become a character's main activity, especially in the comedies. This activity is usually manifested in the reversal of contrary roles (man/woman, servant/master) by means of disguise, an expedient of consolidated comic tradition that does not threaten the social order, as it is limited to tolerated moments of license—for example, at Carnival.

More rarely, a character appropriates the typical features of a parallel social group, opening up microconflicts that will not necessarily be resolved in the comedy's final harmonization. Such cases, in the variegated universe of Shakespeare's macrotext, shed light on the obscure, insurmountable barriers between social groups. These barriers, taken for granted by the Elizabethan audience, did not become the cause of open conflict; but to modern audiences they cause unexpected gaps in the construction of a character, sudden moments when the character abandons the strict confines of a well-codified identity.

When we explore the subtle distinctions between social roles, it is difficult not to project onto the Elizabethan world our own sensitivity, our own idea of "class." It is equally difficult to resist the temptation of reading literary texts as historical documents *tout court,* expecting to find in them a precise and consistent use of the terminology that marks membership in a given social group. Also, in the indeterminate borderland between bourgeoisie and gentry, in the exchange of certain key words in the characteristic vocabulary of each group, it is possible to glimpse traces of a social hierarchy that still resists the upheavals of modern times.

In plays with a court setting the hierarchy of social relationships is clarified by the presence of the sovereign, a fixed point around which the courtiers are obliged to rotate, etiquette manual in hand. In the city, the boundaries between groups are more difficult to define, especially when authority appears to be absent or ineffectual as regards the social structure. The most subtle skirmish is that between the two groups which are most conspicuous and most difficult to define reciprocally: gentlemen and merchants. The "rhetorical assertion of social status"[1] reflected in the dialogue becomes especially important when it helps illuminate the difficult coexistence of these two identities—which are parallel, not overlapping.

In *The Comedy of Errors, The Taming of the Shrew,* and *The Merchant of Venice,*[2] merchants play a dominant role occupying a city scene devoid of higher authority.[3] In these three comedies, authority is represented by a duke whose sole function would appear to be to ensure that the laws of the market are observed. In *The Comedy of Errors,* the duke begins the play with a strict defense of the rules of commerce, using terms that soften the solemnity of the edict with a frank admission of familiarity with the language of commerce:

Duke. Thy substance, *valued at the highest rate,*
Cannot amount unto a hundred marks;
Therefore by law thou art condemn'd to die
(1.1.23–25; emphasis added)

The characters in *The Merchant of Venice* expect a similar approach from the Doge, justifying it, however, with motivations that raise it to a higher level of abstraction:

Antonio. The duke cannot deny the course of law:
. . . .
Since that the trade and profit of the city
Consisteth of all nations.
(3.3.27–31)

In *The Taming of the Shrew,* the duke never appears (the protagonists' domestic quarrels do not interfere with the tranquil procedures of business); he is evoked as a threatening presence in order to persuade the Pedant to assist the plans of Lucentio, in terms similar to those in *The Comedy of Errors*. The speed with which the story is believed is proof of its plausibility.

The three comedies thus provide interesting material for an inquiry aimed at defining the specific space of the merchant, and

The Comedy of Errors: All the World's a Market

Arriving at Ephesus, a city where *mart* is a synonym for public space, Antipholus of Syracuse sets out on a sightseeing tour in which "Peruse the traders" comes before "gaze upon the buildings," confirming the central role of merchants that is made dramatically evident from the first scene. The same scale of priorities comically regulates the words of the Abbess when she seeks an explanation for the odd behavior of the other Antipholus:

> *Abbess.* Hath he not lost much wealth by wrack of sea?
> Buried some dear friend? Hath not else his eye
> Stray'd his affection in unlawful love . . .
> (5.1.49–51)

The economic loss occasioned by a shipwreck is more traumatic than a bereavement, more traumatic even than the passion of love, which traditionally is taken as the driving force of a comedy plot. Among merchants, class solidarity is greater than that of citizenship. Far from reporting to the authorities the presence of a Syracusan, Antipholus' partner suggests to him a way of eluding the local law: "Therefore give out you are from Epidamnum" (1.2.1). In such a context it is hardly surprising that business matters prevail over private considerations; the declaration "I am invited, sir, to certain merchants, / Of whom I hope to make much benefit" (1.2.24–25) is a socially acceptable excuse for refusing an invitation to dinner.

Besides the comical exploration of the customs of the merchants, who seem to be dominated by an all-pervading desire to reduce all aspects of human life to the level of commerce, *The Comedy of Errors* brings to the fore a definition of "reputation" that is also closely linked to the world of business:

> *Sec. Merchant.* How is the man esteem'd here in the city?
> *Angelo.* Of very reverend reputation, sir,
> Of credit infinite, highly belov'd,
> Second to none that lives here in the city . . .
> (5.1.4–7)

Angelo is also aware of the risks of losing one's credit: "This touches me in reputation" (4.1.72). This is the bourgeois reply to the courtiers' "honor," a reply that is reassuring in its concreteness and simplicity because it sees the individual in relation to his commercial trustworthiness. This is a definition of the ego which leaves no space for doubt or zones of dim obscurity and which is therefore bound to be questioned by the incomprehensible behavior of the two Antipholuses.

At Ephesus, no parallel social group comes to challenge the precise identity of the merchants or to undermine their solidity. If they sense a danger, they see its source in a category of individuals who are socially neither their superiors nor their inferiors but explicitly outsiders—witches, sorcerers, casters of spells—who can safely be blamed for the proliferation of errors. This gives rise to a social context with such clear-cut confines that "the major characters increasingly experience a feeling of claustrophobia."[4] In this city-market, the problem of relations with a class that is felt to be socially higher simply does not exist: "gentlewoman" and "gentleman" are generic terms, courtesy titles employed to indicate strangers (Antipholus of Syracuse uses them for Adriana and the Second Merchant) or to underline the respectability (in the commercial sense) of a character, as, for example, Angelo does when he alludes to his creditor.

If sadness and melancholy are frequently mentioned in relation to the two Antipholuses, this does not mean that these two solid members of the bourgeoisie have appropriated a typically aristocratic foible. It is more of a strategy that serves to extend their physical similarity, of which only the spectators are from the beginning aware, also to their mental character. At the beginning of the play, the Syracusan slips into his discourse with the merchant an apparently incongruous allusion to his tendency to be "dull with care and melancholy" (1.2.20), the victim of commonplace low spirits which the servant's jests drive away. The dramatic function of this remark becomes clear in Act 5, when Adriana recalls her husband's strange behavior in the days before he is reunited with his twin: for the entire week, Antipholus of Ephesus was "heavy, sour, sad, / And much, much different from the man he was" (5.1.45–46). The imminent denouement of the comedy of errors also seems to involve a rapprochement of characters.

In *The Comedy of Errors,* the merchant successfully combines his role in the community with his pursuit of wealth over distant seas. His ego is so monolithic that, in order to produce in it the corrosions that set the comic mechanism in motion, Shakespeare is obliged to use the device of duality. The crisis does not come from the outside world, from the attempt of a stranger to query the centrality of the merchant or from ambition inducing the merchant to encroach on the gentlemen's territory; it comes from a refined jest that is presented as being totally within the social group. The behavior of each Antipholus is perfectly rational and consistent with the merchants' code of conduct, but the physical similarity is sufficient to fuse two responsible businessmen in one madcap figure. The happy ending restores to both Antipholuses not only their family but also a full and serene awareness of their social status. Their "reputation" is safe because, despite all appearances, the behavior of the twins never seriously jeopardized it.

The Taming of the Shrew: The Merchant-Gentleman

The society of *The Taming of the Shrew* is more variegated and moves within less precise confines because, in Shakespeare's Padua, there is some interaction between merchants and gentlemen. Editors of the play have always shown a measure of circumspection when distinguishing between the two groups. Regarding Petruchio, there are no doubts: the rough pretender to Kate's hand is "a gentleman of Verona" who deliberately adopts another style of language and behavior but nonetheless never abandons his essential social role:

Petruchio. Good Kate, I am a gentleman . . .
. . . .

Katherina. If you strike me, you are no gentleman,
And if no gentleman, why then no arms.

(2.1.217–21)

Kate, in fact, jumps to the wrong conclusion: Petruchio can indulge in exhilarating acts unbecoming a gentleman without risking being caught up by them and without losing his external badges of rank. Alone among the characters in *The Taming of the Shrew,* he indubitably belongs by birth to the gentry, which, for the other characters, is a conquest related to economic achievement and subject to continual control. Petruchio has the traditional credentials of the gentleman: country house, retainers, arms, and matrimonial intentions—the search for a woman "rich enough to be Petruchio's wife" (1.2.66).[5] Katherina is not unworthy of him and he would not be unworthy of Portia (what a pity we cannot see him pitting his wits against the lady of the riddles). His social position is as certain as that frequently repeated in the text of Vincentio, who is, and clearly remains until the very end "a merchant of great traffic through the world" (1.1.12) and "a merchant of incomparable wealth" (4.2.98).

Baptista occupies an interesting social niche halfway between these two points. Editors of the play now tend to call him not "a rich gentleman" (Cambridge, 1928; Arden, 1929) but more generically "a rich citizen" (Arden, 1981; Cambridge, 1984), reflecting the difficulty of clearly defining the status of a character who rubs shoulders with gentlemen but lives "more toward the market-place" (5.1.8), who is known in Padua as "an affable and courteous gentleman" (1.2.97), and who relies on his wealth in his search for a suitor, of whatever social class, to his daughter's hand. Baptista has succeeded in fitting so well into the social group immediately above that of the merchants that his origins are forgotten even by that master of social codes whom we know Petruchio to be, despite his rough diamond exterior. It is he who reassures Vincentio about his future daughter-in-law's social background, guaranteeing that Bianca is "of worthy birth" (4.5.64). However, the insistence in various points of the text on the two sisters' upbringing gives rise to the suspicion that their blood is not particularly noble: we know that Kate, albeit with scarce success, has been "brought up as best becomes a gentlewoman" (1.2.86), and we are offered ample examples of the education of the gentle Bianca, almost as if to underline the fact that her aristocratic ways are a conquest, and not an inborn heritage of class.

There is, however, one moment when Baptista relinquishes the standards of behavior typical of the gentry, and resumes the mercantile qualities that he has never completely forgotten. The event is so exceptional that it is clearly marked for the spectator by precise verbal signals. After having defined himself a gentleman—"Was ever gentleman thus griev'd as I?" (2.1.37)—Baptista identifies a mercantile element in the marriage contract which he has just stipulated for Katherina:

Baptista. Faith, gentlemen, now I play a merchant's part,
And venture madly on a desperate mart.
(2.1.319–20)

As this remark is followed by an even harder round of bargaining—a veritable auction—for Bianca's hand, the daughter/money exchange is clearly not considered unworthy of a gentleman. The negotiation between Baptista and Petruchio regarding Kate's dowry, a typical feature of Elizabethan marriage customs, would not have been interpreted by the audience as a surrender to the uncultivated manners of an inferior class but rather as a perfectly acceptable verbal shorthand between two characters of the same social class. The eccentric element in Baptista's behavior, which to his mind delineates the confines of mercantile behavior and is unacceptable for a gentleman, is instead understood perfectly well by Tranio:

> *Tranio.*   'Twas a commodity lay fretting by you,
> 'Twill bring you gain, or perish in the seas.
>
> (2.1.321–22)

Katherina is rated as "a questionable piece of goods that Baptista has done well to get off his hands";[6] to get rid of her, a gentleman is authorized to adopt a merchant's ways, without this entailing any loss of status. For the "rich citizens" of Padua, "a merchant is one who takes risks."[7] Commerce and hazard thus go hand in hand, as commerce means the projection of one's interests beyond the city walls. In a less compact society than Ephesus, the social space that typifies the merchant extends outside the confines of the city. This characteristic is not, however, seen as an enrichment but rather as a diminution, as an absence of part of oneself, almost like a social disease of the ego. The gentleman is entirely enclosed within his role as a pillar of the community's social stability, which is guaranteed by a well-tried system of matrimonial alliances. As Petruchio aptly points out, for the gentleman, "venture" can only mean a game of chance: "I'll venture so much of my hawk or hound" (5.2.72). The merchant's ethos, on the contrary, is characterized by a potentially eversive attraction toward the unknown, by a dubious interest in the exotic opportunities offered by distant markets. In such a context, "venture" acquires the negative connotation of a form of hazard that jeopardizes the gentleman's scale of values.

When listing their riches, Gremio and Tranio show that they know very well what this scale of values is: first come town houses, embellished with everything that fashion makes indispensable; then real estate, which not only provides an income but also suggests links with the landed gentry; and last of all, to be admitted only as a dire necessity, there is the ownership of the argosies which carry the merchants' wealth about the oceans. If one compares the importance of merchant ships in the universe of *The Comedy of Errors* and *The Merchant of Venice* with the reluctant, embarrassed hints in *The Taming of the Shrew,* one can perceive the great distance the merchants of Padua have put between their present status and the origins of their wealth. In Padua, as at Ephesus, the merchants move within a social hierarchy that is conveniently truncated, devoid of extremities. The "lower members" are servants whose survival depends on the merchants' goodwill, while the "upper members" are represented by the unpredictable Petruchio. Kate's suitor, sure of the rank to which he was born, has no qualms about becoming related to Baptista, nor any interest in deflating his future father-in-law's aristocratic pretensions.

While the framework of the comedy farcically presents the impossible incursion of the proletarian Sly into the world of high aristocracy, the Players enact the felicitous integration of the merchants in a gentry that is so careless of its class privileges that the servant Tranio has no difficulty impersonating his master. In Padua, Shakespeare would seem to be saying, social climbing is not a crime, no threat to law and order. This was a positive message for the audience of merchants and burghers watching the play. It was also a deceptive message, as it is entrusted to the double fiction of a play-within-the-play, almost as if to suggest that in real life things do not quite go that way.

The Merchant of Venice: Forever a Merchant

The illusion of social harmony created by *The Taming of the Shrew* is quickly dissipated by what is the bitterest of Shakespeare's comedies, in which the importance of the merchant is signaled in the title and confirmed in the frontispiece to the Quarto:

> The most excellent / Historie of the *Merchant* / *of Venice*. / With the extreame crueltie of *Shylocke* the Iewe / towards the sayd Merchant, in cutting a iust pound / of his flesh: and the obtayning of *Portia* / by the choyse of three chests.

The protagonist is thus "the merchant of Venice," as yet without a name, defined simply by his social status. The secondary plot is added as an afterthought, as if the author of this informatory notice sensed the difficult caesura between the two parts, and recognized that, in the declaredly fairy-tale dimension of the secondary plot, there was no room for "the sayd Merchant."

From his very first words, however, Antonio begins to encroach upon the territory of a different identity, that of a gentleman tormented by an inexplicable melancholy which should make him akin both to Portia and to Orsino in *Twelfth Night,* but certainly not—at least, in his intentions—to the two quarrelsome Antipholuses in the *Comedy of Errors.* In this way, he comes to occupy the most ambiguous zone of the play: "he is a hybrid figure because he declares himself to be aristocratic and passive and yet is active as a merchant on the level of the action of the play."[8] Salerio and Solanio immediately recall him to his real status as a "venture merchant," a figure they describe in terms Baptista would have been the first to agree with: someone whose mind is elsewhere, not in the Venetian space of the Rialto but on the high seas with his ships. This is an explanation Antonio does not reject as absurd, but simply as not applicable to his particular case because not all his fortunes are at sea. Solanio's rejoinder, "Why then you are in love," stresses the affinity between "venture merchant" and "lover" as persons who are physically present in the space represented but who project elsewhere an essential part of their identity. Once again, the implication is that of a damaging division of the merchant's ego.

Antonio's drama lies precisely in this gap between what he declares he is and what he in fact is: "too much a merchant to be a tragic hero."[9] Antonio belongs to a different class from Bassanio ("a scholar and a soldier," as he is defined by Nerissa, who knows a gentleman when she sees one), and yet would like to live on the same plain of absolute friendship, uncontaminated by commerce, to be the young man's patron in accordance with courtly practice. Bassanio is "anxious to wive it wealthily in Belmont like Petruchio in Padua,"[10] but he is not denigrated by his scarce morality any more than Antonio, the "quantifying bourgeois," is elevated by his nobility of spirit.[11] Antonio is a gentleman in his behavior and is recognized as such by Salerio (2.8.35) and Lorenzo (3.4.6), minor characters who are his social inferiors. In Baptista's Padua, his preeminence would be beyond discussion; but in Venice he succumbs to the dual attack of Shylock and Portia. Shakespeare only had to transfer from the framework to the play the representatives of two classes, one clearly lower and the other clearly higher than that of the merchants, to destroy any illusion that a general social harmony had been achieved.

Shylock is the first to disparage Antonio's ambitions to improve his social standing:

Shylock.   Antonio is a good man.
Bassanio.   Have you heard any imputation to the contrary?

Shylock. ... my meaning ... is ... that he is sufficient,—yet his means are in supposition.

(1.3.11–15)

These words bring Antonio back to the reality of the Rialto where, as at Ephesus, reputation is based on commercial solvency, not on the sense of honor that permeates the chivalrous universe of Belmont. To prepare the way for the crucial trial scene, Shakespeare allows ample space for the speeches of Salerio and Solanio, which, together with those of Shylock and Tubal, draw the complete picture of the ruin of a merchant in terms that would have been familiar to the audience: from the highly emotional moment of the shipwreck to the more banal and humiliating arrival of the creditors. This temporary abandonment of the fairy-tale of the riddles takes us to the heart of a bourgeois drama rarely portrayed in the theater of the time. Antonio has lost his money, and therefore his reputation, which is the merchant's honor:

Shylock. ... a bankrupt, a prodigal, who dare scarce show his head on the Rialto, a beggar that was us'd to come so smug upon the mart.

(3.1.39–41)

The comparison between the situation before and after the event is the same as that used by the duke when he asks Shylock to renounce his claim to "a pound of this *poor merchant's* flesh" (4.1.23), reminding him that the losses heaped on Antonio's head are "Enow to press a *royal merchant* down" (4.1.29, emphasis added).

On the level of social identity, Antonio's existence as a character is so strongly linked to his professional status that he sees death by Shylock's hand as the work of Fortune, which for once has forsaken its perverse "... use / To let the wretched man outlive his wealth" (4.1.264–65). Once wealth and credit are gone, the merchant no longer exists, and he gives way to man seen as an empty physical shell, who views "with hollow eye and wrinkled brow" (line 266) an anonymous age of poverty, a *not having* that becomes a devastating *not being*. Shylock's lawsuit brutally presents Antonio with the substantial difference between himself and Bassanio. Even without money, Bassanio remains an aristocrat, while, without money, Antonio is nothing.

This is a devastating discovery for Antonio, but it is not the worst that is to happen to him. His most dangerous adversary, the greatest obstacle preventing closer friendship with Bassanio, is—

nor could it be otherwise—the mistress of Belmont. Portia's castle is the anti–Venice, a fabled place where money is not earned or loaned—it simply exists as an unlimited resource that is drawn upon to guarantee the solution to any problem that may blemish the surface perfection. It is a place where love is won by resolving riddles, not by lending money—and is therefore off limits to Antonio. To make this clear to him, the mistress of Belmont does not mince her words. "Which is the merchant here? and which the Jew" (4.1.170) asks Portia/Balthazar, clearly marking, with exemplary economy of language, the zone separating the two litigants from the rest of the court, from the space of the aristocracy where Bassanio casually takes up his position beside the duke. Within the merchant's space, Antonio is able to distinguish himself by his refinement and the social acceptability of his way of conducting business, compared to the despised usurer, but he cannot make elite society forget that Shylock is more his equal than Bassanio. Between the two habitués of the Rialto lies a "conflict . . . of mercantile ideals" but no substantial difference.[12] During her cross-examination, Portia often uses the name "Shylock" as well as "the Jew," whereas Antonio is the victim of a merciless, reiterative stategy. He is persistently called "the merchant" (4.1.201, 229, 259, 295) until the duke's sentence awarding him half the Jew's money makes him a "sufficient" man once again, and restores to him some semblance of identity that can be accepted by the mistress of Belmont (4.1.365–69). Inevitably, this identity is that of a merchant, which Antonio—abandoning all ambitions of playing a leading role in the world of comedies—resigns himself to accepting, as he could never have done in Act 1, with "life and living" (5.1.286). His visit to Belmont, where, as a result of the quarrel about the ring, he is only "welcome notwithstanding" (5.1.239), cannot but be concluded by a courteous but firm expulsion with the only option of "a return to Venice and to business, to a world in which his identity as merchant bestows some power."[13] Only on the Rialto can he be "royal," but only insofar as that adjective qualifies "merchant." As Portia remarks, when she resumes residence in Belmont:

Portia.	A substitute shines brightly as a king Until a king be by, and then his state Empties itself, as doth an inland brook Into the main of waters. . . .

(5.1.94–97)

Gentlemen can behave as merchants, invade the territory of the Rialto, and return to their own world; but the merchant can appear "royal" only in the absence of the real thing.

While Shylock's social inacceptability is immediately apparent, Antonio might turn out to be the new man capable of harboring within himself the values of the aristocracy and the pragmatism of the new merchant class, happily combining the hard reality of commerce with the fantasy world of the fairy-tale. This prospective does not, however, materialize. The failure of his integration in the comedy's final harmonization is particularly serious because it is precisely in Antonio that, theatrically speaking, this highly symbolic fusion could have taken place: the fusion of Belmont and the Rialto, of the high aristocracy that dominates the universe of the romantic comedies and the merchants, who are usually presented in farcical circumstances. Antonio represents the ambition of a new class to enter the theater in the protagonist's role. His failure demonstrates how this process, at the end of the 1590s, is still far from complete. Only Bassanio, like Petruchio, can move from one social group to the other with absolute ease.

Notes

This article appeared in different form in *Shakespeare e la sua eredità*, ed. Maria Grazia Caliumi (Parma: Zara, 1993), 141–48.

1. Frank Whigham, "Ideology and Class Conduct in *The Merchant of Venice*," *Renaissance Drama,* n.s. 10 (1979): 93.
2. All quotations from the Comedies are taken from the Arden editions.
3. On the role of the merchants, see John McVeagh, *Tradefull Merchants: The Portrayal of the Capitalist in Literature* (London: Routledge & Kegan Paul, 1981); Laura Caroline Stevenson, *Praise and Paradox: Merchants and Craftsmen in Elizabethan Popular Literature* (Cambridge: Cambridge University Press, 1984); and Jean-Christophe Agnew, *Worlds Apart: The Market and the Theater in Anglo-American Thought, 1550–1570* (Cambridge: Cambridge University Press, 1986).
4. Wolfgang Riehle, *Shakespeare, Plautus and the Humanist Tradition* (Cambridge: Cambridge University Press, 1990), 79.
5. He may be "one of the new landed gentry," as suggested, on the basis of Kate's pun on "arms," by Carol F. Heffeman, "*The Taming of the Shrew:* The Bourgeoisie in Love," *Essays in Literature* 12:1 (Spring 1985): 5. The key term is *land,* which distinguishes him from the merchants.
6. George R. Hibbard, "*The Taming of the Shrew:* A Social Comedy," in *Shakespearean Essays,* ed. Alwin Thaler and Norman Sanders (Knoxville: University of Tennessee Press, 1964), 21.
7. Ralph Berry, *Shakespeare and Social Class* (Atlantic Highlands, N.J.: Humanities Press International, 1988), 25.
8. Angela Locatelli, *L'eloquenza e gli incantesimi* (Milan: Guerini e Associati, 1988), 78.
9. Leslie A. Fiedler, *The Stranger in Shakespeare* (Paladin: Frogmore, 1974), 75.

10. Harry Levin, "A Garden in Belmont: *The Merchant of Venice*, 5.1," in *Shakespeare and Dramatic Tradition: Essays in Honor of S. F. Johnson,* ed. W. R. Elton and W. B. Long (Newark: University of Delaware Press, 1989), 17.

11. Terry Eagleton, *William Shakespeare* (Oxford: Blackwell, 1986), 45.

12. John W. Draper, "Usury in *The Merchant of Venice,*" *Modern Philology* 33:1 (August 1935): 37. See also, Walter Cohen, "*The Merchant of Venice* and the Possibilities of Historical Criticism," *English Literary History* 49:4 (1982): 765–89; and Michael Ferber, "The Ideology of *The Merchant of Venice,*" *English Literary Renaissance* 20:3 (Autumn 1990): 431–64.

13. Nancy Elizabeth Hodge, "Making Places at Belmont: 'You are welcome notwithstanding'," *Shakespeare Studies* 21 (1993): 169.

Three Kings, Herod of Jewry, and a Child: Apocalypse and Infinity of the World in *Antony and Cleopatra*

GILBERTO SACERDOTI

> . . . Let me be married to three kings in a forenoon, and widow them all: let me have a child at fifty, to whom Herod of Jewry may do homage . . .

We are in Cleopatra's palace at Alexandria in about 31 BC. A handmaiden is jesting with a soothsayer who is reading her hand. But we are also in the second scene of the first act of *Antony and Cleopatra,* that is, in London in the year AD 1608. In the opening scene, Antony has declared to Cleopatra, when she asks him how much he loves her: "there's beggary in the love that can be reckon'd." If Cleopatra wishes to know how far his love extends, "then must thou needs find out new heaven, new earth." This lovers' *bavardage* (curiously concluded with a quotation from *Revelation*) is interrupted by the arrival of news from Rome. As the merest mention of Rome (where Fulvia is) arouses Cleopatra's jealousy, Antony has no desire to hear the news. As far as he is concerned, Rome can melt in the Tiber. The messengers see confirmation of the rumors about his "dotage" and express the hope that things may go better the following day. Thus the first scene closes. The second introduces us into the palace and begins with a bantering exchange between the handmaidens and a soothsayer endowed with "prescience" (1.2.20) who knows how to read "In nature's infinite book of secrecy" (1.2.9). The frivolous discussion revolves around the handmaidens' future. "O that I knew," Charmian exclaims, "this husband, which, you say, must charge his horns with garlands!" (1.2.3–5). But, as the soothsayer's predictions do not regard this cuckolded, begarlanded husband, she presses him further:

> Good now, some excellent fortune! Let me be married to three kings in a forenoon, and widow them all: let me have a child at fifty, to whom Herod of Jewry may do homage . . . (1.2.25–30)

A few lines before, a servant has advised her to be attentive to the soothsayer's oracles. Should we too be attentive to Charmian's oracular fantasies, or does the fact that they are fantasies exonerate us from doing so? The more convenient solution would seem to be the latter, for otherwise it is difficult to see how we can fail to reach certain conclusions about the "child"—conclusions that become most awkward when we consider the context. The Arden edition contains the following note: "Furness cites, and unwillingly inclines to accept, the suggestion of Th. Zielinski that in Charmian's speech the child is Christ." Furness's "unwillingness" is comprehensible; yet, what else is one likely to think of this "child," whom one hears mentioned in the same breath as "three kings" and "Herod of Jewry"? We have two alternatives: either we yield to reluctance and speak no more of the matter, considering it just the fantasy of a servant-girl; or we must devote to the question a degree of attention at least equal to that of the reluctance. I opt for the second alternative.

Regarding Charmian's idea of becoming a mother at the age of fifty, Steevens makes the following observation: "This is one of Shakespeare's natural touches. Few circumstances are more flattering to the fair sex than breeding at an advanced period of life."[1] That may be. But the naturalness seen by Steevens contrasts somewhat comically with the profound *unnaturalness* of the situation, starting with Herod himself, who—as Dover Wilson points out—"was the last person in the world to do homage to an infant." Yet, however unnatural, Herod's posture is so diametrically opposite that which he adopted vis-à-vis another Infant that the conclusions on the nature of the "child," far from being dissipated, are instead consolidated. Charmian's fantasy in some way implies that she shares a certain "prescience" with the soothsayer. To put it another way, if the soothsayer reads in the book of nature, the handmaiden for her part seems to be influenced by the reading of a Book that has yet to be written, without foreknowledge of which, however, Herod's behavior lacks a script to invert. Since Herod, as Jones points out (New Penguin), is he who "martyred the Holy Innocents in his attempt to kill the infant Christ," one is bound to agree with him that "Charmian is being extravagantly ambitious in hoping for his homage" (p. 195). This ambitiousness implies foreknowledge of the behavior of the historical Herod, that is, of the Book that deals with such behavior. Neither Dover Wilson nor Jones dared hazard the possibility of the acceptance of a Christological hypothesis; yet, in the end, both suggest the possibility of a hypothesis that one might define as super-Christological. Indeed, there is no other alternative, as Charmian's child carries off a triumph superior to that of the Infant Jesus who, in 31 BC, was not yet incarnate but whose vicissitudes are the negative of the image created by the handmaiden.

We must also note, however, that if the soothsayer is the only one to show familiarity with nature's infinite book of secrecy, the handmaiden is not the only character who knows the Book of Holy Scriptures. The Bible is used by Antony himself in the opening lines, which are notoriously crucial in all Shakespeare plays. As we have seen, when asked by Cleopatra how great his love is, Antony declares that there is beggary in the love that can be reckoned. But the Queen is not satisfied and demands physical proof of the immeasurability of his love. And, as the whole universe—whether in Alexandria in 31 BC or in London in AD 1608—is immeasurable, Antony is compelled to deduce: "Then must thou needs find out new heaven, new earth." This is an interesting expression, as regards not only the actual concept it expresses but also the words selected to express it. To indicate to Cleopatra the need of this "discovery," the triumvir chooses to borrow what is perhaps the best-known sentence in *Revelations:* "And I saw a new heaven and a new earth: for the first heaven and the first earth were passed away." Let us for the moment disregard the fact that this passage may have sounded extremely "prophetic" in 1608, when the old Aristotelian universe seemed on the point of "passing away," tottering as it was, ever more fearfully, undermined by Copernicanism and shaken by its disturbing variations. Let us simply say that the protagonist of the play begins by quoting from the culminating chapter of *Revelation*.

If, therefore, the Roman Antony appropriates the future apocalyptic production of St. John, there is no reason why the Egyptian handmaiden should not have recourse to a prediction in the Gospel of St. Matthew. If it is an extrinsic ornament in the first case, in the second it is indeed one of the "natural touches" in which Shakespeare, the imitator of nature, excels. And if that is so, we have possibly dwelt too long on Charmian's child and Antony's heaven. If, instead, we reflect that, after all, we are in the seventeenth century, and that an apocalyptic cosmological quotation of this type, pronounced by a "libertine" fed by "Epicurean cooks" (2.1.23–24), may not be merely a decorative way of starting a play in which it is said that "truth should be silent" (2.2.108); and if we reflect that the imitation of nature may lead to a very special kind of "natural touch," where nature is an "infinite book of secrecy"— if we entertain such considerations, then we have yet to reach a conclusion. Let us, therefore, reexamine Charmian's image, in the awareness that she is not the only one to manipulate the Scriptures.

Herod is paying homage to a child. Why? What significance can this development have in his behavior toward children? Can this development be extraneous to his feelings toward a particular child? For, if the King of the Jews developed a bloody aversion to infants, it was because of a very definite Infant. Three kings had arrived one day in Jerusalem and inquired: "Where is he that is born King of the Jews? For we have seen his star in the east, and are come to worship him." On hearing these words, Herod was "troubled." He summoned the high priests to find out the place "where Christ should be born," and they replied to him: "In Bethlehem," quoting Micah 5:2: "out of thee [Bethlehem] shall he come forth unto me that is to be ruler in Israel." If, therefore, Herod "sent forth, and slew all the children . . . from two years old and under," it was because of his "trouble" at the prospect that a child might be recognized by his people as "Christ" and "king of the Jews" (Matthew, 2:2–16).

It is hardly surprising that Herod was "troubled," for he had only two alternatives: either recognize the Child as "Christ," and therefore the lawful "king of the Jews," thus forfeiting the throne; or keep the throne by eliminating the Child. Herod opted for the second solution, but the handmaiden seems to be presenting the first. What conclusion can one draw, if Herod is doing homage to a child, other than that he is recognizing Him as "Christ" and "king of the Jews"? This suggests that Herod has been *converted*. But it is unlikely that the conversion of the king of the Jews, who desired to kill the Infant Jesus lest He be recognized king by the Jews, could have occurred without such recognition by the Jews themselves—in which case the "extravagantly ambitious" spectacle provided by Charmian is a touch no less naturally apocalyptic than Antony's apocalyptic quotations. For, among the upheavals that were to precede the revelation of a new heaven and a new earth, the final conversion of the Jews, which in the fullness of time would crown the conversion of all the peoples of the world, was among the most spectacular and most widely expected events in Protestant millenarism in general and in English millenarism in particular. Indeed, Charmian's image is a concise but eloquent representation of that conversion of the Jews which was one of the "necessary conditions without which the millennium could not take place."[2]

Both biblical intrusions into the Plutarchan tale—within the space of a few lines—are thus of an apocalyptic nature that a contemporary audience would have recognized without any great difficulty. There is nothing, for example, to prevent our imagining a group of Puritans hostile to the theater who are waiting for the spectators at the theater entrance in order to admonish them about the imminence of the fullness of the times—and who, for the purpose, use the same points in the Scriptures so casually pronounced on stage. Chapter 21 of *Revelation* falls pat to Antony's purpose when he wishes to declare to the "strumpet" (1.1.13) who is the object of his "devotion" (1.1.5) that his immeasurable love beggars the measurable old universe. Verse 1 reads: "And I saw a new heaven and a new earth: for the first heaven and the first earth were passed away." But verse 8 promises "second death" in "the lake that burneth with fire and brimstone" for "the unbelieving, and the abominable . . . and whoremongers . . . and idolaters." To put St. John's words in the mouth of a "libertine" in order that he may certify his "devotion" to a "strumpet" may well have given rise to some suspicion of "incredulity" or "idolatry" in what was happening on stage. But with these words still ringing in his ears, what would one of those Puritans have thought of Charmian's lines if he had seen the play? Would he have accepted, without batting an eye, the image of Herod kneeling before a child? Or would he have felt inclined to anticipate the Christological hypothesis of Thomas Zielinski? And, in this case, let us suppose that he was interested in millenaristic literature, and that before the performance he had happened to glance at the title of a newly printed book by Draxe, *The Worlds Resurrection*—a work completely dedicated to a subject well known to him and also treated by Perkins, Hooker, and many others.[3] What "unwillingness," a few lines away from Antony's apocalyptic utterances, could have prevented him from recognizing, in that king of the Jews kneeling before a child, the emblematic representation of one of "the necessary conditions without which the millennium could not take place"?

At this point, the situation precipitates. Just as our spectator could not have been unfamiliar with the words Antony takes from St. John or with the story of the three kings, Herod, and a child narrated by Matthew in the second chapter of his Gospel, so too he could not have been unfamiliar with the first chapter of the same Gospel, which tells of the conception of the child—a chapter with which the handmaiden also seems to be familiar. The mother of the Child whom one day the Jews were to recognize as king "was found with child of the Holy Ghost" before lying with her spouse. Regarding this working of the Holy Ghost, as noted by St. Augustine (quoted in the classic comment on St. Thomas), "it is understood that in every working of the Holy Ghost God operates in Unity and Trinity."[4] The bridegroom, "a just man," who "was minded to put her away privily," was dissuaded from doing so by an "angel of the Lord" who in a dream thus addressed him: "Fear not to take unto thee Mary thy wife: for that which is conceived in her is of the Holy Ghost." And so the husband "took unto him his wife," although "he knew her not." Now, if all the interest in a comparison between the evangelical narration and the handmaiden's fantasies simply lay in the possibility of proving their cryptoblasphemous nature, we might hardly need bother with it. But, as the comparison enables us to proceed to a second comparison, and to discover something that is not simply blasphemous, let us proceed.

The comparison is quickly made. Charmian, competing with the prescience of the soothsayer, an expert in the deciphering of "nature's infinite book of secrecy," foresees for herself a cuckolded but garlanded husband—that is, one to whom homage is paid, who, indeed, is venerated precisely because he is cuckolded: the garlands interwoven around the horns indicate a cuckolding which, for Warburton, is "rich and honorable," for Malone, "contented," and for Steevens, "triumphant." The maiden then foretells a marriage with three kings which takes place and is over within a forenoon. In the same sentence in which Charmian predicts for herself this single and triple marriage, she expresses her hope of becoming the mother, at the age of fifty, of a child to whom Herod will do homage. It is impossible to establish whether the child is the son of one, two, all three, or none of the kings; thus, the child's conception remains a mystery. What is certain, however, is that the maiden, as her fantasies show, is a marriageable girl aged about twenty and consequently—as the play is set around the time of the battle of Actium in 31 BC—her fiftieth birthday, and therefore the birth of the child to whom Herod pays homage, would coincide more or less with the birth of the Child to whom Herod did not, in fact, pay homage. When the more realistic soothsayer rejoins: "You have seen and prov'd a fairer former fortune / Than that which is to approach," Charmian deduces: "Then belike my children shall have no names" (1.2.33–35), meaning—as Case, Dover Wilson, and Jones in concert point out—"my children will be bastards." Alas, her fantasies are no more than wishful thinking; a contented cuckold for a husband, the single and triple marriage with three kings, the king of the Jews kneeling before her child—these are not certainties. The only certainty is that her children will be bastards (including the child to whom Herod pays homage). This is the conclusion to be drawn from the imperfect correspondence of foreknowledge based on the reading of "nature's infinite book of secrecy" and foreknowledge influenced by the prereading of another Book. What, then, would our Puritan have thought? Is it not more likely that, rather than admire the naturalness of the poet's touch, he would have suspected Shakespeare of veiled yet horrendously blasphemous and libertine derision of those points in the Gospel story that best lent themselves to such treatment? Was it a mystery that such abominations were not uncommon on the stage? Had it not come out, some fifteen years earlier, when Richard Baines denounced Marlowe to the Privy Council with a list of the "most horrible blasphemes and damnable opinions" that Baines himself and other "good & honest witnes" had heard him utter, that Shakespeare's illustrious colleague was wont to declare, inter alia, "that Christ was a bastard and his mother dishonest?"[5]

The problem at this point is not simply to establish whether something of the sort is or is not as it appears in, as it were, the watermark, when we hold the handmaiden's remarks up to the light. One should, rather, ask oneself whether this blasphemy is *all* that it appears, also because it so happens that in this particular play "levity" (2.7.119) may act as a "wild disguise" (2.7.122) of some "graver business" (2.7.118). To establish whether this blasphemy is really all that it appears in the watermark, it is necessary to compare Charmian's fantasies not only with its future precedents in the Gospel but also with Antony's borrowings from *Revelation*. Once again, Marlowe comes in useful; or, rather, the context in which his "damnable opinion" was set, for also in Marlowe such "levities" were not devoid of some "graver business." As it is precisely this "graver business" that will provide us with the correct basis for comparing Antony's apocalyptic terminology with Charmian's apocalyptic fantasies, it will be necessary to open a parenthesis.

The above-quoted blasphemy is the sixth of the nineteen "opinions" of Marlowe's reported by Baines to the Privy Council in May 1593: Marlowe "came to a soden & fearful end of his life" three days later.[6] The first "opinion" read: "That the Indians and many Authors of Antiquity have assuredly writen of aboue 16 thousand yeares agone wher at Moyses Adam is said proued to haue liued within 6 thowsand yeares." The second says: "He affirmeth that

Moyses was but a Jugler, & that one Heriots being Sir W. Raleighs man can do more than he." And the fourth: "That the first beginning of Religion was only to keep men in awe." And the fifth: "That it was an easy matter for Moyses being brought vp in all the arte of the Egiptians to abuse the Jewes being a rude & grosse people." And the ninth: "That if there be any god or any good Religion, then it is in the papists, because the seruice of god is performed with more ceremonies, as Elevation of the mass, organs, singing men, shaven crownes, &c that all protestants are Hypocriticall asses." And the tenth: "That if he were put to write a new religion, he would vndertake both a more Excellent and Admirable methode and that all the new testament be filthily written."

We thus learn that it was Marlowe's "opinion" that the story of the Creation was one of the deceptions used by Moses in order to found a religion—that is, to keep men in awe and rule over them at will—not a difficult task, as the Jews were ignorant, while Moses knew the arts of the Egyptians and was thus in a position to claim for himself divine authority, impressing the common people with feigned supernatural miracles which in reality were no more than tricks of Egyptian natural magic. According to Marlowe, as we are told by Kyd (arrested and tortured a few days before for being in possession of a paper denying Christ's divinity), "Things esteemed to be done by divine power might have as well been done by observation of men."[7] Since the deciphering of nature's infinite book of secrecy had made great strides since the days of the Egyptians, his friend the mathematician and cosmologist Thomas Harriot, Ralegh's counselor for thirty-five years, may well have produced miracles greater than those of Moses. If we consider the Jewish and Christian religions—religions based not on the book of nature but believed to have been revealed by a divinity superior to nature—they are an *instrumentum regni,* not a manner of knowing God. And, as an *instrumentum regni,* the Catholic religion is superior to Protestantism because it contemptuously exploits all its ceremonial pomp to impress the "rude and grosse people." If one is to be content with such a religion, one might as well keep the old form, which, as a deception, works better and is less hypocritical in its cynicism.

As can be seen, this gross blasphemy is part of an anti-Christian set of beliefs which itself is not gross. The concept of religion as an *instrumentum regni* is clearly of Machiavellian and "Averroist" origin. As for the pre-Adamites and the confutation of the story of the Creation, this opinion, which was typical of libertine disbelief but which "was rather rare at the time in England,"[8] takes us straight to the Harriot who could perform miracles greater than those of Moses. When Nashe wrote, "I hear say there be Mathematicians abroad, that will prove men before Adam"; and "impudently they [that is, English atheists] persist in it, that the late discouered Indians, are able to shew antiquities, thousands [of years] before Adam,"[9] the atheist mathematician who speaks of pre-Adamites on the basis of American antiquities must certainly be Harriot, who had traveled through Virginia on Ralegh's behalf. In fact, if Harriot spoke of pre-Adamites and, as Aubrey was subsequently to recall, "he did not like (or valued not) the old storie of the Creation of the World"; if "he could not beleeve the old position; he would say *ex nihilo nihil fit*"; if "he made a Philosophical Theologie, wherein he cast off the Old Testament, and then the New-one would (consequently) have no Foundation." If, in conclusion, "he was a Deist,"[10] it was not only because he had traveled in America but because his atomistic Copernicanism brought him to extend the universe to infinity in space and in time. The atomist theory, in fact, implied "the eternity of matter, and clashed not only with official Aristotelianism but also with the Christian dogmas of the Creation and God's omnipotence," so that "it is evident that his philosophical thinking had ventured along paths that led him away from some essential dogmas of Christianity."[11] Not unwisely, Harriot published nothing that could compromise him, which did not, however, prevent him from being surrounded, throughout his life (first in Ralegh's service, then in Northumberland's) with an aura of impiety. His name was frequently mentioned in law courts, where he was branded as a master of "atheism," "Epicureanism," and "magic." Even at an advanced age, he complained to Kepler that he could not "philosophize freely."[12]

Marlowe and Harriot were not the only ones to speak of pre-Adamites and deny the story of the Creation. In the heart of England, the philosopher Giordano Bruno had done precisely the same thing, in the *Spaccio* he dedicated to Sidney in 1584. But here, too, it was no isolated chance remark but part of an argument in a precise cosmological context. That same atomist, infinitist and Copernican context that made it inevitable for Harriot to depart from "some essential dogmas of Christianity." We know today that Harriot and Northumberland's circle of friends knew and appreciated the works of Bruno, with a special predilection for those in which the Lucretian aspects were to the fore.[13] If Bruno's idea of a new, infinite universe disconcerted Kepler, Harriot—moving, like Bruno, from atomist and "Epicurean" premises—was, on the other hand, ready, with Bruno, to support the idea of an infinite universe, the mere idea of which inspired in Kepler "an indefinable occult horror."[14]

All this is of great interest. Having decided to investigate Charmian's "levities," we have found, together with an "apocalyptic" posture of Herod, certain implications similar to those pronounced in Marlowe's sixth "damnable opinion." And, having extended our attention to other "opinions," we have discovered that the first speaks of pre-Adamites, and the second quotes Harriot, who, in his turn, supported the first on the basis of a cosmological opinion said to be "rather rare at the time in England," and for that very reason easily identifiable—that is, that of the physical infinity of the universe. This opinion transformed the old closed world into the new infinite universe that has dominated modern thought ever since. In so doing, however, it attributes to physical nature certain qualities that previously were uniquely God's prerogative and thus shakes the very foundation of Christianity. For, if God communicates even His most divine attributes to nature, the most suitable text for knowing God is the Book of Nature, not the self-confessedly supernatural Book of the Scriptures. Finally, this opinion was one which, all over Europe and in England in particular, had been preached by Giordano Bruno, who put the immeasurability of the universe at the center of his "gospel," as can clearly be shown from the very titles of works we know today to have been much read in important circles of English scientists, artists, and aristocrats: *De infinito, universo e mondi; De immenso*. . . . These opinions will now provide us with an appropriate context in which to examine Antony's apocalyptic-cosmological pronouncements. This, in turn, will enable us to make a comparison with those of Charmian and to draw the consequences. Let us reconsider the two main characters' opening words:

Cleopatra.	If it be love indeed, tell me how much.
Antony.	There's beggary in the love that can be reckon'd.
Cleopatra.	I'll set a bourn how far to be belov'd.
Antony.	Then must thou needs find out new heaven, new earth.

(1.1.14–17)

What Cleopatra demands is factual proof ("indeed") of Antony's love, which, to be really "true," must be very great. But the problem is precisely that: *how much?* With fair eloquence, Antony points out that a measurable love is a miserable love: a love that is not miserable, such as his, cannot be other than immeasurable. But Cleopatra insists on having concrete proof, and asks Antony to tell her the "bourn" of his love. As *bourn* is a term used to mean the boundary between fields, her request is inequivocal: she wishes to know how great is the field of Antony's love. A parlous problem! Any field, however large, is measurable and would ipso facto be proof of a miserable love. But where was it possible to find an immeasurable field, if not only all the fields of the world put together but also all the heavens and the universe were notoriously measurable? Was not the universal field bounded by the sphere of the fixed stars? Therefore, however great it might be, the universe was nevertheless measurable—ergo proof of a beggarly love. The situation thus offers only one possible solution: Do you wish, Cleopatra, an immeasurable field that is concrete proof of my immeasurable love? "Then," ergo, "must thou needs find out" a new universe that is infinite because, as a proof of infinite love, the entire old measurable universe is inadequate and always will be.

The main characteristic of this new universe—its physical infinity—is deducible, *hic et nunc,* from the logical organization of the lines just uttered, which—as signaled by the word *then* (ergo) introducing the final proposition—compose a syllogism. Having established that a measurable love is a miserable love, and having also established that it is required to know how great is the field of love, it may be deduced that necessarily a new universe must be discovered. From these premises it is not only possible, but also necessary, to deduce a dual discovery: (1) the new universe will necessarily be immeasurable; (2) the old measurable universe is necessarily miserable. To make her discovery, Cleopatra (and we with her) need only draw the consequences of those same lines which decree the absolute necessity of doing so. The text is more than sufficient for this to be done, and we could very well stop here. But, as others in England had made this same discovery, employing precisely this kind of argument, and as it was a discovery pregnant with so many different philosophical and religious implications that it is hard to overestimate it, we will pause to consider its precedents.

There is no doubt that Bruno was a leading proponent of the concept of an infinite universe. But there is also no doubt that, just as this concept found early support precisely in England, with Harriot and his circle, so also it was precisely in England that, even before Bruno, the idea of a Copernican universe devoid of any "bourn" was first formulated—it was in England that "countless stars" for the first time outreached their hitherto impassable sphere, expanding "in Sphaericall altitude without ende." This breaking of the boundaries occurred in 1576, on a page of the *Perfit*

Description of the Caelestiall Orbes (the translation by Thomas Digges of Copernicus' *De Revolutionibus*). But, whereas Copernicus had left the "bourn" of his universe intact, in Digges' diagram we see a "countless" multitude of stars that cover the page entirely, expanding "in Sphaericall altitude without ende." And if the stars *must* stretch without end it is because they "may wel be thought of us to be the gloriouse court of the great god, whose unsercheable worcks invisible we may partly by these his visible conjecture, to whose infinite power and majesty such an infinit place surmounting all other both in quantitye and qualitye only is conveniente."[15] If only an "infinit place" is "conveniente" (that is "seemly") for the infinite divine power, it is clear not only that the universal field *must* be infinite but also that a finite field would lead to "unseemly" conjectures regarding God. On the one hand, we have an old finite universe with blasphemous connotations, in that it implied a limitation on divine power; and, on the other, a new infinite universal field which is the sole seemly manifestation of a divinity whose attributes include not only infinite power but also infinite love. The similarity to the picture presented by the syllogism contained in the protagonists' opening words in Shakespeare's play in 1608 is striking, even if in Digges there is no trace of apocalyptic language—differently from Bruno, who later would use identical arguments. Before considering this aspect, let us take a moment to explore the figure of Digges.

Thomas Digges was the pupil and friend of John Dee, Sidney's master of philosophy. He was also a protégé of Edward Dyer, himself a member of the circle orbiting around Sidney (to whom the *Spaccio della bestia trionfante* and *Eroici furori* are dedicated) and of Greville (the amphytrion of the *Cena delle ceneri*).[16] Before translating Copernicus, Digges had, with Dee, produced a study of the new star which, in 1572, appeared in the sky above the moon. This publication was no fortuitous precedent, as there was a close link between interest in new stars (the nova in Cassiopeia in 1572 and the star *in pede Serpentarii* in 1604) and in comets (those of 1577 and 1607) and interest in a new universe. Indeed, it was the widespread public interest aroused by these phenomena that contributed more than anything else to the collapse of Aristotelian cosmology, which allows for no changes in the sky above the moon.[17] It thus followed: (1), that the new stars were miracles, divine transgressions of nature's law, the reappearance of the star of Bethlehem announcing the return of Christ on earth, the conversion of the Jews, the imminence of the revelation of a new heaven and a new earth; or, (2), that they "signified" the need to discover a new non-Aristotelian universe. Or possibly both. Kepler himself, in *De nova stella in pede Serpentarii*—where he spoke of his "indefinable occult horror" for Bruno's hypothesis, a hypothesis accepted by Harriot (of an infinite universe)—did not disdain to hint at the imminence of the Second Coming and the conversion of all the peoples of the world, starting with the Jews.[18] Digges' translation of Copernicus went through seven editions, the last in 1605. In 1942, Dover Wilson for the first time drew attention to the fact that the Leonard Digges, who contributed warm memorial verses not only to the First Folio in 1623 but also to the 1640 edition of Shakespeare's poetry, was the son of Thomas Digges. This coincidence was pointed out by Dover Wilson in order to cast doubt on the conclusions of his own essay—conclusions that confirmed the general opinion of Shakespeare's total deafness toward all matters relating to the birth of new universes, even if "it was not Shakespeare's way" to remain silent before events of such importance.[19] Nor is it likely that these were the only links between Shakespeare and the Digges family. According to Kermode, "almost certainly," Shakespeare also knew

> Sir Dudley Digges, ardent in the Virginian cause, whose brother Leonard contributed memorial verses to the First Folio, and whose mother married Thomas Russel, the "overseer" of Shakespeare's will. Both Dudley Digges and William Strachey contributed laudatory verses to Jonson's *Sejanus* in 1605 and Shakespeare had acted in the play. Shakespeare's friend Heminge was at Digges's wedding, and signed as witness.[20]

Whether or not Shakespeare was a sort of "family friend" of the Diggeses, the fact remains that in 1608 there were in Europe only three new universes capable of satisfying the cosmological requirements established by Antony and Cleopatra's syllogism. Of these three infinite universes, two (that of Digges and that of Harriot) were English in origin, and the third (Bruno's) had been created by an Italian who constructed it and placed it on the market precisely in London, in a limited circle of aristocratic patronage that included both scientists and artists. Digges' new universe interests us not only because it offers an "infinit place" but also because of the way its necessity is argued. Bruno's new universe attracts our attention as well. For, if Digges believed that a finite universe would represent an "unseemly" concept of divinity, Bruno believed that the universe, "being effected and originated by an infinite cause and infinite principle, must, by its corporal capacity and its manner, be infinitely infinite."[21] That is what he wrote in the first of his

"English" dialogues, the Copernican *Cena* (*Supper*) at Greville's residence; but, to the judges in Rome he would later repeat: "I hold to an infinite universe, that is, the effect of the infinite divine power, because I deemed it unworthy of the divine goodness and power to produce a finite world, when it could produce beyond this world another and others infinite."[22] Although this argument is only hinted at in Digges, Bruno dwells on it on several occasions. Thus, in *De infinito* (also published in England), he violently attacks a concept which to him is tantamount to blasphemy.[23] What Bruno proclaims with such passionate eloquence, however, is precisely the fundamental idea underlying both Digges' opinion and Antony and Cleopatra's syllogism: that a finite universe would be "unworthy" of a God possessing "goodness" and "power," because an "infinite cause" *must necessarily* produce a "corporally" infinite effect. Were that not so, God would be "powerless" or "otiose" or "envious." Clearly, from this particular viewpoint of Bruno's, a measurable universe would be the beggarly proof of a beggarly love; just as in the opening lines of the play, so here it becomes of vital importance to discover a new immeasurable universe. It is no less interesting that just as *Antony and Cleopatra* begins with a syllogism that obliges us to seek out a new immeasurable universe, so too Bruno had already used the syllogistic technique to make similar deductions, as we read—again, in *De infinito*—when he demonstrates the physical infinity of the universe on the basis of "a couple of syllogisms":

> I construct and present a couple of syllogisms in the following manner. If the first efficient wished to do other than that which he wishes to do he could do other than that which he does; but he cannot wish to do other than that which he wishes to do. Therefore, whosoever says the effect is finite makes the working and the power finite.

And again:

> The first efficient can but do that which he wishes to do; he does not wish to do that which he does not. Therefore, whosoever denies infinite effect denies infinite power.[24]

Here, then, are two further syllogisms that enable us to discover: (1) the necessity of a new infinite universe; and (2) the beggarliness of the old universe. Not only were there notable precedents, in England, for the new universe that Cleopatra is about to discover in 1608, there were also precedents for the argument of its "ontological" necessity, even for the formal logical technique used to demonstrate it. It is all the more notable that Bruno's new infinite universe also presents a third precise connection with that which Cleopatra "must needs find out": apocalyptic terminology.

This occurs in the third book of *De immenso,* where Bruno, after praising Copernicus for having recognized that the earth is a body that rotates around the sun, warns him that all this would "serve no purpose" unless he recognized that "the space beyond" the fixed stars "cannot be limited since such a power must have fitting qualities." "Therefore," he continues:

> do not propose either heaven or the primum mobile; they are now dissolved, as was foretold by the true voice of the prophet it would come to pass in this our age, since the favor and will of the Gods come upon us with the speed of truth, which will be followed by the judgement of the righteous and the foundations of a holy religion and which will be succeeded, in this world, by the long awaited century. The gods of darkness and the obscure errors caused by the weight of a false balance shall be cast to the Beast; long did they hide the truth and give up to cruel generals the spirits of mortals, wandering in the night. The species of the divine nature shall shine resplendently from the holy breast throughout the whole amplitude and the only true moderator of such an immense work shall be recognized in his greatness.[25]

Here, Bruno is explaining the full meaning of the "true voice of the prophet" who had "foretold" the "dissolution" of the old heaven—what St. John had prophesied at Patmos was the abolition of the "bourn" of the universe. This abolition had occurred at that very moment in time, considering that he, Bruno, had just proceeded to abolish it. Thus, the apocalyptic event coincides not with a crushing by God of the old heaven in order to reveal a new one but with the demonstration of the need to abolish that which sets a "bourn" on the spreading of the divine nature into the whole amplitude. Having autonomously initiated the millennium, nothing prevents Bruno from activating the rest of the apocalyptic picture. Hence the triumph of a single "holy religion" for all the peoples of the world. Hence the defeat of false gods. Hence, lastly, the "judgement of the righteous." The apocalyptic picture could not be more traditional, were it not for three things: this manner of inaugurating it abolishes the very concept of the Apocalypse; the new "holy religion" supplants Christianity; and the false gods are worshiped by all the Christian sects. Here, what occurred seven years earlier with the Eucharist, in the Copernican *Cena* at Greville's residence, is repeated with the Apocalypse. On that occasion, too, Bruno had presented himself as an interpreter of the "religious" implications of the Copernican truth, which Copernicus himself had not understood. Just as, in the one case, his extension of the Copernican universe acquires an apocalyptic meaning that removes all value from the Christian Apocalypse, so, in the other case, his Copernican supper acquired eucharistic connotations that undermined the foundations of his rival's Eucharist. For Bruno, this duality was innate in his "discovery" of an infinite universe; it made physically manifest and communicated to all humanity the "incarnation" of an infinite God in an infinite nature, and therefore inevitably assumed a religious significance that was both eucharistic and apocalyptic. Except that *his* was the "true" Eucharist, *his* was the "true" Apocalypse; this is transparent in his scorn for the corresponding Christian doctrines. In Bruno's view, the "true" religion had been, if anything, the philosophical, magical, natural, and civil religion of the ancient Egyptians, which was founded on nature's infinite book of secrecy and which, with Hermes, had professed the universal animation and the movement of the earth.[26]

We have thus concluded our exploration, the purpose of which was simply to trace out a background in order to facilitate close examination of certain "levities"—levities which, precisely because they were levities, might be the "wild disguise" of some "graver business." The journey of exploration has been somewhat protracted, but I hope I may be forgiven when I recall that it was undertaken because a Herod kneeling before the bastard son of an Egyptian handmaiden did not seem to me solely an example of Shakespeare's natural touch. Nor was it easy for me as a result to accept as a natural "touch" that Antony should begin by uttering syllogisms about the need to discover a new immeasurable universe, with quotations from the *Book of Revelation*. I thus reconsidered Herod, the child, and the mother and discerned, on one hand, an "apocalyptic" situation and, on the other, a Marlovian type of blasphemy. I then examined the context in which Marlowe pronounced it, noting that the new universe of his friend Harriot corresponded to the most novel characteristics of the new universe which, according to Antony, it was necessary to "find out": its infinity. And, as there were only three new infinite universes in Europe in 1608, and all three in London, I thought it useful to examine them and compare them with Antony's. Harriot's Epicurean and atomist universe was infinite, but there was no trace in Harriot of the "ontological" argument that only an infinite effect corresponds to an infinite cause; nor were there any traces of syllogisms or an apocalyptic terminology. Digges' universe made summary use of the "ontological" necessity, but not of syllogisms and

Revelation. I then examined Bruno's universe, which not only used the "ontological" argument, syllogisms, and *Revelation* but also developed these themes in such a way that the use of a "wild disguise" to conceal a certain "graver business" ceased to seem extravagant. This context enables me to proceed to a final comparison between the two scenes I have analyzed: the loving *bavardage* of the peerless couple and the happy daydreams of the handmaiden.

Once the "apocalyptic" character has been recognized, this comparison is quickly made. It might, indeed, be limited to the observation that one is a demonstrative syllogism and the other a maidservant's picture-story. Antony's syllogism and Charmian's daydreams offer us two exemplarily antithetic approaches to an equally "apocalyptic" configuration. In the first case, there is nothing to wait for. What is necessary is a discovery, one that we ourselves can make, here and now. In the second case, there is nothing to find out. The only thing to do, therefore, is to wait—for a cuckolded and contented husband, for a single and triple marriage, for motherhood at the age of fifty, for Herod kneeling before a child. In the first case, the apocalyptic event described by John in the Scriptures coincides with a mental event: the discovery, through the use of our mental faculties, of the most formidable of the secrets "in nature's infinite book of secrecy"—the infinity of nature itself. In the second case, the apocalyptic event has to consist of the historical realization of the fantasies of a maidservant, based on the book of the Scriptures.

There is another connection between the two scenes. As we have seen, the handmaiden's fantasies conceal a gross Marlovian blasphemy. However, was there not a blasphemy—less gross, yet possibly more serious—in the opening syllogism? Was it not to cancel this blasphemy that it was absolutely essential to find out a new heaven and a new earth? If we had to find out a new universe, it was because the old universe was, per se, a blasphemy. *Blasphemy* means "irreverence," "revilement," "calumny." Is not the attribution to God of the qualities of powerlessness, inactivity, or envy (as must necessarily be the case if a physical bourn is set on His work) tantamount to irreverence, revilement, and calumny of God—that is, the most sacrilegious of blasphemies? In the ultimate analysis, which is more blasphemous? To jest coarsely on the supernatural circumstances of the conception of a certain Child while offering another version so natural as to arouse the admiration of an illustrious critic for the natural touch with which an illustrious writer imitates nature? Or to believe that God, envious of nature, should have committed an act of self-mutilation lest He should communicate to nature His own infinite glory? In a nutshell, is the sixth of Marlowe's "damnable opinions" more blasphemous than the setting of a limit to the universe? The answer depends on one's point of view, but in the seventeenth century there were substantially only two points of view: that of the wise and philosophers, on the one hand, and that of theologians and common people, on the other. To understand which is the more "damnable," from the first point of view, we can refer to Bruno. "Among the wise," says Philotheus in *De infinito,* commenting on the two syllogisms that proved the infinity of the universe, the setting of a limit on the universe "is scandalous and detracts from the greatness and excellence of God." For it is from the "truths of nature" that conclusions are drawn regarding the "excellence of the creator of nature," and it is therefore not possible to confine nature without drawing detrimental conclusions about its creator.[27] Marlowe's sixth opinion, on the other hand, is damnable only from the supernatural point of view which the theologians teach to the common people, because, from the point of view of the wise and philosophers, it is difficult to see how the natural conception of a child can offend the "truth of nature" and consequently the "excellence of the creator of nature."

That the "Everest" of the Shakespearean corpus (as Wilson Knight defines *Antony and Cleopatra*), eight years after the burning of Bruno, should have begun with a syllogism demonstrating the absolute necessity to find out a new physically infinite universe is extremely interesting. It may even be a "natural touch," in such a naturally gifted poet at this historical moment of cosmic upheavals. To use Dover Wilson's words, "it was not Shakespeare's way" to remain silent before matters of such import.

If, to find out a new heaven and a new earth, it is sufficient to consider the few lines that pronounce the absolute necessity to do so, before I conclude I must confess that, in order to discover them, I made use of the results of an analysis of an entire series of other "levities," all of which are, however, dedicated to the masking of the same "graver business." For, if the protagonist of this drama is—as Cleopatra tells us—a "perspective"—that is, an optical prism[28]—then the *whole* drama is constructed like an optical prism. "Perspectives" were very fashionable in the seventeenth century. They were made by painting a figure *(A)* on a surface. A second surface was then taken, on the back and front of which figures *B* and *C* were painted. The second surface was then cut into strips, which were applied at right angles to the first surface. The perspectives showed figure *A* when viewed frontally—and figures *B* and *C* when viewed from the right or left side. Unless the perspective was viewed sideways, from the right or left, it was impossible to see figures *B* and *C*. If the perspective was viewed not only frontally but also from right and left, it showed not just one figure but all three. This device was so well known and provided such an appropriate parallel to the functioning of a poem that has more than one meaning that Galileo used it to illustrate and criticize Tasso's allegorical poetry.[29]

So, too, if observed frontally, this "Roman play" shows only its immediate surface, which is the story told by Plutarch. If observed from the side, however, it reveals a second, unsuspected, surface, one that is not so much Roman as "Egyptian," and that has everything to do with the "discovery" that absolutely must be made as soon as the protagonists utter their first words—a "discovery" Bruno had presented in England as a return to the light of the true ancient Egyptian philosophy after the "darkness" of Christianity. Of this second surface, I have only analyzed and juxtaposed strip number one (the opening cosmic-apocalyptic syllogism) and strip number two (the handmaiden's fantasies). If the overall picture thus gains in coherence and precision, as I hope I have been able to show, it is only after analyzing and juxtaposing all the "Egyptian" strips that we can see, in its entirety, the back and the front of a single formidable truth which "*should* be silent" but which, in fact, speaks, albeit with most ingenious caution. But, as the space at my disposal is finite, I refer the reader elsewhere.[30]

Notes

An earlier Italian version of this article appeared in *Intersezioni*, 2 (1994).

1. Quoted in the *Arden* edition. See *Antony and Cleopatra,* ed. M. R. Ridley (London: Methuen, 1967), 11. Line references are taken from this edition.
2. Christopher Hill, "Till the Conversion of the Jews," in *The Collected Essays of Christopher Hill.* Vol. 2: *Religion and Politics in 17th Century England* (Brighton, 1986), 271. Protestant interest in the conversion of the Jews was nothing new; see, for example, the Hussites in the fifteenth century and the compilers of the Geneva Bible of 1557. In 1590, Andrew Willet devoted an entire treatise to the subject, *De Judeorum vocatione;* in 1608, Draxe published *The Worlds Resurrection or the general calling of the Jewes;* the matter is treated by "William Perkins, Richard Hooker and many others from the turn of the century onwards," Hill, "Till the Conversion," 270, 271, 293n, 294n.
3. Ibid.
4. Compare N. Tommaseo, *I santi evangeli col commento che da scelti passi de' padri ne fa Tommaso d'Aquino,* ed. R. Ciampini (Florence, 1973).

5. Compare J. Shirley, *Thomas Harriot: A Biography* (Oxford: Clarendon Press, 1983), 182–83. Marlowe's blasphemy repeats that imputed to the Earl of Oxford, who had been accused of questioning the Trinity, expressing the coarsest doubts of the Virgin's purity, treating St. Joseph as a complacent husband, affirming that the Scriptures authorized *paillardise* more than Aretino, and defining religion a political lie (see P. Lefranc, *Sir Walter Ralegh écrivain* (Paris, 1968), 341).

6. Lefranc, *Sir Walter Ralegh*, 369.
7. Ibid., 375; and Shirley, *Thomas Harriot*, 182.
8. Lefranc, *Sir Walter Ralegh*, 378.
9. *Works*, ed. McKerrow, I.172 and II.176; compare Shirley, *Thomas Harriot*, 186–87.
10. *Brief Lives*, ed. O. Lawson-Dick (London: Secker and Warburg, 1949), 123.
11. Lefranc, *Sir Walter Ralegh*, 352.
12. Letter dated 13 July 1608, *Kepleri Opera omnia* 2, ed. C. Frisch (Frankfurt, 1857–71), 74: "Ita se res habent apud nos, ut non liceat mihi adhuc libere philosophari." Compare Lefranc, *Sir Walter Ralegh*, 350.
13. H. Gatti, *The Renaissance Drama of Knowledge: Giordano Bruno in England* (London: Routledge, 1989), 199n.
14. *De stella nova:* "Brunus . . . infinitum facit mundum . . . Quae sola cogitatio nescio quid horroris occulti prae se fert"; compare Erwin Panowsky, *Galileo as Critic of the Arts* (The Hague, 1954).
15. Compare F. R. Johnson and S. V. Larkey, "Thomas Digges, the Copernican System and the Idea of the Infinity of the Universe in 1576, *Huntington Library Bulletin* 5 (April 1934). Although infinite, Digges' space is not homogeneous, as it is for Bruno; see M. A. Granada, "Bruno, Digges, Palingenio: omogeneità ed eterogeneità nella concezione dell'universo infinito," *Rivista di storia della filosofia*, 1 (1992): 47–73.
16. F. R. Johnson, *Astronomical Thought in Renaissance England* (Baltimore: Johns Hopkins University Press, 1937), 157; Lefranc, *Sir Walter Ralegh*, 356; Shirley, *Thomas Harriot*, 180.
17. C. D. Hellman, *The Comet of 1577: Its Place in the History of Astronomy* (New York, 1944).
18. Compare C. Webster, *From Paracelsus to Newton* (Cambridge: Cambridge University Press, 1982).
19. J. D. Wilson, "Shakespeare's Universe," *University of Edinburgh Journal* (Summer 1942).
20. F. Kermode, ed., *The Tempest* (New Arden), Introduction, pp. xxvii–xxviii.
21. *Dialoghi italiani*, ed. G. Aquilecchia (Florence, 1958), 104.
22. *Cena*, ed. G. Aquilecchia (Turin: 1955), 165n.
23. Compare *Dialoghi italiani*, 380–81, 383–84.
24. Ibid., 385.
25. Translation of Italian version, in C. Monti, *Opere latine* (Turin, 1980), 572–73.
26. F. Yates, *Giordano Bruno e la traduzione ermetica* (Bari, 1969), 266–67.
27. Ibid., 386–87.
28. *Antony and Cleopatra*, 2.5.117–18.
29. E. Panowsky, *Galileo*, 46–47.
30. G. Sacerdoti, *Nuovo cielo, nuova terra. La rivelazione copernicana di "Antonio e Cleopatra"* (Bologna: Il Mulino, 1990); "'Cosa significa questo?' Sopra uno 'strano trucco' shakespeariano in *Antonio e Cleopatra*," *Intersezioni*, XII, 1 (April 1992); "Tre re, Erode di Giudea e un bambino," XIV, 2 (August 1994).

Part Three:
Language and Ideology

A National Idiom and Other Languages: Notes on Elizabethan Ambivalence with Examples from Shakespeare

VANNA GENTILI

I

The poets of the English Renaissance—by which I mean the phase of a literary movement that flourished somewhat later than it did on the Continent and is conventionally considered to coincide with the last four decades of the sixteenth century—that is, more or less corresponding to the reign of Queen Elizabeth—were spasmodically involved in transforming English into a literary language capable of competing on equal terms with other languages that elsewhere had authoritatively established themselves. It was literary language that would be so expanded and diversified as to be a valid instrument in each of the genres that were already so illustrious in the rest of Europe, especially in the area of Romance languages: the epic, lyric, romance, essay, and drama.

Similarly, a process of expansion and diversification had occurred in the sixteenth century which transformed England from a producer and exporter (mainly of wool and woven products) into a producer and exporter of various textiles, including some that required new and more complex technology (passing from the traditional cheap broadcloth to expensive and greatly sought after new draperies). This expansion and diversification had, to a large extent, become possible thanks to the decisive contribution of Flemish artisans welcomed by the Tudors (in some cases, even enticed) as exiles from Catholic domination.[1]

The literary language was enriched and made more articulate by means of lexical, morphological, and rhetorical borrowings from the ancients and moderns. Native archaisms were reexhumed. With due adjustments, the everyday vernacular was rehabilitated. What today would be termed special registers were widely drawn upon (the language of law, theology, commerce, the sea, and the artisan world). Whole pieces were incorporated from botanical, zoological, astrological, and alchemical nomenclatures—not always, let it be said, with universal approval.

For example, in his authoritative contribution as illustrator-glossator of Spenser's first work, the *Shepherd's Calendar* (1579), "E. K." praises the reexhuming of "good and natural" old English words that had long fallen into disuse. At the same time, he is harshly critical of those who, in their desire to strengthen the fabric of a national language, wrongly deemed to be "bare and barren"—both in prose and poetry—have chosen to patch up its "holes with pieces and rags of other languages, borrowing here of the French, there of the Italian, everywhere of the Latin. . . . So now they have made our English tongue a gallimaufry or hodgepodge of all other speeches."[2] On the opposite side, in his note "To the Understander" in the second part of his translation of the *Iliad* (*Achilles' Shield,* 1598), the scholarly poet, George Chapman, supports the legitimacy—and, indeed, the utility—of lexical borrowings for the enrichment of "the ceaseless flowing river of our tongue."[3] A river deposits its sediment and swells with waters conveying new material. That is what Chapman must have thought when he took it as a metaphor for the language of his day, in which he, without any doubt, perceived the constant declining of sedimented words and forms and the pressure of new words and new forms.

F. W. Bateson has shrewdly remarked that at the base of the Elizabethans' copiousness is a distrust of the signifying capacity of the language at their disposal. Poets, not daring to attribute an entire meaning to a single word or phrase, reiterated, commented, and amplified. Spenser is the most macroscopic example, but he is by no means alone.[4] To Bateson's observation, I would add that Spenser, like others—and even more than others—seems to wish to *translate* himself, expanding every phrase or annotating it. This self-translation, to which Spenserian criticism has perhaps devoted insufficient attention, is, in my opinion, a specific operation distinct from another, equally evident procedure of Spenser's: the transparent paraphrase of his various models (Virgil, Ovid, the Italian heroic poets, and so on). This operation, while recognizably distinct, is also incorporated in this kind of paraphrase.

Thus, a poetic creation such as *The Faerie Queene* is, like a multilevel translation, in some kind of exponential development. As we can also note, a translation like the one Chapman makes of Homer amplifies and modernizes the original text with the torrential contributions of the copious and ever-developing national idiom. One example may suffice: *Iliad,* X, 93–94: οὐδέ μοι ἦτορ/ ἔμπεδον (literally: "nor is my heart firm"), in Chapman becomes "my heart, the fount of heat, with his extreme affects made cold."⁵ The amplification introduces the figure of oxymoron, common enough in sixteenth-century Petrarchism (heat/cold). The explanation reflects contemporary physiology and psychology: the heart as the motor and the extreme "affects" causing short circuits.

In other words, this manneristic language—which provides its own self-commentary, bejewels itself, makes itself up, and dons a mask as if before a mirror—proceeds by trial and error. I would say that the Elizabethans were self-conscious about their language, in the dual sense of the term: first, in the more modern meaning, current since the nineteenth century, of denoting embarrassment, excessive preoccupation with one's appearance or behavior, for the way in which others see or judge us; and, second, in the older, more philosophical and etymologically literal meaning of self-awareness.

This self-awareness declared itself with pride. In *An Apology for Poetry* (written about 1580 but published posthumously in 1595), Sir Philip Sidney reviewed the physical and phonic qualities of the English language. He explored the proportion between vowels and consonants, and the availability of words with all three varieties of stresses (oxytone, paroxytone, and proparoxytone) which distinguish English, to its advantage, from Italian ("so full of vowels"), from German (where the excessive consonants "cannot yield the sweet sliding fit for a verse"), from French, which has no words stressed on the antepenultimate syllable, and from Spanish, which has very few. "The English is subject to none of these defects." In conclusion, if poetry was not properly esteemed in England, the fault lay not with the poets but with the "poet-apes," those servile imitators of classical or Petrarchan models; while "our tongue is most fit to honour Poesy, and to be honoured by Poesy."⁶ When he wrote the *Apology,* Sidney, who rightly may have thought himself destined to set an example for a poetry that would do the English language honor, had good reason to be hard on his contemporaries. Spenser, whom he appreciated with some reserve—in particular as regards his use of the archaisms praised by "E.K."—had so far produced only *The Shepherd's Calendar.*

Nearly twenty years later, the prestige of the English language was celebrated in the poem *Musophilus, or a General Defence of Learning* by Samuel Daniel, another impressive "national" literary figure who, according to tradition, succeeded Spenser as poet laureate in 1599, the year of the publication of *Musophilus* in his *Poetical Essays*. The English language was a glory, an immense treasure accumulated in England, the fruits of which would eventually be carried to distant lands, to enrich and civilize unknowing populations and regions as yet still undiscovered:

> And who, in time, knows whither we may vent
> The treasure of our tongue, to what strange shores
> This gain of our best glory shall be sent,
> T'enrich unknowing nations with our stores?
> What worlds in th'yet unformed Occident
> May come refin'd with th'accents that are ours?[7]

(957–62)

The English celebrated by Daniel was thus a language of conquest, and at the same time a language for the conquered, who had no language (as certain Spaniards said of the American Indians). In this sense, it was a language that was conceived of as unique and universal, with a sort of repression of the existence of the many other known languages.

II

What is repressed returns as fear. For insular England, satisfied geographical separateness also meant satisfied linguistic separateness, a proud self-sufficiency which, however, proved to be feeble and indeed useless in foreign countries in the face of the impenetrable barrier of the languages of other peoples.

When Thomas Mowbray Duke of Norfolk is condemned by the king to exile, he fears only one deprivation of the many that may descend on an exile: the supreme source of unbearable suffering, the impossibility of using his native tongue, which he has *learned* for forty years of his life, and the consequent sentence to perpetual dumbness, to "speechless death," since an adult is unable to *learn* a new language:

> The language I have learnt these forty years,
> My native English, now I must forgo,
> And now my tongue's use is to me no more
> Than an unstringed viol or a harp,
> Or like a cunning instrument cas'd up—
> Or being open, put into his hands
> That knows no touch to tune the harmony.

> Within my mouth you have engaol'd my tongue,
> Doubly portcullis'd with my teeth and lips,
> And dull unfeeling barren ignorance
> Is made my gaoler to attend on me.
> I am too old to fawn upon a nurse,
> Too far in years to be a pupil now:
> What is thy sentence then but speechless death,
> Which robs my tongue from breathing native breath?[8]
> (*Richard II*, 1.3.159–73)

The English fear of the alloglot, which Shakespeare sets out in the lament for the Duke of Mowbray, seems not to have affected a monarch like Queen Elizabeth, if we recall one of her most famous pronouncements:

> I am your anointed Queen. I will never be by violence constrained to do anything. I thank God I am endued with such qualities that if I were turned out of the Realm in my petticoat I were able to live in any place in Christome.[9]

It is hard to establish on which or how many of her "qualities" Elizabeth based her conviction that, even abroad, she could regain the imaginary condition of a sovereign who not only has been uncrowned in her own country but has also banished and even caught out in a typically feminine déshabillé—a "petticoat" which, whether worn inside or outside the skirt, is certainly not the ultimate garment of a gentlewoman's dress. Did the queen rely on her political prestige overseas? Very few foreign potentates, however, were willing to recognize it, compared with those who were hostile. Or did she rely on qualities of character increased by the special tenacity that a woman in power doubly developed in comparison with the Prince-Man of the Renaissance—as she had to come to terms not only with the insidious snares of false friends and counselors, or declared enemies within and without the court, but also with the barriers of an apparatus invented, controlled, and constituted by men? Or did she rely—or also rely—on her claimed knowledge of other languages (Latin—she translated Seneca—or Italian, according to more or less reliable sources; not to mention French)? We cannot tell.

Whatever the case, even if it is likely that in the collection of her memorable sayings there is some interference from legend, the citation refers to the historical person of Elizabeth, not to a literary representation of the Queen. On the contrary, it is certain that one sixteenth-century literary projection of the English monarch, that of the triumphant Henry V in Shakespeare's play, did not need to know other languages in order to crown his military victory on foreign soil with a political marriage.

The famous scene of the wooing of the French princess centers on a dialogue with no precedent in *Henry V*'s historical sources (Holinshed's *Chronicles* [1587] and *The Union of the Two Noble Families of Lancaster and York* by E. Hall [1548]), while the dialogue occurs in the anonymous play, *The Famous Victories of Henry V* (published in 1598), Shakespeare's probable direct source, or an analogue from a previous lost play on which Shakespeare and the anonymous author both drew. In our case, the important thing is that the dialogue in the *Famous Victories* (the only scene, incidentally, presented in reliable form in the printed version of 1598, compared with the rest of the text, which is extremely corrupt and bristling with repetitions) is a monolingual dialogue, all in English, while Shakespeare's is bilingual or, perhaps I should say, a medley of two languages.

Katherine speaks French, and her lady-in-waiting, Alice, acts as her interpreter, translating her virtuously coquettish remarks into a bad English in which grammar and in particular pronunciation reproduce the patterns of French. The interpreter is overridden by the princess who ventures forth, stumbling like her interpreter, along the steep paths of the foreign language. The result is a *franglais* which adds comic tones to a scene that in the epilogue of *2 Henry IV* had already been announced as "merry." The brevity of the women's mixed-language comments contrasts with the long tirades of Henry who, using his own language, denounces with feigned humility the military rusticity of his speech:

> I'faith, Kate, . . . I am glad thou canst speak no better English; for if thou couldst, thou wouldst find me such a plain king that thou wouldst think I had sold my farm to buy my crown. I know no ways to mince it in love, but directly to say, "I love you": then if you urge me farther than to say, "Do you in faith?" I wear out my suit. Give me your answer; i'faith, do: and so clap hands and a bargain. How say you, lady?
>
> (*Henry V*, 5.2.122-32)

The royal will is such that it has no need of *translation* to be understood and satisfied; communication, for Henry, is ensured by his extraverbal position as victor, sovereign, and man. It is only at the end of his gallant assault, with the outcome now clear, that the king—who has already provided a full answer in English to Katherine's "political" question ("Is it possible dat I sould love de enemy of France?")—blurts out a translation of his answer into French:

> . . . I will tell thee in French, which I am sure will hang upon my tongue like a new-married wife about her husband's neck, hardly to be shook off. Je quand sur le possession de France, et quand vous avez le possession de moi—let me see, what then? Saint Denis be my speed!—donc votre est France, et vous êtes mienne.
> (5.2.184–91)

Now, the *defeated* Duke of Norfolk in *Richard II* is obsessed by the fear of living and dying speechless in lands where other tongues are spoken. The *victorious* Henry V, already so insular in his youthful escapades as Prince Hal, the companion of Sir John Falstaff (see the two parts of *Henry IV*), is still tenaciously insular within the bulwark of his language when on French soil he has defeated King Charles VI and, by offering to marry his daughter, uses the wedding bond to seal a treaty on the basis of a relationship of strength that is all in his favor. The barrier to his monolingualism is, in fact, sidestepped at another level, by virtue of a condition of superiority that we might call praeterlinguistic.

In *The Tempest*, Prospero experiences both conditions, that of the exile imagined by the Duke of Norfolk and that of the conqueror exercised by Henry V. But this lies in a territory that does not belong to established potentates, to the world of political exchange, a territory where recognized foreign languages are not spoken. Also, Prospero uses his native tongue as a universal language of communication (the actual English of the stage representation replaces Italian, according to conventional theatrical pretense). This language, this "treasure" he bestows—as Samuel Daniel foreshadowed—upon those who, on "strange shores" are "unknowing," incapable of speech, but who can become "refin'd with th'accents that are ours." By teaching Caliban words, Prospero not only reveals to the "monster" the meaning of things, but also gives him the capacity of thought:[10]

> I pitied thee,
> Took pains to make thee speak, taught thee each hour
> One *thing* or other: *when thou didst not, savage,*
> *Know thine own meaning, but wouldst gabble* like
> A thing most brutish, *I endow'd thy purposes*
> *With words that made them known.*
> (*The Tempest,* 1.2.355–60; emphasis added)

The triumph dreamed by Samuel Daniel, however, does not materialize on the island. The nature of the alien, the savage, does not change with the culture transmitted to him by the white man, the lord of civilization:

> But thy vile race,
> *Though thou didst learn,* had that in't which good natures
> Could not abide to be with; therefore wast thou
> Deservedly confin'd into this rock,
> Who hadst deserv'd more than a prison.
> (1.2.360–64; emphasis added)

Caliban, able to remember his initial gratitude as a subhuman who has been well treated and even trained (lines 334–40), but now excluded from the little human consortium created by Prospero, proclaims his linguistic failure:

> You taught me language; and my profit on't
> Is, I know how to curse. The red plague rid you
> For learning me your language!
> (1.2.365–67)

III

Literary rivalry with the Continent, ambivalence toward antiquity, nationalistic pride, the imperial dream of a universal and civilizing language, and a sense of inadequacy and isolation are distinctive features of the cultural climate of Shakespeare's day, which was characterized by the dialectic of trust/distrust in the native tongue. All these features are reflected in the problem of translations.

These problems affected Shakespeare differently from the way they did many of his contemporaries and immediate predecessors. Unlike poets who were also translators, such as Sidney and Spenser (who, however, never considered writing for the theater), or other poets and translators who also wrote plays (such as Kyd, Marlowe, Chapman, and Daniel), Shakespeare was not an assiduous reader of the classics in the original. Unlike Ben Jonson, he had no desire to gloss his "Roman" plays with citations from the Latin *auctoritates;* nor did he produce translations from modern languages. Indeed, in the disorderly transpositions and clumsy simulations that mark the interlinguistic exchanges between Henry V, Katherine, and Alice (together with numerous, analogous other examples in his plays), one is tempted to read a parody that reveals the fragility and unreliability of any translation from one language to another.

> Bless thee, Bottom, bless thee! Thou art translated.

Thus, Quince laments the metamorphosis of his friend, who now wears an ass's head (*A Midsummer Night's Dream*, 3.1.113–14).

This, for Shakespeare, is not an exceptional use of the verb *to translate*—it is virtually the norm. Throughout the canon, the verb is most often used in the sense of change, conversion from one condition to another, from one feeling to another. Although established for more than two centuries, the meaning of the verb as an interlinguistic transposition is not that of Shakespeare except, in some cases, by allusion, when it is taken as a metaphor to signify transcodifications between extra-verbal levels; or, as in *Hamlet*, from the extra-verbal to the verbal. When the King comes on stage, after Hamlet has dragged off Polonius's body following his harrowing exchange with his mother, he exhorts the distressed Queen to translate her signs of desperation into words:

> There's a matter in these sighs, these profound heaves,
> You must translate. 'Tis fit we understand them.
>
> (4.1.1–2)

In *The Merry Wives of Windsor,* the literal sense of the expression "translate into English" is distorted by Pistol, who gives "English" quite a different meaning, already foreshadowed in Falstaff's assertion:

> ... Briefly, I do mean to make love to Ford's wife. ... she discourses, she carves, she gives the leer of invitation; ... and the hardest voice of her behaviour, to be *Englished* rightly, is, 'I am Sir John Falstaff's.'

Even the most resistant aspects of Mistress Ford's behavior, if Englished—that is, expressed in words—"say" ("the hardest voice"): "I am Sir John Falstaff's." Hence Pistol's remark:

> He hath studied her will, and *translated* her will—*out of honesty into English.*
>
> (1.3.40–47; emphasis added)

This use of the verb *translate* by Shakespeare is, in my view, part of his wider metaphorical use of terms belonging to the semantic area of verbal communication ("language," "tongue," "speech," "discourse," and so on). One should consider, for example, in *2 Henry IV* (4.1.30–52) all Westmoreland's apostrophe to the Archbishop of York, who has taken the side of the king's opponents, in which the metaphorical use of "speech," "tongue," etc. (taking the place of actions and functions) rotates around the words *translate yourself,* blaming the *transformation/deformation* of the prelate's nature and functions, as also the *transfer* of his episcopal see:

> Wherefore do you so ill translate yourself
> Out of the speech of peace that bears such grace
> Into the harsh and boist'rous tongue of war.
> (4.1.47–49)

IV

A great theme underlies these considerations: all Shakespeare's plays, we may say, enact the comedy, and the tragedy of the word/thing relationship: the celebration of the power of language, and the uncovering of its snares. From this viewpoint, the problem of translation would also appear to project over the absolute horizon postulated in statements like that made by George Steiner: "inside or between languages, human communication equals translation,"[11] which, to my mind, means that translation is the equivalent of at least three of the functions described by Jakobson (referential, phatic, and metalinguistic).

Setting aside this great theme, my contribution is intended to focus only on the relationship between the national idiom and other languages, in order to remark on some of its aspects. I referred at the beginning of this essay to the Elizabethan cultural context, recalling the positions taken up in theory and in literary practice by a few writers—"E. K.," Spenser, Sidney, Daniel, and Chapman (the last as a theoretician, translator, and imitator of the classics). Passing, with Shakespeare, to the field where theory and poetic praxis satisfy or clash with the primary needs of performability on the stage, I indicated—also with just a few examples—the ways in which the playwright expresses the various levels of his contemporaries' awareness of the value of the national language in the attitudes of certain of his characters in *Richard II, Henry V,* and *The Tempest.* I then suggested that Shakespeare's very use of the verb *translate,* eluding all direct reference to the concrete activity of translating from one language to another, can be taken as an indication of a certain indifference (if not suspicion) as regards this kind of intellectual activity, which he himself never in fact attempted—but of which, as we shall soon see, he made wide and skillful use.

It may be useful at this point to recall how, in the linguistic tissue of Shakespeare's theater, the relationship between native and other languages is subjected to contaminations and inversions according to complex modalities which, for simplicity's sake, can be reduced to two types of operation.

The first type consists of the inclusion of passages of "other" languages in the text: Latin, and modern languages, together with various more or less cryptic hybrid forms, are used with multiple functions which accurate research can distinguish and classify, and of which many, even at first comparison, show a considerable difference from the intertextual, plurilinguistic devices of other contemporary playwrights—from Lyly, Kyd, and Marlowe to Jonson and Marston. I would say, in general, that, in Shakespeare, these passages either *collide* or *collude*. When they collide, they have effects of estrangement, like the Latin of the pedants in *Love's Labour's Lost;* when they collude, they suggest compliant understandings, as in the much–debated "miching mallicho" in *Hamlet* (3.2.135).

If the first type of operation is interlinguistic, the other is infralinguistic. Or, to put it differently, English becomes a conglomeration of languages with the inclusion, for example, of regional dialect forms phonetically transcribed with their misleading pronunciation, blunders, malapropisms, neologisms produced by pedants and rustics, plus various other distortions which the reader of Shakespeare frequently comes across. The frequency is certainly higher in the comedy register (which is also present, as we know, in the tragedies); but here, too, the infralinguistic interplay often produces resonances that audibly clash with the comic effect.

The operation implies procedures I would define as infratranslation, specimens of which are plentiful. One need only consider the two parts of *Henry IV* and especially *The Merry Wives of Windsor*, in which the English of certain characters who "hack" it, or "make fritters of" it (3.1.72, 5.5.144) is subjected by others to corrective reformulations, which, in turn, generate further paraphrases.

As I wish to give just one example, I will take it from a more sophisticated kind of character, one that is more ambiguous than the Welsh or Scots speaker, than the clown with his malapropisms, or the pedant with his absurd erudition. I am thinking of the professional fool who, like other characters of different status, is capable of producing quotations in foreign languages, inventing neologisms, and disrupting the link between sound and sense but whose particular ability lies in the way he plays with all possible combinations of formal, logical, and argumentative rhetoric within the framework of current language.

In their working with words, Touchstone in *As You Like It,* Feste in *Twelfth Night,* Lavatch in *All's Well That Ends Well,* and the nameless Fool in *King Lear* are masters of translation within the English language, on the synchronic and diachronic levels, with their translations from the cultured lexis of Latin-Romance origin into the everyday Anglo-Saxon lexis (or vice versa), and with countless types of explicit transposition.

If I may so put it, I will take Touchstone as my touchstone. In the third and fifth acts of *As You Like It,* Touchstone, transported to an Arcadia where the lords have lost their substantial prerogatives in the social hierarchy, is somehow alienated, a court employee in a state of forced unemployment. (Life there, as he says to the shepherd Corin, "in respect it is in the fields, it pleaseth me well; but in respect it is not in the court, it is tedious," 3.2.17–19). His satirical volleys are still fundamentally courteous toward the lords in exile; toward the natives of this Arcadia, however, he turns the "malignant" face of the fool (a figure intrinsically two-faced, both in his effective anthropological and cultural dimension and in his folkloric and literary representations, a figure generated by the complex duplicity which, albeit by different routes, permeates the Graeco-Hebraico-Christian vision of "folly"). The "malignant" face is shown with a certain aloof superiority which seems to parody that of the conqueror-colonizer foreseen by Samuel Daniel.

To induce the rustic William to cede his Audrey to him, Touchstone overawes him with his learned language and humiliates him with his simultaneous translation into "boorish:"

> Therefore you clown, *abandon*—which is in the vulgar *leave*—the *society*—which in the boorish is *company*—of this *female*—which in the common is *woman*. Which together is, abandon the society of this female, or clown thou *perishest;* or to thy better understanding, *diest;* or, to wit, I *kill* thee, make thee away, *translate* thy life into death, thy liberty into bondage. *I will deal in poison with thee, or in bastinado, or in steel. I will bandy with thee in faction; I will o'er-run thee with policy;* I will *kill thee a hundred and fifty ways.* Therefore *tremble and depart.*
>
> (5.1.45–57; emphasis added)

When he pronounces his death threat, Touchstone interrupts his interpretation for the benefit of the clown. After using the verb *translate* in the sense, as I have said, that Shakespeare prefers—that is, of the passage from one condition to another (in this case, from life to death, from freedom to slavery)—the fool gives vent to a series of variants on ways to persecute and kill that are so elaborate, unpalatable, that poor William is terrorized into doing that which in conclusion is imposed on him in two words of Latin-Romance origin: "tremble and depart." Without a word of objection, William takes his leave and abandons Audrey to his rival.

V

Unlike the verb *translate,* the noun *translation* occurs only once in the entire Shakespeare canon, with direct reference to a literary object. The tokens of love that Dumaine has sent her, complains Katharine in *Love's Labour's Lost,* are a pair of gloves

> and moreover,
> Some thousand verses of a faithful lover;
> A huge translation of hypocrisy,
> Vilely compil'd, profound simplicity.
>
> (5.2.49–52)

Does this mean a bad translation from a "hypocritical" text, which is the interpretation given by Cesare Vico Lodovici in his Italian translation ("E qualche migliaio di versi di fedele amore, una interminabile traduzione da un testo d'ipocrisia mal combinata e estremamente sciocca")?[12] Or is it, instead, a poor text, the work of Dumaine himself, who clumsily *translates* hypocrisy into sincerity? In either case, the word *translation* helps give a negative connotation to certain contemporary love poetry, considered to be mediocre imitation.

As we know, the debate on translation in the Renaissance takes up a series of points of reference to the past, from Cicero and Horace to St. Jerome and Maimonides and Dante in the *Convivio.* Before then, however, and even in the period of humanism (witness Erasmus), the dominant theme is that of the three "great" languages—Hebrew, Greek, and Latin—of the translation from one of these languages to another or, at most (and rarely), from one of them to a modern language.

In the sixteenth century, national languages acquired the status of noble languages, and the need began to be felt of reciprocal translatability, especially for literary works.

England, which had had its great medieval translators (Bede, Alfred, Aelfric), but no school comparable to that of Toledo, played a marginal role in the theoretical questions that engrossed the literary figures of sixteenth-century Europe (in France, for example, Etienne Dolet, Thomas Sébillet, and Du Bellay). This may also have been a consequence of the dialectic between the isolationist spirit and the sense of isolation I have mentioned.

At the time of *Love's Labour's Lost,* the debate on translation (here, as throughout, I refer only to literary translation, mainly poetic) tends in Europe to pivot on a question I would call aesthetic rather than semantic; that is, whether it is possible to render in another language the qualities of the original, its "eloquence" (including decorum, figures of speech, harmony, and wit). There is a prevalence of negative responses, especially in the case, not of the noble and fertile exercise of translating from the "great" languages, but of translations from modern languages—"easy languages," as Don Quixote calls them toward the end of the second part of Cervantes' novel (1615), in the episode of the visit to the printing-house in Barcelona (chap. 62):

> But despite all that, it appears to me that the translation from one language to another, unless it be from the most noble of languages, namely Greek and Latin, is like looking at a Flemish tapestry from the back; although one can see the figures they are full of threads that obscure them and they do not have the same even surface as they have on the front; translation from easy languages requires no more ingenuity or eloquence than that required to copy from one sheet of paper to another.[13]

The fine metaphor of the tapestry viewed from the wrong side must have become widely known, thanks to *Don Quixote;* it is, for example, recalled in a couplet in James Howell's *Familiar Letters:*

> Some hold translation not unlike to be
> The wrong side of a Turkish tapestry.[14]

This opinion seems to have become a mere commonplace to be repeated, as in this case, with a variation of marketable goods: from a product of the nearby familiar provinces of Flanders to the more exotic product of an eastern land, which frequent contacts had now made better known.

Apart from this literary type of mistrust, we may presume that in the Elizabethan age there were also some who—even without the precise comparative exercises that occupied the attention of authors in the second half of the seventeenth century and in the eighteenth century—were aware of, or at least suspected, the large number of errors which, especially in the case of the shift from one translation to another, could make the original unintelligible or completely alter its meaning.

This mistrust, whether of one type or the other, must have been shared by Shakespeare, who, in addition to using sources written in his own native language, used tales, anthologies, and collections that had been "Englished" through a process of one or more linguistic mediations, including such classical works as Plutarch's *Lives,* translated by Sir Thomas North from Amyot's French version.

It is on this uneven field that Shakepeare performed his work of "adaptation": pruning, innovating, inventing, ingeniously bending his source material to the laws of stage representation, not disdaining, when he thought fit, to maintain or rather to simulate the literariness or the particular features of the genre to which the source belonged. When he had a translation before him, he was obviously not troubled by a philologist's scruples to seek out the original text, or even to make casual spot checks (unlike those who translated into a modern language the Latin version of a Greek text, who would declare—often truthfully—that they, too, had consulted the original).

We can only admire the extremely useful labors of the many twentieth- and late-nineteenth-century exegetes who, comparing a passage of Shakespeare's text with the English translation of the source from which it was drawn, discovered phrases or sentences not to be found in that translation and, instead, seem closer to phrases or expressions in the original (or intermediary) Italian, French, Spanish, or even Latin text. But, when the discovery of individual coincidences (the famous "verbal parallels") are all put together—along with other elements (such as contemporary school curricula)—in order to build up monumental conjectures regarding Shakespeare's "learning," there is the risk that the image of the playwright at work may be totally distorted, to be replaced by that of the scholar locked in his study poring over tome after tome. No one can say that Shakespeare did not also have the original text or an intermediary translation which he used for his plots. Nor can it be said that he was unaware of the extent to which a text can be corrupted as it passes from one language to another.

Among the many cruxes in Shakespeare's plays, in addition to those attributable to the notoriously precarious manner of the transmission of the actual texts of the plays, there are several inconsistencies that may originate from the sources used. There are few cases, however, in which the distortions perpetrated by a translator (which, in some cases, were due to ideological reasons and not mere carelessness or ignorance) induced Shakespeare to follow him if that involved breaking his firmest rule: dramatic credibility. Traps of this nature he carefully avoided, transforming or eliminating anything that did not suit his need.[15]

Inversely, an error of translation (which may, indeed, not have been a real error but only an ambiguity) sometimes inspired him to find a solution that is dramaturgically more effective. We can take as an example Pompey's bleeding statue in *Julius Caesar*, which is not mentioned, as it is in Plutarch, at the moment of the assassination but is moved forward in time to the Forum scene, with Antony's re-evocation in his funeral speech:

> Even at the base of Pompey's statue
> (Which all the while ran blood) great Caesar fell.
> (3.2.190–91)

Plutarch's Greek original (*Life of Caesar*, 66) goes as follows:

παρῆχεν ἑαυτόν [. . .] πρός τήν βάσιν ἐφ'ἧς ὁ Πομπηίου βεβηχεν ανδριάς. Καὶ πολὺ χαθήυαζεν αὐτὴν ὁ φόνος

Literally translated, as it appears in the Loeb edition, the passage reads: "[Caesar] sank . . . against the pedestal on which the statue of Pompey stood. And the pedestal was drenched with his blood."[16]

In Greek, grammatical gender distinguishes the pedestal (βάσις, feminine) from the statue (ανδριάς, masculine). But, in Amyot's French version the distinction is lost, as both the terms used (*base* and *image*) are feminine. Moreover, Amyot turned Plutarch's second main clause into a subordinate: "qui en fût toute ensanglantée."[17] The sense of the relative clause is clear: a physical event is being described—the blood of Caesar, flowing from his wounds, bathes the base of the statue. North keeps the relative clause, qualifies "blood" with "gore," and transforms Amyot's passive into an ambiguous active: "[Caesar] was driven . . . against the base whereupon Pompey's image stood, which ran all of a gore blood."[18] In his edition of the *Lives*, George Wyndham sees a "blunder" by North in this passage which subsequently misled Shakespeare.[19] But it seems to me that there is no reason why we should not interpret North's sentence in the realistic meaning it had in the original and in Amyot.

The fact remains that Shakespeare alters the text of his source with very few modifications: "which ran all of a gore blood" becomes in the above-quoted line in *Julius Caesar:* "which all the while ran blood." But what modifications they are! A spatial "all" becomes a temporal "all the while"; away goes "of," which only interrupts the direct transitive link between "ran" and "blood"; and out goes "gore," which denotes the blood at the foot of the statue as that which flows from Caesar's wounds and then coagulates. These slight modifications, however, are sufficient to impress on the event the inequivocal sign of the supernatural prodigy of a bleeding statue, an extraordinarily useful sign to give further emphasis to the tone and manner of Antony's oration—a prodigy, above all, the dramaturgical need for which is prepared by the figuration of another statue spouting blood, not to be found in Plutarch or in any other source: that of Caesar, according to the dream of Calphurnia which he himself relates (2.2.76–82).

The dramaturgical transformation of the source material thus takes place on three levels. On the temporal level, Pompey's statue is brought forward, from the moment of the assassination to the moment of its re-evocation in a flashback, and is anticipated by Caesar's statue in Calphurnia's dream. On the iconic level, this oneiric element, with its supernatural overtones, generates an isotopy that will be concluded by the prodigious nature attributed to Pompey's statue. On the verbal level, this prodigious nature is achieved by some modifications of North's original sentence, by way of a slight *retranslation* from what was already English into the "other" English of the poet-playwright.

To define such an operation of metamorphosis, one might well take the verb *to translate* in the meaning of "transformation," which Shakespeare often gives it. The best comment on this transformation, however, one which I have chosen as an epitome of the many he performs, comes to us in his celebrated description of the poetic process:

> And as imagination bodies forth
> The forms of things unknown, the poet's pen
> Turns them to shapes, and gives to airy nothing
> A local habitation and a name.
> (*A Midsummer Night's Dream*, 5.1.14–17)

Notes

An earlier Italian version of this article appeared in *Rivista di letterature moderne e comparate*, 39, 2 (1986).

1. C. Hill, *Reformation to Industrial Revolution* (London: Penguin Books, 1969), 86–88; C. M. Cipolla, *Storia economica dell'Europa preindustriale* (Bologna: Il Mulino. 1974, 308–21).

2. In *Elizabethan Critical Essays,* ed. G. Gregory Smith, 2 vols. (Oxford: Oxford University Press, 1904), 1: 129–30. Here, as in all other quotations from sixteenth- and seventeenth-century texts, I have consistently modernized the spelling regardless of the criteria used by individual editors.

3. *Elizabethan Critical Essays* 2: 304–307 (305).

4. Bateson, *English Poetry and the English Language: An Experiment in Literary History* (Oxford: Oxford University Press, 1934), chap. 2, "Elizabethans, Metaphysicals, Augustans."

5. *The Iliads of Homer* . . . Done According to the Greek by George Chapman, ed. R. Hooper (London, 1865), I: 212.

6. Sidney, *An Apology for Poetry,* ed. G. Shepherd (London-Edinburgh, 1965), 140–41.

7. Daniel, *Musophilus,* ed. R. Hirnelick (West Lafayette: Indiana University Press, 1965).

8. For the text of all quotations from Shakespeare, as well as line numbering, I follow the respective New Arden editions.

9. *The Oxford Dictionary of Quotations* (1959), 198, note 3.

10. The speech, which I quote as being Prospero's (since, logically, it belongs to him) is, in fact, given to Miranda in the 1623 Folio (the only original edition we have of *The Tempest*). Various modern editors—as, indeed, also Dryden and Theobald—attribute the speech to Prospero. Frank Kermode keeps the attribution to Miranda, although admitting that the speech is more appropriate for Prospero. He also points out that Caliban's response is directed to both father and daughter; see *The Tempest* (New Arden, 1954), page 32 and note.

11. G. Steiner, *After Babel: Aspects of Language and Translation* (London: Oxford University Press, 1975), 47. In relation to this, see the fine essay by Inga-Stina Ewbank, "*Hamlet* and the Power of Words," *Shakespeare Survey,* 30 (1977): 85–102, which persuasively defines the protagonist as "the most sensitive translator in the play" (p. 95), a play in which each character requires a "translation" or "translates" for another.

12. Shakespeare, *Teatro,* ed. C. Vico Lodovici, (Turin: Einaudi, 1964), 2:148.

13. English translation from M. De Cervantes, *El ingenioso hidalgo Don Quijote de la Mancha,* ed. L. A. Murillo, 3 vols. (Madrid: Clásicos Castalia, 1978) 2:519. The original reads:

> Pero, con todo esto, me parece que el traducir de una lengua en otra, como no sea de las reinas de las lenguas, griega y latina, es como quien mira los tapices flamencos por el revés, que aunque se veen las figuras, son llenas de hilos que las escurecen, y no se veen con la lisura y tez de la haz; y el traducir de lenguas fáciles, ni arguye ingenio ni elocución, como no le arguye el que traslada ni el que copia un papel de otro papel.

On this passage, and another at the beginning of the first part of *Quijote* (chap. 6), where there is a discussion about the translatability of *Orlando furioso,* see Lore Terracini, "Una frangia agli arazzi di Cervantes," in *Lingua come problema nella letteratura spagnola del Cinquecento (con una frangia cervantina)* (Turin: Stampatori, 1979), 287–322. In this essay (written in 1968), Terracini, with amused acumen, traces the Spanish sources and polemic references that lie behind the two passages in Cervantes and concludes that, despite certain qualifications and concessions, the "firmest and most insistent" concept expressed by the author is "the condemnation of translation" (page 308).

14. Howell, *Epistolae Ho-Elianae: Familiar letters, Domestic and Foreign,* Book I, ed. O. Smeaton (1645), letter no. 6 (London, 1903).

15. Here I must describe a stimulating personal experience I had during the course of research on *Julius Caesar* (compare V. Gentili, "Sul *'Julius Caesar'*: Plutarco, Appiano, e i contesti culturali," in *Le forme del teatro,* ed. G. Melchiori, 3 (Rome: Edizioni di Storia e Letteratura, 1984), 95–158; Gentili, "Shakespeare's *'Julius Caesar'* and the Elizabethans' Roads to Rome," in *Shakespeare Today: Directions and Methods of Research,* ed. K. Elam (Florence: La Casa Usher, 1984), 187–212). Examining the text of the second book of Appian's *Civil Wars* in the English translation (1578) by W[illiam] B[arker] (which, in my opinion, is a further source of *Julius Caesar*), I thought it would be useful to find the reason for what seemed to me a strange error by the English translator in a passage regarding Antony's funeral oration. A comparison with the sixteenth-century Spanish, Italian, and French translations, as well as with two different Latin versions that circulated at the time, revealed a curious series of additions, omissions, and misunderstandings that could not all be explained by the use of Latin versions based on different Greek codices. The translators' misunderstandings, together with the fanciful and implausible solutions chosen by each of them, indicate—in this particular case—how cultural and ideological distance or extraneousness from the original text in the end constitutes an impenetrable, confusing barrier. I would imagine that other accurate comparisons between samples of Renaissance translations in various languages from classical (and possibly also modern) texts would confirm the interference of cultural barriers.

16. *Plutarch's Lives,* ed. B. Perrin, 1959.

17. *Les Vies des Hommes Illustres Grecs, et Romains, Comparees l'une avec l'autre par Plutarque de Chaeronee. Translatees de Grec en François par Messire Iacques Amyot lors Abbé de Bellozane, à présent Euesque d'Auxerre* . . . A Lausanne par François Le Preux . . . 1574, page 896. I refer to the fifth edition (Lausanne, 1574), as I am of the opinion that Sir Thomas North did not follow the previous editions (compare V. Gentili, "Sul *'Julius Caesar,'*" 145–46, note 22).

18. *The Lives of the Noble Grecians and Romanes, Compared together by . . . Plutarke of Chaeronea . . . Translated out of Greeke into French by Iames Amyot . . . and out of French into Englishe, by Thomas North* . . . Imprinted at London by Thomas Vautrouiller and Iohn Wight, 1579. For easier consultation of the passage in question, see *Narrative and Dramatic Sources of Shakespeare,* ed. G. Bullough, 5, *The Roman Plays* (London: Routledge and Kegan Paul, 1964) 5:86.

19. George Wyndham, Introduction to *Plutarch's Lives . . . Englished by Sir Thomas North* . . . (London, 1895–96 [The Tudor Translations], I: lxxiii–iv), W. W. MacCallum, author of a well-known, meticulous study (*Shakespeare's Roman Plays and Their Background* [London: Macmillan 1910]), see pp. 184–86, is of the same opinion.

"But thou didst understand me by my signs": The Instability of Signs in *King John*
ROBERTA MULLINI

> Clauditur hoc saxo, clarus rex ille Ioannes,
> Qui quondam nituit, Anglica regna tenens,
> . . . .
> Attamen ornatum gladio capitisque corona,
> Dextra decens virgam, levaque sceptra tenet.
> Aurea vestis erat propior, quam serica texit,
> Calcar erat pedibus, annulus in digito.
> (Ioannis illustrissimi Anglorum Regis Epitaphium)

The story of John Plantagenet, used by Reformation propaganda as an antecedent to the events that occurred during the reign of Henry VIII and recalled to public memory both in learned treatises (for example, by William Tyndale in *The Obedience of a Christen Man,* 1528) and in the theater (by John Bale in *King Johan,* 1538), became a genuine myth of the origins of Tudor historiography, which Shakespeare—though interested, rather, in reinterpreting more recent English history—could not well ignore. If we accept the widely held belief that *The Troublesome Raigne of John King of England* was written before *King John,* we may surmise that Shakespeare wished to rewrite the story, remodeling the background episodes, if not the main events, with regard not so much to the version presented by Bale as to that proposed by the anonymous author of the more recent play.[1]

In the present cultural climate, in which British and American scholars are reexamining critical and hermeneutical attitudes and reading the Shakespeare canon in the context of production and of an extratext capable of accounting for authorial choices and ambiguities, the *histories* have not yet been recognized as places of representation and representability, either of context or extratext.[2] Two works in particular—at the beginning and at the end of the Shakespearean Tudor myth, respectively—appear to be affected by this lack of interest: *King John* and *Henry VIII*, even if *King John*, it is true, has recently attracted the attention of certain scholars.³

The parallels between the story enacted by *King John* and events related to the struggle between Elizabeth and Mary Queen of Scots have, over the years, received considerable attention⁴ and are still the basis of certain works that analyze cruxes of the Shakespearean text and their relationship with the epochal historical context of production.⁵ Although this is a fertile field of inquiry, as is also the exceptional female presence in the play,⁶ I will here seek the textual traces—if possible, justifying them—of judgments of indeterminacy, confusion, and uncertainty that have succeeded each other since Tillyard took his stand.⁷

The Medieval World

"Anno MCLXXII apparuit signu(m) igniferu(m). Anno MCLXXIII discordia orta est. . . . Anno MCXCIX [mortuus est] Ric(hardus) rex et Joh(anne)s successit": these basic events of English history, traditionally related as the history of kings, are the stages recorded in a psalter from an Anglo-Saxon Benedictine abbey.⁸ It is indeed scarcely more than a list of dates and names; but, interestingly, it records that in the year 1173 keen conflicts arose within the royal family ("from 1173 onwards," writes J. Gillingham, "Henry was plagued by rebellious sons"⁹), the "discord" which was to lead to the episodes narrated in Shakespeare's play and which was foreshadowed by omens of misfortune ("signum igniferum"). Very likely, the presage was added to the chronicle at a later date, in the light of the importance the discord had in subsequent English history; yet the interpolation indicates that the reign of King John, even in the Middle Ages, was deemed to have been "troublesome" from the start, having begun under an "unlucky star."

Shakespeare thus set his tale in that remote medieval period, with all the allusions to the contemporary Elizabethan scene abounding in the play. However, the process of modernization—or, rather, of actualization—of the events does not pass only by way of more or less veiled references to the problems of the succession to the throne of Elizabeth or to contemporary matters such as England's struggle against Spain. As in *King Lear*, the medieval epoch—a legendary past in the tragedy, a historical past in *King*

John—is caught in a moment of profound crisis, when some bastions of its sign system are beginning to fail.[10] Lear, who is the king, divides the reign, dismembering that which is indivisible (the body politic), and ceases to be king. John is the sovereign of a kingdom that is already shattered (not for nothing did he gain the nickname "Lackland"), because too many bodies natural aspire to it or exert power over it. It is true, as Barbara Traister has observed, that John lacks a body politic and possesses only the "one body"[11] (the physical body), but it is also true that the play contains many, perhaps too many, characters who manifest, or have manifested, "symptoms" of regality. Apart from Arthur, legitimate heir to the throne of England as son of Geoffrey, third son of Henry II, and obviously John himself, who has succeeded Richard the Lion-Heart, there is regality in the Queen Mother, Eleanor of Aquitaine, proud protectress of her sons and of the feudal state inherited from her great husband, and also in the Bastard, who so resembles the late King Richard and in the play bears his authority, if not his title. To these we must add the King of France and the Dauphin, supporters of Arthur's rights, of his memory, of their own dynastic claims and of the desires of the Church. There are thus many "bodies natural," each with one or more reasons for managing the single "body politic," England, which Henry II's decisions regarding the distribution of the land among his sons had already transformed with respect to the extent of the Plantagenet domain.

The feudal system allowed the construction of Henry II's great empire. With its far from amicable division among his sons, however, Henry himself promoted a process of disgregation which called into question the law, feudal loyalty, and relations with the supernational power of the Church and undermined the entire system. We must not forget that Henry II was also the king who opposed the power of Rome, in the person of Thomas Becket, Archbishop of Canterbury, slain in 1170 by four of Henry's knights. History has handed down the story of the "misunderstanding" between the Plantagenet sovereign and the knights who killed Becket. G. M. Trevelyan declares that, as a consequence of the Archbishop's reiterated demands,

> Henry's ungovernable temper broke out in a cry of rage that inspired four of his knights to steal away from his court and murder his enemy in Canterbury Cathedral.[12]

And Gillingham writes:

> "Will no one rid me of this turbulent priest?" Henry's heated words were taken all too literally by four of his knights. Anxious to win the king's favour they rushed off to Canterbury. . . .[13]

Both historians thus recognize the king's "innocence" and state that Becket's murder was due to a misinterpretation of the sovereign's words.

It is no coincidence that in the theater of Reformation propaganda, Thomas Becket is presented not as a martyr but as a negative figure. Bale, in *King Johan,* has him condemned by Imperyall Majestye with the same arguments as those adduced by Henry II in his battle against the Archbishop:

> But Thomas Becket ye exalted without reason
> Because that he dyed for the Churches wantom lyberte,
> That the priestes myght do all kyndes of inyquyte
> And be unponnyshed.[14]

In a monologue in the same play, King Johan rehabilitates his father's memory, asserting that Becket was killed "with owt the kynges consent" (line 1291).

The story of Becket and Henry II does not come into Shakespeare's play, and the struggle between John and the Church (central to *King Johan* and a repetition of his father's struggle) is only marginal. These events are, however, in the background, recalled to the Elizabethan audience by the incomprehension between John and Hubert (3.2.69–76 and 4.2). Indeed, these events seem to be the "original guilt" that still loomed over the English sovereign, the same as that matrix of royal behavior that lay behind the clash between Elizabeth and her secretary, Davison, with regard to the death sentence decreed for Mary Queen of Scots, which Lily Campbell rightly sees hinted at in *King John.*[15]

The Instability of the Sign

The medieval symbolic world rested on the fixity of the sign, on the "recognition of a biunivocal (and not arbitrary) correlation between the plane of expression and the plane of content, of their substantial inseparability."[16] The word "is perceived as an icon, an image of content."[17] The doctrine of "the king's two bodies" can indeed be reduced to the substantial unity of expression and content—that is, the body natural as an expression of the body politic, such that even if the former should come to harm, the latter continues to exist, requiring merely a new "expression" (a new body natural) for the dynastic succession. The concept of the Crown was, in turn, often assimilated to that of the body politic,[18] even if the physical crown represented, more accurately, the unity of the bodies natural and politic, as John of Grandisson, Bishop of Exeter, averred in 1337: "The substance of the nature of the Crown is found chiefly in the person of the king as head and in the peers as members."[19]

"Doth not the crown of England prove the king?" John asks the citizens of Angiers (2.1.273), but the reply repeats that which has already been said in the previous lines: "he that proves the king, / To him will we prove loyal" (lines 270–71). In other words, crown and king are no longer conjoined, the expression (the physical crown) is no longer a direct reference to the content (the king). The "biunivocal correlation" has ceased to exist, the sign is no longer such; indeed, its substitute function (crown for king) now refers only to the lack of content, like Lear's crown, which after the division of the kingdom is, like him, "an O without a figure" (1.4.189–90).[20]

There are, in fact, many moments in which *King John* manifests the crisis of the sign system through the lack of correspondence between expression and content. It matters little whether this is a result of the hierarchically more elevated crisis factor, to which I have just referred, or, vice versa, whether the sum of so many partial incongruities has led to the general upheaval. The fact is that the image of the medieval world presented in the play is that of a universe whose linchpins are beginning to vacillate, in which that which is expression rarely finds confirmation in consolidated contents, ranging from items of clothing (the "lion's hide" over the shoulders of the King of Austria which should be replaced, in the Bastard's words, by a "calve's–skin," 3.1.55) to the exposal of adultery, which brings into doubt the correspondence between the birth of a son in wedlock and the son's legitimacy, and to the inconsistency between the sovereign's thoughts and his words.

The King of Austria, responsible for the death of Richard the Lion-Heart, wears a lion's skin to indicate his courage and also the totemic possession of his enemy's qualities, although in fact the garment scarcely befits his cowardice and insignificance.

Political marriage, an ancient practice for the acquisition or safeguard of possessions, is intended also in *King John* to bring peace and put an end to the quarrels between France and England. The union of Blanche and the Dauphin does not, however, prove to be a positive element of concord, to the extent that Blanche immediately sees herself as a victim of dynastic maneuvers, of that power which, expressed in the two enemy armies, will "whirl asunder and dismember me," since "Whoever wins, on that side shall I lose" (3.1.256 and 261).

Constance's unbound tresses (3.3), interpreted by Cardinal Pandulph as a sign of madness, are not that at all, and Constance contests the erroneous decoding of her condition:

> I am not mad: this hair I tear is mine;
> My name is Constance; I was Geoffrey's wife;
> Young Arthur is my son, and he is lost!
> I am not mad; I would to heaven I were!
> For then 'tis like I should forget myself:
> O, if I could, what grief should I forget!
> Preach some philosophy to make me mad,
> And thou shalt be canoniz'd, cardinal;
> For, being not mad but sensible of grief,
> My reasonable part produces reason
> How I may be deliver'd of these woes,
> And teaches me to kill or hang myself:
> If I were mad, I should forget my son,
> Or madly think a babe of clouts were he.
> I am not mad; too well, too well I feel
> The different plague of each calamity.
>
> (3.2.45–60)

The outward signs of madness, visible in Hamlet as related by Ophelia to her father (2.1.77–84),[21] and cunningly simulated by Hamlet well knowing how they will be interpreted, are, however, accompanied in the tragedy by a language that imitates a condition of madness: the "antic disposition" (1.5.180) includes both "th'exterior" and "the inward man" (2.2.6), in order to ensure the successful impact of the feigned madness on its intended addressees. But, in Constance, the outward aspect is not an unmistakable symptom of madness and cannot be read as such. Indeed, "Constance insists that the vehemence of her grief is evidence of her sanity,"[22] thus cancelling the relationship between expression and content.

The Signs of the Body

The human body, the paradoxical copy of a god that is acorporeal yet visible in the perfection of Christ, presents itself as an image of beauty, an expression that raises a question of moral content. Thomas Aquinas defines beauty as the possession of *integritas, proportio* and *claritas;* lacking the first, human beings "*turpia sunt.*"[23] In the medieval world anything affecting the integrity of the body (illness and deformity) was considered a sign of guilt and sin because of the relation between exterior and interior, the devil thus being represented as utter monstrosity. In contrast, the king, in his physical body, must be beautiful and healthy (any illness of the sovereign is menacingly reflected in the body politic) and—thanks to his thaumaturgic power—he must also be able to cure his subjects' diseases. *King John* says nothing about John's beauty or otherwise, but presents the king's body as prey to humors and passions (Salisbury affirms, in 4.2.76–77, "The colour of the king doth come and go / Between his purpose and his conscience) and to "This fever," "this tyrant fever" (5.3.3, 14). Indeed, just when the king's natural body is about to fall prey to a poison-induced dryness—that is, when the king's illness might mean the ruin of the body politic—the salvation of the realm arrives, with the death of this "confounded royalty" (5.7.58) and the succession of Henry III.

Beauty as a sign of regality is reserved in the text to Arthur, as seen in his mother's impassioned portrait:

> If thou, that bid'st me be content, wert grim,
> Ugly, and sland'rous to thy mother's womb,
> Full of unpleasing blots and sightless stains,
> Lame, foolish, crooked, swart, prodigious,
> Patch'd with foul moles and eye-offending marks,
> I would not care, I then would be content,
> For then I should not love thee: no, nor thou
> Become thy great birth, nor deserve a crown.
> But thou art fair, and at thy birth, dear boy,
> Nature and fortune join'd to make thee great:
> Of nature's gifts thou mayst with lilies boast
> And with the half-blown rose.
>
> (2.2.43–54)

Neither history nor Shakespeare's text, however, reserves anything to this royal body, this kingly beauty that would merit the crown. Only when this body natural is dead will its correspondence with the body politic be recognized, in the words of the Bastard, "How easy dost thou take all England up / From forth this morsel of dead royalty!" (4.3.142–43).

There is another human body that is invested with the failure of the relationship between expression and content, this time with reference to a physiognomy that closely correlates outward appearance and inward behavior. When John believes that Hubert has performed the order (because at this point it is confirmed as being indeed an order to kill Arthur), the king's rage and insecurity are violently dashed against the "murderer":

> . . . Hadst thou not been by,
> A fellow by the hand of nature mark'd,
> Quoted and sign'd to do a deed of shame,
> This murther had not come into my mind;
> But taking note of thy abhorr'd aspect,
> Finding thee fit for bloody villainy,
> Apt, liable to be employ'd in danger,
> I faintly broke with thee of Arthur's death.
>
> (4.2.220–27)

Hubert bears on himself the *signs* of evil (never, may it be said, indicated elsewhere in the text), his body reveals his character, for nature, just as it has blessed Arthur with benevolent signs of kingliness, has "mark'd, quoted and sign'd" Hubert with traces of aberration. Once again, however, the "biunivocal correlation" is not respected. The spectators already realize that the mark of the assassin does not necessarily correspond with the body, however deformed it may be.

The Signs of the King

In the universe of medieval signs, to be king one had to be publicly crowned. It was not sufficient to be the king's son, or to be appointed king by one's predecessor—there had to be a ceremony, a ritual which, with the holy unction, indicated the acquisition of the status of king. Indeed, it was only in the reign of Edward I and thereafter that the King of England acquired his title on the death or burial of his father, even before the official ceremony of the coronation.[24] Prior to 1272, the coronation bestowed on the king the status of one who was "anointed by the Lord," a sort of eighth sacrament which shared with priestly ordination the character of nonrepeatability. Shakespeare's John, on the contrary, is crowned twice, or rather three times, respecting the historiographical source.[25] The text contains no trace of the first, true, ceremony; the second is reported as one that has already occurred ("Here once again we sit, once again crown'd," 4.2.1) and that is strongly criticized by the nobles, in the only scene in which Shakespeare seems to be hinting at problems related to the Magna Carta, without however ever explicitly mentioning them. The third is represented, without pomp, in the first scene of the fifth act, when John again receives the crown ("The circle of my glory," line 2) from the hands of Cardinal Pandulph, who presents it to him again as a sign of "Your sovereign greatness and authority" (line 4), as a demonstration of the king's submission to the Pope and the consequent annulment of the interdiction. If, however, the first and second coronations marked John's contested coming to power (it is not surprising that Shakespeare chose not to present them on stage, thus depriving the king of a ceremonial moment of great sign value[26]), the third takes on the significance of a surrender to an external and supernational power. The crown and the ceremony, elsewhere signs of "greatness and authority," now indicate something quite different.

If the crown is (or ought to be) the sign of the king, so too are the seal and the royal decree, since both function as confirmations of the sovereign's word—a word which, however, must be neither ambiguous nor uncertain. The apex of the hierarchical pyramid, both in the feudal world and for some time afterward, was considered to be free of all blame. In 1765, Sir William Blackstone, in his *Commentaries on the Law of England,* pointed out that the sovereign:

> is not only incapable of *doing* wrong, but even of *thinking* wrong: he can never mean to do an improper thing: in him is no folly or weakness.[27]

In contrast, therefore, in the incipit of *King Lear,* in the exchange between Kent and Gloucester regarding the irresolution (madness?) of Lear's decisions, the audience can begin to perceive that "something is wrong," for the sovereign must not show "folly or weakness." John's weakness is manifest from the beginning of the play, following the reiterated accusations of usurpation aimed against him. This weakness is not madness; rather, it derives from the problem of the succession to the throne, which constitutes the main interest of critical studies devoted to the play. But, in addition, John reveals yet another weakness—one much more intimate, one related to his person: his hesitation between word and action. Francis Bacon remarks in his essay, *Of Empire,* that

> The difficulties in princes' business are many and great; but the greatest difficulty is often in their mind. For it is common with princes (saith Tacitus) to will contradictories; "*Sunt plerumque regum voluntates vehementes, et inter se contrariae*": for it is the solecism of power to think to command the end, and yet to endure the mean.[28]

In a prince not up to his task, the Machiavellian clash between the end and the means leads to contradiction. John shows as much in the dialogue with Hubert in 4.2.

The original decision to get rid of Arthur had been clear in the monosyllabic exchange between Hubert and the king:

King John.   Death.
Hubert.   My lord?
King John.   A grave.
Hubert.   He shall not live.
King John.   Enough.
     I could be merry now. Hubert, I love thee.
                                                            (3.2.76–77)

The audience does not get the impression that the order imparted to Hubert is in any way veiled. Possibly the order is merely implicit in the previous lines ("Hubert, throw thine eye / On yon young boy . . . Thou art his keeper," lines 69–74); in the next lines, however, the command is so explicit that there is scarcely any need of the writ mentioned in 4.2.215 (*Hubert.* "Here is your hand and seal for what I did"). Therefore, there can be no doubt: John ordered the murder of his nephew. Yet, in their next encounter, after Hubert has spared young Arthur's life, the sovereign rebukes the courtier for mistaking his "humours for a warrant / To break within the bloody house of life" (lines 209–10). Possibly mindful of the "misunderstanding" between his father, Henry II, and the four knights that led to the murder of Thomas Becket, the king places himself in the long line of rulers whose meaning is misinterpreted: "It is the curse of kings to be attended / By slaves . . ." (lines 208–209). The king admits that he may be subject to changing moods and humors but not to acts of madness such as to drive him to demand the death of a child. Indeed, in the same scene (4.2), just before the dialogue quoted above, John recognizes that Hubert does *not* present the signs of the melancholy that might persuade him to explicitly ask Hubert to commit the crime. In other words, John has his own definition of melancholy, as a disease and a predisposition of the mind toward crime, which, in this scene, he does not discern in his "assassin." But at this point, in 4.2, the king is hesitant to confess his abject wish to Hubert; subsequently, he openly utters the order, only to repent of it two scenes later. What, then, is the king's word worth? "Mad world! mad kings! mad composition!" are the Bastard's first words immediately after he has witnessed the matrimonial agreements of sovereigns who a moment earlier were enemies (2.1.561), when he realizes that the world is "unhinged," with no rules, if even sovereigns can change their minds, turning like weathercocks, and "break faith upon commodity" (line 598). Not only is John's word unreliable, so too is that of all those who call themselves king, as Constance reiterates when she defines Austria and France "these perjur'd kings" (3.1.37).

The king's word is subject to the same changeability and uncertainty as the sign that characterizes the medieval world portrayed in *King John*. The sovereign himself points out its instability: "But thou didst understand me by my signs," John affirms in rebuking Hubert (4.2.237). The "signs," as we have seen, were perfectly clear words, even if now he claims to have spoken "darkly" and not "in express words" (4.2.232, 234). He thus claims to have emanated "symptoms," not signs, and denies any willful purpose to his previous affirmations. Hubert understood him, though, reading the "signs" as such, above all because the king's word means what it says; it has, almost by statute, performative value. But this is no longer true. In a world where possession of the crown does not itself identify the sovereign, the king's word no longer maintains the "biunivocal correlation between the plane of expression and the plane of content."

The discrepancies, the incongruities in the text of the play, and the inconsistencies of which it is accused—all, in my opinion, are merely a reflection of the friction between Tudor historiography (John's reign as the myth of origins) and Shakespeare's interpretation of a world passing through a critical period. Indeed, in *King John* even more than in the other histories, Shakespeare is often obliged to be ambiguous precisely because he is dealing with a subject which, although the most remote in time of his national histories, is among those which caught the main attention of Reformist interpretations.

The epitaph, taken from Bale, emphasizes (to my mind, quite deliberately) all the symbols of regality which, on the contrary, are lacking in Shakespeare's play.[29] Clearly, the propaganda implicit in these lines—that John was a martyr to papal interference in English history—does not question the legitimacy of Plantagenet authority. However, the officially established image, still evinced in *The Troublesome Raigne* and even before from *King Johan*, did not interest Shakespeare, who chose not to represent a king with sword, crown, seal, scepter, and gilded raiment. On the contrary, with a critical reinterpretation of the official sources, Shakespeare presents on stage a character whose very right to wear the kingly symbols is brought into question. And he does so by putting to the test, on various occasions, the relationship between expression and content, assessing its instability, changeability of rapport, and loss of certainty. In this light, the actual symbols of regality found in John's tomb, when it was opened on 30 June 1529, seem a posteriori to remind one, by their extravagance, of the unconfessable dynastic and political necessity of defining John as king, however reluctantly.

Notes

An earlier Italian version of this article appeared in *King John: dal testo alla scena,* ed. Mariangela Tempera (Bologna: CLUEB, 1993).

1. On Shakespeare's work as a historiographer, I agree with P. Pugliatti, who stresses the playwright's critical contribution to the interpretation of England's past and present: "Shakespeare's historical writing was not, as was prescribed to the historians of his time, an act of re-production; it was rather an act of production," an account of history implying "on the one hand a critique of the reproductory procedures of contemporary historiography, and on the other the need to add glosses and comments in the dialogue with tradition" ("'Rex fictae in fabula vera.' Towards a Study of Invention in Shakespeare's History Plays," *Strumenti critici,* 8:1 (1993): 19–35, 29 and 26.

2. Compare Pugliatti, "Dall'evento storico alla storia dell'evento: Shakespeare e la storia inglese," *Messana* 3:14 (1993): 79–89.

3. I refer to studies in the collection edited by D. Curren Aquino, *King John: New Perspectives* (Newark: University of Delaware Press, 1989), and to D. Womersley, "The Politics of Shakespeare's *King John,*" *Review of English Studies,* n.s., 11:160 (1989): 497–515; and J. Dusinberre, "*King John* and Embarrassing Women," *Shakespeare Survey* 42 (1990): 37–52.

4. In particular, Lily B. Campbell, *Shakespeare's Histories* (London: Methuen, 1947); and Marie Axton, *The Queen's Two Bodies* (London: Royal Historical Society, 1977).

5. Compare the essays in *King John: dal testo alla scena,* ed. M. Tempera (Bologna: CLUEB, 1993).

6. Phyllis Rackin, "Patriarchal History and Female Subversion in *King John,*" in D. Curren Aquino, *King John: New Perspectives,* 76–90; and Dusinberre, "*King John* and Embarrassing Women."

7. E. K. Chambers (1925) defined *King John* an "incoherent patchwork" (cited by E.A.J. Honigman, editor of the Arden edition of the play [London: Methuen, 1967], xxxi, note 2; the following quotations are taken from this edition). E.M.W. Tillyard, *Shakespeare's History Plays* (London: Chatto & Windus, 1944), expressed the opinion at the beginning of the chapter on *King John* that "Shakespeare huddles together and fails to motivate properly the events of the last third of his play" (p. 215). The charge is repeated in the closing pages of the same chapter: "In construction the play lacks unity. . . . In sum, although the play is a wonderful affair, full of promise and of new life, as a whole, it is uncertain of itself" (232–33). Tillyard's view is reiterated by Robert B. Pierce, *Shakespeare's History Plays: The Family and the State* (Ohio State University Press, 1971): "*King John* is a rich but untidy play," page 144; and by Edna Zwick Boris,

Shakespeare's English Kings, the People and the Law (London: Associated University Presses, 1978), in which the difficulty of arriving at a "unified interpretation" of the play is put down to "inconsistencies" in the text (131).

8. The *Psalterium,* an illuminated volume which unfortunately lacks some of the first pages (the genealogy of the English sovereigns stops with John's ascension to the throne, while the last date reported is 1204, that of the death of "alianoris regina franciae et angliae"), probably dates back to the 14th century, considering its binding and calligraphy. It is preserved in Italy, in the Imola Town Library. Curiously, it bears the signature "Tho. Mo.," and Thomas More has therefore been conjectured as its possible one-time possessor.

9. "The Early Middle Ages," in K. O. Morgan, ed., *The Oxford History of Britain* (Oxford: Oxford University Press, 1990 [1988]), 145.

10. Serpieri, "Il crollo della gerarchia medioevale in *King Lear,*" *Il piccolo Hans* 19 (July–September 1978).

11. Traister, "The King's One Body: Unceremonial Kingship in *King John,*" in Aquino, *King John,* 91–98.

12. Trevelyan, *History of England* (London: Longmans, Green, 1926), 155.

13. Ibid., 145.

14. Lines 2597–2600. The quotation is taken from the text given in P. Happé, ed., *The Complete Plays of John Bale,* 2 vols (Cambridge: D. S. Brewer, 1985–86).

15. Campbell, *Shakespeare's Histories,* 162–64.

16. Jurij M. Lotman and Boris Uspenskij, "Sul meccanismo semiotico della cultura," in Lotman and Uspenskij, *Tipologia della cultura* (Milan: Bompiani, 1975), 49.

17. Jurij M. Lotman, "Il problema del segno e del sistema segnico nella tipologia della cultura russa prima del XX secolo," in Lotman and Uspenskij, eds., *Ricerche semiotiche* (Turin: Einaudi, 1973), 56.

18. Ernst H. Kantorowitz, *The King's Two Bodies: A Study in Medieval Political Theology* (Princeton: Princeton University Press, 1957), 358ff.

19. Ibid., 362.

20. *King Lear,* Arden edition, ed. K. Muir (London: Methuen, 1972).

21. *Hamlet,* Arden edition, ed. H. Jenkins (London: Methuen, 1982).

22. J. Dusinberre, "*King John* and Embarrassing Women," note 7.

23. Umberto Eco, *Il problema estetico in Tommaso d'Aquino* (Milan: Bompiani, 1970), esp. 89–153, 157–65, and 92.

24. Kantorowitz, *King's Two Bodies,* 329: "Edward did not have to wait until his coronation, which was consummated only in 1274, to assume full power; he, too, began to count his regnal years, contrary to the hitherto valid practice in England, from the day of his accession."

25. R. Holinshed (*Chronicles,* 3, 1587, 165.i) attests that in 1202, with regard to the second coronation, "king Iohn, comming ouer to England, caused himselfe to be crowned againe at Canterburie" and that for the "third," in 1213, "shortlie after (in like manner as pope Innocent had commanded) he [king John] tooke the crowne from his own head, and delivered the same to Pandulph the legat. . . . Then Pandulph keeping the crowne with him for the space of fiue daies in token of possession thereof, at length (as the popes vicar) gaue it him againe" (177, i, ii). G. Bullough, ed., *Narrative and Dramatic Sources of Shakespeare,* 8 vols. (London: Routledge & Kegan Paul, 1962), 4:31–32, 40. It should be remembered that *The Troublesome Raigne* gives the second coronation more space than does *King John,* representing it on stage (1:1538ff.) in solemn tones.

26. On the lack of rituality and ceremony in *King John,* see Traister, "The King's One Body," 92–93.

27. Quoted in Kantorowitz, *King's Two Bodies,* 4.

28. The essay was written in 1612 and amplified in 1625. The quotation is taken from *Essays or Counsels Civil and Moral of Francis Bacon* (London: Collins, n.d.), 170.

29. The epitaph refers to a discovery made at Worchester on 30 June 1529, when stonemasons building a new tomb for the king found the remains of the old sepulchre. The text was transcribed by Bale in his copy of the *Annales Regum Angliae* by Nicholas Trevet (cited in *The Complete Plays of John Bale,* ed. P. Happé, 1: 151; 2: 1–2, 9–12).

"Let her witness it": The Rhetoric of Desdemona

MICHELE MARRAPODI

I

"O, falsely, falsely murder'd,"[1] miraculously whispers Desdemona after being stifled by Othello. Her temporary resurrection has, to some extent, the same symbolic and thaumaturgic function as Hermione's return to life,[2] with the obvious difference that in the idyllic and pastoral atmosphere of the romance—in which symbolism and suggestion blend in *mythos,* replacing the individual tensions and the pathos of tragedy—the jealousy of Leontes does not have irreparable consequences, and the queen's feigned death contributes to the process of expiation and rebirth of a monarch and a reign. Nor is Desdemona's dying voice exhausted in the framework of a natural, predictable epiphenomenon subsequent to the horrid and grotesque events of certain Jacobean tragedies in which an exasperated delight in horror is often related to the revival of certain elements of the medieval *danse macabre,* and to intertextual legacies from Italian Senecan tragedies.[3] In *Othello,* Desdemona's last words perform a specific dramatic purpose, one profoundly linked to the moral significance of the play and to the consistency of her own characterization. The iteration "falsely, falsely" helps revive in the Moor, even if only gradually, a human conscience that Iago's "poison" has monstrously altered, while at the same time being anaphorically associated with the previous, highly effective iteration in line 85 ("O Lord, Lord, Lord!"), which imbues the whole episode with unmistakable religious connotations.[4] The rhetorical figure prevalent throughout the final scene does indeed appear to be *geminatio,*[5] accentuating, by force of repetition, the pathos of Othello's "heavy hour."[6]

Desdemona's second pronouncement, "A guiltless death I die" (5.2.123), once again emphasizes her innocence; while the third and last, in reply to Emilia's question, is no longer, as R. B. Heilman says, "a denial of wrongdoing, but the acting of goodness: the assertion not of one's innocence or goodness but of that of the evildoer, shielding him but, more than that, forgiving him:"[7]

Emilia. O, who has done this deed?
Desdemona. Nobody, I myself, farewell:
Commend me to my kind lord, O, farewell!
(5.2.124–26)

According to Heilman, Desdemona "represents the world of the spirit which Iago must by philosophical necessity destroy."[8] Hers is a metaphysical bond that transcends the natural confines of human love and triumphs over Iago's perverseness. Yet the power of this spiritual force is not sufficient to rid Othello of his egoism. The Moor realizes he has lost a faithful companion, but "he does not know," Heilman states, "that he has lost the woman who could forgive him and ask him to think well of her. This is his ultimate obtuseness."[9]

This limitative judgment on Othello reflects, as it were, on the dramatic role of the heroine, reducing the significance of her miraculous return to life, which Heilman himself stresses and exalts. My claim in this essay is that the two characters move on two parallel planes which are closely related and therefore interdependent. Desdemona's death represents a victory over evil, inasmuch as it leads to Othello's redemption, to his purification, and to the reestablishment of a moral and spiritual order. Only from this perspective does her temporary resurrection acquire a symbolical connotation which marks the victory of the spirit over the flesh, of the soul over the body, of divine powers over human frailties. The regained union of the two lovers is expressed not only by the overturning of the deceitful world of disrupted and subverted values ideologically represented in the blasphemous and oppositive language that is typical of Iago and other Shakespearean villains ("Heaven/hell," "true/false," "fair/foul," "white/black," and so on)[10] but also by the gradual process of resolution of the subtle and cunning game of antitheses and oxymorons which the Ancient's astute rhetoric has implanted in the mind of the Moor.[11] Desdemona's words thus acquire dramatic significance if uttered *for* Othello, for his moral salvation and catharsis; if, in other words, they can provoke an expected, albeit tragic, denouement. That her conative appeal is addressed to the Moor, in particular, is evident from the stress placed on the information and on who is to receive it: "falsely, falsely," "A guiltless death," "Commend me to my kind lord." It is a stress that characterizes the entire linguistic code of the sequence and of the character, moves along a dual performatory and deictic track,[12] and acts first on the external axis (guiding the spectators' attention) and then on the internal axis (influencing Emilia and Othello) in an action operating on the three levels—rhetorical, ideological and allegorical—of dramatic discourse.

In Desdemona's calvary, we may perceive an echo of the Christian myth of the Passion of Christ, which is meaningful only insofar as it serves to redeem humanity: "Father, forgive them; for they know not what they do" (Luke, 23:34). Similarly, the Moor's self-portrait of a man who loved "not wisely, but too well" suggests an identification with Mary Magdalene, the fallen woman, who was forgiven "for she loved much" (Luke, 7:47), an image that contrasts with the sense of guilt and remorse expressed in the successive *similitudo* of the "base Indian" who "threw a pearl away, / Richer than all his tribe" (Matthew, 13:45–46).[13]

The biblical background to this and other plays is part of the semantic richness of Shakespeare's dramatic language and derives from conventions and the *ethos* of the age and from the general polysemy of the theatrical text. The purely Christian view of *Othello* and other tragedies, offered by a certain kind of monistic interpretation which sees in the main characters explicit and unequivocal theological allegorizations, is contrary to the purpose of Shakespeare's dramatic art and of theater as a genre.

Much of *Othello* criticism, indeed, has been devoted to complicated but sterile disquisitions on the theme of the Moor's salvation/damnation, using religious parameters that are highly implausible, if not contrary to the theological doctrine of the time.[14] Commenting on these paradoxical positions, Roland M. Frye aptly points out:

> Shakespeare emerges . . . as a man who seems to have known Christian doctrine intimately, though not on any professional plane. His references to the commonplace topics of theology are never introduced into drama for doctrinaire reasons, and the action of the plays is never subservient to the presentation of any systematic theology.[15]

Edward Hubler's ironic remark is even more straightforward: "Unless we are told where a character goes when he goes off the stage, he doesn't go anywhere at all."[16]

The religious aspect is therefore simultaneously present in the text with the other sign pointers, but acts—as always in Shakespeare—on an ethical and moral plane rather than on a specifically theological one. Whatever the case, the figure of the heroine takes on a greater dimension than is generally recognized; her function—as the present essay will attempt to demonstrate—is not merely marginal or parallel to the agon between Othello and Iago but becomes fundamental and essential for the dynamic of the action and for the realization of an allegorical opposition between Good and Evil on which the Moor has to make his own choice.

II

The inconsistency of some critical judgments in the evaluation of Desdemona—the accusation that she is either excessively passive or too intolerant and rebellious—is as mistaken as the tendency to see her as a detached "Christ-like figure."[17] In order to point out the contradictions of past criticism, with a view to a reassessment of the character of Desdemona, I will briefly summarize the traditional positions of some highly influential historical scholars.

For John W. Draper, Desdemona's characterization shifts considerably after Act I.[18] In the Council scene, Desdemona—like Portia—faces a public trial in which, with exceptional confidence, she claims the right to choose her own husband. This stand, so contrary to the custom of the age, is explained by Draper as an attempt on Shakespeare's part to reconcile two diametrically opposed cultures, Elizabethan and Venetian. In the later acts, the rigid social conventions of Venetian culture override the more flexible Elizabethan ways, which allowed a certain liberty; and Desdemona's character becomes suddenly docile, submissive, obedient to her husband's strangest whims, with a totally passive and childlike behavior which Draper sees reflected in a change in the rhythm of her language.[19] According to this view, Shakespeare thus made the play more plausible to the Elizabethan public and in particular diverted the spectator's attention from the fact that she "wooed a husband for herself" and "deceived a father and made him die of bitterness"[20] with a gesture of defiance and rebellion that was to cause his death.

G. Bonnard rejects the theory of the two cultures but agrees with Draper's overall interpretation.[21] The secret marriage and Desdemona's resolute, undaughterly attitude toward her father are explained by the strong attraction that binds her to the Moor. Othello also commits a tragic error when he allows her to accompany him to Cyprus at a time of a dangerous war with the Turks, showing—from the very beginning—that his reason is dominated by passion, which, ironically, he believes he can keep under control. This makes the two lovers "defenceless against evil," for they are both devoid "of common sense, of reason, of all awareness of the life around them."[22]

Margaret L. Ranald is even more outspoken in her condemnation of Desdemona's "gross revolt."[23] Desdemona is "hardly the perfect maiden according to Elizabethan ideals of feminine and filial conduct." Indeed, "she is not really the perfect wife according to the same code."[24] The parameters of comparison are the "courtesy books" of the age, which Ranald analyzes, concluding that Desdemona's attitude is totally contrary to contemporary conventions. It is only in the last two acts that she seems to acquire a truly docile, meek, and submissive character; but, at this point, her previous conduct has precipitated the tragedy. This would remove, in Ranald's opinion, a great deal of blame from Othello's shoulders, and it does explain the twisted image Iago has of her.

S. N. Garner draws our attention to the aspect of social and racial disparity.[25] The tragedy revolves around the impossible, ill-auspicious union of two lovers of different races, cultures, and customs. Desdemona does not fall in love with Othello but with a virile, heroic, military image she has not found among her Venetian suitors. "She must recognize in Othello," states Garner, "a dignity, energy, excitement, and power that all around her lack. Since these qualities are attributable to his heritage, she may be said to choose him because he is African, black, an outsider."[26] That is why—when his behavior changes—she appears confused, bewildered, helpless. In her remark about Lodovico (4.3.35), and even in her final words, Garner reads an admission of her fatal initial error of marrying the wrong man. Othello, too, is a victim of faulty judgment. He marries a woman he cannot fully know, owing to the evident divergence between their respective cultures; whereas Iago is the only character who understands the diversity, exploiting it for his own ends. For this reason, Garner concludes, "*Othello* is surely one of Shakespeare's bleakest tragedies." In contrast to other tragedies, the protagonists die without catharsis and anagnorisis, for "Desdemona and Othello are finally denied even that knowledge."[27]

These unfavorable, sometimes even contradictory, judgments conceal the post-Romantic and Bradleyan tendency that privileges the narrative texture of the play and considers the characters in psychological terms of plausibility and apparent reality, as if they were actual living creatures totally detached from a fictitious dramatic context obeying its own code of *situational* communication that is basically rhetorical and paralinguistic—that is, operating also at a supersegmental level with many kinesic, proxemic, mimetic and gestural implications.[28]

Unlike prose fiction, claims Alessandro Serpieri, discussing the specificity of dramatic language, "the theater is bound by its nature to the process of enunciation; it needs a pragmatic context; its temporal axis is always based on the present; its space is *deixis*."[29] The entire communicative potentiality of dramatic language—both at the syntagmatic, interactive, and correlational level among the *dramatis personae* and at the paradigmatic, metalinguistic, and extrascenic level—is established by means of "a continuous interrelation of instances of discourse in a deictic performative dimension, with multiple opportunity for relations of reciprocal simulation on stage, within the primary simulation which is that instituted from the start between stage and public."[30]

The multidimensional nature of theatrical communication was aptly summed up by the Elizabethans in the term *actio,* which was an essential feature of the oratory and eloquence of ancient authors. In this regard, Wolfgang G. Müller cites a number of examples in Shakespeare, as well as Francis Bacon's essay *Of Boldnesse,* of which I give here the significant opening remarks:[31]

> It is a triuiall Grammar Schoole Texte, but yet worthy a
> wise *Mans* Consideration. Question was asked of *Demosthenes;*
> *What was the Chiefe Part of an Oratour?* He answered, *Action;*
> what next? *Action;* What next again? *Action.*[32]

The chiastic construction of Hamlet's *comunicatio* "suit the action to / the word, the word to the action" (3.2.21–22) has to be interpreted in this light, as is clear from Hamlet's own words:

> Speak the speech, I pray you, as I pronounce it to you,
> trippingly on the tongue; . . . Nor do not saw the air too
> much with your hand, thus; but use all gently . . . O! it
> offends me to the soul to hear a robustious periwig-pated
> fellow tear a passion to tatters, to very rags, to split the
> ears of the groundlings, who for the most part are capable
> of nothing but inexplicable dumb-shows and noise.
> (3.2.1–14)[33]

In an exemplary essay on character construction in *Othello,* Giorgio Melchiori uses the term "action pointers" to define the linguistic and paralinguistic elements implied by this specific meaning of the word "action."³⁴ "Under the heading of 'action' we can include the implicit stage directions in the speeches and all those expressions, exclamations, demonstrative pronouns and adverbs and other deictic parts, which are not really part of a rational argument but verbal gestures, or, as I prefer to call them, action pointers."³⁵

Thus, if we analyze the rhetorical pointers and structures, whose purpose is to suggest individual characterization and provide the text with an accurate interpretative key, some of the contradictions and aporias of certain critical views that overemphasize verbal content will be overcome, and Shakespeare's own directions will be more easily identified. In this regard, a valuable essay by Vanna Gentili has stigmatized the racist and sexist attitudes of certain critical stands, from the eighteenth century to A. C. Bradley, and restored to the figure of Desdemona a role of prime importance and active participation which does not seem to be given adequate recognition in the play.³⁶ This is because Desdemona must struggle against the twisted image the diabolical Iago has made of her and projected on to the stage world. She thus appears to operate, as it were, on two levels: a *real* level, expressed by what she is and says; and an *imaginary* level, represented by what is said or thought of her. The dramatic irony lies in the fact that, in Othello's mind, the second level gradually takes the place of the first, and she "precipitates from that slender surface of social certitudes on which she has hitherto proceeded and finds herself obliged to engage in direct communication with Othello, who lacks the referents which he has been unable to grasp."³⁷ This assessment of Desdemona thus stops short at a sort of involution which the character presents. In the final scenes (4.2, 4.3, 5.2), Desdemona, confused as to her own identity, "helpless within the tight confines of her private existence, regresses . . . to an obstinate yet voluble infantile behavior." Her last message "is solely a desperate negation of everything: she blames herself for her death."³⁸

Similarly, Alessandro Serpieri, in a stimulating and detailed monograph,³⁹ speaks of the "sudden infantile regression of Desdemona, who, overwhelmed by Othello's unjust vituperative fury, *becomes a child again,* and begins to have self doubts and to desire a 'consolatory' punishment."⁴⁰ This immature image of the character, which contrasts with the "capricious and rebellious" figure in Act 1, is interpreted in psychoanalytic terms:

> First disobedient, not only to her father but also to her nation and the codes of tradition; then obedient to the point of masochism, frightened,

bewildered. Attracted by the "different," a fetishist . . ., a character drawn to the world of the imagination, she now perceives, with an intensity that will increase until the end, the dark side of that "different" which she had seen as something "marvellous."[41]

Consequently, Serpieri denies Desdemona the charismatic strength of love that produces catharsis and favors nemesis. *Othello* becomes "a psychoanalytical play that invests the episteme of an age." There is no nemesis, since the hero "is not punished within a motivated sacrificial context," and because "his tragedy seems to have no immediate external effect, through purification of the passions."[42] In Serpieri's view, the rhetorical figure that characterizes Iago's idiolect is litotes, together with the other tropes of suspension and dissimulation; while, for Othello, it is hyperbole. As for Desdemona:

> She moves in a linguistic field that is dramatic and of difficult interpretation: overwhelmed by Othello's unconventional hyperbole . . . in one bound she leaps over the taboos of her culture. She is zestful, clear-headed, adventurous; but she is also a prisoner of her imagination. . . . For when she is assaulted by Othello's destructive fury, which she cannot understand, she is compelled to take refuge in *regression* and, consequently, in a childlike language of extraordinary dramatic effect.[43]

Giorgio Melchiori's opinion is somewhat different. In his view, Desdemona's language "exhibits a constant simplicity and propriety of grammatical and syntactical patterns that reveal a proper education in the art of speaking. . . . Desdemona's is the rhetoric of the natural aristocrat and remains such throughout, uncontaminated (unlike that of Othello) by Iago's influence."[44]

This observation seems to me extremely useful for defining Desdemona. Her manner of speech is, in fact, completely antithetical to that of Iago: Desdemona's is univocal, exclamative, paraphrastic, tending toward the *affirmation* of human and divine qualities, in touch with human reality and existence and symbolizing the world of truth and being. Iago's, on the other hand, is ambiguous, contrastive, reticent, dependent on *negation* and expressing a simulating and dissimulating will whose purpose is deception and persuasion, using refined rhetorical techniques of suspension and suggestion, and concealing in tautology and *amplificatio* a mask of apparent virtue. According to Heinrich F. Plett, the typology of the characters corresponds so closely to the general strategy of the stylistic models employed in the play that it is possible to distinguish three different rhetorical types in Iago, Othello, and Desdemona.⁴⁵ In Plett's view, Desdemona, like Cordelia, represents the anti-rhetorical character par excellence who has no need of oratory to assert her values and her identity ("What shall Cordelia speak? Love, and be silent." *King Lear,* 1.1.62);⁴⁶ hence, the contrast with Iago, who, on the contrary, uses rhetoric to conceal his true feelings and to convince his listeners.

I therefore believe that, parallel to the traditional interpretation which relegates Desdemona to a minor role, wholly subordinate to the main agon between Othello and Iago, it is possible to make an allegorical reading which privileges the eternal conflict between Good and Evil in the age-old terms of the Morality Play and illuminates—in a kind of moral *psychomachia*—the obscure and indefinite aspects of the two extreme and most complex characters in the play.⁴⁷

III

In the great scene in the Council Chamber (1.3), Brabantio asks his daughter, who has been summoned to give evidence about her flight and marriage to Othello: "Do you *perceive* in all this noble company, / Where most you owe obedience?" (1.3.179–80).⁴⁸ Desdemona's reply shows from the start that she distinguishes clearly between duty and affection, between a daughter's love and a wife's. It is no coincidence that she uses the same verbal voice and form as her father, but she resolves their ambiguity and tendentiousness by using a markedly emphatic form that also operates on the deictic level: "*I do perceive here* a divided duty" (181). The "divided duty" she mentions does not concern only her feelings but refers, above all, to her father's convictions. Hence, the attempt to correct Brabantio's false principles and perverse social ethic by using the didactic method of comparison ("so much *duty* as *my* mother show'd / To *you,* preferring *you* before *her* father," 1.3.186–87), which from these first lines testifies to the prevalently didascalic nature of all her linguistic code. Like Iago and Roderigo, Brabantio judges by appearances, by what he believes to be upright and natural, and consistent with rigid social and cultural rules which impose on him fixed moral and racial principles: Othello is a black, a soldier, a savage; so why should Desdemona "fall in love with what she fear'd *to look on?*" (1.3.98). It is interesting to note the frequent use of verbs of perception which serve to underline the mistaken reliance on man's deceptive outward senses.⁴⁹ The constant Shakespearean dichotomy between seeming and being, illusion and reality, is thus already beginning to take form in Act 1, marking all the sign pointers of the play's linguistic structure. Desdemona realizes at once that this "division" is irreparable. Like Cordelia, she must struggle against a world of false ethical and moral values, a world based on outward show and appearances. Once more, however, she makes an attempt at communication with her father, ironically yet again disrupting the linguistic code to which he is accustomed. To Brabantio's refusal to keep her with him, pending the Moor's return, she rejoins:

> I would not *there* reside,
> To put my father in impatient thoughts,
> By being in his *eye*.
>
> (1.3.241–43)

and then asks the Duke if she may follow her husband, whose true qualities she alone has been able to read in his mind: "*I saw* Othello's visage in *his* mind, / And to *his* honours, and *his* valiant parts / Did *I my* soul and fortunes consecrate" (1.3.252–54). In these words, Desdemona not only shows a capacity for profound insight that is denied to the other characters, but also, by stressing the blackness of Othello's face, she implicitly rebuts the stereotyped, racist prejudices just pronounced by Iago, Roderigo, and Brabantio.[50] Indeed, the Duke, led by Desdemona's calm, balanced, but highly effective rhetoric, cannot but declare, at the conclusion of the Council meeting, "Your son-in-law is far more *fair* than black" (1.3.290); while Brabantio marks his exit from the stage and from the play with a couplet which once again demonstrates his misjudgment and his spiritual "blindness" and which opens up the metaphorical pathway along which, from this moment onward, Iago's perfidious imaginative and rhetorical techniques will proceed:

> *Look* to *her*, Moor, have a quick *eye to see:*
> *She* has deceiv'd *her* father, may do *thee*.
>
> (1.3.292–93)

IV

The first scene in Act 2 offers us, in the comic remarks—rich in obscene double entendres—which Iago exchanges with Desdemona, the only episode in which the two characters face each other. They meet again, it is true, on later occasions, but their exchanges are shorter and less significant; for the conflict between Desdemona and Iago is played out at a distance, indirectly, on a symbolic-allegorical plane. Hence, the relative importance of this sequence, which, however, has generally been underestimated or judged in terms of an alleged violation of the rules of decorum. Yet, in the words of Madeleine Doran, "English dramatists never were slaves of decorum"[51] and Shakespeare, after Desdemona has declared "I am not merry, but I do beguile / The thing I am, by seeming otherwise" (2.1.122–23), contrives to make his heroine perceive some aspects of the Ancient's ambiguous nature and attack his disrespectful misogyny. Thus, Iago's improvised womanhating couplets are taken as "old paradoxes, to make fools laugh i' the / alehouse" (2.1.138–39); his use of antinomy and *vituperatio*, of which he is so fond, is evidence of "a heavy ignorance, that praises the worst best" (2.1.143); while his egocentric and nihilistic attitude marks him as "a most profane and liberal / counsellor" (2.1.163–64).

These intuitive flashes take on particular importance as metalinguistic acts of communication with the spectators, who have already been offered, in the opening scene, an early example of Iago's oppositive and scurrilous language ("an old *black* ram / Is tupping your *white* ewe," 1.1.88–89) and of his vindictive purposes, expressed in the opening conversation with Roderigo ("*I* follow *him* to serve *my* turn upon *him*," 1.1.42) and in the soliloquy closing Act 1 ("to abuse Othello's ear" 1.3.393).

Iago's ambiguity is also conveyed by rhetorical articulation. The denial "I am not what I am" (1.1.65), which inverts the affirmation of the word of God "I am that I am" (Exodus, 3:14), testifies, as in Viola (*Twelfth Night,* 1.3.155), to the use of dissimulation, a false identity. But, while Viola's disguise is entirely an external feature, being part of the *topos* of the comedy's skirmishes of love, Iago's stresses the duplicity of his nature and is related to the malefic and deceitful behavioral code of the Vice in the morality plays ("those fellows have some souls, / And such a one do I profess myself," 1.1.54–55).

Bernard Spivack, who has written the most convincing and perceptive analysis of the villain that I know of, cites numerous moralities in which the treatment of the vices and the seven deadly sins presents notable affinities with the character construction of Iago.[52] We also find in Thomas Dekker's *The Bel-man of London* the distinctive traits of the Vice perfectly reflected in Iago:

> All *Vices* maske themselues with the vizards of *Vertue*; ...
> They borrow their names, the better and more currantly to
> passe without suspition: for murder will be called *Manhood*,
> *Dronkennesse* is now held to be *Phisick*, *Impudence* is
> *Audacitie*, *Ryot*, good fellowship.[53]

This capacity for dissimulation characterizes all Shakespeare's villains. In *Richard III*, for example, the Duchess of York, mother of the future usurper, is sorry that Richard's behavior "should steal such gentle shape / And with a virtuous vizard hide deep vice" (2.2.27–28); for Hamlet, the corruption and deceit that govern Denmark are summed up in the proverbial saying, "that one may smile, and smile, and be a villain" (1.5.108); and Lady Macbeth urges her husband "Look like the innocent flower, / But be the serpent under't" (1.6.66–67).

Iago, more than other villains, bases the whole success of his diabolical plan on this capacity. His ambivalence is emblematically suggested in his pagan oath in Act 1 ("By Janus, I think no," 1.2.33); the multiform nature of the Vice is also to be seen in his use of different models of simulation in relation to the aims he is pursuing and the persons he is dealing with. According to Brian Vickers,[54] who has analyzed the function of this villain's use of prose,

> Iago's prose persuasions lie not so much in their revelation of his character but in his ability to vary his argument to suit the nature of his listener . . . his arguments to Roderigo depend on proving that Desdemona is a character of shallow, changeable appetite, whereas those to Cassio turn on his proof that she is kind and virtuous; again to Roderigo he must play upon the dupe's self-interest and wish for revenge, while to Cassio he must rescue his victim's contrite condition by belittling the value of reputation. . . . we are keyed up to the act of watching him in the act of persuading others, and varying his whole style, argument, character, even his metabolism to suit the purpose.[55]

Vickers speaks of Iago's "chameleon ability," the demoniac quality he manifests with morbid pride when he speaks in verse.[56] In Act 2, Scene 3, in which he persuades Cassio to seek Desdemona's intercession in order to regain his rank, Iago identifies himself with the traditional archetypal image of the enemy of man:

> How am I then a villain,
> To counsel Cassio to this parallel course,
> Directly to his good? Divinity of hell!

> When devils will their blackest sins put on,
> They do suggest at first with heavenly shows,
> As I do now.
>
> (2.3.339–44)

The use of rhetoric as a means of dissimulation naturally dominates the great temptation scene. The *aposiopesis* "Ha, I like not that" (3.3.35) initiates the subtle work of hidden persuasion that characterizes Iago's operating strategy. He uses all the tropes of suspension, but also interjections, hesitations, deictics, and paralinguistic elements which produce a shift from the first phase of *reticentia* and *interruptio* to the successive phase of *descriptio actionis,* the effectiveness of which constitutes the true phantasmal force of his words:

> *Iago.*   *Ha*, I like not *that*.
> *Othello.* What dost *thou* say?
> *Iago.*   *Nothing*, my lord, or *if*— *I* know *not what*.
> *Othello.* Was not that Cassio parted from *my* wife?
> *Iago.*   Cassio, my lord? . . . *no,* sure, *I cannot* think *it,*
>   That *he* would sneak away so *guilty-like,*
>   Seeing *you* coming.
>
> (3.3.35–41)

The gradual persuasion of Othello passes through a number of ironic "recitations" of various "*ocular* proof(s)" which serve to destroy the ethical, moral, and sensorial convictions of the Moor—that is, create a dramatic confusion of illusion and reality. Thus, the imaginary *actio* of adultery is visualized in the crude, bestial terms of mating animals: "Would *you,* the supervisor, grossly *gape on,* / Behold her topp'd?" (3.3.401–402). The evidence of the betrayal is strengthened in the psychological impact of the account of Cassio's dream (3.3.425–32), and of how Cassio uses Desdemona's handkerchief ("such a handkerchief— / I am sure it was *your* wife's—did *I* today / *See* Cassio wipe *his* beard with," 3.3.444–46); and finally in the ironic *dubitatio* of the word play on the verb *to lie,* with which Iago, at the beginning of Act 4, sardonically leaves the Moor the choice of the most painful solution ("With her, on her, what *you* will," 4.1.34).

Othello now sees through Iago's eyes; illusion has supplanted reality. The slender defensive arguments presented by the Moor are, moreover, related to the visual faculties, to external reality (". . . *she* had *eyes,* and chose *me*. No, Iago, / *I*'ll *see* before *I* doubt, when *I doubt,* prove," 3.3.193–94), which Iago cunningly puts to his own good use ("*I* speak *not* yet of proof; / *Look* to your wife, *observe* her well with Cassio; / Wear your *eye thus*, not jealous, nor secure," 3.3.200–202). The moment is thus ripe for the most deceptive and convincing proof: the pantomime of Cassio's confession. Iago passes from the *descriptio actionis* to the representation of the *actio* itself,[57] which Othello sees only in the kinesic, mimetic and gestural terms in which it is presented to him:

> . . . *mark* the *jeers*, the *gibes*, and notable *scorns*,
> That dwell in every region of *his* face
> For *I* will make *him* tell the tale anew,
> *Where, how, how oft, how long* ago, and *when,*
> *He* has, and is again to cope *your* wife:
> *I say,* but *mark* his *gesture.*
>
> (4.1.82–87)

This is, without any doubt, one of the most extraordinary scenes in the entire Shakespeare canon. On the one hand, it marks the climax of Iago's triumph, the moment when his utopia of illusion and deceit—as Rosa Maria Colombo puts it—achieves its most concrete and real application;[58] while, on the other hand, it is the apotheosis of theater, the living proof of the tremendous flexibility and performativity of Shakespearean drama after the great experience of *Hamlet.*[59]

V

Desdemona's style of rhetoric tends, on the contrary, not toward the *reduction* of information but rather toward its *augmentation.* The oratorical character of her linguistic code is directed toward the performance of a "defensive" and/or "declarative" function with which she attests, affirms, and manifests her metadramatic role.

I have already shown how in Act 1 Desdemona efficaciously defends Othello from the charge of seduction and the use of magic arts, and how she implicitly declares her own values by denouncing her father's perverse social ethic. This same rhetorical strength, known to the classical rhetoricians as *energeia,*[60] she puts to use, though with tragic results, in her defense of Cassio:

> . . . I'll *perform* it
> To the last article; my lord shall never rest,
> I'll watch him tame, and talk him out of patience;

> His bed shall seem a school, his board a shrift,
> I'll intermingle every thing he does
> With Cassio's suit; therefore be merry, Cassio,
> For thy *solicitor* shall rather die
> Than give thy cause away.
>
> (3.3.21–28)

In the scene following this, after the dramatic cross-examination about the missing handkerchief—which Desdemona attempts to exorcise of the magic power against evil attributed to it by Othello ("Then would to God that I had never seen it!," 3.4.75)—she once again refers to her forensic role ("my *advocation* is not now in tune," 3.4.120); at the same time, she reaffirms her understanding of her husband, her confidence that he will be able to reconsider and to return to his former reason and love. Significantly, the Moor's behavior is generalized: Othello is described in the guise of *Everyman,* and therefore subject to the natural weaknesses of man:[61]

> Men's natures wrangle with inferior things,
> Though great ones are the object.
> 'Tis even so; for let our finger ache,
> And it indues our other healthful members
> Even to that sense of pain; nay, we must think
> Men are not gods;
> Nor of them look for such observances
> As fits the bridal: . . .
> But now I find I had suborn'd the *witness,*
> And he's *indicted* falsely.
>
> (3.4.141–52)

Act 4 marks the passage of Desdemona's role from "forensic" to "declarative." Ironically, Desdemona is now obliged to defend *herself* from an unknown accusation. In her own defense, she once again uses the only parameters she knows: attesting her qualities with illocutionary speech acts, the purpose of which is to affirm human and divine values. But there is no longer any communication between Othello and Desdemona ("Upon my knees, what does your speech import? / I understand a fury in your words, / *But not the words.*" 4.2.31–33). The "music" that united their souls has been interrupted and subverted by Iago, and the Moor translates every declaration by his wife into its opposite. It is significant that he expresses himself in the contrastive language of Iago: *affirmation* is transformed into *negation* and *antimetabole:*

Othello.	Why, what art thou?
Desdemona.	Your wife, my lord, your *true* and *loyal* wife.
Othello.	Come, *swear* it, damn thyself, Lest, being like one of *heaven,* the *devils* themselves Should fear to seize thee, therefore be double-damn'd, *Swear* thou art *honest.*
Desdemona.	*Heaven* doth *truly* know it.
Othello.	*Heaven truly* knows, that thou art *false* as *hell.*

(4.2.34–40)

Desdemona realizes that the confusion in Othello's mind is due to a reversal of the normal linguistic codes ("fair/foul," "true/false," "heaven/hell")[62] and she tries to re-establish contact with him through the illocutionary force of her own declaration of faith, stressing the true meaning of the referents she uses:

Desdemona.	By *heaven,* you do me wrong.
Othello.	Are not you a strumpet?
Desdemona.	No, as I am a *Christian:* If to preserve this vessel for my lord From any *hated foul unlawful* touch, Be not to be a strumpet, I am none.
Othello.	What, not a whore?
Desdemona.	No, as I shall be *saved.*

(4.2.83–88)

But the attempt fails. The chaos ruling Othello's mind prevents him from distinguishing Good from Evil, reality from appearance.[63] The most he can manage is oxymoron, the antithetical coexistence of terms, combining in the same line contrary ethical and religious values. Thus, Desdemona, already described as a "fair devil," now seems to him a "*black* weed" which yet exhales sweet fragrance ("why art so lovely *fair?*," 4.2.69). It is natural that Desdemona should be upset and bewildered by Othello's conduct ("How have I been behav'd," 4.2.110); even so, she does not abandon the ethical and spiritual paradigms she has followed thus far. The "eternal villain," whose slanderous acts are to Emilia's pragmatic mind the only logical explanation of Othello's change, she immediately forgives ("If any such there be, heaven pardon him!," 4.2.137). The "unutterable" accusation that her husband has laid against her is significantly answered by her Christian oath ("Here I kneel," 4.2.153), which anaphorically recalls to the spectator's mind the other, pagan oath between Othello and Iago by which the latter takes absolute possession of the Moor's power of reason ("I am your own for ever," 3.3.486). Desdemona's distress at Othello's insulting words is not, however, sufficient to destroy her love. Indeed, she prophesies to Iago: "his unkindness may defeat *my life,* / But never taint *my love* (4.2.162–63), and in the following scene she declares to Emilia, when the latter says she wishes she had never met her husband,

> So would not I, my love doth so approve him,
> That even his stubbornness, his checks and frowns,—
> Prithee unpin me,—have grace and favour in them.
> (4.3.19–21)

Her mention of Lodovico soon afterwards has often been misinterpreted and should, rather, be seen in relation to the similar, structurally parallel sequence in Act 2, Scene 3. Here, Cassio speaks of Desdemona with respect and admiration ("a most exquisite lady," "a most fresh and delicate creature," 2.3.18, 20), while Iago loads his own remarks with subtle erotic allusions to present her to him in a provocative light ("it sounds a parley of provocation"; "happiness to their sheets!," 2.3.21, 26). This exchange of isotopies, or change of topic,[64] is one of the character's most effective rhetorical techniques, and Emilia, like Iago, takes on the role of temptress in Act 4, Scene 3, shifting Desdemona's remark to the level of physical and sexual attraction:

Desdemona.   This Lodovico is a *proper man.*
Emilia.   A very *handsome man.*
Desdemona.   He speaks well.
Emilia.   I know a lady in Venice would have walk'd bare—
   foot to Palestine for a *touch* of his nether *lip.*
(4.3.35–39)

This enticing function of Emilia is further confirmed in her later remarks when she tries to make her mistress accept her own falsely feminist materialistic credo, according to which she declares herself ready to betray her husband for all the riches of the world ("who would not make her husband a cuckold, to make him a monarch?," 4.3.74–75). Desdemona's categoric refusal to do likewise contrasts allegorically with Iago's successful temptation of Othello:

> Good night, good night: God me such usage send,
> Not to pick bad from bad, but by bad mend!
> (4.3.104–105)

VI

Desdemona's words in Act 5 are few but significant. She leaves her tragic story on tiptoe, in silence, as she has always acted. But we have seen that her language—rather than conforming to an evocative "rhetoric of silence" (*Rhetorik des Schweigens*), as suggested by Plett[65]—manifests itself, despite the limited number of utterances, as an illocutionary force, characterized by a grave and solemn sense of sacrality and devotion which acts in the play with a marked and lasting epideictic and hierophantic action.

With the aid of the distinction made by Flavia Ravazzoli on the levels of rhetorical communication,[66] I will list below some of the more significant examples of the two contrary rhetorical codes of Iago and Desdemona:

DESDEMONA	VS	IAGO
Amplifying axis		*Attenuating axis*
Heaven keep that monster from Othello's mind!		I am not what I am.
Heaven doth truly know it.		By Janus, I think no.
By heaven, you do me wrong.		Nay, it is true, or else I am a Turk.
No, as I am a Christian.		I am nothing if not critical.
No, as I shall be sav'd.		As honest as I am.
O heaven, forgiveness.		As I am an honest man.
Nay, heaven doth know.		I dare presume, I think, he is honest.
If any such there be, heaven pardon him!		I am a very villain else.
Then heaven have mercy on me!		I bleed sir, but not kill'd.
Then Lord have mercy on me!		From this time forth, I never will speak a word.
O Lord, Lord, Lord!		

One may note that some rhetorical structures are similar ("*as I am a Christian*" vs "*as I am an honest man*") but are different in their intent or, rather, in what Ravazzoli defines as "lexicalized" and "pragmatic" axiality.[67] The first of these is expressed purely by linguistic means and participates in the direct increment of information; the second also involves extralinguistic, psychological, social, and intersemiotic aspects. This classification is clearly not absolute, and there are continuous interchanges giving rise to a multiplicity of possibilities. It does, however, seem possible to distinguish in Desdemona's linguistic code a massive presence of apodeictic affirmations (that is, *statements*)—*metasememes* in the Belgian group's nomenclature—often tending toward didacticism and operating on the level of lexicalized communication;[68] whereas Iago makes obsessive use of the tropes of negation and suspension (*understatements* and *overstatements*)—*metalogisms* for the Liège group—whose oblique purpose is to persuade without revealing one's intentions and which are essentially conveyed along the axis of pragmatic communication.

All that remains to be said is a word about the outcome, the results which the two characters achieve. In this respect, it is clear that it is particularly in Acts 3 and 4 that Desdemona loses the contest with Iago (when he succeeds in imposing on Othello the phantasmal fabula that will lead him to commit murder, employing with perfidious mastery all the metalogical and paralinguistic means that the evolution of the play makes available to him) because she expresses herself with illocutionary speech acts that do not produce—in Austin's terms—perlocutionary effectiveness.[69] Desdemona's sole outright verbal victory occurs in Act 1, in the Council scene, when it is no coincidence that she is in perfect moral and spiritual harmony with Othello. For her words to have perlocutionary effectiveness, for the final defeat of Evil and for the reconquest of Othello, Desdemona must accept to the full her metadramatic role, even to the point of self-sacrifice in order to favor the catharsis of the hero, and this charges her with still more allegorical and moral significance. In addition to the tragedy's basic actantial triangle, proposed by Alessandro Serpieri[70]—agonist (Othello), antagonist (Iago), object of desire (Desdemona)—I would claim the existence, within the semiotic folds of the dramatic texture of the play, a different triangulation with a change of vertex: Othello as the "object of desire" in the allegorical conflict between Desdemona and Iago.

This more active and positive role of Desdemona clearly implies a greater sense of awareness in the character. Indeed, she immediately perceives the mental chaos lying beneath the apparent calm of Othello's great soliloquy, the grotesque and contradictory sense of justice that dominates his thoughts ("Be thus, when thou art dead, and I will kill thee, / And love thee after." 5.2.18–19), and roundly declares as much:

> *Othello.* Think on *thy* sins.

Desdemona.	They are loves *I* bear to *you.*
Othello.	And for *that thou* diest.
Desdemona.	*That* death's *unnatural,* that kills for *loving.*

(5.2.40–42)

Yet, it is precisely on Desdemona's martyrdom, her Christian resignation, that the Moor's rehabilitation depends. After a moment of bewilderment following his wife's unexpected forgiveness, Othello gradually returns to the rediscovery of lost values, to the resolution of the opposites and the antitheses Iago has inculcated in him. The "just grounds" on which he believes he has proceeded—ironically questioned by Emilia with the correct use of terms on which he instead has equivocated ("angel/devil," "heaven/hell," "white/black," "true/false," and so on)—prove mere calumny; and he takes cognizance of his tragic error, which at first may appear to him only "pitiful" but soon to his eyes becomes the sacrilege that will cast him into hell:[71]

> . . . when we shall meet at count,
> This look of thine will hurl my soul from heaven,
> And fiends will snatch at it.

(5.2.274–76)

The "heavenly" creature he has offended and brutally murdered, described first in terms derived from the theory of humors as "hot, hot and moist" (3.4.35),[72] now appears to him "cold, cold, my girl, / Even like *thy chastity*" (5.2.276–77); while Iago is for the first time recognized publicly by Othello as *devil-Vice,* epithets which from this moment onward all the other characters also use for him:

> *I look down* towards *his* feet, but that's a fable,
> If that *thou* be'st a *devil, I* cannot kill *thee.*

(5.2.287–88)

Othello can now see with the inward eye of the mind and discover that which mere outward sight is unable to discern.

Notes

An earlier Italian version of this article appeared in *Nuovi Annali della Facoltá di Magistero dell'Università di Messina,* 2 (1984).

1. Act 5, scene 2, line 118. Line references are to M. R. Ridley's Arden edition (London: Methuen, 1958), which is based on the First Quarto of 1622.

2. *The Winter's Tale,* 5.3. For other Shakespearean works cited, I have used W. J. Craig's edition, *Shakespeare: Complete Works* (London: Oxford University Press, 1905).

3. A good example is John Webster's *The Duchess of Malfi,* in which the murder of the Duchess (4.2), preceded by a macabre dumb show and Bosola's sinister singing, presents a notable series of parallels and contrasts with the death of Desdemona.

4. On this exclamation by Desdemona and its dramatic function, see my article, "*Othello:* 5.2.85: 'O Lord, Lord, Lord!,'" *The Blue Guitar* 2 (1976): 211–17.

5. For the examination of the rhetorical structures of the play, I have used in particular: H. Lausberg, *Elemente der literarischen Rhetorik* (München, 1949); Groupe N, *Rhétorique générale* (Paris: Larousse, 1970); P. Dixon, *Rhetoric* (London: Methuen, 1971); and the contemporary treatise by George Puttenham, *The Arte of English Poesy* (1589), in particular chaps. 10–22, included in the collection edited by G. Gregory Smith, *Elizabethan Critical Essays,* 2 vols. (Oxford: Oxford University Press, 1904), 2:1–193.

6. The most significant instances are: "My wife, my wife, my wife; I ha' no wife" (98); "What needs this iteration? woman, I say thy husband. . . . My friend, thy husband, honest, honest Iago" (151–55); "Villainy, villainy, villainy! (191); "O! O! O! (199); "cold, cold, my girl" (276); "O Desdemona, Desdemona, dead, / Oh, Oh, Oh" (282–83); "what you know, you know" (304); "O fool, fool, fool!" (324).

7. Heilman, *Magic in the Web: Action and Language in 'Othello'* (Lexington: University of Kentucky Press, 1956), 215–16.

8. Ibid., 218.

9. Ibid., 217.

10. On the simulating and dissimulating function of the villain's rhetorical language, see Wolfgang G. Müller, "The Villain as Rhetorician in Shakespeare's *Richard III,*" *Anglia* 102 (1984): 37–59.

11. See my article, "A horned man's a monster, and a beast': Notes on Shakespeare's Treatment of Jealousy as Metamorphosis in *Othello,*" *The Blue Guitar* 3–4 (1977–78): 151–71.

12. John Austin defines as "performatory" the category of verbs, used in the first person singular of the present indicative, which are not descriptive, emotive, or persuasive in character and do not give rise to true or mendacious declarations, as, for example, in the verb forms "I bet," "I swear," "I promise," "I do," "I say," etc. See Austin, "Other Minds," *Proceedings of the Aristotelian Society,* supplement vol. 20 (1946), cited in M. Weitz, *"Hamlet" and the Philosophy of Literary Criticism* (Chicago: University of Chicago Press, 1964), 220–22. See also, Austin, *How To Do Things with Words* (Oxford: Oxford University Press, 1962). A good example of the application of a semiotic approach to Shakespeare is to be found in *Come comunica il teatro: dal testo alla scena,* ed. Alessandro Serpieri et al. (Milan: Il Formichiere, 1978). Serpieri's introductory chapter, "Ipotesi teorica di segmentazione del testo teatrale" (pp. 11–54), provides a clear methodological exposition. In this regard, see also the pioneering essay by Marcello Pagnini "Per una semiologia del teatro classico," *Strumenti Critici,* 12 (1970), 121–40, and the long theoretical introduction by Paola Pugliatti in *I segni latenti: scrittura come virtualità scenica in "King Lear"* (Messina-Florence: D'Anna, 1974), 23–81. For a general survey of the semiotics of the theatrical text, see Keir Elam, *The Semiotics of Theatre and Drama* (London: Methuen, 1980), Jurij Lotman, "Semiotica della scena," *Strumenti critici,* 44 (1981), 1–45, and Marco De Marinis, *Semiotica del teatro* (Milan: Bompiani, 1982).

13. On Shakespeare's wide use of the Bible, see R. Noble, *Shakespeare's Biblical Knowledge* (London: Society for Promoting Christian Knowledge, 1935); and N. Shaheen, *Biblical References in Shakespeare's Tragedies* (Newark: University of Delaware Press, 1987). On Shakespeare's use of biblical myths and archetypes, see Northrop Frye, *The Great Code: The Bible and Literature* (London: Routledge & Kegan Paul, 1982).

14. Let us recall the most important doctrine. Othello's damnation is sustained for a variety of reasons, by the following: H. Granville-Barker, *Prefaces to Shakespeare* 4 (London: Sidgwick & Jackson, 1945); S. L. Bethell, "Shakespeare's Imagery: The Diabolic Images in *Othello*," *Shakespeare Survey* 5 (1952): 62–80; P. N. Siegel, "The Damnation of Othello," *PMLA* 68 (December 1953): 1068–78; *Shakespearian Tragedy and the Elizabethan Compromise* (New York: New York University Press, 1957): 119–41; *Shakespeare in His Time and Ours* (London: University of Notre Dame Press, 1968), 22–68; and A. Gerard, "Egregiously an Ass: The Dark Side of the Moor," *Shakespeare Survey* 10 (1957): 98–106. Among the critics who believe in Othello's salvation, see, in particular, K. O. Myrick, "The Theme of Damnation in Shakespearian Tragedy," *Studies in Philology* 38 (1942): 221–45; and I. Ribner, *Patterns in Shakespearian Tragedy* (London: Methuen, 1960), 91–115. A more modest proposal is advanced by G. R. Elliott, *Flaming Minister* (Durham: University of North Carolina Press, 1953), who believes that Othello's refound awareness merits him at least a place in Purgatory, pp. 234ff.

15. Frye, *Shakespeare and Christian Doctrine* (Princeton: Princeton University Press, 1963), 9; on the discussion of some of the critics mentioned, see pages 19–42.

16. Hubler, "The Damnation of Othello: Some Limitations on the Christian View of the Play," *Shakespeare Quarterly* 9 (1958): 256.

17. See, for example, H. Granville-Barker, *Prefaces to Shakespeare,* 121–26.

18. Draper, "Desdemona: A Compound of Two Cultures," *Revue de Littérature Comparée* 13 (1933): 337–51; by the same critic see also, "Changes in the Tempo of Desdemona's Speech," *Anglica* 1 (1946): 149–53; and *The Othello of Shakespeare's Audience* (Paris: Didier, 1952).

19. Draper, "Changes in the Tempo of Desdemona's Speech," 153.

20. Draper, "Desdemona: A Compound of Two Cultures," 351.

21. Bonnard, "Are Othello and Desdemona Innocent or Guilty?" *English Studies* 30 (1949): 175–84.

22. Ibid., 184.

23. Ranald, "The Indiscretions of Desdemona," *Shakespeare Quarterly* 14 (1963): 127–39.

24. Ibid., 128.

25. Garner, "Shakespeare's Desdemona," *Shakespeare Studies* 9 (1976): 233–52.

26. Ibid., 243.

27. Ibid., 250.

28. See J. L. Styan, *The Elements of Drama* (Cambridge: Cambridge University Press, 1960); *Shakespeare's Stagecraft* (Cambridge: Cambridge University Press, 1967); *Drama, Stage and Audience* (London: Cambridge University Press, 1975); and above, note 12.

29. Serpieri, "Ipotesi di segmentazione del testo teatrale," 15 (italics in original; my translation).

30. Ibid., 25. See also W. Nigel Dodd, "Conversation, Dialogue and Exposition," *Strumenti critici* 44 (1981): 171–91.

31. Müller, "The Villain as Rhetorician in Shakespeare's *Richard III*." According to Müller, "there is one part of rhetoric which forms the connecting link between rhetoric and the art of acting—namely, *actio,* the management of voice and body during the delivery of a speech" (55–56). Müller also cites examples in *Julius Caesar, Othello,* and *Coriolanus,* plus numerous other contemporary instances. For this point, see also, Serpieri, "La retorica a teatro," *Strumenti Critici* 41 (1980): 149–79.

32. *Essays by Francis Bacon* (London: Oxford University Press, 1937), 47; italics in original.

33. See also, in the preceding scene, lines 584ff.

34. Melchiori, "The Rhetoric of Character Construction: *Othello,*" *Shakespeare Survey* 34 (1981): 61–71.

35. Ibid., 62.

36. Gentili, "L'immaginario contro Desdemona," *Nuova DWF* 5 (October–December 1977): 29–54.

37. Ibid., 53; my translation.

38. Ibid., 53–54.

39. Serpieri, *"Othello": l'Eros negato. Psicoanalisi di una proiezione distruttiva* (Milan: Formichiere, 1978).

40. Ibid., 171; italics in original; my translation.

41. Ibid., 172.

42. Ibid., 216, 217.

43. Ibid., 228; italics in original.

44. Melchiori, "The Rhetoric of Character Construction," 67.

45. Plett, "'Action is eloquence': Zur rhetorischen Aktionstypik in Shakespeares *Othello,*" *Germanisch-romanische Monatsschrift* N. F. 32 (1982): 1–21.

46. See W. R. Elton, *King Lear and the Gods* (San Marino, Cal.: The Huntington Library, 1966), pages 75–84.

47. On the complex allegory of Iago, see B. Spivack, *Shakespeare and the Allegory of Evil* (New York: Columbia University Press, 1958); and "Iago—Vice or Devil?" *Shakespeare Survey* 21 (1968): 53–66; also, S. E. Hyman, *Iago: Some Approaches to the Illusion of His Motivation* (London: Elek, 1971).

48. Here and in other lines quoted, the emphasis is mine.

49. See Heilman, *Magic in the Web,* 50–73; and M. S. Adams, "Ocular Proof in *Othello* and Its Source," *PMLA* 79 (June 1964): 234–41.

50. See Melchiori, "Rhetoric of Character Construction"; and, by the same, "O thou blacke weede," *Shakespeare Quarterly* 32 (1981): 355–57.

51. Doran, *Endeavors of Art: A Study of Form in Elizabethan Drama* (Madison: University of Wisconsin Press, 1954), 246.

52. Spivack, *Shakespeare and the Allegory of Evil,* esp. chaps. 3 and 4, pages 60–129.

53. Dekker, *The Bel-man of London,* in *Non-Dramatic Works of Thomas Dekker,* ed. A. Grosart (London, 1885), 3:116; cited in Spivack, *Shakespeare,* 155 (italics in original).

54. Vickers, *The Artistry of Shakespeare's Prose* (London: Methuen, 1968).

55. Ibid., 336.

56. To quote Madeleine Doran, "Othello's goodness is sufficient to meet and conquer any recognizable evil; the terrible thing is that the evil he meets *is not recognizable for what it is.*" *Endeavors of Art,* 305; emphasis added. See also, M. C. Bradbrook, *Themes and Conventions of Elizabethan Tragedy* (Cambridge: Cambridge University Press, 1935), esp. chap. 3.

57. Plett, "'Action is eloquence'," 10.
58. Colombo, *Le utopie e la storia: saggio sull'"Othello" di Shakespeare* (Bari: Adriatica, 1975), 110: "the deceit will be all the more subtle, and the illusion all the more atrocious, the more effectively the 'proof', i.e. the scenic action, reflects to him, like a distorting mirror, a grotesque image of the worries that torment him, a farcical exasperation of the tragedy of his life: Cassio's scorn for the woman who loves him will represent to his eyes both the degradation of Desdemona and derision of himself the courtesan excluded from the social order and tolerated only as an instrument of pleasure will represent a caricatural distortion of his own position of excluded; and the sudden appearance of Bianca and the desecrated handkerchief the absurd end result of jealousy." (my translation).
59. See Serpieri, *"Othello": l'Eros negato,* 157: "It is a double scene: realistic for Iago and Cassio . . . , phantasmal—but real—for Othello, for whom it is played. But the actual addressee of the whole representation—that of Iago and Cassio and that of Othello—*is* the spectator, who witnesses both the scenic and communicative levels and, more precisely, of the divarication between sign and referent . . . which occurs between the two levels" (italics in original).
60. Doran, *Endeavors of Art,* 233 and 252–53. See also Dixon, *Rhetoric,* 40–41.
61. It is interesting to note that even when Desdemona uses litotes ("Men are not Gods," 146), it is employed in a "positive" sense and in defense of the person accused.
62. See Bradbrook, *Themes and Conventions,* 63. "'Heaven' and 'hell' were definite parts of the stage, associated with their appropriate inhabitants."
63. See Styan, *Elements of Drama.* In Styan's view

> The language through which Othello and Desdemona speak is written to raise the scene from the level of domestic melodrama. . . . The ground of the discussion has shifted to heaven and hell, and the issue in Othello's mind becomes one less of his own jealousy and more of the horror of a foul and mortal sin clothed in innocence. . . . he asks her, "Are you not a strumpet?" and Desdemona swears by her religion and in her hope of heaven that she is not. By using these words Shakespeare raises her from the level of the misunderstood wife to be a representative of Christian martyrdom, while Othello, speaking for heaven with the promptings of hell and Iago behind him . . . is deceived in both worlds. . . . It is neither the self-torture of Othello nor the torture of Desdemona that is behind our scene, but the composite picture of man in his pride doubting his own element of divinity, and in his doubt reversing all he holds valuable until the reason and coherence of life is confused, slackened, degraded, "Perplex'd in the extreme" (37–38).

64. Serpieri, "La retorica a teatro," 158–61.
65. Plett, "'Action is eloquence'," 14.
66. Ravazzoli, "Appunti di nuova retorica, tra semantica e pragmatica," *Strumenti critici* 44 (1981), 154–70. "The definition 'amplifying axis' covers the various rhetorical figures based on the analogic-substitutive mechanism: simile, allegory, allegorism, metaphor, metonymy, synecdoche, hyperbole, antonomasia, prosopopoeia, *amplificatio,* etc.: the *metasememes* of the Liège group and also . . . all tropes in the proper sense. The 'attenuating axis' includes all the figures of negation, reticence, and (pseudo) contradiction: the *metalogisms* of the Belgian group" (page 158, italics in original; my translation).
67. Ibid., 157.
68. Groupe N, *Rhétorique générale,* esp. chaps. 4 and 5.
69. Austin, *How To Do Things with Words.* See also Serpieri, "Ipotesi teorica di segmentazione del testo teatrale," 24, and Elam, *Semiotics of Theatre and Drama,* 157–59.

70. Serpieri, *"Othello": l'Eros negato,* 288–89.

71. In my view, the question raised by some critics as to whether or not Othello's words are dictated by self-dramatization does not arise. Othello is not a living person but an artistic creation; and his words, if not contradicted by the other characters, must be taken as true and sincere. The theater communicates only what pragmatically occurs on stage. Everything extradramatic (that is, external to all the elements constituting the text) belongs exclusively to our sensitivity and our involvement in the play. Othello's stoicism, which is part of the dramatic convention of the age, cannot coexist with the hypothesis that Othello, in his last speech, "is *cheering himself up*," as suggested by T. S. Eliot ("Shakespeare and the Stoicism of Seneca," in *Selected Essays* [London: Faber, 1932], 111), nor with recourse to self-dramatization by an egocentric and egotistic "man" (F. R. Leavis, *The Common Pursuit* [London: Chatto & Windus, 1952], 136–59). Strangely enough, similar critical misgivings also appear in more recent interpretations. In Stephen Greenblatt's *Renaissance Self-Fashioning* (Chicago: University of Chicago Press, 1980) Othello's sexual anxiety is aroused by Desdemona's open nature and Iago's insinuations about Desdemona's appetite. In her frank admission of love to the Moor in Act 1, Greenblatt finds "the cause of Desdemona's death, for it awakens the deep current of sexual anxiety in Othello, anxiety that with Iago's help expresses itself in quite orthodox fashion as the perception of adultery" (p. 250). An attack on Greenblatt's theory of "cultural poetics" comes from Graham Bradshaw's *Misrepresentations: Shakespeare and the Materialists* (Ithaca: Cornell University Press, 1993) which aims at discovering the partiality of the new historicist and cultural materialist approaches, but Bradshaw's search for textual verities misses in the same scene the important issue of Desdemona's dramatic function, discounting her capacity of discernment in the play: "Whatever Desdemona thought she was looking at when 'saw Othello's visage in his mind,' she didn't see the mind of the murderer" (p. 213). Some genuine new proposals in the definition of the characters of Desdemona and Othello are to be found in the anthology of neo-feminist and gender studies *Shakespearean Tragedy and Gender,* ed. Shirley Nelson Garner and Madelon Sprengnether (Bloomington: Indiana University Press, 1996), specifically within the essays by Lena Cowen Orlin, Margo Hendricks, and Mary Beth Rose in Part Two, pp. 171–238.

72. On the dramatic significance of the sequence and on Othello's full recovery, see my article, "'A horned man's a monster, and a beast'" esp. pages 165–71.

"Great mischiefs mask in expected pleasures": The Rhetoric of Expectation and the Rhetoric of Surprise in English Baroque Theater

FRANCO MARENCO

The opening quote comes from the end of Thomas Middleton's *Women Beware Women* (ca. 1620). The line is spoken by the Duke of Florence—one of the Jacobean theater's many arrogant, treacherous characters and the chief corruptor in the story of Bianca Capello, which Middleton adapted from Malespini's *Ducento novelle*. What is meant by "expected pleasures" is some theatricals arranged by the duke to celebrate his marriage to Bianca. Many obstacles have been surmounted, and his obstinate desire is about to be satisfied; but "great mischiefs" lie in wait, prepared under cover of this final ceremony. Each character has plotted the death of his rival, and now, as the celebrations reach their height, the crisscrossed vendettas start to claim their victims—but in strange, unexpected ways. The carnage at once appears the result of chance and error rather than precise intentions. Revenge comes in the figure of a grand finale, common to the various plots but contrary to their individual drift. The desires of those who have hatched them are warped; each success (that is, each death) is marked by the utterance of grotesque lines or perfidiously ironic commentary on the story of each character, who, at the same time, is an executor and a victim of chance.

It is hard to avoid interpreting this finale in a metadramatic sense. Indeed, the author prompts us to do so by personifying the play's diegetic soul, as it were, in the Duke of Florence, and allowing him to fall victim to one of many inevitable errors. The duke wanders around the stage reading a parchment outlining the script of the ceremony and its pleasant allegory but is unable to make head or tail of it. The horrible, inexplicable events he witnesses together with us are not mentioned in this plan; nor do they follow any prearranged order. Amid all this coming and going, running here and falling there—which is always half-joyful celebration, half-dark tragedy—there is the blissfully ignorant duke, who at every line stumbles across something unforeseen, some unexpected deformation of the original text, which he nevertheless doggedly continues to consult with infinite incredulity: "What's the conceit of that?"; "This swerves a little from the argument . . ."; "Why sure, this plot's drawn false; here's no such thing!"; "I have lost myself in this quite . . ."; down to the supremely ironic "Read, read; for I am lost in sight and strength"—pronounced when he is finally given a "confession" of "the full scope, the manner and intent" of the inexplicable mess (5.2.118, 121, 127, 140, 181).[1] The duke is standing at the threshold of death. Around him the allegorical mask has reached the height of confusion, with corpses piling up on top of each other, while he is trying to understand what on earth is going on, still striving against all odds to make the play remain faithful to an abstract design, to a rational order.

This work of Middleton's was written about thirty years after Thomas Kyd's *Spanish Tragedy* and twenty years after *Hamlet*, and it shows. The unbroken chain of deceit, betrayal, and misunderstanding that unleashes vengeance at the Spanish court in the former tragedy and at the Danish one in the latter is revived by Middleton after countless similar experiments by his fellow dramatists, set in an Italian context and raised to the level of a tragic system par excellence. It is not simply offered as a tribute to an audience well versed in the conventions of the genre and ever hungrier for new sensations and emotions; rather, it is presented as an inevitable outcome and epitome of the entire genre itself, a genre which declines the status of a "mournful order of reality" (as Benjamin would say) and which adopts instead disorientation and arbitrariness as the basis of its strategies. Thus, it sets up a subtle game of recognition and contrast between stage and spectators, a game in which satisfaction of the audience's expectations is linked to frustration of the expectations of the characters. Against all temptation to read these plays with the requirements of the realistic theater in mind, let us stress once again: it is a genre that bases the success of mimesis on the failure of diegesis. It is thus a theater of irony and the grotesque which worms its way into the tragic archetype, subverting it and discarding its traditional construction. A theater, therefore, that is obliged to make ever more frequent use of surprise, *coups de théâtre*, the magnification and repetition of *peripeteia;* that invents the metadramatic mechanism of displaying a written script only to empty it of all meaning and direction—a twist we feel entitled to read, both as a proud profession of independence from the written tradition and as a parodic commentary on the impermanence of all performances and the instability of all texts.

The tragedies of Kyd and Shakespeare also use the device of the play-within-the-play—condensed allegories of the main plot, illusions which become instruments of truth. Shakespeare places "The Murder of Gonzago" at the center of *Hamlet,* while Kyd uses "Soliman and Perseda" as an anti-catastrophe, a prelude to the finale, which provides a precedent for Middleton. Both Kyd and Middleton display an attitude of supreme irony toward characters who are acting out as fiction the real story of their own lives, characters who condemn in the roundest terms vices which the audience knows full well they are guilty of. In Kyd's work, the play-within-the-play is a fierce tragedy, while in Middleton's it is a harmless pastoral-mythological affair based on conventional sentiments. This inevitably leads to a heightening of the sense of euphemism—namely, the distance and disproportion between the fable that is being enacted and the feelings nurtured in secret. Between the last decade of the sixteenth century and the third decade of the seventeenth—before the cataclysm of Puritanism, that is—the English theater took on an ever more pronounced sensationalist character and established an increasingly solid pact with its audience. This pact was based on a clear metadramatic awareness—that is, on the exposure and ironic highlighting of the mechanisms that guaranteed the theater's great popularity: vice, scandal, and violence were not only shown, but were shown to be part and parcel of the theatrical business. Such developments mark the deepening of the crisis which the humanists' proudly celebrated subject had already fallen prey to.[2]

One does not need to leave the English stage far behind in order to find the archetype of these suspended and disconcerting solutions. In my opinion, it is to be found, not in a theatrical text, but in the first version of Sidney's *Arcadia*. This work—a strange hybrid of genres and of piled-up structures—is scrupulously arranged according to a dramatic design and is set in a land with unmistakably literary antecedents: the idyllic *locus amoenus* announced by the highly traditional title. This setting, however, gradually loses its utopian character and takes on the increasingly real and threatening appearance of a land in the throes of political disorder. In such a changeable context are played out the adventures of two princes, whose behavior is governed by the acknowledged codes of chivalry—they fall in love and don disguises in order to accomplish their amorous designs. What they fail to notice is that such actions lend themselves to various interpretations, interpretations which are no longer prompted by the ideals of the past but by the pressure of a new, disquieting present. This, too, is a case of protracted euphemism, of absolute divarication between the conventions of composition employed and the implications of the plot; hence the persiflage, the ironic dismantling of both pastoral and chivalric traditions, which Sidney performs in the name of the revolution in individual consciences brought about by the Reformation.

What is most of interest to us is the peculiar structure of *Arcadia*'s ending, which offers not one but two antithetical denouements. In the first, the two princes are condemned to pay with their lives for the sins they have committed in pursuit of their hedonistic ends. The judge who imposes this sentence on them is a foreign sovereign famous for his humanity and justice. Nor is the sentence changed when, in a predictable moment of pathos, the miraculous recognition is forced on everybody: this same sovereign is father to one prince and uncle to the other. In the second ending, the sentence is changed, because the main charge against the princes turns out to be unfounded; thus, they are at last free to marry their princesses, be reconciled with their august relation, and live happily ever after. Nevertheless, this succession of surprises does not sort everything out. The real offenses the princes have hidden behind a screen of conventional rhetoric go unpunished; none of the ethical problems raised by the story is really solved. Everybody can heave a great sigh of relief, as long as logic and justice are forgotten. Indeed, the impulses of feeling and reason stirred up in the reader are deliberately played off against each other and shown to be irreconcilable. Here, too, amid all the final jubilation, there remains one bewildered character: the Duke Basilius. Ultimately to blame for all the misfortunes that have befallen Arcadia, he seems to represent the common consciousness, which can never make head or tail of the trials of life, nor ever understand the ways of Providence. This is the text's innermost meaning: its fabula has already been outlined by an oracle that speaks at the beginning of the romance. The truth is there on display for anyone who wishes to see it; but at every step, the signs are misinterpreted. In the end, when the providential script has at last revealed itself, it is too late: it doesn't help stave off disaster, but merely serves to humble the pride of reason, in the characters as well as the reader.[3]

"GREAT MISCHIEFS MASK IN EXPECTED PLEASURES" 249

The weakening of the subject as conceived by the humanists is thus already apparent here. It is also apparent that a highly intricate game is being played with the audience's expectations. Whereas Sidney's work allegorizes the corruption of human nature and the impossibility of understanding the designs of Providence, the dramatists indulge in a savage, almost perverse, portrayal of that corruption, deriding reason's attempts to find a remedy or consolation. And, whereas Sidney employs pure irony at the expense of literary traditionalism, in the work of the dramatists, irony takes on a tone of turbid excess, eventually reaching the point where it becomes a mockery of faith and virtuous planning, a parodistic countermelody to the most tried and tested textual strategies.

The hatred shown to the theater by the most industrious section of English society—namely, those for whom Puritanism provided a rallying point—was not born of mere petty moralism. It was a symptom of a conflict between two cultures: one, bound to the old communitarian ethos, pivoting around times of feasting and celebration when classes were brought together; the other bound to discipline and social selectivity, which aimed to suppress, rather than guarantee, such opportunities for imaginative subversion. The preachers addressed the latter culture, while the dramatists spoke to the former, and pulled out infinite resources to get their message across—above all, sudden reversals of signs, ambiguities of meaning, sensational *coups de théâtre,* irreparable catastrophes in which their rare virtuosity had free rein. Their audiences could indulge in an unbridled passion for surprise and for what was already a highly modern form of suspense. Although it steered clear of any form of theorization, the English Baroque theater's hallmarks came to be the weakening and confusion of traditional genres, and the hypertrophy of the Aristotelian *peripeteia*.[4]

The basic aesthetic rule governing this genre was formulated by Thomas Cartwright in an apparently complimentary digression—which is in fact a most enlightening description of the audience's role in an ideal theater. It appears in a long eulogistic poem published in the 1647 edition of the works of John Fletcher:

> None can prevent the fancy, and see through
> At the first opening; all stand wondering how
> The thing will be until it is.[5]

This fine formula invites us to imagine the work of the sixteenth- and seventeenth-century English dramatist as a continuous effort to formalize unpredictability, that is, as a creation of the conflict between will and desire, between rational and irrational development of the plot. It must be said that the English cultural scene did not provide ideal conditions for performing this task. Indeed, above all in the sphere of tragedy, home-grown English drama bore the indelible hallmark of moralism, which expressed itself through archetypes and allegorical plots, wherein it was apparent from the outset how "the thing" would turn out.

As the name suggests, the "fall of majesty" that the theater had long dramatized alongside the popular series of didactic poems called *The Mirror for Magistrates* meant infinite variations on a single, constant theme: the damnation of those in positions of power who had indulged in private vices and thus neglected the common good—a perfectly predictable basic plot. Thanks to the combined influence of court ideology and Protestant thought, it was, above all, the new historiography and travelogues that developed a model of history, which could be used for didactic purposes and interpreted as a synecdoche of the inscrutable yet infallible design of Providence: "[He] who feeleth this inclination in himself," wrote Edward Hayes in a preface addressed to the investors in Sir Humphrey Gilbert's colonizing voyage to America in 1583, "by all likelihood may hope, or rather confidently repose in the preordinance of God, that in this last age of the world (or likely never) the time is compleat of receiving those Gentiles into his mercy, and that God will raise him an instrument to effect the same."[6]

Just like determinism today, providentialism then meant the consolidation of all finalist and eschatological ideologies, such as millenarianism, while the writing of texts, inside this framework, implied the immediate and literal interpretation of the event and the drawing of an unambiguous, circular plot line that excluded all surprises and anything new. The dramatist had to take numerous cultural factors into account. Among the most complex and deeply rooted in his audience was what we might call a rhetoric of prophecy—which, of course, took various forms, such as vaticination, placing curses or solving riddles—rhetoric that made no attempt to formalize the unpredictable any easier. To a great extent, the development of the Elizabethan and Jacobean theater can be seen as the history of rivalry between two opposing rhetorical strategies, which shared an uneasy coexistence until the structures of prophecy were gradually supplanted by the structures of the unpredictable.

As we have seen, Sidney had pointed the way to possible integration of these two strategies. He had placed the problem of human destiny and its predictability at the center of the text's symbology and composition. He had also formulated it in apparently traditional terms by resorting to a typical feature of the Alexandrian romance—the oracle that makes an initial prediction, couched in obscure terms, of everything that subsequently happens; he had, however, introduced a new dimension, one that was allegorical in a Christian rather than Classical sense. He employed the oracle as a sign of a secret logic underlying the plot—ever present, yet always misunderstood, always contrasting with the carelessness and pride of characters given over wholly to the vain search for pleasure and the equally vain conviction that they understood everything. Every single *peripeteia* in the romance meant that their convictions were disproved, that their selfish quests were frustrated.

What ultimately was under attack was the humanist conception of the dignity of man—a conception of human nature not reformed by a dose of Calvinistic humility. In Sidney, surprise becomes evidence of the vacuity of reason as well as a sort of parodistic picklock vis-à-vis every recognized literary genre, either tragic or comic. Hence, the ending to *Arcadia*—which is left hanging between the two alternative outcomes, "tragic" and "comic," so as to disorientate the reader and problematize his choices.

Such symbolizations made it possible to establish a dialectic among the various strategies, to integrate them; and the theater wasted no time in capitalizing on this development. Shakespeare springs to mind immediately, since his theater abounds with prophecies expressed in a variety of forms: commanders have dreams on the eve of battle; before they die, victims put curses on their executioners. Then there are oracles in the Classical mold or simple witticisms or jokes that allude to important developments; all these elements combine in various ways to create doubt and suspense. The plays *Richard III* (ca. 1591) and *Macbeth* (1606) seem particularly relevant to our discussion.[7] If there is one character who can be described as the very embodiment of predictability, it is Richard, since he is a throwback to ancient theatrical techniques—to the medieval figure of the Vice—which makes him prone to announcing his own crimes before committing them, leaving the audience disconcerted by such "innocent" wickedness: "I am determined to prove a villain" and: "As I am subtle, false, and treacherous," etc. (1.1. 30, 37). Richard knows exactly what he needs in order to pursue his evil ends:

> Plots have I laid, inductions dangerous,
> By drunken prophecies, libels, and dreams . . .
>
> (1.1.32–33)

Plots, allusions, prophecies, slander, and dreams: the tools of the schemer are the tools of a theater director who is about to put on his drama of power struggle and death at the English court. Richard is all preparation, foresight, and masterly direction, as it were; there is nothing but irony toward the other characters. By making the audience privy to his every single move, he isolates himself from the rest of the cast, threatens them constantly, thanks to his superior knowledge and ability to manipulate, and carries the theatergoers along with him in his ruthless entertainment. This inexhaustible plot-hatching is matched by the equally inexhaustible passivity of the victims. At bottom, only death can confirm the expectations raised.

The drama's *agon*—that is, the opposition it builds to the control Richard exerts over the plot—is provided by the two heads of the contending royal houses, the Duchess of York and Queen Margaret, who perform the function of a tragic chorus as they constantly inveigh against the usurper and make repeated predictions of his downfall. Thus, the basic design of the play is contained in the dialectic between the destiny that is knowable and the destiny that is actually realized: between expectation and frustration. Such a design reappears in the shape of a *peripeteia* marking a reversal of fortune, when Richard at last must confront a real rival, who will subsequently dethrone him and found the Tudor dynasty. Once again, the course of history is indicated and conditioned by a prophecy; only this time matters are complicated by a misinterpretation of the prophecy. The surprise hits Richard himself when he mistakes the name of Rougemont in the homophone Richmond. Now the deceiver is himself deceived, the supreme plot-hatcher is himself the hostage to a misunderstanding. Now the master of irony is himself persecuted by a double meaning, by the foreseen presenting itself as unforeseeable.

Macbeth, too, is a great tragedy of expectation, of time that either never seems to pass or passes too quickly, thus upsetting every calculation. The course the drama will follow is outlined in the first scenes in which the account of the battle and of Macbeth's heroic feats is inserted between the witches' riddle-prophecies. Macbeth's destiny is fixed; but, as immediately becomes clear, it is fixed outside the bounds of his conscious intentions and is thus beyond his control. Macbeth will always waver, remain ever uncertain as to the real value of the witches' words:

> This supernatural soliciting
> Cannot be ill; cannot be good:
> If ill, why hath it given me earnest of success,
> Commencing in a truth? I am Thane of Cawdor:
> If good, why do I yield to that suggestion
> Whose horrid image doth unfix my hair,
> And make my seated heart knock at my ribs,
> Against the use of nature?
>
> (1.3.130-37)

Here, condensed in a few lines, are the various motifs that make up our discussion and mark the difference between the young Shakespeare, author of *Richard III*, and the mature Shakespeare, author of *Macbeth*. In the latter play, prophecy, the correct interpretation of destiny, works not against but in favor of surprise. Prophecy itself becomes a source of apprehension, doubt, internal rebellion and finally of *peripeteia* precisely when it becomes clear it is an unnatural and scandalous source of truth. The dramatic mechanism is deprived of its traditional providential connotation and is left hanging precariously in a valueless vacuum. Such secularization—"What! Can the Devil speak true!" (1.3.107)—provokes indignation and disbelief, both in Macbeth and in us. Just like him, we wonder what good can come from a truth that unfixes one's hair and makes the heart knock at one's ribs. What *Macbeth* achieves is an absorption of temptation in the "supernatural," a supernatural that divides because it presents itself as divided between the equal possibilities of truth and untruth. Such a supernatural is, in a perfectly modern way, neither "good" nor "ill." It is neutral and volatile, tending now in one direction, now in another, because it is only able to keep its promises, to pay and not disappoint, insofar as it is "against the use of nature."

This is how the strategy of order is integrated dramatically with the strategy of disorder and the unforeseen. After the first three scenes, the word *good* will become synonymous with "evil," and vice versa: "Fair is foul, and foul is fair" (1.1.10). Truth will emerge easily; yet it will continue to spring surprises. The subversion of nature announced during the opening of the play continues to reign supreme. This is reaffirmed in the great confrontation scene between Macbeth and Lady Macbeth (1.7) and in the series of crimes that make up the usurper's career. It is this subversion, this inversion of perspectives, which renders Macbeth's fate both certain and surprising at the same time—wholly natural, yet incredible in natural terms. Toward the end of the play, when Macbeth visits the witches for the second time, he sees the signs of the retribution that awaits him but interprets them as "sweet bodements" (4.1.96)—sweet because according to any natural logic they are impossible:

> That will never be:
> Who can impress the forest; bid the tree
> Unfix his earth-bound root?
> (4.1.93–96)

The last hope Macbeth clings to, the prophecy that none of woman born can vanquish him (5.3.6–7), is in the same vein. When, against all expectations, this prophetic truth finally comes to pass, it represents, at the same time, the denial of a misinterpreted prophecy, which leaves Macbeth torn in two:

> And be these juggling fiends no more believ'd,
> That palter with us in a double sense;
> That keep the word of promise to our ear,
> And break it to our hope.
> (5.3.19–22)

As a final example of this mixing of strategies I now turn to one further example of revenge tragedy, John Webster's *The White Devil* (1612).[8] The spirit of the plot is embodied in the character of Vittoria Corombona: she is the "white devil", and this oxymoronic epithet gives us an idea of the multiple, contradictory and disconcerting expectations in which female characters in revenge tragedies had come to be shrouded. Vittoria is referred to as "diversivolent"—which, editors tell us, means "sower of discord"—though a philologically closer, and dramatically more suggestive, equivalent would be "multidesirous." The plot's structure betrays traces of the old prophetic strategy, for example in the dream that Vittoria relates in 1.2. when she urges the Duke of Bracciano to remove the barriers standing in the way of their marriage. There is no lack of ghostly apparitions crying for revenge (4.1; 5.4) or predictions of imminent deaths (5.4.79–86). It immediately becomes apparent, however, that such devices are sensational expedients superfluous to the development of the plot—mere quotes from other dramas, inserted here and there to propitiate success. Furthermore, these scattered devices are not so much integrated as piled up with others, which belong to the opposite series of expedients designed to deceive and disappoint, to continually disorientate and reorientate the audience's expectations. Among such devices may be mentioned the disguise under cover of which the revenge is carried out, which enables the speakers' secrets to be discovered, or love intrigues and mistaken identities. These are all clearly imitations of Shakespearean archetypes, borrowed this time from *Measure for Measure.*

In the *White Devil*, there is confusion rather than fusion between motifs of various origin: the collective folk memory that had contributed so much to sixteenth-century theatrical culture is replaced by a *literary* memory, drawing on a stock of images and conventions which no longer bear any relation to their original archetypes. Nevertheless, they are not bandied about as the simple ingredients in a game of illusion, but are integrated into a new function that paves the way for what will be the realistic delineation of characters. If the protagonist is the desiring subject who bestows dramatic tension on the play, her brother Flamineo is the driving force behind all the deception. Like Shakespeare's Richard III, he announces his misdeeds, comments on them smugly, reveals the crimes of others, and assesses them with a cynical smile on his face. Unlike that great master of dramatic speech, Flamineo is subservient to it. He is a tragic master servant—the first great descendant of Iago. What is modern about this protagonist is his final abandonment of any attempt to plan or worry about the future, the conscious narrowing of his horizons to encompass nothing but the most immediate present (now prophecy is no longer possible, everything must be surprising):

> I do not look
> Who went before, nor who shall follow me;
> No, at myself I will begin and end.
>
> (5.6.253–55)

Flamineo speaks these words when his resources have at last run out, a few lines after having produced his final *coup de théâtre*—and all the more sensational insofar as it is a double one. His back to the wall and his enemies about to take their revenge upon him at any moment, he visits Vittoria with two brace of pistols and ambiguously asks her and her maidservant Zanche to kill him and themselves together. The two women shoot Flamineo only and start to exult over his death. Flamineo falls to the ground and speaks his dying breath. He insists that Vittoria kill herself, too (which she has not the slightest intention of doing). Then suddenly the dying man stands up again, reveals that the pistols were loaded with blanks, and launches into a misogynist tirade. In a rapid succession of surprises, a typical villain shows himself willing to die, moralizes, dies, and comes back to life in what is a complete triumph of fiction. For a moment, theatrical flair seems to guarantee him immortality, but this too is mere illusion; revenge still awaits him. For Flamineo, the plot of deception is life itself; but the audience perceives it as a sign of a condition shared by all the characters, deceivers and deceived alike. Each character bears his own truth, but such truth is imprisoned in a circle of unreliability, falsification and funereal illusion and is thus deprived of efficacy.

I believe it is no exaggeration to say that the scene of Vittoria's trial (3.2) represents an important paradigm of the entire Baroque episteme. In it, two contrasting desires clash—the accusers' desire for revenge and Vittoria's desire for life and power. With great skill, the author balances these two desires, allowing first one and then the other to win over the audience's heart and mind. We know that Vittoria is guilty, but Cardinal Monticelso's indictment sounds totally empty. He does not address himself to facts but to Vittoria's reputation, which facilitates her self-defense. The accused vindicates her own illegitimate love, shows that Monticelso's eloquence lacks any substance, that it is a signifier deprived of signified—or, rather, that it depends on an inadmissible signified, partiality and the desire for revenge, which puts accuser and accused on the same plane. It is clear that the author builds the scene so as to keep the audience's reactions divided and unreconciled to the very end, in order to envelop the entire drama in a sense of indecision and suspension. In the end, it is the word, human speech—not just dramatic speech—which is declared to be in a state of crisis.[9]

The game of expectations performed in the English Baroque theater, the misunderstandings and revelations, the unsolvable oxymorons and *coups de théâtre* have a long history. This history began when the lack of confidence in the ideology of the humanists' sovereign subject was formalized. It ended when significance itself, and communication, were disrupted by a sense of crisis, in stagecraft writ small and in society writ large.

Notes

1. All references are to the New Mermaids edition by Roma Gill (London: Benn, 1968).

2. It would be too long to retrace here the excellent work that, since Foucault's controversial propositions, has been done on the rise of modern subjectiv-

ity. Two outstanding books that deal, among other authors, with the Elizabethan and Jacobean dramatists are Stephen Greenblatt's *Renaissance Self-Fashioning* (Chicago: Chicago University Press, 1980); and Catherine Belsey's *The Subject of Tragedy* (London: Routledge, 1985). In the present paper, the occurrence of a "crisis" so early in the history of subjectivity is related to what seems to me a possible key to some important developments in the Renaissance and Baroque periods throughout Europe—that is, the confrontation between old and new ways of conceiving the role of man's reason in society—in England, for short, between humanism and Puritanism. This is itself an old opposition, which nevertheless receives new light from contemporary studies. It does not receive full attention in either Greenblatt's or Belsey's works—the latter especially being preoccupied with the subject as product of "liberal humanism," perhaps too bold a move on the way of modernization.

3. For an exploration of this allegory, I refer the reader to my studies of Sidney, *Arcadia puritana: L'uso della tradizione nella "Old Arcadia" di Sir Philip Sidney* (Bari: Adriatica, 1968); and "Double Plot in the Old *Arcadia,*" now in Arthur F. Kinney, *Essential Articles for the Study of Sir Philip Sidney* (Hamden, Conn.: Archon Books, 1986), 287–310. For more extended treatment, see Rosanna Camerlingo, *From the Courtly World to the Infinite Universe: Sir Philip Sidney's Two* Arcadias (Alessandria: Dell'Orso, 1993).

4. I develop this argument in "From Romance to Ritual: Memory and the Community in Shakespeare's Last Plays," in Keir Elam, ed., *Shakespeare Today: Directions and Methods of Research* (Florence: La Casa Usher, 1984), 117–33; and in "'Let us see Desdemona smother'd', ovvero gli imprevisti di una canonizzazione," in Grazia Caliumi, ed., *Shakespeare e la sua eredità,* Atti del XV convegno dell'Associazione Italiana di Anglistica (Parma: Zara, 1993), 21–32.

5. "Commendatory verses" (1647), in D. Klein, ed., *The Elizabethan Dramatists as Critics* (New York: Philosophical Library, 1963), 147.

6. Edward Hayes, "A report of the voyage . . ." in D. B. Quinn, ed., *The Voyages and Colonising Enterprises of Sir Humphrey Gilbert,* 2 vols. (London: The Hakluyt Society, 1940), 2:387.

7. All references are to the Arden Methuen editions, by A. Hammond and K. Muir, respectively.

8. All references are to the New Mermaids edition by Elizabeth M. Brennan (London: Benn, 1966).

9. See my "Crisi della parola e tecnica della rappresentazione nel teatro barocco inglese: Webster e Middleton," in Franco Marenco, ed., *Thomas Middleton e il teatro barocco in Inghilterra* (Genoa: Il Melangolo, 1983), 9–38.

From Shakespeare to Dryden: Three Dramatic *Incipits*
VIOLA PAPETTI

> In Corneille's *Discours de l'utilité et des parties du Poème dramatique* we can read:
> Je voudrois donc que le premier acte contînt si bien le fondament de toutes les actions, qu'il fermât la porte à tout le reste.
> (variant of 1660 edition)

The generative dynamics of choice and refusal of possible courses of action could not have been better defined in its twofold and contrary function. (Neoclassical theater makes special use of the vertical intensity of the discourse that follows the limited, interdicted, horizontal ramification of actions.) But the dramatic *incipit*—known in rhetoric as the protasis—is usually shorter than the first act, which, generally, is already given up to activities of choice and orientation of the separate threads of the plot.[1] I therefore use the term *protasis* (or *incipit*, or *protatic* complex or macrosequence) as the initial syntagm of the dramatic text, whether it is preceded by the antefact or not. I have chosen it as a privileged place of analysis because of its intense codifying action within the modern dramatic text—paradoxically deprived as it may be of specific expositive intention.

"The beginning has a determinant function as a model," according to J. M. Lotman; "it is not only the testimony of existence but also the substitute of the later category of causality. To explain the appearance means indicating its origin."[2]

Protasis, the threshold or way into dramatic time and place, separates non-action from essentially mimetic action and a strategically ordered narrative program. Often in tragedy—possibly always—the protatic nucleus is the rapid and incisive dramaturgical *mise en abîme*. It is an enunciated enunciation that marks the theatrical event while at the same time marking the manner of its happening. Hence, the interest of the contrastive analysis of dramatic texts of different historical periods which share a common *fabula* but not the same plot or the scenic space where the performances take place. The late seventeenth-century remakes of *The Tempest, Antony and Cleopatra,* and *Troilus and Cressida,* of which Dryden was the main if not the only begetter, are subject to one and the same intention: to establish the truth of the "Shakespeare" phenomenon, to redeem him from his primitive condition—in other words, to enunciate him in a different cultural context.

My intention here is to make an analytical comparison of some contiguous levels of dramatic protasis: (1) action; (2) dialogic strategy; (3) the position of the audience, whenever the residual text gives us more indications. The late-seventeenth-century ideological world left visible traces of its impact on theatrical theory and practice; the dramatic signifier is marked by a sudden and irreversible change.

Metaphorical Tempest and Metonymic Tempest

The protatic macrosequence (1.1.1–102) of *The Tempest 1674,* by Shakespeare-Davenant-Dryden-Betterton, is divisible into 26 microsequences that can be defined by empirical criteria: entrance or exit of characters, turns in speaking, deictic orientations that often coincide in their marking of narrative-spectacular caesura.[3]

In this particular type of protasis "en action," the tempest/shipwreck event constitutes a paradoxical use of catastrophe functioning as an *incipit*. This end/beginning violently excludes other courses of dramatic action, establishing the island as the only possible place for action, a primitive "theater of the world," closed within itself. The relationship between the Elizabethan protatic complex and late-seventeenth-centuries remakes, modified from the original on the basis of the constitutive codes of the scenic signifier, invites one to imagine a hypothetical text that contains them all and sets them side by side—a metatext rich in all the variants of stage practice and theatrical writing, of the shadow area of the collective imagination that distinguishes and realigns them. This is an exemplary description of the fracture that can traverse a dramaturgic tradition.

The full use of the stage space of the new Italian-style theater (Dorset Garden) requires a rewriting of the verbal text that names the various parts of the stage: upstage, downstage, perspective effect. An incredible number of stage properties denote this, and the parts of the ship, even the waves—some thirty, compared to the four mentioned in *Tempest 1623*—suggest movement and lead to practical action. The modern verbal text—especially *Tempest 1674*—performs the function of anchoring the dramatic figuration (Barthes) and illustrating the syntax of visual and auditory codes, and at the same time expunges from itself the task of naming the metaphoric invisible, the theme of death by water. The almost total cancellation of metaphoric discourse brings with it the development of metonymic discourse, which is frequently iconic and apparently denotative. The false innocence of this theater marks the desire of the Stage to contain its sensual Addressee, to structure itself as "consumer" theater, *tout court*.

In Shakespeare's *Tempest*, on the contrary, the characters enunciate what they "know," they do not simply "do." They speak not just to comment on the actions they perform but to open the gates of the imagination to the theme of death and its rich implications.

The shipwreck enacted in the three *Tempests* is not a continuous, single event that can assume a form in the spectator's memory or after a rapid reading; the binary structure of the action also remains the basis of the revised versions. The mariners' actions have one purpose only: to save the ship. They are regarded by those who perform them as consequential and necessary. They form a sequence of composite actions linked by this common purpose, which is destined to fail because the ship is, in fact, wrecked, while Prospero's aim will, instead, be achieved: to initiate the second tempest—the magical redemption of the guilty.[4]

To the first ordered series of events is added the disordered series of the actions of the nobles, which provoke a pause, an obstacle. Their speech acts ignore necessity and logical concatenation and seek to interpret the future in ways no less magical than the magical plan in which they are unwittingly caught up. Their speech acts do not require the support of gestures or stage action—voices are sufficient. The social conflict dividing the two groups is also symbolically represented by the difference in the kind of action: pragmatic and intentional in the mariners, cognitive and intensional in the nobles. In the framework of this verbal clash, the conflict is enunciated as a relationship between name and event—active and operative in the nobles, absent in the boatswain.

> What cares these roarers for the name of King?
> (*The Tempest*, 1.1.16–17)

From the grouping of microsequences thus structured and empirically identified, it is possible to deduce that the audience is so situated as to face the content of the Italian-style theater through *proxemic actions, phonic actions, expressive speech acts or speech acts descriptive of practical activity in course.*

The zero level of the presentation or perception of space and time is a here-now enunciation that goes by without comment (microsequences 5, 9, 12). They are acts of transference of the (actors) mariners crossing the stage, the effect of which is to make the horizontal scenic plane coincide with a conventional place—"deck of the ship" or even "all visible space." Although contained in broader microsequences, where there is an exchange between characters, they impose themselves directly on the attention of the spectator, who finds himself in the position of an observing "you." The spectator is in a similar situation when he hears the cries of terror coming from a space that is not visible but inward. These are expressive phonic acts (microsequences 21, 24, 27) which occur within an exchange between characters but which are separate and parallel, and which enunciate another space and an imminent, frightening future.

A different modality of the spectator's direct involvement is provided by the microsequence in which Gonzalo apostrophizes fate. This is a monologue addressed to the audience, rather than a verbal exchange between two noblemen. Gonzalo, a sorry remnant of the rich Shakespearean character, puts the spectator in the particular position of a "you-we," emerging from collective anthropological consciousness. (In the remaining microsequences, the spectator clearly is in the traditional "he" position, the standard vertex of dramatic communication.) At a more complex level, the positioning of the spectator takes place by means of *a meditated activity of the verbal text in order to create effects of spatiotemporal 'débrayage',* that is, enunciation from the here-now place-time of a place-time projected in the not here-not now enunciated.[5]

All the microsequences reflect this orderly distribution of the action in the englobed and englobing places of the scene—its dramatic extension in an inevitable and conclusive future. The speech acts are glosses of practical actions, commands that orient the collective action of the mariners on the horizontal, vertical, and perspective plane, or descriptions of a state that are assessments of the general situation or forecasts based thereon. The real scene is duplicated in the nominated scene.

The presupposed spectator is a Hobbesian spectator. In the emanatistic model of matter there are premises for a sensorial dramaturgy: the object world presses on the senses with the acuteness and celerity of its motions, which continue in the person as psychic and oneiric motions ("for motion produceth nothing but motion").[6] The sense organs do not perceive immaterial images or ideas originating from the object, but mechanical-type modifications instead. Not only is the theater of scenographic and mechanical effects fully justified, but it rises to the dignity of a specular (or hyperbolic) model of the real world and its apperception. Even theatrical machines could be thought to have the larva of a soul, as the Hobbesian soul was the larva of a machine. The spectator watching *T1674* was quantitatively struck by the considerable increase in names *primae intentionis,* the continual glossings, and the incessant production of practical acts. The exaggerated movement becomes the seme of "imminent catastrophe." The actors' bodies—material substances—function as agents and the spectators' bodies as patients of movement by contact, a mechanistic and baroque version of Aristotle's "empathy."

The protasis of *T1623* ends with Gonzalo's speech (eliminated in *T1674*):

> Now would I give a thousand furlongs of sea for an acre of barren ground, long heath, broom, furze, anything. The wills above be done! but I would fain die a dry death.
> *(The Tempest,* 1.1.64–67)

In this momentary, total suspension of the scenic action, Gonzalo utters the ancient mythologeme of the return to the earth, of the individuality of the body, compared to the anonymity of death by drowning perpetrated by the sea. "Dry death" is a difficult icon with regard to a spectacular *béance* which is death in its full reality. In Shakespeare's text, Gonzalo's anthropological motifs are freely circulating metaphoric constellations, flights entrusted to a single voice that have no raison d'être in the narrative-spectacular logic of *T1674*. Gonzalo's function as an ideologic, interpreting character is, in the later play, much reduced, even if he remains an augur, a decoder of signs. He still reads in the face of the boatswain the symptoms of a cultural death ordained by human justice. In the gynecomorphous ship, he is aware of perfidious feminine sexuality communicating with destruction. These, however, are mere fragments of the wider Shakespearean metaphoric discourse.

In *T1623* the boatswain wonders:

> What, must our mouths be cold?
>
> (1.1.52)

Are the mouths cold because they are full of water (or because they lack alcohol, as some have suggested?), or are they simply mouths of the dead? If the last hypothesis is true, the cold mouths of those about to die by water have the function of the matrix of the second metaphoric nucleus, the marine mouths that imprecate and gape wide open to swallow bodies. The latent cohesion between the two nuclei induces a sense of necessary identity between those about to die and the agents of death. One dies of the death that resembles one (a human death), of that which penetrates us or lets itself be penetrated, death by water, or that which coherently assimilates us to the general landscape.

Owing to the operation of *detractio* performed on Shakespeare's text, the second metaphoric nucleus is canceled and the line pronounced by the boatswain (now Trincalo) stands out, isolated and even more ambiguous at the beginning of the last two microsequences. The cold mouths have now become a separate sign, a symbolic apex that is retranscribed in the practice of Hobbesian perspective theater. They act as an enigmatic background to the hectic stage action, a presupposed prediction against which excited voices and rapid motions clash.

Protasis as a Theatrical Necessity

"The very first scene of *Antony and Cleopatra* is a clue to all the elements that follow," as B. Beckerman has said.[7] This exceptionally elaborate protatic complex is in three parts, of which the first and third are a frame to the middle part, a close dialogue between the protagonists. According to Beckerman, this *incipit* contains, *in nuce,* not only the motifs that will later be developed, but is also an example to which we should refer to understand the dynamic strategy of the whole work. A dual point of view is created in the dialogues between Philo and Demetrius (lines 1–13, lines 57–63): the Roman vision and that of the audience, which incorporates and transcends it. The event to be judged is the dialogue-duel between Cleopatra and Antonio, the paradigm of which is "Cleopatra's teasing and testing" which gives way to Antony's "overriding image of rapture," a dynamic constant that is repeated throughout the play. This is, therefore, a dramatized prologue, which, in its tripartite structure, defines the relationships to be explored, determines the purpose of the events, and anticipates the modalities of the action.

The protasis of *Antony and Cleopatra* has already attracted the attention of Mark Rose, who describes it as a masterpiece of economy, a most simple and elegant design that has a precedent in the opening scene of *King Lear*.[8] "Design" is not an isolated metaphor for Rose, since his analysis of Shakespeare's dramatic text is continually supported by terms, procedures, and references typical of the aesthetics of the visual arts. The audience would thus be making a mental journey within the play, just as the eye runs over a series of narrative frescoes. At times, Rose seems to forget that as the dramatic scene is a scenic potentiality capable of being enjoyed yet lost in time, the audience cannot make a visual summary (an easy memorial synthesis) except in the absence of the object of their contemplation. They cannot enjoy the synchronic view of a story, but only undergo an effect. The effect of this "frame scene" in particular would therefore be analogous, according to Rose, to that of certain Renaissance perspective paintings, and specifically to the famous *Ambassadors* by Holbein (1533). J. Baltrusaitis devotes an entire chapter to this intriguing case of anamorphosis, identifying the structure of a double composition, in which each part emanates its point of view and is counterpoised to the other within the same frame.[9] Hence, the theatrical quality of the representation consisting of a first part and a second part, a dynamic formation of meaning merely by counterposition. Rose interprets the *Antony and Cleopatra* triptych as an anamorphic composition. The imaginative analogy is based on the intuition of an oppositive formation of meaning in action that is also in the dramatic text.

Being irreconcilable and equally convincing, the perspectives of the frame and centerpiece vibrate endlessly in our minds. The scene as a whole is contrived to provide a completely ambiguous view of Antony.

Closer analysis of this singular protatic triptych reveals a structure of action constructed in depth, a movement toward and from the thematic center, which is not homogeneous but composed of two different types of action. The intended event is that between Philo and Demetrius, the former invested with the role of the active sender, the latter with that of the passive receiver. They represent the polarity that makes theater possible; between Demetrius' question and Philo's answer there is a process of dramatic enunciation. But Philo leads up to the question with a brilliant evocation of the "figure" of Antony (actantial *débrayage*), fragmented in metonymic subjects, projected from its natural background, war, into a legendary then/there. The eyes that were "goodly," that "glowed like plated Mars [then] bend, now turn . . . devotion [now]; the captain's heart (then) is bellows and fan (now)." The name of Cleopatra, on two occasions replaced by a sacral insult, is marked by the possessive *'s:* "a gipsy's lust," a "strumpet's fool." Lust, the attribute that defines her, is the fire of that negative alchemy that causes the transformation of Antony, the pillar of the world, the cosmogonic phallic symbol, into a mere object, the symbol of subjugated masculinity. The three suppressions/additions that stand for the name of the unnamable (a tawny front, gipsy, strumpet)—always in final and conclusive position—leave their mark on the Antony of today, like an indelible scar.

Philo. Nay, but this dotage of our general's
O'erflows the measure. Those his goodly eyes,
That o'er the files and musters of the war
Have glowed like plated Mars, now bend, now turn
The office and devotion of their view
Upon a tawny front. His captain's heart,
Which in the scuffles of great fights hath burst
The buckles on his breast, reneges all temper
And is become the bellows and the fan
To cool a gipsy's lust. Look where they come!
Take but good note, and you shall see in him
The triple pillar of the world transformed
Into a strumpet's fool. Behold and see.
(*Antony and Cleopatra,* 1.1.1–13)

In the closing part of the triptych, which re-equilibrates and terminates the Philo-Demetrius relationship, there is the enunciation of the expectation of the double receiver for the theatrical event. The protatic complex, in this case, is action crowned by success, inducing a request: "Let the curtain rise! Let the dramatic enunciation open upon itself, let it be revealed!"

Demetrius. Is Caesar with Antonius prized so slight?
Philo. Sir, sometimes, when he is not Antony,
He comes too short of that great property
Which still should go with Antony.
Demetrius.   I am full sorry
That he approves the common liar who
Thus speaks of him in Rome, but I will hope
Of better deeds tomorrow. Rest you happy!
(1.1.57–63)

The stage action contained between the two moments in which it is enunciated (requested, commented on) finds in performance the variety and casualness of a real happening. The arrival of the messenger announcing a forbidden message marks the irruption of the outside world into the closed wordplay of the lovers. This forewarning of danger that separates the dialogue into two parts is reintegrated by Cleopatra in her violent inquisitorial project, a tortuous search for the truth eluded by the inertia of Antony's hyperbolic comment (1.1.14–56). The sequence is divided into seven conversational exchanges between Antony (A) and Cleopatra (C).[10]

Cleopatra's supremacy in the couple relationship is immediately proved by her role in the dialogue. It is she who asks the questions, or rather sets the theme and orders comment (our love, its quantity). Antony emphatically rejects the definition by quantity but agrees to a definition by extent, enunciating a boundless value: their love coincides spatially with new heaven and new earth (A2). For the second time, Antony avoids getting caught up in the implication of the conversation: "provide a definition of some kind of measurable value, which can generate a norm and discipline for the lover."[11] His reply is so hyperbolic and overwhelming, however, that it puts a stop to all further questions. The commentative tenses used (present, imperative, future) do not determine an existential here-now, but the non-place and non-time of logical or paralogic discourse. They signal happenings in a world devoid of referentiality.

The messenger, however, comes from the referential world. The "background," the elsewhere he has left (Rome), comes within the space of the couple, *res bina* of cosmogonic dimensions, and lacerates and besets the lovers. Recognizing immediately that the relationship with the referent will oblige Antony to measure their love pragmatically, Cleopatra constructs the message that Antony would prefer to hear only summarily, and imagines Fulvia and Octavian, who assert Antony's moral obligations, first in a story and then in a dialogue in the story. Rome's will is asserted as pure will, realized in the domain of the politically known world, and therefore endowed with quantity and extent. The messengers are its menacing, and often menaced, signals. Here, their appearance, invoked and denied throughout the dialogue-duel, becomes the hidden figure, the cuttlebone floating over the floor in Holbein's *Ambassadors*. Like all anamorphic "Vanities," it means "death," the ineluctable promise of all passion.

In this historical/existential agon, Antony agrees to match the political power of the Empire against that of the human couple—the one of clay, composed of perishable material and indifferent to the ends to which it is destined; the other supreme among human enterprises, its matter the nobility of life, a splendid paragon (A5).

An unexpected move by Cleopatra sets Antony himself as the missing theme, the split-off element of the couple (C5). Antony, who now systematically refuses the dialogic domination of his interlocutor, tries a new and diversely orienting theme: the use of the time spent in love, the time of pleasure, without memory, but intensely real, capable of being counted and treasured (A6).

This is followed by Cleopatra's only peremptory move: "Name the threat, hear the ambassadors!"—let the message at last be uttered that will not belie her own message, but rather will bestow futurity on it (C6).

Antony's winning reply is to choose the queen herself as the theme, in her dual existential and mythical accepted meaning, a place of passion and of precious transformations. There is no place for a messenger in the narrow existential space of the couple; in their mythical projection, they are and are not named. His proposal is to wander in the night through the deserted streets of Alexandria, watching without being seen, surrounded by the silence of the "background," now recognized and declared to be nonexistent, emptied of substance, disseminated through the shadows.

Can There Be Protasis Without Antony and Cleopatra?

The theory of dramatic action elaborated by prescriptive French criticism subtracts action (and the segment of action) from the accidentality of natural experience and the incongruence of the romantic taste of performance. Action has to be single, finalized, conventional, with steps and progressions that steadily mark its development, inextricably linked from start to finish. In *All for Love* (1678), the catastrophe and not the antefact is enunciated at the opening of the protatic complex. Dryden's purpose was to achieve a perspective arrangement of the semantic-narrative units, of the threads of the plot, the outcome of which (the catastrophe) is also the pole of attraction of the play's movement.

> Therefore, as in perspective, so in tragedy, there must be a point of sight in which all the lines terminate; otherwise the eye wanders, and the work is false.[12]

The perspective effect is of the type known in painting as "accelerated": the Shakespearian text having been promoted to a "natural perspective," the circumscribed time-place of the catastrophe is cut into it (after Actium, in Alexandria). This enmeshment of the beginning in the end bestows on the tragedy a sort of false movement toward the solution so that the end is always present at every point of the action. The expedient of the *liaison des scènes* is the presupposition of stereoscopic vision. The necessary and fatal concatenation of events is subtly exalted, and the play is better entitled to adopt the form of absolute drama.[13] Dryden is a playwright expunged from dramatic discourse but is within the project in the same way as the Hobbesian geometer.[14]

To maintain the linearity and essentiality of action, tragedy has two possibilities: either to open up in depth, making the character a perspective place, inhabited by a single immeasurable passion that reduces the character to a hieroglyphic sign of substance; or to accept the confrontation scene as an ample perspective, symmetrically balanced and rhetorically moved, of contrasting passions and ideologies. Use of the unity of place cancels "Alexandria" as a category of narrativity (the rich East-West opposition is indeed weakened in *All for Love*), and requires that rhetorical places, multiple perspectives of the word, open up on stage.

In the preface to *All for Love,* Dryden compares himself not with Shakespeare, as one might expect, but with Racine. Dryden had no intention of sacrificing to precious abstraction, to an extreme and vertiginous skillful interpretation of passions, the evident vitality of the confrontation scene, a gift of the city to the theater, of oratory to rhetoric, substance and not ceremony among men. (Along with Montaigne, he complains: "Nous ne sommes que cérémonie; la cérémonie nous emporte, et laissons la substance des choses.") In Dryden's tragedy, the confrontation scene establishes an alternation of perspectives that does not destroy the unity of the play—as Kibédi Varga[15] fears—but iterates its effects, operating analogously with the visible transformations prepared by the scenographer, the subsequent scenes that open and close upon themselves. Text and spectacle proceed in parallel fashion in accordance with the desires of the audience, passing from expectation to wonder. By means of the confrontation scene, the audience is actively involved, inscribed in the text; the arbiter of different situations, it formulates partial judgments. The procedures of deliberative discourse, both in the persuasion scenes and the accusation scenes, capture the "impassioned thought" of the Hobbesian spectator. According to Richard L. Larson, the confrontation scene, in its double meaning, constitutes an excellent alternative to battles, descriptions, surprising actions, lyrical passages and soliloquies:

> Dryden's artificial management of his persuasions and accusations establishes a rhythm for the action; the variations within the repetitive pattern help to emphasize the characters' unfortunate mistakes, and to make the tragic dénouement produce pity. Because it records vividly the bases for his characters' behavior, Dryden's structure is well planned to achieve the effects he desired.[16]

The problem of the distance between the first text and the second does not arise in the case of *All for Love*. The protatic complex of *All for Love* is not a remake of that of *Antony and Cleopatra*, but only a parallel text, springing from the same *fabula*, in which the relationship between the level of the plot and that of discourse is abnormal—a minimum advance in the plot (reduced to its final part) corresponds to a maximum extension of the verbal surface (the confrontation scene). The beginning signifies the end with a subtle interplay of references: the macrocosm, the initial *topos* of this upside-down world, contains the microcosm, the final death of the lovers. Dryden's text has the effect of a palindrome. An empirical scheme of verbal turns may make it easier to understand the modalities of this singular neoclassical protasis, from which the two protagonists are mimetically absent.

1st cycle	*2nd cycle*	*3rd cycle*
1. S1–M1	3. A1–S3	6. M2–A4
2. S2	4. A2–S4	7. S6–A5
	5. A3–S5	8. S7–A6
		9. S8–A7
		10. S9–A8

The first cycle consists of two monologues, separated not so much by the weak intervention of Myris and the entrance of Alexas, not seen by the characters on stage, but by the different function which they assume in the perspective construction of the catastrophe. Thematically, they proceed from the general to the particular. The first is an exquisite (Ovidian) poetic passage on the upside-down world, run through by the feeling of catastrophe; the second is a description of sepulchral vault with a ghost. Serapion, with the rapid effect of internal *débrayage*, relates the horrid scene that predicts the ruin of Egypt and the strong emotion he has felt: terror and pity. The cathartic passions of catastrophe have possessed him, and he himself has become an emblem and example of a tragic spectator. This two-part complex proceeds temporally from the (implicit) future to the past perfect, the past, and the threshold of the (as yet unsaid) present.

In the second cycle, Alexas reveals himself, taking the initiative in the dialogue, characterizing Serapion and himself, operating the passage between two levels of discourse: that emerging directly from the *fabula,* with the strong tension of the "end as beginning" theme, and that of the *plot,* "antefact as beginning." The spectator, in the traditional "he" position, is invited to scan the scenographic horizon (A5) in order to find there the Roman camp, a dark menace looming over the Egyptian presence which occupies the foreground, the here-now space of enunciation and the proscenium. After Myris's question (third cycle), the variety of the information is ensured by the shifting of the authoritative Alexas to the position of the answerer. Although the principle of cooperation and the rules of quality, relation, and manner are respected, Alexas constructs for himself a dominant position toward his questioner. He exceeds in quantity (he is somewhat brighter than Serapion), he uses conversational implication, he cooperates with Serapion in sharing, distributing, expanding the points of the antefact, and producing *débrayage* effects. In this way, the only point of view of this protatic complex is formed: the Egyptian point of view. The fated couple appears here only as causation of the end, mentioned by Alexas: Cleopatra, fluidly clasping the powerful ruin of Antony; and Antony, a prey suspended between the approaching hands of his persecutors and the airy hands of Cleopatra.

"Well, you know the State of Things" (A8) closes the unilinear protasis of *All for Love,* which conclusively establishes a statute for the seventeenth-century spectator, split and metonymic: ear for the poet and eye for the scenographer.

Can There Be Protatic Function Without Protasis?

The armed Prologue in Shakespeare's *Troilus and Cressida* derives from the fabula and draws the attention of the audience to the fabula. It is intended to make dramatic irony emerge from the fabula before the process of mythologization begins. The Prologue enunciates the dramatic scene ("In Troy there lies the scene"), the argument ("the quarrel"), the antefact, the cancellation of the protasis as a unique place of protatic function ("our play Leaps o'er the vaunt and firstlings of those broils, Beginning in the middle"). The armed Prologue is a metaphoric irruption of the real into the space of fiction. It comes from war (reality), from which it bears the awareness of the conventional and already decided nature of the play. It invokes judgment of the play by the audience, as unpredictable and arbitrary as the outcome of war.

> Like, or find fault: do as your pleasures are:
> Now good, or bad, 'tis but the chance of war.
>
> (30–31)

As promised, *Troilus and Cressida* begins *in medias res*. The identity is immediately established between personal test (scene 1) and collective test (scene 3), between erotic and heroic achievement, between woman and city (to be taken, held, or lost). After this, only a continuous process takes place. "Nothing exists in the perfect tense, and nothing is ever really or permanently done."[17] If, as hypothesized, the fabula centers on the dramatic archetype of the Trial, both Apollonian and Dionysian, here it is not a case of passing or failing. It is uniquely a case of its being (incessant desire, necessary challenge to death) and of the enunciation in relation to the two-faced figurations that delimit it, Fortune and Time, coadjuvant or contrasting.

> Tell me, Apollo, for thy Daphne's love,
> What Cressid is, what Pandar, and what we.
> Her bed is India; there she lies, a pearl.
> Between our Ilium and where she resides,
> Let it be call'd the wild and wand'ring flood,
> Ourself the merchant, and this sailing Pandar
> Our doubtful hope, our convoy and our bark.
>
> (1.1.98–104)

> In the reproof of chance
> Lies the true proof of men. The sea being smooth,
> How many shallow bauble boats dare sail
> Upon her patient breast, making their way
> With those of nobler bulk;
> But let the ruffian Boreas once enrage
> The gentle Thetis, and anon behold
> The strong-ribb'd bark through liquid mountains cut,
> Bounding between the two moist elements
> Like Perseus' horse. Where's then the saucy boat
> Whose weak untimber'd sides but even now

>   Co-rivall'd greatness? Either to harbour fled,
>   Or made a toast for Neptune.
>
>   (1.3.33–45)

The test is not governed, or governable, by the hero, but is endlessly reproposed, seeking temporary and multiple heroes, different circumstances, derisive or contradictory solutions that are a denial of a final solution and instead favor a perspective of tests, none of which has the dignity of a final regenerating catastrophe. Historical man acts and suffers obscure and shapeless events. History is progress toward a non-goal; it is simply the movement of an illusionistic oriflamme, the barbaric ire that enflames Troy and Troilus.

"The aim of Dryden in adapting *Troilus and Cressida*," according to Kenneth Muir, "was to make a tragedy out of it, a tragedy based on a misunderstanding."[18] The subtitle, *Truth Found Too Late* (1679), announces the formal and substantial intention. The synchronicity of Shakespeare's text (temporally simultaneous scenes, evanescence of causal nexuses) is transformed in the linearity of Dryden's rewriting. The ordering energy of the plot sets the three-part action (beginning, middle, end) in motion toward the denouement. Not only is the fantastic, mysterious urgency of the fabula lost ("this hybrid and hundred-faced and hydra-headed prodigy," as Swinburne was to define it), but also the archetype of the Trial is removed.[19] In actual fact, there was no Trial but only an erroneous linearization, a mistaken *dispositio* of the situations. Dryden does not question, or test, the high honor of the soldiers or the low honor of Cressida. The fabula is based on a cult archetype, on Honor as an abstract, demanding, coercive sign that subordinates destiny and character. The weakness of this dramatic premise lies in the absence of choice between Honor and Duty, morality or passion, in its ineluctable, gratuitous, exterior character. An honored Cressida is not a sufficient guarantee for the refoundation of the mythical world, for the return of the heroes.

The protatic function is disseminated by Dryden in different places: (a) in the prologue; (b) in the preface; (c) in the inversion of the first two macrosequences.

The prologue, in its rough metatextual intention, enunciates the author of the new version (Dryden of Shakespeare, Shakespeare of Homer) as a preliminary and necessary condition of the text, and therefore as a protatic character par excellence who brings to the stage the incessant rewriting of texts, an author who is a sign of the epochality of the text, who operates and undergoes the rewriting, a querulous and impotent ghost destined to haunt the threshold of drama

> See, my loved Britons, see your Shakespeare rise,
> An awful ghost confessed to human eyes!
> Unnamed methinks, distinguished I had been
> From other shades, by this eternal green,
> About whose wreaths the vulgar poets strive,
> And with a touch, their withered bays revive.
> Untaught, unpractised, in a barbarous age,
> I found not, but created first the stage.
> And, if I drained no Greek or Latin store,
> 'Twas, that my own abundance gave me more.
> On foreign trade I needed not rely,
> Like fruitful Britain, rich without supply.
> In this my rough-drawn play, you shall behold
> Some master-strokes, so manly and so bold,
> That he who meant to alter, found 'em such,
> He shook, and thought it sacrilege to touch.
> Now, where are the successors to thy name?
> What bring they to fill out a poet's fame?
> Weak, short-lived issues of a feeble age;
> Scarce living to be christened on the stage!
> For humour farce, for love they rhyme dispense,
> That tolls the knell for their departed sense.
> Dulness might thrive in any trade but this:
> 'Twould recommend to some fat benefice.
> Dulness, that in a play-house meets disgrace,
> Might meet with reverence, in its proper place.
> The fulsome clench, that nauseates the town,
> Would from a judge or alderman go down,
> Such virtue is there in a robe and gown!
> And that insipid stuff which here you hate,
> Might somewhere else be called a grave debate;
> Dulness is decent in the church and state.
> But I forget that still 'tis understood,
> Bad plays are best decried by showing good.
> Sit silent then, that my pleased soul may see
> A judging audience once, and worthy me;
> My faithful scene from true records shall tell,
> How Trojan valour did the Greeks excel:
> Your great forefathers shall their fame regain,
> And Homer's angry ghost repine in vain.[20]

In the preface—which precedes the *Grounds*—the author gives way to the critical ego that has performed the rewriting and indicates the operations of suppression on the stylistic level ("his whole style is so pestered with figurative expressions, that it is affected as it is obscure").

(a) cancellation of obscurities (metaphors, metaphoric constellations, motifs) and archaisms:

I undertook to remove that heap of rubbish . . .
I have refined his language, which before was obsolete;

(b) addition-suppression at the level of plot and discourse:

I new modelled the plot; threw out many unnecessary persons; improved those characters which were begun and left unfinished . . . and added that of Andromache.
The beginning scenes of the fourth act are either added or changed wholly by me; the middle of it is Shakespeare altered and mingled with my own; three or four of the last scenes are altogether new. And the whole fifth act, both the plot and the writing, are my own additions.

(c) new linkings:

I made . . . an order and connection of all the scenes;
I have so ordered them that there is a coherence of 'em with one another, and a dependence on the main design . . .

The inversion of the first two macrosequences is part of the operation of new linkings, with the result that the *incipit* of the tragedy is substantially modified. The *Troilus 1679* opens with the third scene of Shakespeare's *Troilus*. The Greek council is placed before the two scenes in Troy in order to invert the hierarchy of values: war makes History and the separate world of the lovers is destroyed in its violent course.

In the case of *Troilus and Cressida,* Dryden's rewriting operates directly (and violently) on Shakespeare's text. The linearization demanded by the hegemony of the plot is plainly signaled by the closure of the syntagm which, recovering its part of protatic function, sets itself as the beginning-cause of the dual story of love and war. The closure coincides with the end of the action (the Greek leaders' debate) and the plan of future action, whereas Shakespeare's text flows into the following sequence with almost naturalistic effect. With a brusque change of attention, Agamemnon asks: "What trumpet? Look, Menelaus," and the Trojan Aeneas advances in the denotable space of the Elizabethan stage. The drastic reduction of the text (Dryden eliminates about half of Shakespeare's lines) causes a change in quality. The dialogic turns are shortened and interlinked according to a rational principle of cooperation which spontaneously observes the rules of quantity (giving an informative contribution appropriate to the request), of relation (reduction of the symbolic dilatation of Shakespeare's language) and of manner (as specified in the introduction). The motif of the test, stripped of its rich referentiality, springs from an accident of the plot: the senseless dallying in the military enterprise. The complementary motif of degree is lowered and reduced by means of a substitution that precedes the *detractio* proper.

> O, when *degree* is shaked, (Shakespeare)
> O, when *supremacy of kings* is shaken (Dryden)

A symbolic figure of society, degree (with which the discord of natural elements and of parts of the social body is in contrast) is replaced by a political and contingent entity, absolute monarchy. Ignoring the historical relationships linking the Greek leaders to Agamemnon, *primus inter pares,* Dryden bestows on him the function and quality of an absolute sovereign. Dryden modernizes him with the clear intention of political propaganda. Seeking a new form for a new substance, Dryden also modifies the sociolinguistic mechanisms regulating the debate. Agamemnon, assimilated to Charles II among his courtiers, holds the absolute power of speech. He confers and revokes it, he foreordains its comment, and demotes it in favor of practical action.

If *immutatio* (substitution) is thus a direct ideological action on the substance, *detractio* (subtraction of quantity or intensity)—which traverses action, dialogue, and character—starts from the form of the substance. Shakespeare's Achilles, possessed with the hubris of the tragic hero, "Grows dainty of *his* worth," while Dryden's, more reasonably and modestly envious of Agamemnon's sovereign power, "Disdains *thy* sovereign charge." (The neoclassical subject lives on the outside, in its relationship with its social environment, by which it is influenced and by which it influences.) Dryden's character does not proceed from history to literature (or from literature to literature) without the filter of that great connective principle of that which is "proper" (the Aristotelian πρέπον, the Renaissance "decorum" which adapts action to dialogue and both of these to the individual character). Not merely a formal relationship between the parts (class, character, language), the "proper" regulates the relationship with the audience and extends as far as the problem of understanding and receiving the play. Seventeenth-century criticism regards as a social and psychological subcategory "usage and custom," or *moeurs* (especially Le Bossu, *Traité du Poème Epique,* 1675) or manners, which Dryden describes in the *Grounds,* following the French text almost word for word.[21] The dramatic performance contains this knowledge of proper behaviors that models the reality-performance-reception relationship. It predetermines, and at the same time verifies, the transparency, fidelity, and consistency of the characters. It interprets—and, in general, comforts—the capacity of the average audience to be—and of seeing itself to be—in society and in a social relationship. Dryden developed his conviction of the centrality of manners as he rewrote *Troilus,* apparently remaining indifferent to the censorial function of this often moralistic and political category.

In *Troilus,* an attempt is made to meet the audience in the space between nature and fiction belonging to the high culture of neoclassicism, where the codes of totally ritualized behaviors, regulated by a grandiose, deductive, and abstract rhetoric are formed. It is this exemplary and coercive theater that invents the (implausible) fidelity of Cressida.

Notes

An earlier Italian version of this article appeared in *Le forme del teatro* II, ed. G. Melchiori (Rome: Edizioni di Storia e Letteratura, 1981).

1. According to Dryden, Aristotle divides a play into four parts, and the *incipit* is defined as the first part of a whole: "First, the *protasis,* or entrance, which gives light only to the characters of the persons, and proceeds very little into any part of the action." From *The Works of John Dryden,* ed. H. T. Swedenborg, Jr. et al., 21 vols. (Berkeley: University of California Press, 1956–), *Prose 1668–1691,* ed. S. H. Monk et al., 17: 23. This is not unlike the modern definition by Heinrich Lausberg, *Elemente der literarischen Rhetorik* (München: Max Hueber Verlag: 1949), 52b, who subdivides the dramatic plot into a preparatory phase of information, or *protasis,* and an active phase, or *epitasis,* potentiating the situation.

Dryden is aware of the two main difficulties threatening a good *incipit*: the unnaturalness of the protatic personage, who disappears immediately after performing his function (like Philo and Demetrius in *Antony and Cleopatra*) and the tedium due the long antefact, "the ruin of the play" (17:39), as in the case of *All for Love.*

Jacques Scherer maintains that it is the discontinuous protasis that represents a problem. It should, therefore, be defined as "l'ensemble de ces faits qui constitue proprement l'exposition. Leur répartition dans la pièce, c'est-à-dire la place que leur énoncé occupe dans les différentes scènes, définira les limites précises de ce premier moment du poème dramatique." From *La dramaturgie classique en France* (Paris: A. G. Nizet, 1977), 51. The perfect protasis may be short and complete, but also discontinuous and pruned of the archaic protatic personages, as well as interesting and plausible. Its typology is rich; the presence of the chorus and the monologue of the hero are the most ancient examples. Typically, Racinian is the protasis with the protagonist and a confidant, sometimes even two confidants (*All for Love* provides a variant of this type) or two heroes (of which Dryden's *Troilus* is a variant). The most interesting distinction, in my view, is that between diegetic or mostly narrative protasis and mimetic protasis—that is, dramatic protasis as defined by Jean-Marie Clément in his treatise *De la tragédie* (Amsterdam and Paris: Moutard, 1784) 2:78–79; quoted in Scherer, *La dramaturgie,* 59.

2. Lotman, *Struktura chudožestvennogo teksta* (Moskva: Ed. Iskusstvo, 1970).

3. Compare Christopher Spencer's edition, *Five Restoration Adaptations of Shakespeare* (Urbana: University of Illinois Press, 1965). References to Shakespeare's plays are taken from the relevant New Arden editions.

4. "In a sequence of simple and/or compound acts there is a given purpose, but the acts may be relatively independent in the sense that even when they condition each other these relations are not planned to realize a specific result. . . . The sequence is unified (is not an arbitrary series of acts) under the identity of agent(s), a continuous period of time, and the execution of the various acts under one purpose." This definition is by Teun A. van Dijk, *Text and Context: Explorations in the Semantics and Pragmatics of Discourse* (London: Longman, 1977), 177.

5. Compare Algirdas J. Greimas and Joseph Courtés, *Sémiotique. Dictionnaire Raisonné de la Théorie du Langage* (Paris: Classiques Hachette, 1979), under *débrayage,* 79–82.

6. Thomas Hobbes, *Leviathan,* ed. C. B. Macpherson, (Harmondsworth: Penguin, 1968), See, in this regard, Aldo Gargani, *Hobbes e la scienza* (Turin: Einaudi, 1971).

7. "Past the Size of Dreaming," in *Twentieth-Century Interpretations of "Antony and Cleopatra",* ed. Mark Rose (Englewood Cliffs, N.Y.: Prentice-Hall, 1977), 99–112.

8. *Shakespeare Design* (Cambridge, Mass.: Harvard University Press, 1974).

9. *Anamorphoses ou magie artificielle des effets merveilleux* (Paris, 1955). Rose does not cite Baltrusaitis, who advances interesting hypotheses regarding the possibility that Shakespeare actually saw anamorphic paintings. The *Ambassadors* was painted in London, and the anamorphic portrait of Edward VI was at Whitehall.

10. Rose, *Shakespeare Design,* 164.

11. For the conversation analysis I have used the catagories of H. P. Grace, *Logic and Conversation,* William James Lectures at Harvard University, (Cambridge: Mass, 1967). Paola Gulli Pugliatti's essay, "Per un'indagine sulla convenzione nel testo drammatico," *Strumenti critici* 39–40 (1979): 428–47, is very useful. Of quite different orientation, and therefore not convergent with my analysis, is the essay by G. R. Hibbard, "Feliciter audax: *Antony and Cleopatra,*" I, 1, 1–24", in *Shakespeare's Styles: Essays in Honour of Kenneth Muir,* ed. Edwards, Ewbank, and Hunter (Cambridge: Cambridge University Press, 1980), 95–109. A2 means Antony's second speech.

12. From *The Grounds of Criticism in Tragedy* (1679), in John Dryden, *Of Dramatic Poesy and other Critical Essays,* ed. George Watson (London: Dent, 1962, 2 vols., I: 244.
13. See Jacques Scherer, *La dramaturgie classique,* 266-84.
14. Thomas Hobbes, *Opera philosophica,* 2d ed., 5 vols., ed. W. Molesworth (London, 1839-45; Aalen, 1966) I:3. "Per ratiocinationem autem intelligo computationem. Computare vero est *plurimum rerum simul additarum summam colligere, vel una re ab alia detracta, cognoscere residuum.* Ratiocinari igitur idem est quod *addere* et *subtrahere,* vel si quis adjugant his *multiplicare* et *dividere,* non abnuam, cum *multiplicatio* idem sit quod aequalium *additio, divisio* quod aequalium quoties fieri potest *substractio.* Recidit itaque ratiocinatio omnis ad duas operationes animi *additionem* et *aubstractionem.*"
15. "La perspective tragique. Eléménts pour une analyse formelle de la tragédie classique," *Revue d'Histoire Littéraire de la France* 70 (1970): 918-30.
16. R. L. Larson, *Studies in Dryden's Dramatic Technique: The Use of Scenes Depicting Persuasion and Accusation* (Salzburg: Salzburg Studies in English Literature, 1975), 28.
17. Northrop Frye, "The Ironic Vision," *Troilus and Cressida. A Selection of Critical Essays,* ed. P. Martin, Casebook Series (London: Macmillan, 1976), 182.
18. "Three Shakespeare Adaptations," *Proceedings of the Leeds Philosophical and Literary Society,* Literary and Historical Section 8:3 (November 1957): 233-40.
19. From *Troilus and Cressida,* ed. P. Martin, 55. On the composition of the play, see also my essay, "Appunti per una lettura del *Troilus and Cressida,*" *Scritti in ricordo di Gabriele Baldini,* ed. Vittorio Gabrieli (Rome: Edizioni di Storia e Letteratura, 1972), 259-74.
20. *Troilus and Cressida,* ed. W. Scott and G. Saintsbury, 2nd ed., 18 vols. (London, 1882-92): 6.
21. In the *Grounds,* Dryden recognizes Le Bossu as the best of the modern critics, without, however, precisely stating the extent of his debt.

Bibliography

This is a bibliography of recent monographs and collections of essays on Renaissance studies published in Italy. Individual articles, reviews, translations, and editions of plays are not listed. A great number of relevant entries can be found in the proceedings of the annual meeting of the Italian Association of English Studies (A.I.A.), and in the following major journals and periodicals devoted to English literature:

Analysis, Pisa (1983–1987).
Anglistica, Istituto Universitario Orientale, Naples (1974–   ).
English Miscellany, Rome (1950–1984).
Studi inglesi, Bari (1974–1978).
Textus, English Studies in Italy, Genoa (1988–   ).

Relevant book reviews are mostly to be found in the aforementioned publications. A periodical review article by Michele Marrapodi, "Elizabethan Studies in Italy," is to be found in *Cahiers Elisabéthains* from No. 37, April 1990, onward.
The most complete and updated bilingual edition of Shakespeare's plays, with translations by various hands, is that by Giorgio Melchiori (9 vols., Milan: Mondadori, 1976–91). The complete works in Italian translations by various hands, without the English text, have been edited by Mario Praz (Florence: Sansoni, 3 vols. 1943–47; 1 vol., 1964). The complete plays have also been translated by Cesare Vico Lodovici (Turin: Einaudi, 3 vols., 1960, and 5 vols., 1964), and the complete works by Gabriele Baldini (3 vols., Milan: Rizzoli, 1963). A bilingual edition of all the works in separate volumes with translations by various hands appears under the general editorship of Nemi D'Agostino and, after his death in 1993, of Sergio Perosa (Milan: Garzanti, 1987–). In the same form, Agostino Lombardo presents his translation of the complete plays (Milan: Feltrinelli, 1991–). Alessandro Serpieri has edited and translated the Q1 and Q2-F texts of *Hamlet* (2 vols., Venice: Marsilio, 1997).

Abbamonte, Lucia. *La maschera e lo specchio del tempo: Ben Jonson, Giacomo I e lo spettacolo del re. Immagini shakespeariane.* Naples: Edizioni Scientifiche Italiane, 1996.

Allegri, Luigi. *Tre Shakespeare della compagnia del collettivo teatro due.* Florence: Liberoscambio, 1983.

Almansi, Guido. *Il ciclo della scommessa dal "Decameron" al "Cymbeline" di Shakespeare.* Rome: Bulzoni, 1976.

Amato, A. ed. *Ben Jonson: Masques.* Rome: Bulzoni, 1966.

Anzi, Anna Cavallone. *Shakespeare nei teatri milanesi del Novecento.* Bari: Adriatica, 1980.

———. *Varie e strane forme: Shakespeare, il masque e il gusto manieristico* Milan: Unicopli, 1984.

———. *Storia del teatro inglese dalle origini al 1660.* Turin: Einaudi, 1997.

Aradas, Isabella. *Macbeth in Italia.* Bari: Adriatica, 1989.

Baccolini, R., V. Fortunati, and R. Zacchi, eds. *Il teatro e le donne. Forme drammatiche e tradizione al femminile nel teatro inglese.* Urbino: Quattroventi, 1991.

Baldini, Gabriele. *Manualetto shakespeariano.* Turin, Einaudi, 1964.

———. *La fortuna di Shakespeare 1593–1964.* 2 vols. Milan: Mondadori, 1965.

Barnabò, Antonella, and Roberta Ferrari. *La presenza di Shakespeare in T. S. Eliot e J. Joyce.* Pisa: ETS Editrice, 1992.

Bartalotta, Gianfranco. *Amleto in Italia nel Novecento.* Bari: Adriatica, 1986.

Bottalla, Paola. *"True plain words:" la dinamica tra "plain style" e "country style" dal tardo Medioevo al Seicento.* vol. 1. Abano: Piovan, 1988.

Bottalla, Paola, and Michela Calderaro, eds. *Counting and Recounting: Measuring Inner and Outer Space in the Renaissance.* Trieste: Edizioni La Mongolfiera, 1995.

Bragaglia, L. *Shakespeare in Italia.* Rome: Trevi, 1973.

Bravo, Paola. *Voci della follia. I tragici folli shakespeariani.* Florence: Libri Atheneum, 1994.

Busi, Anna. *Othello in Italia, 1777-1972.* Bari: Adriatica, 1973.

———. *Il teatro della metamorfosi. Saggio su "The Revenger's Tragedy."* Bari: Adriatica, 1988.

Caliumi, Grazia, ed. *Shakespeare e la sua eredità.* Parma: Zara, 1993.

———. *Studi e ricerche sulle fonti italiane del teatro elisabettiano.* Rome: Bulzoni, 1984.

Capone, Giovanna. *Ben Jonson: l'iconologia verbale come strategia di commedia.* Bologna: Pàtron, 1969.

Cappelli, Domenico. *Saggio sullo strutturalismo. Saggio sul "King Lear" di W. Shakespeare.* Cassino: Garigliano, 1978.

Cappuzzo, Marcello. *Da Duncan a Malcolm: la tragedia di Macbeth.* Messina: Peloritana, 1972.

Caretti, Laura, ed. *Il teatro del personaggio: Shakespeare sulla scena italiana dell'800.* Rome: Bulzoni, 1979.

Carotenuto, Silvana. *La voce di Mnemosine: Percorsi teatrali da William Shakespeare a Robert Wilson.* Naples: Istituto Universitario Orientale, 1990.

Carpi, Daniela. *Sintomi di modernità. Trasformazioni di convenzioni drammatiche nel teatro rinascimentale inglese.* Bologna: Compositori, 1990.

Carpi, D., G. Franci, and G. Silvani. *Raccontare i giardini.* Milan: Guerini, 1993.

Castorina, Giuseppe G., and Vittoriana Villa, eds. *La fortuna della retorica.* Chieti: Méthis Editrice, 1993.

Cataldi, Antonietta. *La stirpe di Falstaff.* Florence: Le Monnier, 1989.

———. *Da poeta a poeta. Il sonetto XXXIII di Shakespeare nella traduzione di Montale e di Ungaretti.* Galatina: Congedo, 1996.

Cattaneo, Arturo. *L'ideale umanistico. Henry Howard, Earl of Surrey.* Bari: Adriatica, 1991.

Chiabò, M., and F. Doglio. eds. *Teatro comico tra Medioevo e Rinascimento: la farsa.* Rome: Centro Studi sul Teatro Medievale e Rinascimentale, 1987.

Ciocca, Rossella. *Il cerchio d'oro: i re sacri nel teatro shakespeariano.* Rome: Officina Edizioni, 1987.

Colaiacomo, Paola. *La prova: saggi da Shakespeare a Beckett.* Rome: Editori Riuniti, 1993.

Colesanti, M. *Stendhal, Racine e Shakespeare.* Palermo: Sellerio di Giorgianni, 1980.

Colombo, Rosa Maria. *Le utopie e la storia: saggio sull'"Othello" di Shakespeare.* Bari: Adriatica, 1975.

Corona, Mario. *La fortuna di Shakespeare a Milano, 1800–1825.* Bari: Adriatica, 1970.

Corradini, Silvia, ed. *Il valore del falso. Errori, inganni, equivoci sulle scene europee in epoca barocca.* Rome: Bulzoni, 1994.

Corsani, Mary. *Il linguaggio teatrale di Thomas Middleton.* Genoa: Il Melangolo, 1979.

Corti, Claudia. *Macbeth: La parola e l'immagine.* Pisa: Pacini, 1983.

———. ed. *Il Rinascimento.* Bologna: Il Mulino, 1994.

———. *Shakespeare illustrato.* Rome: Bulzoni, 1996.

Cosentino, Giacomo. *Crisi e valore nel "Coriolano" di Shakespeare.* Catania: Cuecm, 1986.

———. *La coscienza della natura umana nel "Coriolano" di Shakespeare.* Catania: Cuecm, 1988.

Crinò, Anna Maria. *John Shirley, drammaturgo di corte.* Verona: Ghidini e Fiorini, 1968.

Curti, Lidia, Laura Di Michele, Thomas Frank, and Marina Vitale, eds. *Il muro del linguaggio: Conflitto e tragedia.* Naples: Istituto Universitario Orientale, 1987.

Curti, Lidia. *Peter Brook e Shakespeare: alla ricerca di un'avanguardia nel teatro inglese.* Naples: Istituto Universitario Orientale, 1984.

———. ed. *Ombre di un'ombra. Amleto e i suoi fantasmi.* Naples: Istituto Universitario Orientale, 1994.

D'Agostino, Nemi. *Shakespeare e i Greci.* Rome: Bulzoni, 1994.

D'Agostino, N., G. Melchiori, and A. Lombardo, eds., *Teatro elisabettiano: Marlowe-Webster-Ford.* Vicenza: Accademia Olimpica, 1975.

D'Amico, Masolino. *Scena e parola in Shakespeare.* Turin: Einaudi, 1974.

———. *Dieci secoli di teatro inglese: 1970–1980* Milan: Mondadori, 1981.

———. *Storia del teatro inglese*. Rome: Newton Compton, 1995.

Deidda, Angelo. *Icone della malinconia. I sonetti di William Shakespeare.* Cagliari: Cuec, 1996.

De Michelis, L. *La vita e le opere di Sir Walter Raleigh.* Palermo: Sellerio, 1993.

Dente Baschiera, Carla. *La recita del diritto: Saggio su "The Merchant of Venice".* Pisa: ETS, 1986.

De Scarpis, V., L. Innocenti, F. Marucci, and A. Pajalich, eds. *Intrecci e contaminazioni.* Venice: Supernova, 1993.

De Stasio, C., M. Gotti, and R. Bonadei, eds. *La rappresentazione verbale e iconica: valori estetici e funzionali.* Milan: Guerini, 1990.

Di Michele, Laura. *La scena dei potenti. Teatro, politica, spettacolo nell'età di W. Shakespeare.* Naples: Istituto Universitario Orientale, 1988.

———. ed. *Otello e le riscritture contemporanee.* Naples: Istituto Universitario Orientale, 1993.

———. ed. *Aspetti di "Othello".* Naples: Liguori, 1996.

Dodd, William. *"Misura per misura:" la trasparenza della commedia.* Milan: Il Formichiere, 1979.

Dodd, William. et al. eds., *Interazione, dialogo, convenzioni. Il caso del testo drammatico.* Bologna: CLUEB, 1983.

Domenichelli, Mario. *Il limite dell'ombra. Le figure della soglia nel teatro inglese fra Cinque e Seicento.* Milan: Franco Angeli, 1994.

Elam, Keir, ed. *Shakespeare Today: Directions and Methods of Research.* Florence: La Casa Usher, 1984.

———. *La Semiotica del teatro.* Bologna: Il Mulino, 1986.

———. ed. *La grande festa del linguaggio: Shakespeare e la lingua inglese.* Bologna: Il Mulino, 1986.

Faini, Paola, and Viola Papetti, eds. *Le forme del teatro. Saggi sul teatro elisabettiano e della Restaurazione.* Rome: Pubblicazione del Dipartimento di letterature comparate della Terza Università degi studi di Roma, 1994.

Farinella, Odetta Tita. *Timon of Athens.* Rome: Bulzoni, 1991.

Fazio, Mara. *Il mito di Shakespeare e il teatro romantico. Dallo* Sturm und Drang *a Victor Hugo.* Rome: Bulzoni, 1993.

Ferrara, Fernando. *Shakespeare e la commedia.* Bari: Adriatica, 1964.

———. *Shakespeare e le voci della storia.* Rome: Bulzoni, 1994.

———. *Il teatro dei re. Saggio sui drammi storico-politici di Shakespeare.* Bari: Adriatica, 1995.

Fusini, Nadia. *La passione dell'origine: studi sul tragico shakespeariano e il romanzo moderno.* Bari: Dedalo, 1981.

Gabrieli, Vittorio, and Giorgio Melchiori, eds. *The Book of Sir Thomas More.* Bari: Adriatica, 1981.

Gabrieli, Vittorio. *La storia d'Inghilterra nel teatro di Shakespeare.* Rome: Bulzoni, 1995.

Gatti, Hilary. *Shakespeare nei teatri milanesi dell'Ottocento.* Bari: Adriatica, 1968.

Gentili, Vanna. *La recita della follia. Funzioni dell'insania nel teatro di Shakespeare.* Turin: Einaudi, 1978.

———. ed. *Trasgressione tragica e norma domestica: Esemplari di tipologie femminili nella letteratura europea*. Roma: Ed. di Storia e Letteratura, 1983.
———. *La Roma antica degli Elisabettiani*. Bologna: Il Mulino, 1991.
———. *Il suicidio in Shakespeare. Negli scenari della psicosociologia contemporanea*. Milan: Angeli, 1996.
Guido, M. Grazia. *King Lear Workshop*. Congedo: Humanitas, 1992.
Guiducci, Roberto. *Studi sociologici su Shakespeare: Analisi dell'Amleto e dell'Othello*. Milan, 1979.
Gozzi, Francesco. *Il silenzio di Dio. Per una lettura di "King Lear"*. Pisa: ETS, 1993.
Innocenti, Loretta. *La scena trasformata: Adattamenti neoclassici di Shakespeare*. Florence: Sansoni, 1985.
———. ed. *Il teatro elisabettiano*. Bologna: Il Mulino, 1994.
Innocenti, Loretta, Franco Marucci, and Paola Pugliatti, eds. *Semeia. Itinerari per Marcello Pagnini*. Bologna: Il Mulino, 1994.
Johnson, A. L. *Readings of "Antony and Cleopatra" and "King Lear"*. Pisa: ETS, 1979.
Kennan, Patricia. *Sidney Defending Poetry*. Bari: Adriatica, 1990.
Kennan, Patricia, and Mariangela Tempera. eds. *Shakespeare from Text to Stage*. Bologna: CLUEB, 1992.
Kennan, Patricia, and Mariangela Tempera, eds. *International Shakespeare: The Tragedies*. Bologna: CLUEB, 1996.
Locatelli, Angela. *L'eloquenza e gli incantesimi: interpretazioni shakespeariane* Milan: Guerini, 1988.
———. *Il Doppio e il Picaresco: Un caso paradigmatico nel Rinascimento inglese*. Milan: Jacabook, 1998.
Lombardo, Agostino, *Lettura del "Macbeth"*. Vicenza: Neri Pozza, 1969.
———. *Ritratto di Enobarbo*. Pisa: Nistri-Lischi, 1971.
———. ed., *Shakespeare e Jonson: il teatro elisabettiano oggi*. Rome: Officina Edizioni, 1979.
———. *Il testo e la sua "performance."* Rome: Editori Riuniti, 1986.
———. ed., *Shakespeare a Verona e nel Veneto*. Verona: Accademia di Agricoltura, Scienze e Lettere, 1987.
———. *Per una critica imperfetta*. Rome: Editori Riuniti, 1992.
———. *Strehler e Shakespeare*. Rome: Bulzoni, 1992.
———. *Il fuoco e l'aria: Quattro studi su "Antonio e Cleopatra."* Rome: Bulzoni, 1995.
———. *L'eroe tragico moderno. Faust, Amleto, Otello*. Rome: Donzelli, 1996.
Lombardo, Agostino, and Neri Pozza, eds. *Atti del Convegno di Studi su Shakespeare e il "Giulio Cesare"*. Vicenza: Accademia Olimpica, 1980.
Maccioni, Giampiero, ed. *Tutto Shakespeare: Primo ciclo, una produzione BBC*. Rome: Raitre, 1984.
———. ed. *Tutto Shakespeare: Secondo ciclo, una produzione BBC*. Rome: Raitre, 1984.
———. ed. *Tutto Shakespeare: Terzo ciclo, una produzione BBC*. Rome: Raitre, 1986.

———. ed. *Tutto Shakespeare: Quarto ciclo, una produzione BBC*. Rome: Raitre, 1987.

Mango, Achille. *Dentro la finzione*. Rome: Kepos, 1993.

Marenco, Franco. *Arcadia puritana*. Bari: Adriatica, 1968.

———. ed. *Thomas Middleton e il teatro barocco in Inghilterra*. Genoa: Il Melangolo, 1983.

Marengo Vaglio, C., P. Bertinetti, and G. Cortese. eds. *Le forme del comico*. Alessandria: Edizioni Dell'Orso, 1990.

Marra, Giulio. *Arte e ideologia in Shakespeare*. Venice: Cafoscarina, 1984.

———. *Il tragico e il comico: Aspetti e saggi shakespeariani*. Rome: Bulzoni, 1991.

Marrapodi, Michele. *"The Great Image:" Figure e immagini della regalità nel teatro di Shakespeare* Rome: Herder, 1984.

———. *La Sicilia nella drammaturgia giacomiana e carolina*. Rome: Herder, 1989.

———. ed. *Il mondo italiano del teatro inglese del Rinascimento: relazioni culturali e intertestualità*. Palermo: Flaccovio, 1995.

Martini, Emanuela. *Ombre che camminano. Shakespeare*. Bergamo: Lubrica, 1997.

Martino, Mario. *Il problema del Tempo nei sonetti di Shakespeare*. Rome: Bulzoni, 1985.

Marucci, F., and A. Bruttini, eds. *La performance del testo*. Siena: Ticci & Grubbi, 1986.

Marzola, Alessandra. *L'impossibile puritanesimo di Amleto*. Ravenna: Longo, 1985.

———. ed. *L'altro Shakespeare: Critica, storia e ideologia*. Milan: Guerini, 1992.

———. *La parola del mercante*. Rome: Bulzoni, 1996.

Melchiori, Giorgio. *L'uomo e il potere*. Turin: Einaudi, 1973.

———. *Le forme del teatro*. Rome: Ed. di Storia e Letteratura, 1979.

———. ed. *Le forme del teatro II: Contributi del gruppo di ricerca sulla comunicazione teatrale in Inghilterra*. Roma: Ed. di Storia e Letteratura, 1981.

———. ed. *Le forme del teatro III: Contributi del gruppo di ricerca sulla comunicazione teatrale in Inghilterra*. Roma: Ed. di Storia e Letteratura, 1984.

———. *Shakespeare: Politica e contesto economico*. Rome: Bulzoni, 1992.

———. *Shakespeare: Genesi e struttura delle opere*. Bari: Laterza, 1996.

Montini, Donatella. *Le lettere di Shakespeare. Saggio sulle funzioni della lettera nei testi shakespeariani*. Rome: Bulzoni, 1993.

Morretta, Mariano. *Misura per Misura: Eros e potere. Codici linguistici e repressione sessuale*. Salerno: Edisud, 1987.

Moretti, Franco. *Segni e stili del moderno*. Turin: Einaudi, 1987.

Mosca Bonsignore, M. *I "masques" di Ben Jonson*. Turin: Giappichelli, 1980.

———. *Vivat Eliza: rappresentazioni in onore di Elisabetta I*. Turin: Tirrenia Stampatori, 1985.

———. ed. *Orchestra or A Poeme of Dauncing*. Alessandria: Edizioni Dell'Orso, 1994.

Mullini, Roberta. *Corruttore di parole: il fool nel teatro di Shakespeare*. Bologna: CLUEB, 1983.

———. *Il fool in Shakespeare*. Rome: Bulzoni, 1997.

Mullini, Roberta, and Romana Zacchi, eds. *Introduzione allo studio del teatro inglese*. Florence: La Casa Usher, 1992.

Nocera Avila, Carmela. *Tradurre il Cortegiano: The Courtyer di Sir Thomas Hoby*. Bari: Adriatica, 1992.

Nocera Avila, Carmela, Nicola Pantaleo, and Domenico Pezzini, eds. *Early Modern English: Trends, Forms, and Texts*. Fasano: Schena, 1992.

Pagetti, Carlo, ed. *Sh/Sf: da Shakespeare alla fantascienza*. Pescara: Libreria dell'Università, 1985.

Pagnini, Marcello. *Critica della funzionalità*. Turin: Einaudi, 1970.

———. *Shakespeare e il paradigma della specularità*. Pisa: Pacini Editore, 1976.

Papetti, Viola, ed. *Le forme del teatro IV. Contributi del gruppo di ricerca sulla comunicazione teatrale in Inghilterra*. Rome: Ed. di Storia e Letteratura, 1989.

Papetti, Viola and Laura Visconti, eds. *Le forme del teatro V. Eros e commedia sulla scena inglese dalle origini al primo Seicento*. Rome: Ed. di Storia e Letteratura, 1997.

Pellegrini, G. *Dal Manierismo al Barocco*. Florence: Olschky, 1987.

Perosa, Sergio. *Shakespeare a Venezia*. Venice: Il Cardo, 1991.

Piazza, Antonella. *L'eclissi minore: la crisi del patriarcato nella tragedia domestica elisabettiana*. Naples: Blue Rider, 1990.

Piglionica, Anna Maria. *L'oro come funzione drammatica in "The Comedy of Errors."* Bari: Adriatica, 1976.

———. *Dalla realtà all'illusione: "The Tempest" e la parola preclusa*. Florence: Olschki, 1985.

Poggi Ghigi, Valentina. *L'ideale tradito: l'uomo di corte nel teatro elisabettiano*. Naples: Guida, 1980.

Portale, Rosario. *Virgilio in Inghilterra: Saggi*. Pisa: Giardini, 1991.

Praz, Mario. *Caleidoscopio shakespeariano*. Bari: Adriatica, 1969.

———. *Studi e svaghi inglesi*. 2 vols. Milan: Garzanti, 1983.

Pugliatti, Paola. *I segni latenti: scrittuta come virtualità scenica in "King Lear."* Messina and Florence: D'Anna, 1976.

———. *Shakespeare storico*. Rome: Bulzoni, 1993.

Quadri, Marcella. *Coriolanus: L'arma della parola*. Pisa: ETS Editrice, 1990.

Raffaelli, Renato. *Variazioni sul Don Giovanni: Mozart, Molière, Scott, Shakespeare e il folclore*. Urbino: Quattroventi, 1990.

Ragazzini, Giuseppe. *Ebrei e usurai nella società e nel dramma elisabettiani: il linguaggio mercantile in Shakespeare e Marlowe*. Bologna: CLUEB, 1984.

Restivo, Giuseppina. *Saggi shakespeariani*. Milan: Elografia Manzotti, 1984.

Rizzardi, Alfredo. *Il primo Shakespeare*. Urbino: Argalia, 1967.

Rizzoli, Renato. *La politica del colpo di scena: Rappresentazione e ideologia nel teatro giacomiano*. Naples: Edizioni Scientifiche Italiane, 1997.

Rosini, Rosanna. *Le vele viola di Cleopatra*. Trieste: Coopstudio, 1988.

Rossi. Sergio. *Ricerche sull'Umanesimo e sul Rinascimento in Inghilterra*. Milan: 1969.

———. ed. *Saggi sul Rinascimento*. 1 Vol. Milan: Unicopli, 1984.

———. ed. *The Tragedie of Othello, the Moore of Venice. Atti del Convegno*. Milan: Unicopli, 1984.

———. *I documenti della cultura italiana in Inghilterra. Il Rinascimento*. 1 vol. Milan: 1986.

Rossi, Sergio, and Dianella Savoia, eds. *Italy and the English Renaissance*. Milan: Unicopli, 1989.

Rota, Felicina. *L'arcadia di Sidney e il teatro*. Bari: Adriatica, 1966.

Rutelli, Romana. *Saggi sulla connotazione: Tre sonetti di Shakespeare*. Turin: Giappichelli, 1975.

———. *"Romeo e Giulietta": l'effabile. Analisi di una riflessione sul linguaggio*. Milan: Il Formichiere, 1978.

———. *Dialoghi con il testo*. Naples: Liguori, 1985.

———. *Quell'oscura innocenza della seduzione*. Naples: Liguori, 1995.

Sacerdoti, Gilberto. *Nuovo cielo, nuova terra: La rivelazione copernicana di "Antonio e Cleopatra" di Shakespeare*. Bologna: Il Mulino, 1990.

Squarzina, Luigi. *Da Amleto a Shylock. Note di regia*. Rome: Bulzoni, 1995.

Segre, Cesare. *Teatro e romanzo*. Turin: Einaudi, 1984.

Serpieri, Alessandro. *John Webster*. Bari: Adriatica, 1966.

———. *I sonetti dell'immortalità*. Milan: Bompiani, 1975.

———. *Otello: l'eros negato, psicoanalisi di una proiezione distruttiva*. Milan: Il Formichiere, 1978.

———. et al. eds. *Come comunica il teatro: dal testo alla scena*. Milan: Il Formichiere, 1978.

———. ed. *Shakespeare: la nostalgia dell'essere*. Parma: Pratiche Editrice, 1985.

———. *Retorica e immaginario*. Parma: Pratiche Editrice, 1986.

———. et al. eds. *Nel laboratorio di Shakespeare. Dalle fonti ai drammi*. 4 Vols. Parma: Pratiche Editrice, 1988.

Serpieri, Alessandro, and Keir, Elam. eds. *Mettere in scena Shakespeare*. Parma: Pratiche Editrice, 1987.

Serpieri, Alessandro, and Keir Elam, eds. *L'Eros in Shakespeare*. Parma: Pratiche Editrice, 1988.

Sestito, M. *Julius Caesar in Italia, 1726–1974*. Bari: Adriatica, 1978.

Silvani, G. *Il ramo spezzato. Tre studi su Christopher Marlowe*. Parma: Istituto di Lingue e Letterature Germaniche, 1981.

Speziale Bagliacca, Roberto. *Crescere corvi: Psicoanalisi di "Madame Bovary" e "Re Lear."* Genoa: Marietti, 1992.

Spinucci, P. *Teatro elisabettiano, teatro di stato*. Florence: Olschky, 1973.

Squarzina, Luigi. *Da Dioniso a Brecht: Pensiero teatrale e azione scenica*. Bologna: Il Mulino, 1988.

———. *Da Amleto a Shylock. Note di regia*. Rome: Bulzoni, 1995.

Strehler, Giorgio. *Inscenare Shakespeare*. Rome: Bulzoni, 1992.

Tarantino, Elisabetta. *Le metamorfosi dell'amore: Lily, Greene, Shakespeare e le origini della commedia romantica*. Rome: Bulzoni, 1996.

Tempera, Mariangela. *The Lancashire Witches: lo stereotipo della strega tra scrittura giuridica e scrittura letteraria*. Imola: Galeati, 1981.

———. ed. *"Macbeth:" dal testo alla scena*. Bologna: CLUEB, 1982.
———. ed. *"Othello:" dal testo alla scena*. Bologna: CLUEB, 1983.
———. ed. *"King Lear:" dal testo alla scena*. Bologna: CLUEB, 1986.
———. ed. *"Romeo and Juliet:" dal testo alla scena*. Bologna: CLUEB, 1986.
———. ed. *"The Tempest:" dal testo alla scena*. Bologna: CLUEB, 1989.
———. ed. *"Antony and Cleopatra:" dal testo alla scena*. Bologna: CLUEB, 1990.
———. ed. *"Hamlet:" dal testo alla scena*. Bologna: CLUEB, 1990.
———. ed. *"A Midsummer Night's Dream:" dal testo alla scena*. Bologna: CLUEB, 1991.
———. ed. *"Julius Caesar:" dal testo alla scena*. Bologna: CLUEB, 1992.
———. ed. *"Measure for Measure:" dal testo alla scena*. Bologna: CLUEB, 1992.
———. ed. *"King John:" dal testo alla scena*. Bologna: CLUEB, 1993.
———. ed. *"The Merchant of Venice:" dal testo alla scena*. Bologna: CLUEB, 1994.
———. ed. *"The Taming of the Shrew:" dal testo alla scena*. Bologna CLUEB, 1997.
Thompson, Ann, and Keir Elam, eds. *Shakespeare's Text(s)*. Special issue of *Textus. English Studies in Italy,* 9/2 (1996).
Trigona, Prospero. *Il tessuto del testo. Henrici Quinti lectura*. Naples: Edizioni Scientifiche Italiane, 1994.
Troisi, Federica. *Troilus and Cressida. La crisi del Rinascimento nel teatro di Shakespeare*. Naples: Edizioni Scientifiche Italiane, 1997.
Troncarelli, Fabio. *Le maschere della malinconia: John Ford tra Shakespeare e Hollywood*. Bari: Dedalo, 1994.
Valentini, Maria. *Shakespeare e Pirandello*. Rome: Bulzoni, 1990.
Valentini, Valentina. *Teatro in immagine*. 2 Vols. Rome: Bulzoni, 1987.
Visconti, Laura. *La scena restaurata. Percorsi intertestuali del teatro inglese nel tardo Seicento*. Pescara: Tracce, 1991.
Watts, Paola, and Montessori, Elisa. *Appunti su "La Tempesta" di Shakespeare*. Rome: Novi, 1988.
Zacchi, Romana. *La società del teatro nell'Inghilterra della Restaurazione*. Bologna: CLUEB, 1984.
Zaniboni, Maria Cristina. *Un'antica passione: Romeo e Giulietta dalle fonti a Shakespeare*. Imola: Galeati, 1988.
Zazo, Anna Luisa. *Introduzione a Shakespeare*. Bari: Laterza, 1993.

Contributors

VITO AMORUSO is Professor of English at the Faculty of Arts, University of Bari. He is the general editor of "Perspectives", a series of critical studies on English and American Literature. Besides several articles and essays on Shakespeare and the Renaissance, he is the author of monographs on Virginia Woolf (1968) and on Anglo-American literature (1971, 1976).

CLAUDIA CORTI is Professor of English at the University of Florence. She is co-editor of *Rivista di Letterature Moderne e Comparate,* and of the series "Studi di Letterature Moderne e Comparate." Her most recent books include *"Macbeth:" la parola e l'immagine* (1983), *Shakespeare illustrato* (1996), and *Silenos: Erasmus in Elizabethan Literature* (1988). She has edited *I contesti culturali della letteratura inglese: Il Rinascimento* (1994).

LAURA DI MICHELE moved from the Istituto Universitario Orientale of Naples to the University of L' Aquila in 1997. She is the author of *L'educazione del sentimento: la crisi del romanzo inglese fra gotico e sentimentale, 1750–1800* (1977), and of *La scena dei potenti: teatro politica spettacolo nell'età di Shakespeare* (1988). She has also written extensively on eighteenth-century literature, women's writing, and contemporary science fiction. Most recently, she has edited a special Shakespeare issue of *Anglistica* (1995), and *Aspetti di "Othello"* (1997).

FERNANDO FERRARA (1927–1996) was Professor of English at the University of L' Aquila, and formerly at the Istituto Universitario Orientale of Naples, where he taught English and Cultural Studies. He was the founder and main editor of *Anglistica,* and general editor of the series "Culture and Society" (Rome). He was the author of *Shakespeare e la commedia* (1966) and of many books and essays on the early modern period. His most recent works include *Shakespeare e le voci della storia* (1994) and *Il teatro dei re. Saggio sui drammi storico-politici di Shakespeare* (1995).

VANNA GENTILI is Professor of English in the Department of Comparative Literature, University "Rome Three." She has written extensively on Shakespeare, Renaissance poetry and drama, and nineteenth-century literature. Her books include *Sidney: Astrophel and Stella* (1965), *La recita della follia* (1977, revised ed. 1992), and *La Roma antica degli elisabettiani* (1991). She has also edited *Trasgressione tragica e norma domestica* (1982).

ANGELA LOCATELLI is Professor of English at the University of Bergamo. She has published books on Shakespeare, Pinter, and modern fiction, and several essays on literary theory. Her most recent books include *L'eloquenza e gli incantesimi: interpretazioni shakespeariane* (1988) and *Il Doppio e il Picaresco: Un caso paradigmatico nel Rinascimento inglese* (1998).

FRANCO MARENCO is Professor of English at the University of Turin. He has written extensively on Shakespeare, Renaissance drama, and modern fiction. He is the general editor of two series of travel books and of a *History of English Literary Civilization*. His books include *Arcadia puritiana* (1968) and *Thomas Middleton e il teatro barocco in Inghilterra* (1983).

MICHELE MARRAPODI is Associate Professor of English at the University of Palermo. He is Associate Editor of *Cahiers Elisabéthains* and Assistant Editor of *Seventeenth-Century News*. He is the author of *"The Great Image"* (1984) and *La Sicilia nella drammaturgia giacomiana e carolina* (1989). His edited volumes include *Shakespeare's Italy* (1993), *Il mondo italiano del teatro inglese del Rinascimento* (1995), and *The Italian World of English Renaissance Drama: Cultural Exchange and Intertextuality* (1998).

GIORGIO MELCHIORI, C.B.E., F.B.A., is Professor Emeritus of English, University "Rome Three." He is Life-Trustee Shakespeare Birthplace Trust, and Honorary Trustee International James Joyce Foundation. He has edited many plays by Shakespeare and his fellow dramatists and published books on Shakespeare, Yeats, and Joyce. His most recent works include *Shakespeare's Garter Plays* (1994), *Shakespeare: genesi e struttura delle opere* (1994), and the New Cambridge edition of *Edward III* (1998). He is currently engaged in the editing of *The Merry Wives of Windsor* for Arden 3.

ROBERTA MULLINI is Professor of English at the University of Urbino. She has written extensively on Medieval and early modern drama. Her books include *Corruttore di parole* (1983), *La scena della memoria* (1988), *Dramma e teatro nel Medievo inglese, 1386–1553* (1992), *Il fool in Shakespeare* (1997), and *Mad Merry Heywood: La drammaturgia di John Heywood* (1997).

MARCELLO PAGNINI is Professor Emeritus of English at the University of Florence, and one of the founding fathers of structuralist and semiotic criticism in Italy. His wide-ranging publications include books on *Struttura letteraria e metodo critico* (1967), *Critica della funzionalità* (1970), *Lingua e musica* (1974), *Shakespeare e il paradigma della specularità* (1976), *The Pragmatics of Literature* (1987), and *Semiosi* (1988).

VIOLA PAPETTI is Professor of English in the Department of Comparative Literature, University "Rome Three." Her publications include books on *Arlecchino a Londra* (1977) and *G. M. Hopkins: Le foglie della Sibilla* (1992), and editions of *A. Pope: Il riccio rapito* (1984) and *J. Keats: Iperione. La caduta di Iperione* (1988). Her edited volumes include *Le forme del teatro V: Eros e commedia sulla scena inglese dalle origini ai primo Seicento* (1997) and *Le forme del teatro VI: Eros e commedia sulla scena inglese dal tardo Seicento al Novecento* (1997).

GILBERTO SACERDOTI is Associate Professor of English in the Department of Comparative Literature, University "Rome Three." He is the author of *Nuovo cielo, nuova terra. La rivelazione copernicana in "Antonio e Cleopatra" di Shakespeare* (1990) and of several essays on Shakespeare and Renaissance poetry.

ALESSANDRO SERPIERI is Professor of English at the University of Florence. He has written extensively on Shakespeare, Romantic and modern poetry, and contemporary drama. His books include *John Webster* (1966), *T.S. Eliot: le strutture profonde* (1973), *I sonetti dell'immortalità* (1975), *Otello: l'Eros negato* (1978), and *Retorica e immaginario* (1986). He has edited Shakespeare's Sonnets (1991), the Quarto and Folio texts of *Hamlet* (1997), and other Shakespearean plays.

MARIANGELA TEMPERA is Associate Professor of English at the University of Ferrara. She is the author of *The Lancashire Witches* (1981) and of many articles on Shakespeare and Renaissance drama. Her edited volumes include *Shakespeare from Text to Stage* (1992), and *International Shakespeare: the Tragedies* (1996). She is currently editing the series of Shakespeare's individual plays From Text to Stage (1984–).

Index

A.I.A., 279
Actio, 225, 232, 233
Adams, M. S., 242 n. 49
Adamson, Jane, 90, 94 n. 31
Adelman, Janet, 92 n. 4
Aelfric, 200
Affirmation, 227, 234
Agnew, Jean-Christophe, 163 n. 3
Agon, 252
Alexander, William, 115; *Julius Caesar,* 115
Alfieri, Vittorio, 8
Alfred, 200
Alighieri, Dante, 199; *Convivio,* 199
Amoruso, Vito, 7, 10, 14, 97
Amplificatio, 227, 243 n. 66
Amyot, T., 201, 202
Anamorphosis, 264
Antimetabole, 234
Aposiopesis, 232
Appian, 205 n. 15; *Civil Wars,* 205 n. 15
Aquilecchia, G., 184 nn. 21 and 22
Aquinas, Thomas, 211
Aquino, D. Curren, 217 n. 3
Arber, E., 150 n. 8
Aretino, Pietro, 184 n. 5
Ariosto, Lodovico; *Orlando furioso,* 204 n. 13
Aristotle, 77, 78, 81, 93 n. 11, 276 n. 1. Works: *Ethics,* 93 n. 11, *Nichomachean Ethics,* 78; *Poetics,* 77
Ascham, Roger, 84
Auden, W. H., 45, 55 n. 3
Augustine, Saint, 170
Austin, John, 238, 240 n. 12, 243 n. 69
Auvergne, Countess of, 64
Axton, Marie, 217 n. 4
Ayrees, H. M., 126 n. 12

Bacon, Francis, 119, 214, 225; *Essays,* 214, 219 n. 28, 225, 242 n. 32

Bailey, Walter, 118; *A Briefe Discours of Certain Bathes,* 118
Baines, Richard, 171
Baldini, Gabriele, 8, 19, 279
Bale, John, 73, 206, 209, 216, 219 n. 29; *King Johan,* 72, 206, 209, 216
Ball, Emma, 146
Baltrusaitis, J., 264, 277 n. 9
Barba, E., 130, 150 n. 3
Barber, L. C., 48, 56 n. 8
Barker, William, 205 n. 15
Baroque theater, 245, 249, 256
Barthes, Roland, 91 n. 1
Bataille, G., 63, 75 n. 17
Bateson, F. W., 188, 204 n. 4
Battenhouse, Roy, 97, 108 n. 1
Bavardage, 165, 181
Beckerman, B., 263
Becket, Thomas, 119, 208, 209, 215
Beckett, Samuel, 10
Bede, (the Venerable), 119, 200
Belsey, Catherine, 91 n. 2, 92 n. 4, 94 n. 29, 257 n. 2
Bene, Carmelo, 21
Benjamin, 246
Benveniste, Emile, 91 n. 1
Bernthal, C. A., 108 n. 2
Berry, Ralph, 163 n. 7
Bethell, S. L., 241 n. 14
Betterton, T., 259
Beza, T., 123
Blackstone, William, 214; *Commentaries on the Law of England,* 214
Blanchot, Maurice, 67, 75 n. 19
Blistein, Elmer, 75 n. 13
Bloch, M., 58, 74 n. 5
Bodley, Thomas, 123
Boito, Arrigo, 8
Boleyn, Anne, 72, 73
Bonnard, G., 223, 241 nn. 21 and 22
Boorman, S. C., 92 nn. 2 and 11
Boris, Edna Zwick, 217 n. 7

291

Bosch, H., 64
Bottalla, Paola, 11
Bradbrook, M. C., 242 n. 56, 243 n. 62
Bradley, A. C., 90, 93 n. 17, 226
Bradshaw, Graham, 244 n. 71
Brennan, Elizabeth M., 257 n. 7
Brooks, Harold F., 43 n
Brown, John Russell, 55 n. 4
Bruno, Giordano, 15, 16, 173, 174, 175, 176, 177, 178, 179, 180, 182. Works: *Cena delle ceneri*, 176, 178, 179, *De immenso*, 174, 179, *De infinito*, 174, 178, 182, *Eroici furori*, 176, *Spaccio della bestia trionfante*, 173
Bullough, Geoffrey, 125 n. 4, 205 n. 18, 218 n. 25
Burckhardt, Sigurd, 50, 56 n. 13
Burghley (Lord), 121; *Advise to his Son*, 121
Busi, Anna, 12
Buxton, John, 79, 93 n. 12

Caesar and Pompey or Caesar's Revenge, 115
Caesarism, 122
Caliumi, M. Grazia, 12, 163 n, 257 n. 4
Calvin, J., 123
Camerlingo, Rosanna, 257
Campbell, Lily, 209, 217 n. 4, 218 n. 15
Capello, Bianca, 245
Cappuzzo, Marcello, 10, 18 n. 8, 55 n. 1
Carnival, 152
Cartwright, Thomas, 249
Cassirer, Ernst, 92 n. 3
Castorina, Giuseppe G., 93 n. 20
Catilina, 110
Cato, 110
Cellini, Benvenuto, 8, 74 n. 4
Cervantes, Miguel de, 200; *Don Quixote*, 200
Chambers, E. K., 151 n. 14, 217 n. 7
Chapman, George, 30, 61, 74 n. 12, 188, 189, 194, 196. Works: *Achilles' Shield*, 188, *The Iliads of Homer*, 204 n. 5, *Ovid's Banquet of Sense*, 61
Charles II, 275
Charlton, H. B., 93 n. 23
Chaucer, Geoffrey, 119
Chinol, Elio, 8, 12, 19
Chivalric tradition, 248
Ciampini, R., 183 n. 4

Cicero, 78, 92 n. 11, 97, 110, 199; *De Officiis*, 78, 92 n. 11, 97
Cinthio, G. B. *See* Giraldi Cinthio, G. B.
Ciocca, Rossella, 10, 11, 18 n. 11, 74 n. 6
Cipolla, C. M., 204 n. 1
Clément, Jean-Marie, 277 n. 1
Clodius, P., 110
Coghill, N., 108 n. 1
Cohen, Walter, 164 n. 12
Colaiacomo, Paola, 10, 18 n. 9
Coleridge, Samuel Taylor, 43
Colombo, Rosa Maria, 10, 18 n. 10, 233, 243 n. 58
Comunicatio, 225
Copernicus, N., 176, 177, 179, 180. *De Revolutionibus*, 176
Corneille, T., 258; *Discours de l'utilité ed des parties du Poème dramatique*, 258
Corsani, Mary, 12
Corti, Claudia, 9, 14, 109
Coup de théâtre, 246, 249, 255, 256
Courtés, Joseph, 277 n. 5
Craig, W. J., 240
Cranach, Lucas (the Elder), 74
Croce, Benedetto, 8
Cuccurullo, D., 75 n. 18
Curti, Lidia, 11

D'Agostino, Nemi, 8, 12, 279
D'Amico, Masolino, 11, 19
dall'Aglio, Gigi, 21
Danby, J. F., 151 n. 11
Daniel, Samuel, 189, 190, 193, 194, 196, 198; *Musophilus*, 189, 190, 204 n. 7
Danse macabre, 220
Danson, Lawrence, 93 n. 23
Dante. *See* Alighieri
Davenant, 259
Dawson, A. B., 108 n. 2
Dawson, Peter, 7
De Berardinis, Leo, 21
De Marinis, Marco, 240 n. 12
De Sanctis, Francesco, 8
Débrayage, 261, 264, 269, 270
Dee, John, 15, 123, 176
Deixis, 225
Dekker, Thomas, 230, 242 n. 53; *The Bel-Man of London*, 230, 242 n. 53
della Volpe, Galvano, 10

Démesure, 111, 115
Derrick, Thomas J., 93 n. 22
Derrida, Jaques, 91 n. 1
Descriptio actionis, 232, 233
Desmet, Christy, 92 n. 2
Detractio, 263, 275
Di Michele, Laura, 10, 11, 15, 18 n. 11, 128
Digges, Dudley, 177
Digges, Leonard, 123, 177
Digges, Thomas, 15, 123, 176, 177, 178, 180; *Perfit Description of the Caelestiall Orbes*, 176
Dispositio, 272
Dixon, P., 240 n. 5
Dodd, W. Nigel, 241 n. 30
Dolabella, 110
Dolet, Etienne, 200
Dollimore, Jonathan, 78, 91 n. 2, 92 nn. 7 and 8
Domenichelli, Mario, 11
Doran, Madeleine, 230, 242 nn. 51 and 56, 243 n. 60
Dorsch, T. S., 125 n. 5
Downame, John, 120
Drakakis, John, 91 n. 2, 94 n. 29
Draper, John W., 164 n. 12, 223, 241 n. 18, 19 and 20
Draxe, 169, 183 n. 2; *The Worlds Resurrection*, 169, 183 n. 2
Dryden, John, 17, 204 n. 10, 258, 259, 272, 274, 275, 276, 278 nn. 12 and 21. Works: *All for Love*, 267–76, 276 n. 1, 277 n. 1; *Of Dramatic Poesy*, 278 n. 12; *The Tempest*, 259–63; *Troilus and Cressida*, 272–76, 277 n. 1
Du Bellay, J., 200
Dubitatio, 232
Dusinberre, Juliet, 217 n. 3, 218 n. 22
Dyer, Edward, 176

E. K., 188, 189, 196
Eagleton, Terry, 164 n. 11
Eco, Umberto, 11, 218 n. 23
Edward I, 213
Edwards, Philip, 277 n. 11
Eedes, Richard, 115; *Caesar Interfectus*, 115
Elam, Keir, 9, 10, 18 n. 7, 20, 74 n, 125 n. 7, 205 n. 15, 240 n. 12, 243 n. 69, 257 n. 4
Eldrige, Richard, 91 n. 1

Eliot, T. S., 244 n. 71
Elizabeth I, 45, 119, 120, 121, 122, 123, 138, 139, 140, 187, 191, 207, 209
Elliott, G. R., 127 n. 22, 241 n. 14
Elton, W. R., 164 n. 10, 242 n. 46
Elyot, Sir Thomas, 78, 97, 136; *The Boke Named the Governour*, 78, 136, 150 n. 7
Empson, William, 98, 104, 108 n. 4
Energeia, 233
Epitasis, 276 n. 1
Erasmus, Desiderius, 77, 199; *Enchiridion*, 77
Essex rebellion, 100
Ethos, 222
Eton, Sara, 92 n. 4
Euripides, 116
Everett, Barbara, 151 n. 19
Everyman, 234
Ewbank, Inga-Stina, 204 n. 11, 277 n. 11

Falzon Santucci, Lino, 55 n. 1
Famous Victories of Henry V, The, 192
Ferber, Michael, 164 n. 12
Ferguson, Margaret W., 92 n. 4
Ferrara, Fernando, 8, 11, 13, 57, 75 n. 18, 151 n. 15
Fiedler, Leslie A., 93 n. 23, 163 n. 9
Fiorentino, Sir Giovanni, 44; *Pecorone*, 44
Fletcher, John, 249; *Commendatory Verses*, 249
Ford, John, 122
Foscolo, Ugo, 8
Foucault, Michel, 79, 91 n. 1, 93 n. 14, 130, 150 n. 4, 256 n. 2
Frazer, J. G., 48
Freud, Sigmund, 57, 75 n. 21
Frisch, C., 184 n. 12
Frye, Northrop, 241 n. 13, 278 n. 17
Frye, Roland M., 222, 241 n. 15
Fulke, William, 123
Furness, A. A., 166
Furnivall, F. J., 75 n. 24

Gabrieli, Vittorio, 8, 278 n. 19
Galilei, Galileo, 183
Gallo, Bruno, 93 n. 15
Gargani, Aldo, 277 n. 6
Garner, S. N., 224, 241 nn. 25, 26 and 27, 244 n. 71
Garnier, Robert, 115; *Cornélie*, 115

Gatti, Hilary, 184 n. 13
Geminatio, 220
Gentili, Vanna, 11, 16, 187, 205 n. 15, 226, 242 nn. 36, 37 and 38
Geoffrey of Monmouth, 126 n. 15
Gerard, A., 241 n. 14
Gilbert, Humphrey, 250
Gill, Roma, 256 n. 1
Gillingham, J., 207, 208
Giraldi Cinthio, G. B., 44, 98; *Hecatommithi*, 44
Girard, René, 81, 93 n. 16
Globe Theatre, 115
Goddard, Harold C., 46, 47, 48, 55 n. 5
Goethals, George R., 91 n. 1
Goldberg, Jonathan, 86, 87, 88, 94 nn. 26 and 28
Golding, Arthur, 112
Grace, H. P., 277 n. 11
Gramsci, Antonio, 79, 93 n. 13
Granada, M. A., 184 n. 15
Grandisson, John of, 210
Granville-Barker, H., 241 nn. 14 and 17
Grebner, Paul, 119
Greenblatt, Stephen, 77, 91 n. 2, 92 n. 6, 244 n. 71, 257 n. 2
Greene, Robert, 12, 17, 27
Greimas, A. J., 277 n. 5
Greville, F., 176, 178, 179
Grévin, Jacques, 115; *César*, 115
Grimalde, N., 93 n. 11
Grosart, A., 242 n. 53
Guarini, Gianbattista, 14, 101; *Compendio della poesia tragicomica*, 101
Guidi, Augusto, 8

Hall, E., 192; *The Union of the Two Noble Families of Lancaster and York*, 192
Halle, John, 123
Hammond, A., 257 n. 7
Happé, P., 218 n. 14
Harner, James L., 8
Harriot, Thomas, 172, 173, 174, 175, 177, 180
Harsnet, Samuel, 123; *A Discovery of Fraudulent Practises*, 123
Hartman, Geoffrey, 92 n. 2
Harvey, Gabriel, 118, 120
Haslewood, Joseph, 126 n. 14
Hayes, Edward, 250, 257 n. 6
Heffeman, Carol F., 163 n. 5
Heilman, R. B., 220, 221, 240 nn. 7, 8 and 9, 242 n. 49
Hellman, C. D., 184 n. 17
Heminge, J., 177
Hendricks, Margo, 244 n. 71
Henslowe, Philip, 115
Hibbard, George R., 163 n. 6, 277 n. 11
Hill, Christopher, 100, 126 n. 19, 127 n. 20, 183 n. 2, 204 n. 1
Himelick, Raymond, 92 n. 3
Hippocrates, 121
Hirnelick, R., 204 n. 7
Hoare, Quintin, 93 n. 13
Hobbes, Thomas, 277 n. 6, 278 n. 14. Works: *Leviathan*, 277 n. 6, *Opera philosophica*, 278 n. 14
Hodge, Nancy Elizabeth, 164 n. 13
Hoenselaars, A. J., 55 n. 1
Holbein, 74, 264, 266; *Ambassadors*, 264, 266, 277 n. 9
Holinshed, R., 192, 218 n. 25; *Chronicles*, 192, 218 n. 25
Holland, Philemon, 116, 125 n. 8
Homer, 188; *Iliad*, 188, 189
Honigman, E. A. J., 217 n. 7
Hood, Thomas, 123
Hooker, Richard, 169, 183 n. 2
Hooper, R., 204 n. 5
Horace, 199
Howell, James, 200, 205 n. 14; *Familiar Letters*, 200, 205 n. 14
Hubler, Edward, 222, 241 n. 16
Hulley, K. K., 125 n. 6
Hunert, J. D., 108 n. 2
Hunter, G. K., 277 n. 11
Hyman, S. E., 242 n. 47

Immutatio, 275
Innocenti, Loretta, 11
Interludes, 148
Interruptio, 232
Isidore of Seville, 121
Italian setting, 122
Izzo, Carlo, 8

Jakobson, R., 196
James I, 71, 73, 97, 119, 122, 124. Works: *Basilicon Doron*, 97, *Daemonologie*, 124
Jardine, Lisa, 94 n. 29
Jenkins, Harold, 218 n. 21
Jerome, Saint, 199

Jesus Christ, 167, 168, 176, 211
Jewel, John, 62, 75 n. 16, 20
Joan of Arc, 65
Johnson, F. R., 184 nn. 15 and 16
Johnson, Samuel, 105, 108 n. 5
Jones, E., 166, 167, 170
Jonson, Ben, 177, 194, 197; *Sejanus*, 177

Kahn, Coppélia, 91 n. 2, 92 n. 4
Kahn, Victoria, 92 n. 10, 94 n. 23
Kantorowitz, Ernst H., 218 nn. 18, 19 and 24, 219 n. 27
Kemp, Will, 146, 150
Kennan, Patricia, 11
Kepler, J., 173, 174, 177; *De nova stella in pede Serpentarii*, 177
Kermode, Frank, 93 n. 23, 177, 184 n. 20, 204 n. 10
Kinney, Arthur F., 257 n. 3
Klein, D., 257 n. 5
Knights, L. C., 93 n. 17
Kocher, P. H., 126 n. 13
Koelb, Clayton, 93 n. 16
Kyd, Thomas, 62, 172, 194, 197, 246, 247; *The Spanish Tragedy*, 75 n. 14, 246

La Penna, A., 126 n. 12
Lacan, Jacques, 91 n. 1
Larkey, S. V., 184 n. 15
Larson, Richard L., 268, 278 n. 16
Lausberg, H., 240 n. 5, 276 n. 1
Lavia, Gabriele, 20, 21
Lawrence, W. W., 98, 108 n. 3
Lawson-Dick, O., 184 n. 10
Le Bossu, R., 276, 278 n. 21; *Traité du Poème Epique*, 276
Leavis, F. R., 90, 108 n. 1, 244 n. 71
Leech, Clifford, 108 n. 1
Lefranc, P., 184 nn. 5–8, 11, 12 and 16
Leggatt, Alexander, 93 n. 23
Leo, F. A., 125 n. 2
Levellers, 100
Leventen, Carol, 94 n. 23
Lever, James, 101
Levin, Harry, 164 n. 10
Liaison des scènes, 268
Life of Sir John Oldcastle, The, 149
Livermore Forbes, Elizabeth, 92 n. 3
Locatelli, Angela, 7, 9, 13, 76, 93 nn. 15 and 20, 163 n. 8

Locus amoenus, 247
Lodovici, Cesare Vico, 19, 199, 204 n. 12, 279
Logos, 113
Lokke, Virgil, 93 n. 16
Lollard, 149
Lombardo, Agostino, 8–9, 12, 17 nn. 1 and 3; 19–20, 55 n, 71, 75 n. 22, 279
Long, W. B., 164 n. 10
Lotman, Jurij M., 77, 92 n. 5, 218 nn. 16 and 17, 240 n. 12, 258, 277 n. 2
Loyola, Ignatius, 119
Lucan, 110, 125 n. 4; *Pharsalia*, 110, 125 n. 4
Luzi, Mario, 19
Lyly, John, 12, 27, 197

MacCallum, W. W., 205 n. 19
Macpherson, C. B., 277 n. 6
Magna Carta, 213
Maimonides, M., 199
Malespini, C., 245; *Ducento novelle*, 245
Malone, E., 170
Manzoni, Alessandro, 8
Marcuse, H., 57, 74 n. 1
Marenco, Franco, 7, 11, 17, 62, 75 nn. 15 and 20, 245, 257 n. 9
Margaret of Anjou, 65, 67
Marlowe, Christopher, 60, 71, 125 n. 4, 171, 172, 173, 174, 180, 182, 184 n. 5, 194, 197; *Edward II*, 71
Marra, Giulio, 11
Marrapodi, Michele, 7, 16, 17 nn. 2 and 4, 18, 55 n. 1, 220, 279
Marston, John, 122, 197
Martin, P., 278 nn. 17, 19
Mary, Queen of Scots, 207, 209
Mason, James, 123; *The Anatomie of Sorcerie*, 123
Maxwell, J. C., 108 n. 1
Mazzini, Giuseppe, 8
McKerrow, 184 n. 9
McVeagh, John, 163 n. 3
Melchiori, Giorgio, 8, 9, 12, 17 n. 4, 18, 48, 49, 56 n. 9, 205 n. 15, 225, 227, 242 nn. 34, 35, 44 and 50, 276, 279
Merchant, W. M., 45, 55 n. 2
Metalogisms, 238, 243 n. 66
Metasememes, 238, 243 n. 66
Middleton, Thomas, 17, 122, 245, 246, 247; *Women Beware Women*, 245

Midgley, Graham, 48, 56 n. 10
Miles gloriosus, 142
Miola, R. S., 126 n. 18
Mirror for Magistrates, 78, 250
Mise en abîme, 258
Molesworth, W., 278 n. 14
Monk, S. H., 276 n. 1
Montaigne, Miguel E. de, 77, 109, 115, 268; *Essais*, 77
Montale, Eugenio, 19
Monti, C., 184 n. 25
Monti, Vincenzo, 8
Moody, A. D., 85, 94 n. 24
Moralities, 148, 228
More, Thomas, 218 n. 8
Moretti, Franco, 10, 18 n. 9
Morgan, K. O., 218 n. 9
Moses, 173
Mosse, M., 85; *Arraignment and Conviction of Usury*, 85
Muir, Kenneth, 218 n. 20, 257 n. 7, 272
Mulcaster, Richard, 138, 139; *The Passage of our most dread Soveraigne Lady, Quene Elyzabeth* . . . , 138, 139, 150 n. 8
Müller, Wolfgang G., 225, 240 n. 10, 242 n. 31
Mullini, Roberta, 9, 11, 16, 206
Mulryne, J. R., 75 n. 14
Munday, Anthony, 100. Works: *Downfall of Robert Earl of Huntington*, 100, *Sir John Oldcastle*, 100, *Sir Thomas More*, 100
Muret, Marc-Antoine, 115
Murillo, L. A., 204 n. 13
Myrick, K. O., 241 n. 14
Mythos, 220

Nanni, Giancarlo, 21
Nashe, Thomas, 173
Negation, 227, 234
Neo-Aristotelianism, 113
Neoplatonism, 50, 54, 113, 120
Neville, Anne, 65
Noble, R., 241 n. 113
North, Thomas, 109, 201, 202, 203, 205 n. 17

Orbetello, Alfredo, 8
Orlin Cowen, L. 244 n. 71
Ovid, 62, 188; *Metamorphoses*, 112
Oz, Avraham, 55 n. 1

Pagnini, Marcello, 9, 10, 12, 18 n. 5, 27, 93 n. 18, 240 n. 12
Panofsky, Edwin, 57, 73, 74 n. 3, 75 n. 25
Panowsky, Erwin, 184 nn. 14 and 29
Papetti, Viola, 11, 17, 258
Parker, Patricia, 92 nn. 2 and 10
Pastoral tradition, 248
Peele, George, 60, 61; *David and Bethsabe*, 61
Peripeteia, 246, 249, 251, 252, 253
Perkins, William, 117, 119, 123, 169, 183 n. 2; *An Exposition of the Creede*, 117, 119
Perosa, Sergio, 12, 279
Perrin, B., 205 n. 16
Pescetti, Orlando, 115; *Il Cesare*, 115
Pico della Mirandola, Giovanni, 77, 92 n. 3
Pierce, Robert B., 217 n. 7
Pietas, 112
Pindemonte, Ippolito, 8
Plett, Heinrich F., 227, 228, 237, 242 n. 45, 243 nn. 57 and 65
Plutarch, 85, 109, 110, 112, 116, 125 nn. 8 and 9, 201, 202, 203. Works: *Life of Caesar*, 202, *Lives*, 109, 110, 113, 201
Poli, D., 124 n
Pompea, 110
Porter, J. A., 151 n. 13
Post-Reformation, 50
Praz, Mario, 8, 12, 19, 279
Privy Council, 171
Protasis, 258, 264, 277 n. 1
Prouty, C. T., 75 n. 13
Providence, 248, 249, 250
Psalterium, 218 n. 7
Psychomachia, 228
Pugliatti, Paola, 9, 10, 18 nn. 7 and 20, 151 n. 15, 217 nn. 1 and 2, 240 n. 12, 277 n. 11
Puritanism, 247, 249
Puttenham, George, 240 n. 5; *The Arte of English Poesy*, 240 n. 5

Quasimodo, Salvatore, 19
Quilligan, Maureen, 92 n. 4
Quinn, D. B., 257 n. 6
Quint, David, 92 n. 10

Rabkin, Norman, 93 n. 17
Racine, J.-B., 268

Rackin, Phyllis, 217 n. 6
Ralegh, W., *See* Raleigh, Sir Walter
Raleigh, Sir Walter, 172, 173
Raleigh, Walter, 108 n. 5
Ranald, Margaret L., 224, 241 nn. 23 and 24
Rat, Maurice, 92 n. 3
Ravazzoli, Flavia, 237, 243 n. 66
Raven, C. E., 127 n. 20
Recorde, Robert, 123
Reformation, 119, 123, 124, 248
Reich, W., 57, 74 n. 2
Reticentia, 232
Retribution, 254
Revelation, 165, 167, 169, 171, 180, 181
Ribner, I., 241 n. 14
Ridley, M. R., 183 n. 1, 239 n. 1
Riehle, Wolfgang, 163 n. 4
Ronconi, Luca, 21
Rosati, Salvatore, 8
Rose, Mark, 264, 277 nn. 7, 9 and 10
Rose, Mary Beth, 244 n. 71
Rossi, P., 126 n. 13
Russel, Thomas, 177
Rutelli, Romana, 9

Sabbadini, Silvano, 10
Sacerdoti, Gilberto, 11, 15, 165, 184 n. 30
Sade, Marquis de, 67
Saintsbury, G., 278 n. 20
Salisbury, Countess of, 64
Sandys, George, 112
Savonarola, Girolamo, 119
Schelling, F. E., 126 n. 11
Scherer, Jacques, 276 n. 1, 278 n. 13
Schwartz, Murray M, 91 n. 2, 94 n. 23
Scot, Reginald, 120, 123; *The Discovery of Witchcraft*, 123
Scott, W., 278 n. 20
Sébillet, Thomas, 200
Seneca, 97, 112, 191; *De Clementia*, 97
Serpieri, Alessandro, 9, 10, 12, 13, 18 n. 6, 20, 44, 56 n. 7, 60, 74 n, 74 n. 10, 150 n. 2, 218 n. 10, 225, 226, 227, 238, 240 n. 12, 241 n. 29, 242 nn. 31, 39, and 40–43, 243 nn. 59, 64 and 69, 244 n. 70, 279
Shaheen, N., 241 n. 13
Shakespeare, William. Works: *All's Well That Ends Well*, 198; *Antony and Cleopatra*, 17, 116, 165–84, 259, 263–67, 269, 276 n. 1; *A Midsummer Night's Dream*, 10, 12, 27–43, 58, 90, 195, 203; *As You Like It*, 31, 41, 198; *The Comedy of Errors*, 15, 153, 154–56, 158, 160; *Coriolanus*, 130, 242 n. 31; *Edward III*, 12, 13, 59, 63–64; *Hamlet*, 10, 20, 30, 76, 83, 106, 195, 233, 246, 247; *1 Henry IV*, 69–70, 129, 130, 131, 132, 133, 134, 135, 140, 142, 146, 147, 148, 193, 197; *2 Henry IV*, 13, 69, 129, 130, 132, 135, 136, 137, 138, 140, 142, 143, 144, 145, 148, 149, 150, 192, 196, 197; *Henry V*, 13, 16, 59, 60, 70, 74 n. 8, 140, 141, 142, 145, 192, 193, 196; *1 Henry VI*, 13, 64–66, 67, 150; *2 Henry VI*, 13, 67, 83, 128; *3 Henry VI*, 66, 67; *Henry VIII*, 13, 59, 72–74, 207; *Julius Caesar*, 14, 82, 83–85, 109–27, 130, 202, 203, 205 n. 15, 242 n. 31; *King John*, 13, 16, 59, 62–63, 128, 206–19; *King Lear*, 42, 58, 106, 198, 207, 214, 228, 264; *Love's Labour's Lost*, 44, 197, 199, 200; *Macbeth*, 9, 10, 17, 41, 251, 252, 253; *Measure for Measure*, 14, 97–108, 255; *The Merchant of Venice*, 13, 14, 15, 44–56, 80, 82, 83, 85–89, 94 nn. 25 and 27, 153, 158, 159–63; *The Merry Wives of Windsor*, 31, 195, 197; *Much Ado About Nothing*, 58; *Othello*, 16, 44, 45, 47, 74 n. 10, 89–90, 131, 220–44; *Romeo and Juliet*, 58; *Richard II*, 13, 16, 17, 58, 59, 71, 191, 193, 196; *Richard III*, 13, 66, 67, 68, 90, 231, 251, 253; *Sir Thomas More*, 12; *Sonnets*, 20, 58, 68, 75 n. 20; *The Taming of the Shrew*, 14, 15, 44, 82, 153, 156–59; *The Tempest*, 16, 17, 20, 58, 80, 193, 196, 204 n. 10, 259–63; *Timon of Athens*, 20, 74 n. 11; *Titus Andronicus*, 20, 90; *Troilus and Cressida*, 17, 74 n. 11, 259, 270; *Twelfth Night*, 33, 59, 160, 198, 230; *The Two Gentlemen of Verona*, 31, 58; *The Winter's Tale*, 240 n. 2
Shaw, George Bernard, 109
Sheperd, Geoffrey, 93 n. 21, 204 n. 6
Shirley, J., 184 nn. 5, 7, 9 and 16
Showalter, Elaine, 92 n. 4
Sidney, Philip, 12, 27, 74, 84, 85, 93 n. 21, 173, 176, 189, 194, 196, 247, 248,

249, 251. Works: *An Apologie for Poetrie*, 84, 189, 204 n. 6; *Arcadia*, 17, 247, 248, 251
Siegel, P. N., 241 n. 14
Silla, 110
Similitudo, 222
Singer, Milton, 91 n. 1
Skelton, J., 73; *Magnificence*, 72
Smeaton, O., 205 n. 14
Smith, G. Gregory, 204 n. 2, 240 n. 5
Smith, Geoffrey N., 93 n. 13
Smith, Robert M., 108 n. 1
Southampton, Earl of, 60
Spencer, Christopher, 277 n. 3
Spenser, Edmund, 29, 64, 118, 188, 189, 194, 196. Works: *Epithalamion*, 29, *The Faerie Queene*, 188, *Shepherd's Calendar*, 188, 189
Spivack, Bernard, 230, 242 nn. 47 and 52
Sprengnether, Madelon, 244 n. 71
Sprezzatura, 107
Squarzina, Luigi, 20, 21
Starobinski, J., 150 n. 1
Steevens, 170
Stein, Peter, 20
Steiner, George, 196, 204 n. 11
Stevenson, Laura Caroline, 163 n. 3
Strachey, William, 177
Strauss, Jaine, 91 n. 1
Strehler, Giorgio, 20, 21
Stubbes, Philip, 68, 75 n. 24; *Anatomie of Abuses*, 68, 75 n. 24
Styan, J. L., 241 n. 28, 243 n. 63
Suetonius, 112, 116. Works: *Lives of the Twelve Caesars*, 116, *Vitae Duodecim Caesarum*, 112
Swedenborg, H. T., 276 n. 1
Swinburne, A. C., 74 n. 12

Tarlton, Dick, 145, 146
Tasso, Torquato, 183
Tempera, Mariangela, 11, 15, 20, 152, 217 n. 5
Tennenhouse, Leonard, 93 n. 23
Terracini, Lore, 204 n. 13
Texeda, Fernando, 123; *Miracles Unmasked*, 123–24
Theobald, L., 204 n. 10
Thomas, K. V., 126 n. 13
Thomas, Saint, 170
Tillyard, E. M. W., 207, 217 n. 7

Tilney, Henry, 146
Tommaseo, Niccolò, 8, 183 n. 4
Topos, 230, 269
Tourneur, C., 122
Traister, Barbara, 208, 218 n. 11, 219 n. 26
Trevelyan, G. M., 208, 218 nn. 12 and 13
Trevet, Nicholas, 219 n. 29; *Annales Regum Angliae*, 219 n. 29
Troublesome Raigne of John King of England, The, 206, 216, 218 n. 25
Tudor myth, 80, 122, 123, 207
Tudor, Mary, 119, 123
Turner, Robert Y., 83, 93 n. 19
Turner, William, 123
Tyndale, William, 206; *The Obedience of a Christen Man*, 206

Udall, Nicholas, 123
Uspenskij, Boris A., 92 n. 5, 218 nn. 16 and 17

van Dijk, Teun A., 277 n. 4
Vandersall, S. T., 125 n. 6
Varga, Kibédi, 268
Vautrollier, Thomas, 125 n. 2, 205 n. 18
Venetian setting, 45
Veneto plays, 44
Venice, 44, 45, 46; as a bourgeois-capitalist society, 54, 55; as a center of commerce and trade, 51; as a contradictory society, 45–46; as a cosmopolitan city, 44–45
Vice, 251
Vickers, Brian, 231, 242 nn. 54 and 55
Vickers, Nancy J., 92 n. 44
Villa, Vittoriana, 93 n. 20
Virgil, 188
Virgilian tradition, 112
Vituperatio, 230

Walker, D. P., 126 n. 13
Walter, J. H., 74 n. 9, 151 n. 10
Warburton, 170
Watson, F. T., 150 n. 7
Watson, George, 278 n. 12
Watson, W., 74 n. 4
Wayne, Valerie, 92 n. 4
Webster, C., 184 n. 18
Webster, John,, 17, 122, 240 n. 3, 254. Works: *The Duchess of Malfi*, 240 n. 3; *The White Devil*, 254, 255

Weimann, Robert, 151 n. 19
Weitz, Morris, 240 n. 12
Westfall, R. S., 126 n. 13
Whetstone, George, 98
Whigham, Frank, 163 n. 1
Whitney, Geoffrey, 112
Whytinton, R., 93 n. 11
Wight, Iohn, 125 n. 2, 205 n. 18
Wilders, John, 55 n. 3
Wiles, D., 149, 151 nn. 15, 17 and 20
Willet, Andrew, 183 n. 2
Wilson Knight, George, 97, 108 n. 1, 182
Wilson, J. D., 151 n. 16, 166, 167, 170, 177, 182, 184 n. 19

Wilson, Thomas, 78, 85, 93 n. 22.
  Works: *Discourse upon Usury*, 85; *Rhetorique*, 78
Womersley, D., 151 n. 19, 217 n. 3
Woodville, Elizabeth, 65
Wright, Edward, 123
Wyatt, T., 123
Wyndham, George, 202, 205 n. 19

Yates, F. A., 127 n. 20, 184 nn. 26 and 27

Zanco, Aurelio, 8
Zeeveld, W. Gordon, 127 n. 22
Zeffirelli, Franco, 21
Zielinski, Thomas, 166, 169